Learn Programming

Antti Salonen

Aug 11, 2018

Learn Programming, first edition

Antti Salonen

CONTENTS:

CHAPTER

ONE

THE BEGINNING

1.1 Introduction

1.1.1 Why this book?

This book is aimed at readers who are interested in software development but have very little to no prior experience.

The book doesn't have any new information compared to what you can find online or in other books; it has two purposes:

1. It includes what I think is important for software development from a large variety of topics, saving the reader from the dilemma "what should I learn"
2. It collates relevant information from lots of sources in one book, saving the reader from going through several separate web sites and books

It aims to contain an overview of almost everything that I think is important for software developers. It doesn't contain *everything*; but it should contain enough for the reader to understand software development, and to be able to read about and understand any topic in further detail as needed.

The book focuses on teaching the core principles around software development. It uses several technologies to this goal (e.g. C, Python, JavaScript, HTML, etc.) but is not a book about the technologies themselves. The reader will learn the basics (or in some cases more) of various technologies along the way, but the focus is on building a foundation for software development.

This book does have the aim of supporting interested people in pursuing a job in software development, though I obviously can't guarantee a job. I'll expand on this further below.

Why are you writing this book?

My wife was asking if she could become a software engineer like I did.

I have some years of experience in software engineering, and also am now hiring and hence interviewing software engineers. I checked the offerings around Computer Science at the local university, but it seems to me like there's a bit of a gap between what industry needs and what the schools are producing, at least in my local area. To some extent this is expected: universities live in the academic world, often without an explicit goal of ensuring the graduates are employed by the industry. To mitigate, universities may offer degrees directed more towards real world, but these run into the risk of not being relevant or effective enough for the industry.

So I ended up teaching my wife what I think is the right stuff. Now, since we also have a little daughter, finding time for both of us at the same time was sometimes difficult, so I'd write down some notes or exercises for her that she could dive into when she had time. I ended up writing more and more and structuring things better and all of it ended up being this book.

So, I'm writing this book to teach my wife all the necessary basics around software development so that she'll be able to land a job. However, the book could be useful to others as well.

No, really, why are you writing this book?

If I'm being completely selfish, it's because I'm hiring software engineers and am finding it difficult to find any. Without going into my specific requirements, I want to include enough in the book that if the reader were to do all of the following:

- Read and understand everything in the book
- Finish all the exercises
- Write at least some personal mini project in some language (shouldn't be a problem after the above two points)
- Interact with the rest of the software development community, may it be through Reddit or other social media, chat, Stack Overflow or GitHub

...then I think that that person should have the *technical* skills to at least seriously be considered for a software engineering position.

(Apart from technical skills, you'll also need the interpersonal skills and common sense, or analytical and critical thinking skills, among others, before I'd consider you for a position. I'm expecting the reader to obtain these some other way than reading this book.)

Do you mean, if I do the points above, I too can become a professional software engineer?

I obviously can't guarantee anything. Actually getting a job depends on the economy and the job market, where you live, what you're willing to do and work for etc. But I do think that after doing all the above points, the reader should have enough or almost enough *technical* skills for many software engineering jobs.

Apart from raising false hopes about getting a job as a software engineer, another reason for this book is that I'm not happy with how the gap between "techies" and "non-techies" is growing. I think more people should be familiar with software. I want to write a book that has very little prerequisites and teaches enough about software and technology so that a "non-techie" is able to get a better understanding about how software affects the world we live in. So even if you don't get a job, you can at least feel proud about having a better understanding of software and its role in the world.

What's in this book?

The book covers a lot of topics but is very shallow.

The book doesn't include *everything* I know, but it includes enough that the reader should be able to follow a software development discussion, and more importantly, learn more about a specific software development subject without a hugely steep learning curve.

Different programming languages such as C, Python and JavaScript are touched upon. Some traditional Computer Science topics such as algorithms and data structures are touched upon. Some topics that are typical in modern software development work environments such as databases, version control and web development are touched upon. Almost nothing is treated in depth.

Although many subjects are treated almost comically lightly, overall the material should be enough for the reader to get a general understanding around software development.

This book is not a replacement for a Computer Science degree, though it does (shallowly) include some parts of one, and complements one in other cases.

You say "engineering", "programming", "development" and "computer science" - what are the differences?

This book teaches software development. This book doesn't teach engineering, but the term "software engineer" is used to describe a person who develops software because that's what we seem to have arrived at as an industry.

More specifically, I'd define the terminology as follows:

- Engineering is something that's very structured, and something you want to learn in a very structured way. In other words, this book definitely doesn't teach engineering.
- Software development is about solving a problem using software: it's not very clean, it's usually not really engineering nor very scientific, but it's useful in practice and there's a demand for it.

Programming, or coding, is one part of software development, among design, testing, writing specifications etc. This book is about software development although programming plays a major part in it.

There's also Computer Science which arguably is separate from both software development and engineering. (It is a science after all. "Computer Science is no more about computers than astronomy is about telescopes.")

You possibly can't have all the technical stuff that one needs in one book!

No, but I can try.

Whatever code you'll be writing after reading this book, you'll need to study the technology for that particular topic in more detail. The goal of this book is not to include everything; the goal is to put together a foundation so that the reader will be able to learn to write almost any software without significant hurdles, as necessary.

What are the prerequisites for this book?

The book is aimed at people with no experience or skills within software development.

Some parts of the book use high school level maths so you should be somewhat familiar with that. You need to have a computer and be able to use it (install software etc.).

The book requires your computer to be able to run a Unix shell and standard Unix tools. Mac, Linux or Windows 10 should all suffice. Older Windows versions may be fine for the purposes of this book but installing the necessary software may be non-trivial.

You should have some skills around analytical thinking and problem solving. I don't know how to teach those. I believe this book does teach them to some extent though, as a side effect.

I do believe that almost anyone who is able to finish high school without significant struggles can learn how to develop software. It's not magic. It does require persistence though; you need to be able to put effort to the book, and it'll take time. I believe someone with the capability to work on the book full time, enough perseverance and help where needed, should be able to finish the book including all the exercises in a matter of months.

It's probably very helpful to have a tutor or someone who's familiar with software development to answer your questions. Use the Internet to your advantage; there are literally thousands of techies online waiting to share their knowledge and answer newbies' questions. Try Stack Overflow, the learnprogramming subreddit, GitHub, or various IRC channels, e.g. those dedicated to specific programming languages.

You must be able to find information online. For example, notice how I used the term "IRC channels"? If you ever do feel the need to ask a question and decide to investigate the IRC bit further, you need to use the Internet to a) find out what IRC is, b) find out what IRC channels there are e.g. for a programming language you're having trouble with, c) how to connect to such a channel and ask your question. This book won't have that information.

The book is free and licensed under the Creative Commons Attribution-ShareAlike 4.0 International License. This means that you're free to share the book in any medium and modify the book for any purpose, even commercially, as long as you give appropriate credit and your distribution uses the same license. See more details at http://creativecommons.org/licenses/by-sa/4.0/. The code in this book is licensed under the MIT license.

How should I work with this book?

The information in this book is very dense. Most sentences are important for the topic at hand, and information is rarely duplicated. I expect the reader to go through the book several times. You might miss a lot of details the first time, or two times, but should eventually be able to understand all of it.

The book uses the pedagogical approach of assimilation, or constructionism; information is provided to the reader in bulk, and learning is facilitated by exercises which ask the student to think for themselves in an effort to learn the material. If you don't understand something, that may be fine. Let it be and come back to it later. There's a chapter dependency diagram at the end of the book which can give indication as to which chapters you need to understand before proceeding. Different topics are interleaved to some degree, allowing the reader to digest some areas while working on others and to better understand the relationships and connections between topics.

I should mention at this point, if it wasn't already clear, that the author has no real pedagogical experience.

Overall, the book is structured into four stages. These are the main topics in the different stages:

Stage	Main topics
The beginning	Basics of computers and programming using C and Python; basics of Unix
Stage 1	Introduction to algorithms and JavaScript; some more in-depth concepts in C and Python
Stage 1.5	Web development using JavaScript and Python; strongly, statically typed languages, especially C++
Stage 2	Larger software using Python and C++ (or optionally e.g. Java); SQL; various intermediate topics (parsing, threads etc.)

If you think there's something unclear about some part of the book or otherwise have any questions or comments, let me know. My email is ajsalonen@gmail.com. You may also create an issue or a pull request in GitHub. I'm also not a native English speaker so any corrections on that front are welcome as well. The book source code is available at https://github.com/anttisalonen/progbook. The book home page is https://progbook.org.

About the author

My name is Antti Salonen. I've worked as a software engineer for a few years and am currently an engineering manager at a tech company. I started writing code when I was about six years old, or 28 years ago, and have written non-trivial code in about 14 different programming languages. I've professionally written medical device software, company internal tools, software for controlling a telescope, and a few other things. I've managed the development of a web app and been a network admin, an engineering team lead, and a small scale software architect. I've written some humble, ugly, open source games as a hobby, and made some minor contributions to some open source projects.

Disclaimer: This book was written in my personal capacity. All the views and opinions expressed in this book are my own and may not reflect those of my past or current employer.

Even though I started programming at a young age, it doesn't mean you're already a lost cause if you didn't. In fact, I know several great software engineers who didn't start programming until much later.

1.1.2 What is software?

> Talk is cheap. Show me the code.
>
> —Linus Torvalds

Software is code that tells computer hardware what to do.

To get started, let's write a very simple software program.

For this, the first thing you need to do is start a terminal with a Unix shell in it.

I can't tell you how to do this exactly as this is operating system (OS) dependent. At least with some versions of Mac OS, you can start the terminal by searching for "terminal" in Spotlight. On Windows 10, you can install "Windows Subsystem for Linux" (WSL). On older Windows versions, there are ways to get a Unix shell like Cygwin but it's more tricky. Searching online is your friend.

In the end, it could look something like this:

Most notably, the Windows cmd.exe or PowerShell are *not* Unix shells. Typical Unix shells characteristics are the at sign ("@") designating your user name and the host name of the computer you're logged on to, a tilde ("~") to designate the home directory and the dollar sign ("$") to designate the prompt. You can use these to identify whether you're running a Unix shell or not.

Exercise: Start a terminal with a Unix shell.

> **Is this "Unix shell" the only way to program?**
>
> No, it's also possible to program in other environments than Unix shell. However, Unix shell is one environment, and it's a pretty good one (author's opinion). If you're familiar with the Unix shell, it shouldn't be very difficult to learn to use another environment should that become necessary.

Apart from the shell, we also need an interpreter and an editor. For this section we'll use Python as our programming language; so let's install the Python interpreter. Again, I can't tell you how to do this; some OSes may have it already installed. To find out if you have it, start your Unix shell and try typing:

```
$ python
Python 3.6.0 (default, Jan 16 2017, 12:12:55)
[GCC 6.3.1 20170109] on linux
Type "help", "copyright", "credits" or "license" for more␣
↪information.
```

> **I'm supposed to type all that?**
>
> Actually you're only supposed to type "python" (without quotes). On the first line, the dollar sign ("$") means the prompt, i.e. the part of the screen where you can type. The first line effectively means "type 'python'". The following lines don't start with the dollar sign so they're meant to demonstrate the possible output from running the previous command.

If you don't have Python, you might see something like this instead:

```
$ python
bash: python: command not found
```

In this case you'll need to find out how to install it. On e.g. Ubuntu, running something like "sudo apt-get install python" might do it. On Mac you may need to install Python from the Python official web site. Although we'll be using Python 2 later in this book, this section will work with either Python 2 or 3 so the version you pick isn't very important for now.

Once you do get to the Python interpreter as shown above you can exit it by typing "exit()" (without the quotes).

Exercise: Install the Python interpreter if your system doesn't already have it. Run it and exit it.

Now that we have the shell and the interpreter, the final bit we need is the editor. An editor is a program that allows writing code files, or text files in general. For now it's enough with an editor that's easy to use, though Notepad, which is installed by default on Windows, won't do. Furthermore, word processors such as Microsoft Word won't do. If you're on a Linux system you can install e.g. gedit. On Windows you could install notepad++. There are other editors available like Atom or Visual Studio Code. It doesn't really matter which one you install now, as long as you end up with a window where you can type text and save it to a file. Here's an example of what an editor could look like:

Exercise: Install and start an editor.

Now we can use the editor to write some code and save it in a file, then use the shell to start the interpreter with our code as input. The interpreter will then run our code.

The next step is to create a file with these contents:

```
print("Hello world")
```

The above is a one-line Python program (which works either with Python 2 or Python 3). When run, it will write the text "Hello world" to the terminal.

Exercise: Create a file with the above contents. Call it "hello.py". Make sure you know in which directory you saved the file. If you're using Windows 10 and WSL, you should be able to find the files you've saved in Windows at /mnt/c/Users/<username>.

Now, we need to navigate to the directory where the file was saved, and run the Python interpreter with our program as the input.

The directory paths are again somewhat OS dependent but you have a few tools that help you locate your file:

- You can find out which files are in the *current directory* in the shell by running "ls".
- You can find out what your current directory is by running "cwd" (current working directory).
- You can change the directory by running "cd" followed by the directory. E.g. if you have a directory called "Documents" in your current working directory and you wish to change your current working directory to that directory, you can do this by running "cd Documents".
- You can change to the *parent directory* by running "cd ..".

Exercise: Run "ls" in your shell to see the contents of the current working directory.

Now we have some idea of how to navigate around the various directories in our Unix shell.

Exercise: Locate your hello.py in the shell. Change to that directory. If you can't find it, try saving to another location. If you're on Windows you may need to consult the Windows documentation on how to find the Windows files from WSL or vice versa. If you're stuck, you may also try to open the editor from the shell e.g. by running "gedit hello.py" (if gedit is the editor you have installed). This way, after saving the file in your editor, the file should be saved in the current working directory.

Now that you have your source file available, let's run the interpreter with your source file as input by running:

```
$ python hello.py
Hello world
```

This should cause the Python interpreter to run your program which will output the text "Hello world" on the screen.

Exercise: Run your program.

If you made it here, congratulations. You've written your first software.

1.1.3 How does a computer work?

> Computers are good at following instructions, but not at reading your mind.
>
> —Donald Knuth

The previous section was a "hook" in that it attempted to get the reader interested without really going into technical details. This section is a bit different. As is characteristic for this book, we won't go very much into specifics but we will cover the essentials about understanding computers as is required for software development.

In order to understand how a computer works, we must first learn a bit about *digital logic.*

The way computers work is mostly defined by physics, and what is possible in electronics. The key is the *transistor,* which is a semiconductor device which makes it possible to construct *logic gates.* Logic gates are physical, very small devices that perform logical operations.

Logic gates take one or more *inputs* and have one or more *outputs.* The inputs and outputs typically are *binary signals;* they're either an electric signal with a low voltage (e.g. 0 volts) or a high voltage (e.g. 3.3 volts). Binary means that there are two possible values, often called 0 (*false*) and 1 (*true*). (One binary digit is also called a *bit.*)

The behaviour of a logic gate can be captured in a *truth table.* Here's the truth table for one of the standard logic gates, the *AND-gate*:

A	B	X
0	0	0
0	1	0
1	0	0
1	1	1

Here, the inputs are labelled 'A' and 'B'. The output is labelled 'X'. The output is 1 only when both A and B are 1 and 0 otherwise, hence the name AND-gate.

The logic gates can be shown in a diagram as well. Here's what the AND-gate would look like in a diagram:

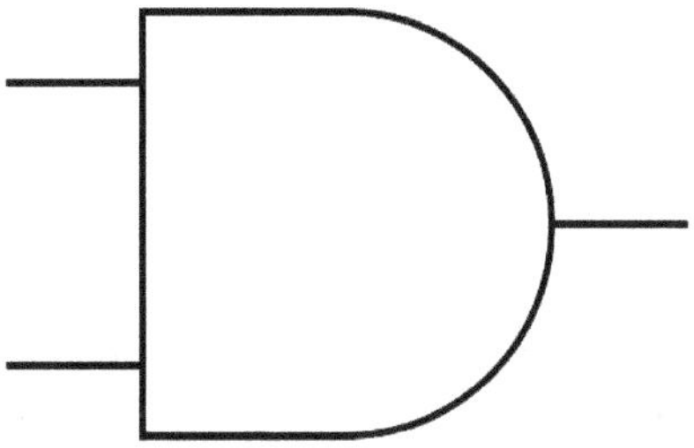

Here, the input signals would enter from the left while the output signal would exit to the right.

Another standard logic gate is the *OR-gate*. It has the following truth table:

A	B	X
0	0	0
0	1	1
1	0	1
1	1	1

The OR-gate outputs 1 when either A or B, or both, have 1. In a diagram it would look like this:

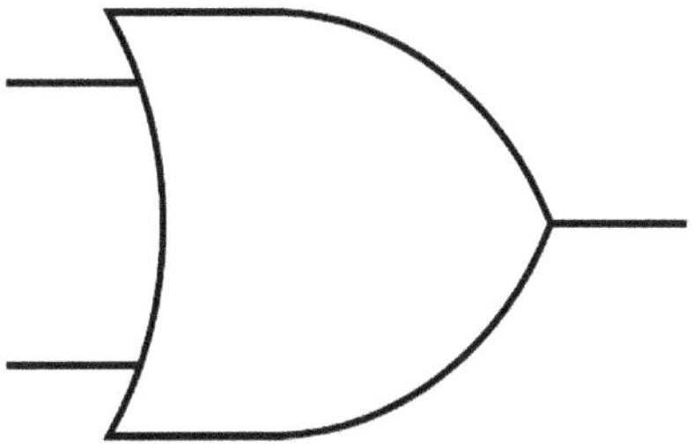

There's also the *NOT-gate*. It has only one input and one output:

A	X
0	1
1	0

It *negates* its input and, in a diagram, would look like this:

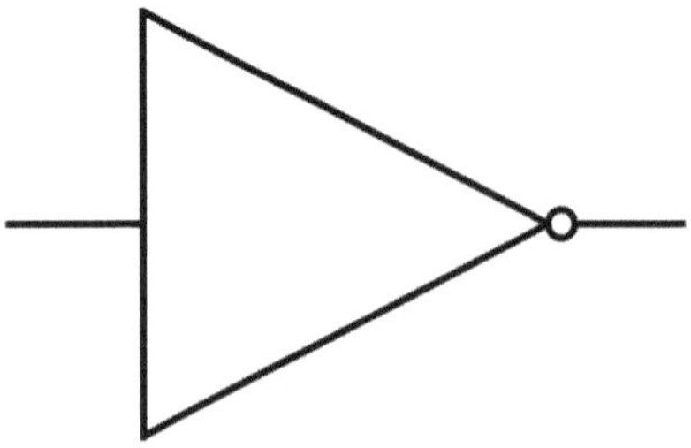

These gates are enough to build complex digital devices including computers (though several million of them may be necessary).

Let's say we wanted to put together a circuit with the following truth table:

A	B	X
0	0	0
0	1	1
1	0	1
1	1	0

That is, it's almost like the OR-gate but if both A and B are 1 then we output 0. (This is also called *XOR-gate*, or exclusive-or.) We could build this circuit by combining what we already have:

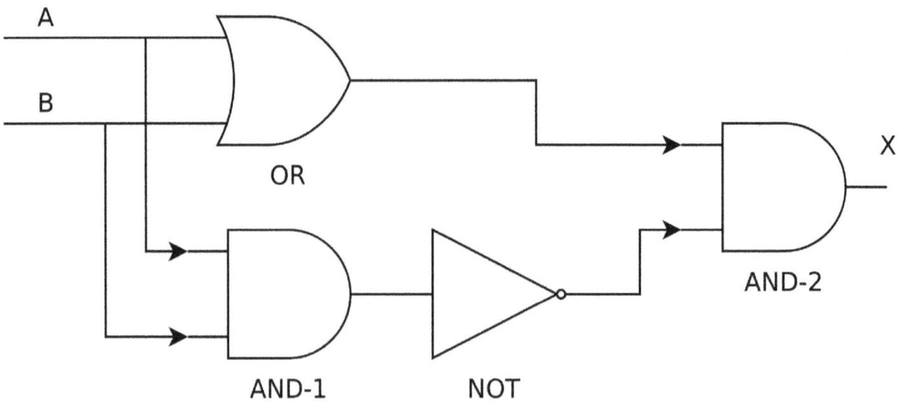

Let's see what we have here:

- We have one OR-gate (labelled OR), two AND-gates (labelled AND-1 and AND-2) and one NOT-gate (labelled NOT)
- The inputs, A and B, are fed both to the OR-gate and AND-1
- The output of AND-1 is negated

- Finally, the output of the OR-gate and the negated output of AND-1 is combined in AND-2. The output of this gate is the output of our circuit.

What happens here is that the output of the OR-gate is always 1 when one of the inputs is 1.

The output of AND-1 is only 1 when both A and B are 1. However, this output is negated, meaning that the output of NOT is 1 always except when both A and B are 1.

Combining the above in AND-2: When both A and B are 1, the output of NOT is 0, meaning that the output of our circuit is 0. In other cases, the output is the same as the output of the OR-gate. Hence the final output is as desired.

We now have a new building block: whenever we need a XOR-gate, we can use this design.

Exercise: Using only the OR-, AND- and NOT-gates, design, with a pen and paper, a circuit with two inputs A and B, and output X, such that the when both A and B are 0, the output is 1. In all other cases the output must be 0.

We can now put together various logical circuits. How about practical use cases?

Addition

One of the first professions that computers made unemployed were the *computers*: people who were given arithmetic tasks such as "123,456 + 789,012", with the goal of computing the correct answer. Indeed digital logic can be used for arithmetic. Let's start with addition.

$0 + 0 = 0$.

$0 + 1 = 1$.

$1 + 0 = 1$.

$1 + 1 = 2$.

Seems simple, doesn't it? Indeed this is quite similar to our OR-gate, except that because our values can only be 0 or 1, we don't have the ability to encode the number 2 in one signal. But we could have another output signal, with the meaning of "the output is two". The truth table for such a circuit would then look like this:

A	B	Output is 2	Sum
0	0	0	0
0	1	0	1
1	0	0	1
1	1	1	0

We could then arrive at the final sum by calculating "output is 2" * 2 + "sum".

This circuit could be designed e.g. like this:

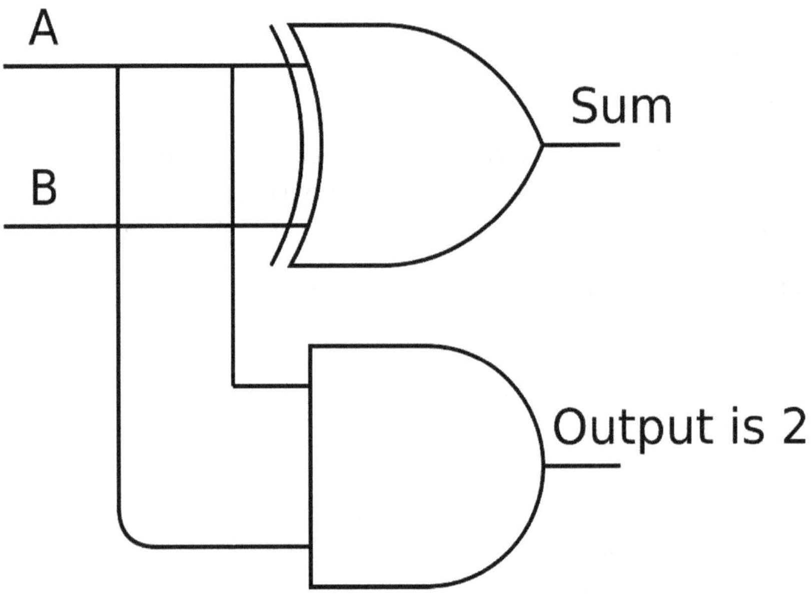

The top gate is a XOR-gate. Hence the "sum" output is A and B XOR'd while the "output is 2" output is A and B AND'd.

What if we wanted to count higher?

2 + 0 = 2.

2 + 1 = 3.

3 + 0 = 3.

3 + 1 = 4.

3 + 2 = 5.

3 + 3 = 6.

We simply add more input and output, and more gates. The truth table could look like this:

A1	A2	B1	B2	Sum has 4	Sum has 2	Sum has 1
0	0	0	0	0	0	0
0	0	0	1	0	0	1
0	0	1	0	0	1	0
0	0	1	1	0	1	1
0	1	0	0	0	0	1
0	1	0	1	0	1	0
0	1	1	0	0	1	1
0	1	1	1	1	0	0
1	0	0	0	0	1	0
1	0	0	1	0	1	1
1	0	1	0	1	0	0
1	0	1	1	1	0	1
1	1	0	0	0	1	1
1	1	0	1	1	0	0
1	1	1	0	1	0	1
1	1	1	1	1	1	0

Here, our inputs are two bits for each number, and we have three bits of output, to capture all possible outputs. The input for either A or B can be any of 0, 1, 2 or 3. 0 is encoded by the pair of bits 0 and 0. 1 is encoded by 0 and 1. 2 is encoded by 1 and 0. Finally, 3 is encoded by 1 and 1. The final output can be calculated from the three bits of output using the formula "sum has 4" * 4 + "sum has 2" * 2 + "sum has 1".

Exercise: Check that the above truth table is correct for some row. Decode what number A, B and output are from the bits.

In similar vein we can do e.g. subtraction and multiplication.

How about comparing whether one number is larger than another one? E.g. for one-bit numbers we'd like the following truth table:

A	B	X
0	0	0
0	1	0
1	0	1
1	1	0

Here, X is 1 when A is greater than B and 0 otherwise. This, too, can be done using digital circuits.

Exercise: Come up with a design for a comparator matching the above truth table.

Now that we're able to construct digital circuits, let's see how they can be used to put together a device with some characteristics not completely unlike those of a smartphone. This is the topic for the next section.

1.1.4 OK, but seriously, how does a computer work?

> On two occasions, I have been asked [by members of Parliament], "Pray, Mr. Babbage, if you put into the machine wrong figures, will the right answers come out?"...I am not able rightly to apprehend the kind of confusion of ideas that could provoke such a question.
>
> —Charles Babbage (1864)

To reduce the modern computer to the essentials, let's build a following, very simple device: a hand-held device with a touch screen. We need to implement very simple functionality for the device:

- If the user taps on the bottom half of the screen, the screen must turn green.
- If the user taps on the top half of the screen, the screen must turn red.

This device is very simple but will cover some of the principles that are shared by nearly all computers, as we shall see.

The following diagram explains the general concept for computers:

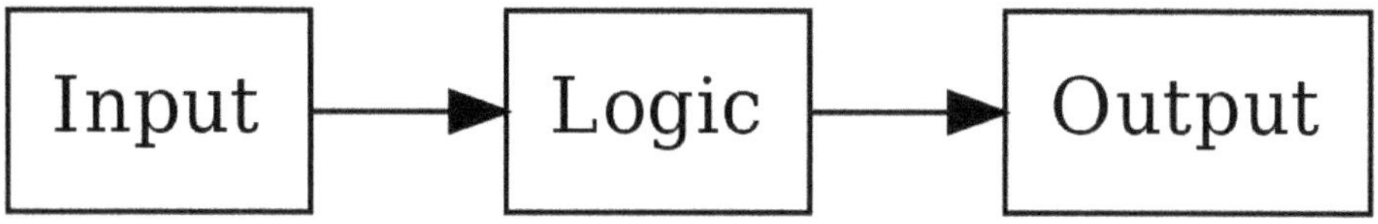

In other words, there's some input, some logic processing the input and creating some output. In our hypothetical device, the input is taps on the touch screen, and the output is what's shown on the display. In our "Hello world" program, there was no input, and the output was a text in the terminal.

To be more specific, the input and output blocks like a touch screen and a display are *digital devices*; they *communicate* with the logic part using binary signals. Generally speaking, the input and output devices come with some kind of a *technical specification* or *data sheet* which describe how to interact with them. In our case, the hypothetical data sheet for our hypothetical touch screen contains the following:

"The X coordinate of the latest tap is output at signal A. The value is either 0 (bottom half of the screen) or 1 (top half)."

Similarly the hypothetical data sheet for the hypothetical display contains:

"To set the colour of the display, set the signals X and Y as desired. The colour is displayed as based on the following table:"

X	Y	Colour shown on the display
0	0	Black
0	1	Green
1	0	Red
1	1	Blue

(This display can only show one colour across the whole screen, i.e. it only has one pixel.)

The logic part in the middle ends up doing at least three things:

- Receives information from the input blocks using logic signals
- Performs the actual logic (in our case, mapping the position of the tap to the output colour)
- Sends information to the output blocks using logic signals

In our case, the logic in Python-like code could look like this:

```
if user_tap_x_coordinate == 0:
    screen_color = 1
else:
    screen_color = 2
```

Here, the variable "user_tap_x_coordinate" represents the touch screen input which holds the X coordinate of the position where the user tapped last. The variable "screen_color" represents the display output which is used to control the colour shown on the display.

In other words, all the logic needs to do is read the input from the touch screen, compare this with predefined values, and depending on the result of the comparison, set the correct signal for the display colour.

Exercise: Write the truth table for this logic. It should have A as the input signal and X and Y as the output signals.

Exercise: Design, using pen and paper, the circuit for this logic.

Software and hardware

We've now designed a device that will display different colours depending on where the user taps the screen. Let's further imagine we mass produce thousands of these devices. The device is an instant hit but a new feature requirement appears: some users would like to change the way the display shows the colours. For example, a user would want the device to show black if the device is tapped anywhere on the bottom half of the screen and blue otherwise.

Because we designed the logic that decides the display colour in the hardware, that is, in the digital logic using logic gates, making this change isn't possible without actually changing the logic and manufacturing a new device with a changed logic. To circumvent this and to make it possible to change the way the colours are displayed without having to manufacture a new device, we can make our device *programmable*. (This e.g. allows app development on current smartphones, though smartphones also use software for e.g. the OS.)

When a device is made programmable, it doesn't contain the logic for its primary purpose in hardware using logic gates. Instead, the logic is stored somewhere else as *instructions*, and the device instead has logic to perform operations *depending on* these instructions. Then, by changing the instructions one can change the behaviour of the device without having to manufacture a new device. We also have to include *memory* on the device. This is where the instructions are stored.

In other words, what's required is:

- Removing the logic in hardware for the primary purpose of the device
- Encoding this logic in a list of instructions instead
- Adding some memory to the device which holds the list of instructions
- Adding logic in the hardware to read and understand these instructions
- Making it possible to change the list of instructions later

Here, the list of instructions is the *software* and the logic that reads and understands these instructions is the *Central Processing Unit*, or *CPU*. Each bit in memory can be implemented using logic gates. Memory can be seen as an array of boxes, each holding either a 1 or a 0, with the ability to change the contents as needed using signals.

We've now covered some aspects as to how a computer works, but haven't yet covered how a CPU works.

CPU

A CPU receives some code in some form and must execute it. Let's take a look at our logic for our original program again:

```
if user_tap_x_coordinate == 0:
    screen_color = 1
else:
    screen_color = 2
```

Now, the above is possibly somewhat understandable to us as humans but it's not really a list. Typically, converting this to a list of instructions would make it look more like this:

```
1: COMPARE A WITH 0
2: IF FALSE THEN JUMP TO 6
3: SET X TO 0
4: SET Y TO 1
5: JUMP TO INSTRUCTION 1
6: SET X TO 1
7: SET Y TO 0
8: JUMP TO INSTRUCTION 1
```

Here, e.g. the first instruction, COMPARE, compares the two operands given to it, and stores the result in memory to be used for the next instruction.

Typically, a CPU needs to *decode* the instructions from the memory. For example, the instruction COMPARE may be defined as the input values "001". This means that the digital logic would read three bits from memory, see if they match the values "001", and if so, perform the comparison. Each instruction has a number that it corresponds to, and when storing the software in memory, the software would need to be stored in the format that the hardware expects for the system to function correctly.

We now have a list of instructions such that each kind of instruction, e.g. COMPARE, SET etc. can be implemented in hardware using logic gates. By implementing each instruction in the hardware and making it possible to modify the list of instructions independently of the hardware we've made our device programmable.

This was a rather high level overview of how a computer and a CPU work, but it should do for now, such that we can start to investigate how to actually write software.

1.1.5 The basics of programming

> And programming computers was so fascinating. You create your own little universe, and then it does what you tell it to do.
>
> —Vint Cerf

It's debatable what the basics of programming are. This section presents the author's view and will cover:

- Variables
- Loops
- Branches
- Functions

We already have a Python programming environment so we'll continue using that. This section will include some code examples. The reader is expected to type these into a file, and then run the Python interpreter with that file as input. For example:

```
print('Hello world')
```

This is the program we wrote a couple of sections ago. Make sure you still know how to create and write such a program.

Exercise: Run your 'Hello world' program.

Exercise: Modify the text "Hello world" (e.g. change it to 'Hallo Welt') in your program and run it again.

It's best not to copy-paste the code from this book but instead type it yourself as this reinforces the learning effect.

Variables

Variables hold some value. The following example defines and uses a variable named 'x':

```
x = 5
print(x)
x = 7
print(x)
```

The above will write '5' followed by '7' in the terminal. 'x' is first defined with the value 5. It is then written out before its value is changed to 7.

You can have several variables, and the assignment can refer to other variables:

```
x = 5
y = 6
print(x)
print(y)
y = x
print(y)
```

Exercise: What does the above code write out? Try it out.

Exercise: Create a program that has a variable with a value 42 and writes it out.

Loops

A loop can repeat a section of code multiple times.

The following is an example of using a loop in Python:

```
for i in range(10):
    print(i)
```

The above will print (write to the terminal) the numbers from 0 to 9. The words "for" and "in" are Python keywords; range() is a Python function that can be used to describe the iterations of a loop; "i" is a variable that is defined using the "for" loop and will hold the current value that is provided by the range() function.

Indentation matters (in Python)

Indentation refers to the whitespace (spaces or tabs) between the start of a row and the start of a text within that row. In the above example, the line containing "print(i)" has four spaces before the word "print". Whitespace must exist to indicate the body of the loop; without it, Python with raise a syntax error. The convention is to use four spaces for each indentation level in Python. Tab characters and spaces must not be mixed in Python.

Here's another loop:

```
x = 5
for i in range(10):
    print(x)
```

Exercise: What does the above code write out? Try it out.

Exercise: Write a program that prints the number 42 five times.

The print() function can also include both text and a variable. This can be achieved using e.g. the following:

```
for i in range(10):
    print('i has the value %d' % i)
```

This looks like it needs some explaining. What we have here is the text "i has the value %d", whereby the fragment "%d" is a *placeholder* for a number. The number for the placeholder is provided by having the percent character ("%") after the text string, followed by the variable the value of which we want to insert to the placeholder. Hence, the above program will print e.g. "i has the value 0", "i has the value 1" etc.

Exercise: Write a program that prints the value of a variable as part of other text five times.

The range() function can also be used to start from another number than 0. To start from 1 you can use:

```
for i in range(1, 10):
    print('i has the value %d' % i)
```

This will print the numbers from 1 to 9, inclusive.

Branches

A branch refers to the if-then structure. This is a branch:

```
x = 5
if x < 10:
    print('x is smaller than 10')
```

Here, we declare a variable named 'x' with the value 5. We then compare its value against 10; if it's less, we print out some text.

The else-part is optional (in Python). If we want to have it, it could look like this:

```
x = 5
if x < 10:
    print('x is smaller than 10')
else:
    print('x is larger than or equal to 10')
```

The if-then-else-statements can be *chained*. In Python, the keyword "elif" (portmanteau of "else if") is used in this case:

```
x = 5
if x < 10:
    print('x is smaller than 10')
elif x < 20:
    print('x is smaller than 20')
else:
    print('x is larger than or equal to 20')
```

Furthermore, the keywords "or" and "and" can be used to combine conditions:

```
x = 5
if x <= 10 and x >= 0:
    print('x is between 0 and 10')
if x < 0 or x > 10:
    print('x is either negative or larger than 10')
```

All the constructs can be combined. Here's a branch within a loop:

```
for i in range(10):
    if i <= 5:
        print(i)
    else:
        print('i is larger than 5')
```

Exercise: What does the above print? Try it out.

Apart from comparing for larger and smaller values, we can also check for equality by using two equals-to characters:

```
for i in range(10):
    if i == 5:
        print('i is 5')
    else:
        print('i is not 5')
```

Here's a loop within a branch:

```
x = 5
if x < 10:
    for i in range(10):
        print(x)
else:
    print('x is too large')
```

Exercise: What does the above print? Try it out.

Exercise: Write a program that prints "Hello world" five times, followed by printing "Hallo Welt" five times. Note that this can be written either with or without using a branch. Write both versions.

Functions

Functions can be used to capture certain code in one block. Here's an example of a function definition and usage:

```
def my_function(variable):
    print('Hello')
    print(variable)
```

(continues on next page)

(continued from previous page)

```
x = 5
my_function(x)
x = 7
my_function(x)
```

Here, we define the function using the keyword "def", followed by the name of the function and the *parameters* to the function. Here, the parameter is called "variable" and is available within the function. The function receives this parameter as input. Like with loops and branches, the function body must be indented. We then call the function twice with different values.

Exercise: What do you think the above program prints? Try it out.

There are also pre-defined functions as part of the Python programming language. We've already used some of them, e.g. range() and the numeric comparator functions (<, <= etc.). print() is also a function (although technically only in Python 3, not in Python 2).

There are a lot more pre-defined functions in Python. For example, the arithmetic operations (+, -, *, /) are all predefined functions. Here's an example of using them:

```
x = 5
y = x * 3 + 2
print(y)
```

The above will print the number 17.

Functions can also *return* values. These can be seen as the output of the function. This way, a function can be seen as something that takes input and produces output, similarly to our logic gates. Here's such an example function:

```
def square(x):
    return x * x

number1 = 5
number1_squared = square(number1)
print(number1_squared)
```

The above will define a variable that holds the value 5, squares it (25), stores the squared value to another variable and prints it out.

Exercise: Define and use a function that takes a number as input and returns that number plus one.

Functions can be combined with branches and loops:

```
def square(x):
    return x * x

for i in range(10):
    print(i)
    print(square(i))
```

The above will print numbers from 0 to 9 as well as the squares of those numbers. The formatting is a bit ugly because we print "i" on one line and the square of "i" on the next line. This can be fixed by using the following construct:

```
def square(x):
    return x * x

for i in range(10):
    i_squared = square(i)
    print("%d %d" % (i, i_squared))
```

Here, we use the placeholder syntax from earlier, but we write two numbers in each line. It's similar to what we did before but when more than one placeholder is used then the values to be inserted in the placeholders need to be enclosed in parentheses (here, "i" and "i_squared").

We don't need to define a variable before printing it out, so we could save some typing by doing the following:

```
def square(x):
    return x * x

for i in range(10):
    print("%d %d" % (i, square(i)))
```

The next program combines functions, branches and loops:

```
def square(x):
    return x * x

for i in range(10):
    i_squared = square(i)
    if i_squared > 10:
        print(i_squared)
```

Exercise: What does the above code print? Try it out.

Loops can also contain loops:

```
for i in range(10):
    for j in range(10):
        added = i + j
        print("i=%d; j=%d; i+j=%d" % (i, j, added))
```

Exercise: Print the multiplication table for numbers from 1 to 10. I.e. the numbers 1 * 1, 1 * 2 etc. up to 10 * 10.

Python also supports *floating point numbers*, i.e. numbers with a decimal point (with the number of supported digits before and after the comma varying depending on the magnitude of the number). Here's an example:

```
x = 5.2
y = 3.4
print('x and y summed is %f' % (x + y))
```

Here, because x and y are floating point numbers, we need to use "%f" as the placeholder instead of "%d". (If we used %d, we'd only see the number rounded down to the first integer.)

Exercise: Define and use a function that calculates the area of a circle. The function should receive the radius as the input and return the area as the output. Use the formula "area = 3.14 * radius * radius". (You can also use the Python built-in power function by writing e.g. "radius ** 2" for radius squared.)

Exercise: Use the above function to print out the areas of circles with radius 1, 2, 3... up to 10.

Exercise: Write a program that, for numbers from 1 to 10, will print the area of the circle with that radius if the area is between 10 and 100.

Exercise: For numbers from 1 to 10, calculate both the area and the square of the number. Print out the difference between the area and the square.

Apart from the standard arithmetic operators and the power function, there's another potentially useful operator, namely *modulo*. It returns the remainder after a division, e.g.:

```
a = 23
b = 3
print('a = %d; b = %d; a / b = %d' % (a, b, a / b))
print('a = %d; b = %d; a %% b = %d' % (a, b, a % b))
```

Exercise: What do you think the above will print? Try it out.

Exercise: Write a program that prints out the numbers between 1 to 10 which, after being divided by 3, have a remainder of 1.

We now have enough in our toolbox to write *FizzBuzz*: FizzBuzz is originally a children's game where each player is expected to tell the next number, starting from 1, except if the number is divisible by 3 then the player should instead say "Fizz", and if the number is divisible by 5 then the player should say "Buzz", and if the number is divisible by both 3 and 5 then the player should say "FizzBuzz". We should write a program that plays this game; from 1 to 100, it should print the correct answer. The correct output should start with:

```
1
2
Fizz
4
Buzz
Fizz
7
8
Fizz
Buzz
11
Fizz
13
14
FizzBuzz
16
```

(continues on next page)

(continued from previous page)

```
17
Fizz
...
```

Exercise: Write a program that produces the correct output, for numbers from 1 to 100.

If you succeeded in all the exercises of this section, congratulations! Not all software engineering applicants are able to write the code to solve FizzBuzz.

1.1.6 Setting up the C toolchain

> C is quirky, flawed, and an enormous success.
>
> —Dennis Ritchie

In the previous sections we learnt some basic programming using Python. In order to get a better understanding of what is general in programming and what is specific to a programming language, we'll learn some basic programming using another programming language, namely C.

We'll start by setting up the C *toolchain*. A toolchain is a set of tools that are used in a chain with the purpose of compiling and running code written in a specific programming language. As you may have noticed, with Python, we executed our Python programs by passing our Python file to the Python interpreter. What happened there, in a nutshell, was that the Python interpreter *interpreted* our code, i.e. read it through and then executed it. C is typically not interpreted but *compiled*. What this means is that the C code is run through a *compiler* which generates an *executable file*, that is, a file with the CPU instructions which the CPU should execute. Only after we've created this executable file we can run it which in turn runs our program. (The Python interpreter is an executable. The official Python interpreter is written in C.)

Now, the C toolchain is a toolchain because in addition to the compiler, you also need the *standard library* which contains the implementations of standard functions in binary form (CPU instructions), the *assembler*, because technically the compiler outputs *assembly language*, which is a human readable format for the CPU instructions which is converted to the actual binary CPU instructions by the assembler (also called the *object file*), and finally the *linker* which links the standard library, our object files and possibly other libraries together to form the final executable. In short, the toolchain looks like this:

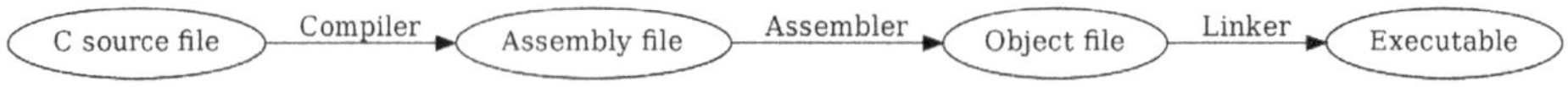

...however, modern C toolchains typically combine all of it in one Unix command so you can usually go from the C source file to the executable in one step. Because of this, in this section from now on, the terms "compiler" and "toolchain" are used interchangeably.

Things do look a bit different if you have several C source files and libraries, namely like this:

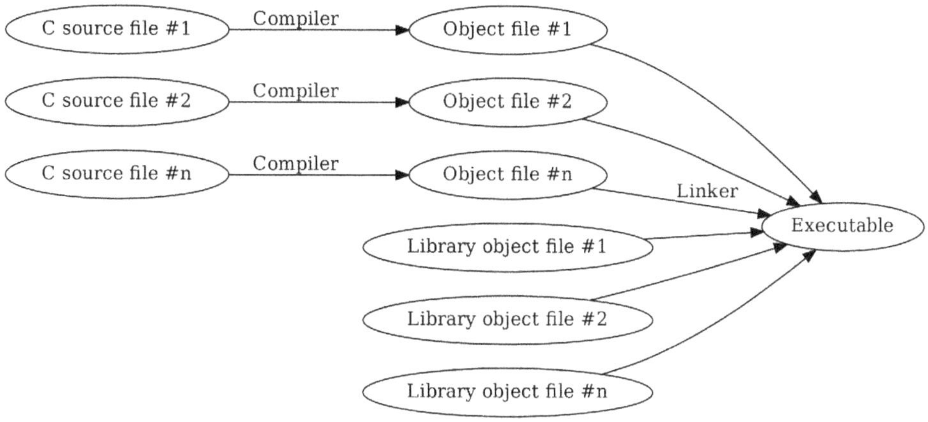

Here, the compiler needs to be called multiple times. But our programs will be one file only, at least for now.

Writing "Hello world" in C

Here's the "Hello world" program in C:

```
1 #include <stdio.h>
2 
3 int main(void)
4 {
5     printf("Hello world\n");
6 }
```

Let's go through this line by line:

- Line 1: We *include* the *header file* called "stdio.h" (standard input and output). The angle brackets ("<" and ">") indicate this header file is expected to be part of the system (as opposed to something we wrote ourselves). Including a file using "#include" causes the *preprocessor* (which is a part of the compiler) to simply include all the contents of that file during compilation. Header file is typically a file that includes *function declarations* of functions that are located in a library; including the relevant header file is recommended when functions of a library are used. In our case, we want to use the *printf* function which outputs text and is part of the C standard library.

- Lines 3-6: We *define* the function called "main". Every C program must have exactly one function called "main" which is the entry point to the program, i.e. the start of the program execution. The keyword "int" means our "main" function returns an integer (as is mandated by the standard) but this isn't relevant for us now. The keyword "void" means our function doesn't receive any parameters. We must start and end the function definition with curly brackets ("{" and "}").
- Line 5: We call the function printf(). We pass it one parameter, namely the *string* "Hello world\n". This causes the function to print the text "Hello world" followed by a *newline character*, a special character that corresponds to enter, or line feed. We must enter the semicolon (";") after the function call to denote the end of the *statement*.

Exercise: Type (don't copy-paste) the above program to a file. Call the file "hello.c".

Installing a C compiler

Let's now ensure we have a C compiler (which in our case includes the assembler, the linker and the standard library) installed.

You may already have one installed. The most common C compilers at the time of writing in Unix systems are *gcc* and *clang*. For now it's not relevant which one you use. You can test if you have gcc installed by running e.g. the following:

```
$ gcc -o hello hello.c
```

If you get no output, then you have gcc installed. You should then have the file "hello" in the current working directory. This is our binary file.

You can also try if you have clang installed using e.g. the following:

```
$ clang -o hello hello.c
```

Again, no output implies clang having successfully run and compiled the program. For both compilers we passed the *command line flag* "-o" which makes it possible for us to define the output file, which we define in the following parameter to be "hello". The last parameter to the compiler is the input C source file.

If you have neither gcc nor clang installed, please install one of them. Again, I cannot tell you how as it is platform dependent; please perform the relevant online searches as necessary.

Once you have been able to compile the "Hello world" program successfully, you can then run the resulting binary file with the following:

```
$ ./hello
Hello world!
```

Here, the prefix "./" means we want to run an executable file in the current directory. As we see, the output is what we passed to printf().

Exercise: Compile and run the "Hello world" program.

Exercise: Remove the characters "\n" from the parameter to printf(). Compile and run again. What changed?

1.1.7 The basics of programming in C

> It has nothing to do with dinosaurs. Good taste doesn't go out of style.
>
> —Linus Torvalds

Variables in C

Now that we're able to compile and run C programs, let's see how to use variables.

A variable is defined in C by first defining the *type* of the variable, followed by the name of the variable. Optionally, the value of the variable can be set when defining the variable. Associating a type with a variable is a way of the programmer telling the compiler how the data is intended to be used. There are several possible types and programs can define new types. For example, *int* and *float* are types (integers and floating point numbers respectively, whereby the number of bits used for storing the data, i.e. the minimum and maximum integer values and the floating point number precision are platform specific).

Once a variable has been defined, it can be used by *assigning* a value to it, using standard operations and functions such as arithmetic and passed to functions such as printf(). Here's an example of defining and using variables:

```
#include <stdio.h>

int main(void)
{
    int x = 5;
    int y = 42;
    int z;
    z = x * 3 + y;
    printf("z is %d\n", z);
}
```

Let's go through this line by line again:

- Line 5: We define a variable named "x". It has type "int". We assign the value 5 to it.
- Line 6: We define a variable named "y". It has type "int". We assign the value 42 to it.
- Line 7: We define a variable named "z". It has type "int". We don't assign any value to it. As a result, its contents are *undefined*; it can contain anything.
- Line 8: We assign a value to the variable "z", namely the result of arithmetic operations.
- Line 9: We print the value of "z". We pass the *placeholder* "%d" to printf(). printf() is a function which takes a *variable number of parameters*. Each parameter is separated by a comma (","). Here, we pass printf() two parameters; the first one is (and must be) the format string. The number of placeholders in the format string defines the number of extra parameters that must be passed. Because we have one placeholder, we must pass one extra parameter. Here, our second parameter is "z". This results in printf() printing the value of "z".

Exercise: Type (don't copy-paste) the above program into a file. Compile it and run the generated executable file.

Exercise: Create a new variable of type "int". Assign a value to it which is dependent on "x", "y" and "z". Print out its value.

Exercise: Create a new variable of type "int". Assign a very large number to it (e.g. 9999999999) and print out its value. Compile and run. What is the output? (If the output is unexpected, this is because the value *overflowed*; the number required more bits than your system allocated for "int".)

Loops

There are several ways to define a loop in C. They're all equivalent but have somewhat different syntax.

A *for loop* has three clauses; the initialisation clause, the controlling expression and the expression to be performed after each iteration. An example may be the best way to illustrate this:

```
1 #include <stdio.h>
2
3 int main(void)
4 {
5     for(int i = 0; i < 10; i++) {
6         printf("%d\n", i);
7     }
8 }
```

- Line 5: We define our loop. The keyword *for* is followed by parentheses, and the parentheses contain the three clauses. The first one defines a variable called “i”. Defining a variable here only makes it available within the loop; using it after the loop would cause a *compiler error.* (It’s said that its *scope* is limited to the loop.) The second clause is an expression that, if evaluated to false, will terminate the loop. The third clause is an expression that is performed after each loop iteration. The syntax “i++” is shorthand for “i = i + 1”; it means “i” is incremented by one.
- Line 6: This is the body of the loop. We print out the value of “i” for each iteration.

The curly brackets (“{” and “}”) can optionally be omitted if the loop body is a single statement (like in this case). However, it’s often beneficial to always include the curly brackets for clarity.

Exercise: Type (don’t copy-paste) the code to a file. Compile it and run it. What’s the output?

Here’s a for loop which also prints out the value of “i”, but in reverse order:

```
#include <stdio.h>

int main(void)
{
    for(int i = 9; i >= 0; i--) {
        printf("%d\n", i);
    }
}
```

As you can see, it's similar, but the variable "i" is instead initialised at 9, the condition is changed such that the loop is repeated as long as the value of "i" is 0 or higher, and the value of "i" is decremented at each iteration.

A *while loop* is similar to the for loop but in some ways simplified. The following program is functionally equivalent to the first for loop example:

```
1  #include <stdio.h>
2  
3  int main(void)
4  {
5      int i = 0;
6      while(i < 10) {
7          printf("%d\n", i);
8          i++;
9      }
10 }
```

- Line 5: We define a variable "i" of type "int" and assign the value 0 to it.
- Line 6: We define our *while loop* by using the keyword "while", followed by parentheses which include the controlling expression similar to the for loop, followed by the loop body.
- Line 7: We print out the value of the variable "i".
- Line 8: We increment the value of "i".

Exercise: Type the above code to a file. Compile it and run it.

Exercise: Rewrite the second for loop example (printing out the value of "i" in reverse order) by replacing the for loop with a while loop.

The third loop construct in C is the *do loop*. It's very similar to the *while* loop but ensures the loop body is executed at least once. Here's an example:

```
#include <stdio.h>

int main(void)
{
    int i = 0;
    do {
        printf("%d\n", i);
```

(continues on next page)

(continued from previous page)

```
        i++;
    } while(i < 10);
}
```

This is functionally equivalent to the while loop example from above. Here, the loop body is executed once before checking whether the control expression evaluates to true. The control expression is evaluated after each following iteration.

Whitespace in C

C is not whitespace sensitive. This means that the number of spaces and newlines between tokens is not relevant. Hence e.g. the first for loop example could equivalently be written like this:

```
#include <stdio.h>

int main(void){

for(
        int i = 0;
        i < 10;
        i++)
    {
        printf(
                "%d\n",
                i
            )
        ;
    } }
```

This will behave exactly the same as the original example. Generally it makes sense to pick one form of indentation and stick with it.

Loops can also contain loops:

```
#include <stdio.h>

int main(void)
```

(continues on next page)

(continued from previous page)

```
{
    for(int i = 0; i < 10; i++) {
        for(int j = 0; j < 10; j++) {
            int added = i + j;
            printf("%d + %d = %d\n", i, j, added);
        }
    }
}
```

Exercise: Print the multiplication table for numbers from 1 to 10. I.e. the numbers 1 * 1, 1 * 2 etc. up to 10 * 10.

Branches

Branches in C are defined using the "if" and "else" keywords. For example:

```
#include <stdio.h>

int main(void)
{
    int x = 42;
    if(x < 20) {
        printf("x is smaller than 20\n");
    } else if(x < 40) {
        printf("x is smaller than 40\n");
    } else {
        printf("x is larger than or equal to 40\n");
    }
}
```

Exercise: Type, compile and run the above program.

As is expected, branches and loops can be freely combined. Here's a branch within a loop:

```
#include <stdio.h>

int main(void)
{
```

(continues on next page)

(continued from previous page)

```
    for(int i = 0; i < 10; i++) {
        if(i <= 5) {
            printf("i is %d\n", i);
        } else {
            printf("i is larger than 5\n");
        }
    }
}
```

Exercise: What does the above print? Try it out.

Like in Python, equality between two values can be checked for using double equality sign ("==").

Furthermore, the tokens "||" and "&&" can be used to combine conditions. "||" means "or" and "&&" means "and":

```
#include <stdio.h>

int main(void)
{
    int x = 5;
    if(x <= 10 && x >= 0) {
        printf("x is between 0 and 10\n");
    }
    if(x < 0 || x > 10) {
        printf("x is either negative or larger than 10\n");
    }
}
```

Exercise: Write a program that has a loop within a branch.

Exercise: Write a program that prints "Hello world" five times, followed by printing "Hallo Welt" five times. Note that this can be written either with or without using a branch. Write both versions.

Functions

We've already seen a function definition with the definition of "main". Here's a definition of a function that takes an int as a parameter and doesn't return anything:

```
1  #include <stdio.h>
2  
3  void my_func(int x)
4  {
5      printf("Parameter: %d\n", x);
6  }
7  
8  int main(void)
9  {
10     my_func(5);
11     int x = 7;
12     my_func(x);
13 }
```

- Lines 3-6: We define our function called "my_func". "void" means it doesn't return anything. "int x" in parentheses means it receives one input variable of type int, which will be named "x" within the function.
- Line 5: We print out the value of the parameter passed to the function.
- Line 10: We call our function.
- Lines 11-12: We call our function again.

Exercise: Type, compile and run the above program.

Here's an example of a function that returns a value:

```
#include <stdio.h>

int square(int x)
{
    return x * x;
}

int main(void)
{
    int x = 5;
    int x_squared = square(x);
    printf("%d squared is %d\n", x, x_squared);
}
```

Here, on line 5, we can see the use of the "return" keyword. Using this will cause the execution of the function to stop and the value after the return keyword to be assigned to the caller of the function, in our case to the variable "x_squared" on line 11.

Exercise: Type, compile and run the above program.

Functions can be combined with branches and loops:

```
#include <stdio.h>

int square(int x)
{
    return x * x;
}

int main(void)
{
    for(int i = 0; i < 10; i++) {
        int i_squared = square(i);
        if(i_squared > 10) {
            printf("%d\n", i_squared);
        }
    }
}
```

Exercise: What does the above program print? Try it out.

As an aside, here's an example use of a floating point number:

```
#include <stdio.h>

int main(void)
{
    float x = 3.4f;
    float y = 4.2f;
    float z = 2.2f * x + y;
    printf("z is %f\n", z);
    printf("z with two digits after the decimal point: %.2f\n",␣
↪z);
}
```

Here we define some floating point variables using the keyword "float". Note that we need to use the letter "f" after the numeric literal to denote a (single precision) floating point number. We can pass a floating point number to printf() using "%f" as the placeholder.

With floating point numbers, it's possible that printf() by default includes several digits after the comma, making numbers more difficult to read. The above code illustrates modifying the placeholder to "%.2f" which tells printf() to only display two digits after the decimal point.

Exercise: Type, compile and run the above program.

Exercise: Define and use a function that calculates the area of a circle. The function should receive the radius as the input and return the area as the output. The types should be float for both input and output. Use the formula "area = 3.14 * radius * radius".

Exercise: Use the above function to print out the areas of circles with radius 1, 2, 3... up to 10. Note that you can pass an integer to a function that expects a float as an input parameter. The compiler will *implicitly* convert an int to a float.

Exercise: Write a program that, for numbers from 1 to 10, will print the area of the circle with that radius if the area is between 10 and 100.

Similarly to Python, C supports operators such as / (division) and % (modulo, or remainder).

Exercise: Write a program that prints out the numbers between 1 to 10 which, after being divided by 3, have a remainder of 1.

As before, we should now have everything we need to write FizzBuzz.

Exercise: Write the code to solve FizzBuzz in C.

1.1.8 Learning to learn

There are a few concepts to point out about learning programming.

When learning a programming language, there are a few different areas that need to be learned. One is the syntax. For example, the syntax for branches in Python looks like this:

```
if a > 5:
    print 'a is greater than 5'
```

While for example in C it would look like this:

```
if(a > 5) {
    printf("a is greater than 5\n");
}
```

Another is the standard library, i.e. the library included as part of the language implementation. For example, as part of its standard library, Python has a module for math functions, called "math":

```
import math

print math.sqrt(5)
print math.pi
```

The "math" module has lots of functions, and the *reference* for them can be accessed in the Python interpreter e.g. by running the following commands:

```
1 $ python2
2 Python 2.7.13 (default, Dec 21 2016, 07:16:46)
3 [GCC 6.2.1 20160830] on linux2
4 Type "help", "copyright", "credits" or "license" for more information.
5 >>> import math
6 >>> help(math)
```

That is, on line 1 we run "python2" in shell to start the Python interactive interpreter. On line 5 we import the math module, and on line 6 we ask for the help for that module.

Exercise: Check out the help for the math module in Python. You can exit the help screen by pressing "q". You can exit the Python interpreter by pressing ctrl+d.

The concept of reference is important: it's a factual listing of a library or a programming language. It typically doesn't include examples or tutorials but is useful for getting a deeper understanding of a subject.

As another example, we will introduce the Unix command "ls", a tool for listing files. In order to gain initial understanding of this tool, this book will give a couple of examples:

```
$ ls
genindex.html  index.html  objects.inv                regex.html␣
↪  searchindex.js  _static
_images        js.html     python_generate_file.html  search.
↪html  _sources         unix.html
$ ls -l
total 108
drwxr-xr-x 2 antti users  4096 Feb  5 23:51 _images
drwxr-xr-x 2 antti users  4096 Feb  7 00:48 _sources
drwxr-xr-x 2 antti users  4096 Feb  5 23:51 _static
-rw-r--r-- 1 antti users  2603 Feb  7 23:33 genindex.html
[...]
```

This example shows that merely running "ls" will list the files, while adding the switch "-l" will give more information, such as the last modify time of the files. However, "ls" has a lot more possible switches which are not all covered in this book, although they will become useful and will to some extent be necessary to use, learn and understand as a software engineer. Hence it'll be important to refer to the reference of the command to get an overview. This can typically be done either by passing the switch "–help" to the relevant command, or reading the manual for the command (by running "man", e.g. "man ls"). For example:

```
$ ls --help
Usage: ls [OPTION]... [FILE]...
List information about the FILEs (the current directory by␣
↪default).
Sort entries alphabetically if none of -cftuvSUX nor --sort is␣
↪specified.
```

(continues on next page)

(continued from previous page)

```
Mandatory arguments to long options are mandatory for short␣
↪options too.
  -a, --all                  do not ignore entries starting with␣
↪.
  -A, --almost-all           do not list implied . and ..
[...]
```

If you run "man ls" you'll open the manual page which you can exit by pressing "q".

Exercise: Open the manual page for ls.

The same principle applies not only to Unix commands, but also to programming languages as well as standard and non-standard libraries. For example, for most programming languages there is either a language specification or reference material available which should be consulted whenever questions arise about a specific behaviour in a programming language. Similarly, libraries typically come with references. The standard library for C is included in the Unix man pages, such that for example running "man scanf" will present a detailed documentation of the scanf() function family. For other libraries, the website of the library or other similar material should be consulted. Many libraries also install their own man pages as part of the library installation.

Terminology wise, this book will use the terms "API" and "library" interchangeably. The acronym "API" stands for "Application Programming Interface" and generally means the interface, i.e. the available functions, variables and other constructs, that a library provides to make use of the library. For example, if one were to use the libcurl library, a library for downloading files via URLs, one would want to find the reference of the library on the web page of the software.

Exercise: Look up the man page for printf().

Exercise: Find the reference of the libcurl library online. See if you can find both the entry point to the reference as well as the reference of a specific libcurl function, for example curl_easy_init().

1.2 Basics of programming in Python and C

1.2.1 Quadratic formula in C

Now that we're able to create some C programs, let's try a bit more complicated one. Let's write a program to solve a quadratic equation.

As you may know, a quadratic equation is an equation $ax^2+bx+c=0$, whereby a, b and c are constants. A quadratic function, when plotted, may look e.g. like this:

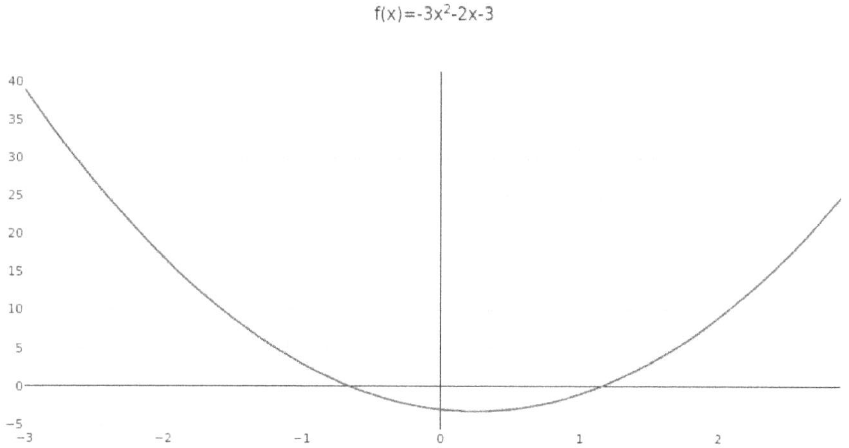

Solving the quadratic equation provides the *roots* of the equation, i.e. the x values at which the x-axis is crossed. For the above function, the roots are at points x=-0.72 and x=1.39. There may be 0, 1 or 2 roots, and the formula to solve the quadratic equation is:

$$x = \frac{-b \pm \sqrt{b^2 - 4ac}}{2a}$$

This mathematical formula can be implemented in C. For example like this:

```
x = (-b + sqrt(b * b - 4.0f * a * c)) / (2.0f * a);
```

The +/- part of the formula causes up to two possible solutions for x to be available; the above C formulation only identifies one.

There may be 0, 1 or 2 roots; the case of 0 roots occurs when the part for which the square root is calculated (also called the *discriminant*) is negative, as a negative number cannot have a real square root. The case of 1 root occurs when the discriminant is exactly 0.

The C function sqrt() is part of the standard C library but there's a twist: in order to use the function, the header file <math.h> should be included. Furthermore, you may need to link your program against the *math library* by passing "-lm" to your C compiler when compiling.

Exercise: Write a program that solves the quadratic equation for a=3.0, b=-2.0, c=-3.0. Print out the number of roots as well as all found roots.

OK, so we now have a program that solves the quadratic equation for some values. What if I asked you to solve the quadratic equation for three, or ten, different functions (a, b and c values), in the same program? There are several ways to approach this but one thing we should avoid is copy-pasting the code to solve the equation multiple times. Instead we should capture this logic in a *function*.

What we require is a function which takes a, b and c as input parameters and returns the roots, as well as an indication as to how many roots were found. Once we have this function we can then call it with different parameters and write out the information about the roots after each call.

Now, there are a few ways this could be approached. An interesting limitation we arrive at is that C can only return one value in a function. However, we can still write our function by using *pointers*.

Pointers

Every variable in C has an *address* in memory. Speaking in metaphors, if a variable was a house, then the value of the variable would be the contents of the house, and the memory address would be the address of the house. A pointer in C is a variable for which the value can be the address of another variable.

Here's an example:

```
1  #include <stdio.h>
2
3  int main(void)
4  {
5          int a = 42;
6          int *p;
7          p = &a;
8          *p = 45;
9          printf("The value of a is: %d\n", a);
10         printf("The value of p is: %p\n", p);
11         printf("The value of what p points to is: %d\n", *p);
12 }
```

- Line 5: We define an integer variable called "a".
- Line 6: We define a variable called "p" which is a pointer to an integer. The asterisk ("*") means the type is a pointer.
- Line 7: We assign a value to "p", namely *the address of* a. The ampersand ("&") means "address of".
- Line 8: We assign a value to *what "p" points to*. The asterisk operator ("*") means *dereferencing* the pointer.
- Lines 9-11: We print out the values of "a", "p" and "*p".

Exercise: What would you expect the output to be? Try it out.

In this example, using the pointer wasn't necessary because if we wanted to change the value of "a", we could have done it directly. However, if you want to change the value of a variable of another function then pointers become useful. What you can do is pass the address of a variable to the other function. The other function can then modify the value of that variable. In this way we can "return" multiple values from a single function.

The following example illustrates the principle:

```
#include <stdio.h>

void increment_by_one(int *p1, int *p2)
{
        *p1 = *p1 + 1;
        *p2 = *p2 + 1;
```

(continues on next page)

(continued from previous page)

```
7  }
8
9  int main(void)
10 {
11         int a = 42;
12         int b = 5;
13         increment_by_one(&a, &b);
14         printf("The value of a is: %d\n", a);
15         printf("The value of b is: %d\n", b);
16 }
```

- Lines 3-7: We define a function called "increment_by_one" which doesn't have a return value and takes two input parameters. Both input parameters are pointers to int.
- Line 5: We assign the value of what "p1" points to plus one to what "p1" points to.
- Line 6: The same for "p2".
- Lines 11-13: In our main function, we define two int variables, and pass the addresses of these to the "increment_by_one" function.

Here, we have a function that takes two pointers and increments the values of the variables that are pointed to by one.

We should now have what we need to create a function that solves the quadratic equation.

Exercise: Write such a function. It should have parameters a, b and c (all floats) as well as r1 and r2 (pointers to floats). It should return an int which is the number of roots found for the given function. In other words, its function *signature* should be e.g. "int quad(float a, float b, float c, float *r1, float *r2)". In your main function, define the variables a, b, c, r1, r2 and number_of_roots. Set the variables such that you can solve the quadratic equation for a=3.0, b=-2.0, c=-3.0. Print out the roots found. Only call printf() within main.

Exercise: Modify your code to solve the quadratic equation for a=3.0, b=-2.0, c=3.0 (positive c instead of negative). This equation has no roots. What happens if you print out the values of r1 and r2?

Now that we have a function that can solve the quadratic equation, we should try solving several equations and outputting the results. For the next exercise, let's assume our goal is to provide the roots for three different quadratic equations, namely:

- x^2-2x-3
- -x^2-x-1
- 2x^2+2x+0.5

How should we structure the code for this? We should keep our solver function clean of side effects by not using printf() in it. Indeed, the ideal main function for this task could look like this:

```
int main(void)
{
    solve_and_print(1.0f, -2.0f, -3.0f);
    solve_and_print(-1.0f, -1.0f, -1.0f);
    solve_and_print(2.0f, 2.0f, 0.5f);
}
```

In other words, for each of the functions to find the roots for, we call a function which does the solving and the printing. We already have a function that can solve the equation so what's left to implement is capturing the behaviour of using the solver function and printing the results.

Exercise: Write a program that solves the quadratic equation for the three functions listed above, and prints the results. Your main function should look like the one above. The function solve_and_print() should take three parameters, a, b and c, call the solver function and print the results of the solver function.

1.2.2 Lots of quadratic equations

Files

Now that we're able to solve multiple quadratic equations, let's step it up one notch. Let's have the goal of calculating the roots of 10,000 quadratic equations and finding the function with the largest root, whereby the definitions of all functions are stored in a file.

You can find a download link at the web site of this book. That file will have one function definition in it.

This file looks like the following:

```
-2.892091 -2.197815 -4.943323
```

In other words, it's a file with one line. The line has three floating point numbers. The numbers represent a quadratic function with values a, b and c respectively.

The C standard library provides an interface for opening, reading, writing and closing files. A file can be opened like this:

```c
FILE *fp = fopen("test.txt", "r");
if(fp == NULL) {
    fprintf(stderr, "Could not open file.\n");
}
```

In other words, there's a standard function called fopen() (for "file open") which takes two parameters. The first parameter is the path and name of the file to open. If no path is given, it is expected that the file is located in the current working directory. The second parameter takes a string which identifies what should be done with the file. The string "r" means the file should be opened for reading only. The string "w" would mean the file is opened for writing; opening a file for writing this way would delete its previous contents. The function fopen() returns a value of type pointer to "FILE". "FILE" is a special type which can be used when reading or writing to a file, or closing it.

If the file could not be opened, a special pointer called *NULL pointer* is returned instead. *NULL pointer* is a pointer which is invalid. We can check whether the pointer is a NULL pointer by using the code like above. The convention is that error messages are written out to *standard error* instead of *standard output* using the fprintf() function like above for reasons that will be expanded upon later in this book.

Exercise: Look up the man page for fopen().

Once you have a file open, you can close it using the following code:

```
fclose(fp);
```

Exercise: Look up the man page for fclose().

How about reading a file? There are several ways to do this. One way we could use is to use the function fread(), but in our case, the function fscanf() suits better. fscanf() is a bit like the inverse of printf(): it takes a format string and the addresses of variables where the contents of the string should be stored, according to the placeholders in the format string. An example is probably the best way to illustrate this:

```
1 float a;
2 float b;
3 float c;
4 int num_read = fscanf(fp, "%f %f %f", &a, &b, &c);
5 if(num_read != 3) {
6     fprintf(stderr, "Could not read three numbers.\n");
7 }
```

Let's go through this line by line:

- Lines 1-3: We define three variables of type float.
- Line 4: We use fscanf() to *read in* the contents of the file. We pass fscanf() five parameters: The first one is the FILE pointer. The second one is the format string. In our format string, we say we're expecting the file to contain three floating point numbers, separated by a space. The last three parameters are the addresses of our floating point variables. We tell fscanf() that we'd like to store the contents of the three floating point numbers from the file to these variables.
- Line 5: We check the *return value* of fscanf(). fscanf() returns the number of variables for which the data could be stored. We passed in three addresses so we expect it to have stored data for three variables. If the return value is not three then something went wrong during

reading of the file; for example, only two numbers were available in the file.

Exercise: Look up the man page for fread() and fscanf().

Digression: what do fread() and fscanf() *actually* do?

The functions fread() and fscanf() are implemented in the C standard library code. The specific code is implementation specific but either of them will probably call the read() function which invokes a *system call* - calling code prepared by the *operating system kernel* which relies on the CPU specific features to transfer the code execution to the kernel, and call a specific kernel function.

The specific kernel function will be a function (typically a C function) which will look up, based on the path of the opened file, which hardware device is responsible for the file. If we assume that a hard disk is responsible for the file, then the kernel code will call the *hard disk device driver* code. This code, which may be specific to the make and model of the hard disk, will communicate with the actual hard disk hardware by setting its registers and reading values. It will do this e.g. to direct the magnetic head on the hard disk to read the data from the correct sector on the hard disk.

Once the device driver has the requested data, it will then provide the data to the caller function in kernel space, which will copy the data back to *user space* - i.e. the memory area where our program is running. The control is finally transferred back to our program and the data we wanted to read is accessible in our variables.

We should now have what we need in order to read a quadratic equation definition from the file referenced above, and calculate its roots.

Exercise: Download the above text file in your computer. Add code in your program to open that file. Read in the contents of that file to three variables. Use your previously written function solve_and_print() to solve that quadratic equation and print the roots.

Larger files

Now that we're able to read in one quadratic equation definition from a file, let's try this for 10,000 equations. You can download a related file on the book web site.

That file contains 10,000 lines, each containing three floating point numbers, each representing a, b and c respectively. Let's see if we can find the equation with the largest root.

Exercise: Download the above file. Modify your program to open that file. Add a loop in your program to loop through your code that reads in the values a, b and c and solves the root for that quadratic equation such that your program reads through all the 10,000 equations and calculates the root for all of them. Note: you may want to *not* print out the roots for all equations as that could create a lot of output.

Aside: Arrays

While this problem can be solved without arrays, you may find it useful to use them.

An array simply contains multiple variables of the same type, such that the variables are all stored next to each other. They can be useful if you need multiple variables of the same type. In other words, instead of writing e.g.:

```
/* don't do this */
int a0 = 0;
int a1 = 10;
int a2 = 20;
int a3 = 30;
int a4 = 40;
```

...you can write:

```
int a[5];
for(int i = 0; i < 5; i++) {
    a[i] = i * 10;
}
```

(The text between /* and */ is a *comment*; you can use these to explain your code.) We don't save very much typing with just five elements, but the more elements you have, the more is saved by using arrays.

Now we can try to find the equation with the largest root, i.e. the equation where we find a root that is arithmetically larger than any other root.

Exercise: Find the equation with the largest root. To do this, you need to note the largest root by having a variable to store this *outside* the loop. For all the roots found for an equation, compare those roots with the largest root found so far. If the root for the current equation is larger than the largest found so far, make note of it by modifying the variable which holds the largest root. Similarly, keep track of the variables a, b and c for the equation with the largest root. Print the a, b and c values of the equation with the largest root at the end.

Phew! We've learned a lot in this section.

1.2.3 Quadratic formula in Python

To improve our programming skills, let's repeat the previous exercises in Python.

This should be easier not only because Python is a higher level language but also because we're already familiar with the problem domain.

From this point on, the book will use Python 2. This is not because Python 3 is a worse language - in fact it's very similar, and probably better - this is mostly due to the author being more used to Python 2. However, because the two languages are so similar you should have no problem picking up Python 3 later on when needed.

It's system specific how to start the Python 2 interpreter. Typically, at the time of writing, there are up to three possible commands you can run:

- "python": If present, this would start the default Python interpreter, which often is Python 2, but could also be Python 3. You can find out which by looking at the first lines of the interpreter output or by running "python –version".
- "python2": If present, this would start the Python 2 interpreter.
- "python3": If present, this would start the Python 3 interpreter.

Exercise: Find out which Python interpreter or interpreters you have installed. If you only have Python 3, also install the Python 2 interpreter.

We can now refresh our thinking behind Python. Comparing Python and C for the first exercise - having some code able to solve the quadratic equation at all - there are a few differences:

- In C, all code must reside in functions. The function called "main" is the starting point for the code. In contrast, in Python it is allowed to have code on the top level, i.e. without defining any functions at all. Code is then executed top down. Functions can also be defined at top level but they won't be executed until the function is called.
- In C, we need to denote the floating point values with an "f" to denote the values as single precision values (as opposed to double precision; typically 32 bits vs. 64 bits of storage). In Python, the denotation isn't necessary (precision is interpreter specific and typically 64 bit).

- In C, in order to use square root, we #include <math.h>, link against the math library with the compiler flag -lm and call the sqrt() function. In Python, we *import math* and call the math.sqrt() function.

We should now have what we need. To get started, here's a simple Python program that calculates one root value:

```
import math

a = 3.0
b = -2.0
c = -3.0
disc = b * b - 4.0 * a * c
if disc >= 0:
    r1 = (-b + math.sqrt(disc)) / (2.0 * a)
    print 'Value of r1 is %.2f' % r1
```

Exercise: Write a Python program that solves the quadratic equation for a=3.0, b=-2.0, c=-3.0. Print out the number of roots as well as all found roots.

Functions and lists

Next up we should encapsulate our quadratic equation code to a function. As C doesn't support returning multiple values from a function we resorted to using pointers. Python handles this differently as it can return *lists* which can contain any number of elements. (To be pedantic, C can return a programmer defined data structure or an array allocated in dynamic memory as well; these topics will be covered later.)

Here are some examples around using lists in Python:

```
l = list()              # l is now an empty list
x = 3
l.append(x)             # l now contains [3]
l.append(x * 2)         # l now contains [3, 6]
l = [x, x * 2, x * 3]  # l now contains [3, 6, 9]
print len(l)            # prints 3 (the number of elements in l)
print l[0]              # prints 3 (the first element of l)
print l[2]              # prints 9 (the third element of l)
y = l[1]                # y is now 6
```

(continues on next page)

(continued from previous page)

```
for element in l:       # for loop - creates a new variable called
↪"element"
    print element       # prints 3, 6 and 9 in separate lines
```

The above also demonstrates the commenting syntax in Python; hash (#) until the end of the line are comments.

Similarly, one can return a list from a function in Python:

```
def return_a_list(x):
    return [x, x * 2]

return_list = return_a_list(3)
for elem in return_list:
    print 'Element in list: %d' % elem
```

The above function returns a list with the input parameter as well as the double of the input parameter. The following code calls that function and prints out the output.

Exercise: Write a function to solve the quadratic equation. It should have input parameters a, b and c and return a list of 0, 1 or 2 elements, depending on how many roots the equation has. In your code outside the function, call the function such that you can solve the quadratic equation for a=3.0, b=-2.0, c=-3.0. Print out the number of roots found (using len()), as well as the roots themselves. Only call "print" outside the function. You can iterate over the list of roots using a for loop.

Now, following our playbook, let's consider the need for solving, and printing, the roots for three different equations. Again, our toplevel code should only contain the following:

```
solve_and_print(1.0, -2.0, -3.0)
solve_and_print(-1.0, -1.0, -1.0)
solve_and_print(2.0, 2.0, 0.5)
```

Here, we should write the function solve_and_print() ourselves, and it should first call our solver function, followed by the necessary print statements to print the results.

Exercise: Write a Python program that solves the quadratic equation for the three functions listed above, and prints the results. Your top level code should look like the one above. The function solve_and_print() should take three parameters, a, b and c, call the solver function and print the results of the solver function.

Files

We can now consider reading files in Python. While files can be opened in Python by using open() followed by a close() to close the file in the end, we can do better by using the *with* statement which will automatically close the file when the "with" statement is exited. The following code snippet illustrates this by opening a file called "test1.txt" for reading and reads all its contents to a string variable called "text":

```
with open('test1.txt', 'r') as f:
    text = f.read()
```

There are a few points to make:

- The built-in function open(), like in C, takes two parameters: the file to open and the mode. The mode is here set to 'r' indicating read mode. If the mode was set to 'w' for write mode, the file contents would be deleted at open.
- With the "with" statement, the name of the variable representing the file object is defined after the "as" keyword - in the above it is "f".
- We then use the file object, which was the output of the open() function, to call its member function read(). The open() function returns a file object, like in C, and the member function read() reads all the contents of the file and returns a string. This string is stored in the variable "text" in the code above.

Exercise: Try opening a file in Python and storing its contents to a variable like above. Print out the contents by printing out the value of the variable.

We now have a variable with text inside, and like in C, we need to somehow *parse* the three floating point variables, a, b and c, from it. Instead of using a function from the scanf() family, Python provides different means:

```
words = text.split()
numbers = list()
```

(continues on next page)

(continued from previous page)

```
3 for word in words:
4     number = float(word)
5     numbers.append(number)
```

Let's see what this code does:

- Line 1: We call the member function split() on "text". This function, turns a string to *a list of strings*, whereby a whitespace (space or tab) defines the number of elements. E.g. evaluating a string "1.23 -2.34 3.45".split() will return ["1.23", "-2.34", "3.45"].
- Line 2: We create an empty list.
- Line 3: We loop through each element in the list of strings.
- Line 4: We *convert* a string to a floating point number by using the built-in float() function. This takes a value of e.g. a string or an int as input and returns a float.
- Line 5: We append the number to our list. In the end we have a list of numbers.

A thing to note at this point is that you can use the Python interpreter to try out different code. After running e.g. "python2" you end up with a prompt (">>>") where you can type any Python expression and see the result.

Exercise: Start the Python interpreter. Set a variable resembling our input string, e.g. "s = '1.23 -2.34 3.45'" (without double quotes but with single quotes). Split it by running "s.split()".

Exercise: Look up the Python documentation for split() by running "help(str.split)" in the Python interpreter.

After the above we should ensure we parsed the correct number of numbers from the file:

```
if len(numbers) != 3:
    print >> sys.stderr, 'Could not parse file correctly'
```

The above demonstrates the Python syntax for writing to standard error, like we did in C. (You will need to "import sys" first.)

Exercise: Add code in your Python program to open the file with a single line from the previous section. Read in the contents of that file to a list, converting the data to floating point numbers. Use your previously written function solve_and_print() to solve that quadratic equation and print the roots.

We can now approach the file with 10,000 equations and find the equation with the largest root. How would we handle a file with 10,000 lines in Python, each holding three numbers? We can first open() the file and read() all its contents to a string like before. After that, we should split that string so we have a list with 10,000 strings, one for each line. This can be done using the following:

```
with open('test.txt', 'r') as f:
    text = f.read()
    lines = text.split('\n')
```

Here, we use the split() member function again, but we pass it the *optional parameter* set to 'n' which denotes newline. This causes the split() function to split the string to a list of strings where each element in the list is a line. Once we have that, we can have a loop that parses the three numbers from each line.

However, there's actually a shortcut in Python for this common use case. We can simply iterate over the file object, which by default provides us with a line for each iteration:

```
with open('test.txt', 'r') as f:
    for line in f:
        # process each line here
```

Exercise: Modify your program to open the larger file from the previous section. Add a loop in your program to loop through your code that reads in the values a, b and c and solves the root for that quadratic equation such that your program reads through all the 10,000 equations and calculates the root for all of them. Note: you may want to *not* print out the roots for all equations as that could create a lot of output.

Exercise: Find the equation with the largest root. As before, to do this, you need to note the largest root by having a variable to store this outside the loop. For all the roots found for an equation, compare those roots with the largest root found so far. If the root for the current equation is larger than the largest found so far, make note of it by modifying the variable which holds the largest root. Similarly, keep track of the variables a, b and c for the equation with the largest root. Print the a, b and c values of the equation with the largest root at the end.

1.2.4 Generating input data using Python

Previously we wrote a program that calculates the roots of 10,000 quadratic equations. You may ask, where did the input data, i.e. the definitions of 10,000 quadratic equations, come from?

The short answer is that is was generated using a Python script. How would we go about generating this file in Python? The file contains 10,000 lines, each having three floating point numbers. The numbers should be random. Python provides a set of random functions, the simplest one being random.random(), which returns a random floating point number between 0 and 1:

```
import random

value = random.random()
print value
```

Writing files in Python is fairly straightforward. We can use the 'with' clause which ensures the file will be closed after we're done with it:

```
with open('test.txt', 'w') as f:
    for i in xrange(5):
        f.write("%f %f\n" % (0.2, 0.5))
```

This program will create a file called test.txt with five times the line "0.200000 0.500000". (If the file existed before, it will be overwritten.)

Exercise: Create the described input file. To make the functions more interesting, don't use the output of random.random() directly, i.e. don't only store numbers between 0.0 and 1.0, but use multiplication and subtraction to generate numbers that are e.g. between -10.0 and 10.0.

1.3 Unix shell

1.3.1 Basic Unix shell usage

> UNIX is simple and coherent, but it takes a genius (or at any rate, a programmer) to understand and appreciate its simplicity.
>
> —Dennis Ritchie

Basic Unix shell commands are quite useful in day to day software development.

Let's assume you have the file with 10,000 lines defining the functions as discussed in "Quadratic formula". In order to inspect this file, you could open it in the text editor, but there are also other, typically easier, ways to achieve this.

In the following, the character '$' means the shell prompt, i.e. you typically type in the shell whatever comes after '$'.

If you wanted to take a quick look browsing a file, you could use the utility 'less':

```
$ less test.txt
```

This will open the file test.txt in 'less', which allows you to read and browse the file. Less has a few useful commands:

- 'q' exits less
- '/' allows you to search in the file - type '/' followed by the string you want to search for, followed by 'return'
- 'n' repeats the previous search
- 'N' repeats the previous search but searches backwards

There are a few more, and you can look up the reference for 'less' to see all of them (by running "man less"). These same commands are to some degree shared across several other Unix tools. For example vim has the same commands for searching.

Let's say you only wanted to see the beginning of the file. You can achieve this using 'head':

```
$ head test.txt
7.269553 3.427526 6.633603
1.980206 -3.655827 -2.629755
-8.687820 -6.930905 -8.731439
-0.608791 -8.126272 -8.652504
[...]
```

This will print the first ten lines of the file. You can adjust the number of lines output by using the "-n" switch. For example, the command "head -n5 test.txt" would only output the first five lines.

The command 'tail' can be used to output the last lines of a file, by default ten:

```
$ tail test.txt
[...]
-7.058864 -5.461025 -8.337095
-0.197971 -1.485949 -0.748672
-3.051099 -9.215679 3.597125
0.868340 -2.444818 -3.173135
```

If you want to search for a string in the file, you can use 'grep':

```
$ grep "1234" test.txt
6.133025 -4.612349 4.969612
-0.904910 -5.976920 8.821234
-6.123416 7.494195 4.350390
-1.123468 0.327963 1.291879
```

This command would print all lines which have the string "1234" in them. The command 'grep' also has a lot of useful switches, for example including lines before or after the line that includes the search string, or inverse search (only print lines that don't have a match).

Exercise: Find out which grep switch makes grep only select non-matching lines.

If you only wanted to print one column of the file, you could achieve this using 'awk':

```
$ awk '{print $1}' test.txt
7.269553
1.980206
-8.687820
-0.608791
[...]
```

This example only prints the first column in the file. ('awk' by default assumed the space is the delimiter character.)

'awk' is actually a programming language capable of much more, but much of the daily use is simple one-liners. Let's say we want to calculate the average of all values in the first column. This can be achieved using 'awk':

```
$ awk '{sum += $1; n++} END {print sum / n}' test.txt
0.0478027
```

What this line means is:

- For each line, take the value of the number in the first column, and add it in the variable called "sum" (automatically initialised to 0). Increment the variable "n" by one (also automatically initialised to 0).
- After the file has been processed, print "sum" divided by "n", i.e. the sum divided by the number of lines.

Another useful command is 'wc', or "word count", which can be used to count the words in a file:

```
$ wc test.txt
10000  30000 284890 test.txt
```

The output includes the number of lines, words, characters and the file name. By adding the switch '-l', only the number of lines and the file name are output:

```
$ wc -l test.txt
10000 test.txt
```

The final command introduced here is 'sed', or "stream editor", which modified the input using a given expression. For example we can use 'sed' to change all space characters in the file to commas:

```
$ sed 's/ /,/g' test.txt
7.269553,3.427526,6.633603
1.980206,-3.655827,-2.629755
-8.687820,-6.930905,-8.731439
-0.608791,-8.126272,-8.652504
[...]
```

Let's break down this expression 's/ /,/g':

- The character '/' is the delimiter; the expression consists of four parts: 's', ' ', ',' and 'g':
- 's': initial command: search (and replace)
- ' ': search for the space character
- ',': replace with the comma
- 'g': do this globally, i.e. not only once per line (the default), but for all occurrences in the file.

Another example is removing all '-' characters from the file:

```
$ sed 's/-//g' test.txt
7.269553 3.427526 6.633603
1.980206 3.655827 2.629755
8.687820 6.930905 8.731439
0.608791 8.126272 8.652504
[...]
```

We can also pass multiple expressions to 'sed' by using the '-e' switch, for example to replace spaces with commas and remove the dashes:

```
$ sed -e 's/ /,/g' -e 's/-//g' test.txt
7.269553,3.427526,6.633603
1.980206,3.655827,2.629755
8.687820,6.930905,8.731439
0.608791,8.126272,8.652504
[...]
```

Unix pipelines

The 'awk' command above lists the first column for all 10,000 lines which might not be what you want. Let's say you only wanted to see the first ten lines, i.e. apply the 'head' command to the output of the 'awk' command. You can achieve this using pipelines:

```
$ awk '{print $1}' test.txt | head
7.269553
1.980206
-8.687820
-0.608791
[...]
```

In this case, head doesn't take a file name as input, but instead reads from standard input, i.e. the output from 'awk'. This is the typical behaviour for Unix commands.

In general, the commands can be combined in any way, giving a lot of power to the user.

Exercise: Find out how many lines in the file have no '0' character in them.

Further Unix shell tips and tricks

man

The command "man" (short for "manual") allows you to browse the documentation of different tools. For example, running "man grep" will display the documentation for grep. The documentation is opened using "less", such that you can browse the text freely and exit with 'q'.

There can be multiple man pages for a single command. For example, "man signal" can mean either looking up the signal() C standard library functions or the general overview of signals. The man pages are categorised by type, such that for example category 1 means commands that can be run, 3 means C standard library functions and 7 means miscellaneous documentation. You can specify which category you mean by including it in your command, for example:

```
$ man 7 signal
```

...will, on some Linux systems, look up the man page on signal in category 7, providing the reader with an overview of signals in Unix.

Exercise: Look up the man page for the command "man".

Exercise: Look up the man page for the C function call "printf".

sort

The tool "sort" sorts its input line by line. By default it sorts alphabetically, but by passing the switch "-n" it will interpret its input data numerically. It by default sorts based on the beginning of each line but this can be changed:

```
$ sort -n test.txt | head
-9.995596 8.887278 2.325502
-9.995454 -0.339710 4.518171
-9.993047 -9.059912 -0.660508
-9.990530 -5.503126 -8.374026
[...]
```

(If your sort command output seems nonsensical, it might be due to the locale set on your shell such that the decimal point is defined as ',' instead of '.', confusing sort. You should be able to fix this by running "export LC_ALL=C".)

The above sorted the data based on the first column. If we wanted to sort by the second column instead, we can use:

```
$ sort -n -k 2 test.txt | head
0.649875 -9.998834 2.834749
-3.819303 -9.998413 -7.295722
0.985071 -9.997176 1.182082
-6.991833 -9.995815 -7.523136
```

"sort" also allows redefining the delimiter character using the "-t" switch. For more information, run "man sort".

Variables

Variable support is typically something that Unix shells have built in. That is, defining variables isn't executing a program per se, but rather using a feature of the shell itself.

Terminology wise, there are different Unix shells (called for example bash, tcsh, zsh), each with different characteristics and quirks, but each one typically implements the same core functionality, namely being compatible with the original Unix shell (sh) and conforming to the POSIX shell specification.

This example defines a variable in bash:

```
$ MY_FILE=test.txt
$ head -n1 $MY_FILE
7.269553 3.427526 6.633603
```

In other words, defining a variable is trivial, and you can use the variable by prefixing it with a dollar sign.

Sometimes you might want to combine the variable with other bits. In those cases it's typically safe to enclose the variable with curly brackets ({ and }). This will make it clear when the variable name starts and ends. For example, if we wanted to combine two variables in one file name:

```
$ MY_FILE_START=test
$ MY_FILE_SUFFIX=txt
$ echo ${MY_FILE_START}.${MY_FILE_SUFFIX}
test.txt
```

Furthermore, you can *export* variables such that they're available to programs started by the shell. These are also called *environment variables* as they form the environment for a program. For example, running "export MY_FILE_SUFFIX=txt" makes the environment variable MY_FILE_SUFFIX available to any programs started by the shell. Programs can then access these environment variables using e.g. C standard library functions. This may e.g. allow you to easily make the input or output files of a program configurable.

echo and cat

The command "echo" simply prints its input. For example:

```
$ echo "hello"
hello
$ echo $MY_FILE
test.txt
$ echo "abc,def,ghi" | sed -e 's/,/ /g'
abc def ghi
```

The command "cat" concatenates files. It can also be used to display the contents of a file:

```
$ cat test.txt
7.269553 3.427526 6.633603
1.980206 -3.655827 -2.629755
-8.687820 -6.930905 -8.731439
-0.608791 -8.126272 -8.652504
[...]
```

Exit codes

Whenever you've finished running a program in Unix, it will return an exit code. The convention is that the exit code 0 means success while non-0 means failure. You can typically see the conditions under which a program returns success or failure by looking at the documentation. For example, grep returns exit code 1 if the search string was not found at all. You can use the special built-in variable $? to access the exit code:

```
$ grep 2345 test.txt
5.145898 3.219212 3.234599
3.323714 3.883829 -4.722345
6.142345 -4.611688 0.817618
-7.761082 9.886385 -5.742345
$ echo $?
0
$ grep 23456 test.txt
```

(continues on next page)

(continued from previous page)

```
$ echo $?
1
```

Multiple commands

You can run multiple commands in series in one line. The following runs "head", followed by "tail":

```
$ head -n 1 test.txt ; tail -n 1 test.txt
7.269553 3.427526 6.633603
0.868340 -2.444818 -3.173135
```

You can also run multiple commands depending on the exit code of the previous execution. The shorthand "&&" means "run the following command only if the previous command succeeded, i.e. returned an exit code 0". The shorthand "||" means "run the following command only if the previous command failed". You can also group commands using parentheses. For example:

```
$ (grep 2345 test.txt && echo "found") || echo "not found"
5.145898 3.219212 3.234599
3.323714 3.883829 -4.722345
6.142345 -4.611688 0.817618
-7.761082 9.886385 -5.742345
found
$ (grep 23456 test.txt && echo "found") || echo "not found"
not found
```

Globbing

Globbing refers to using special characters to match multiple files. An example is "*.py" which means "all files with the extension .py in the current directory". For example, to find out the number of lines in Python files:

```
$ wc -l *.py
 156 conf.py
```

(continues on next page)

(continued from previous page)

```
   8 gen.py
   4 rand.py
   3 with.py
 171 total
```

Seq

The command "seq" simply outputs a sequence of numbers:

```
$ seq 1 5
1
2
3
4
5
```

This might not be very useful by itself but can be handy when combined with other tools.

Find

Find is useful for finding files, and optionally performing operations on them.

For example, let's assume you have a directory with subdirectories, with the directory and subdirectories having lots of Python files. Let's further assume you had used the Python "with" statement in some of the files and would like to see how, but you can't remember which files exactly use "with". Find and grep to the rescue:

```
$ find . -name '*.py' -exec grep with {} +
./conf.py:# extensions coming with Sphinx (named 'sphinx.ext.*')␣
↪or your custom
./with.py:with open('test.txt', 'w') as f:
```

Let's go through this point by point:

- We execute find with several parameters

- The first parameter is '.', i.e. search in the current working directory (as well as subdirectories)
- Search for files with the extension '.py'
- For each found file, run "grep with $filename". The notation {} means the found file name will be used here, and the final '+' means the grep command will be run once with all the files as parameters. For example, if the find command found three Python files, ./a.py, subdir/b.py and subdir2/c.py, it would execute "grep with ./a.py subdir/b.py subdir2/c.py".

The output has two lines: one with grep matching in conf.py, where a comment using the word "with", and another in with.py where the Python with statement was used.

If we only wanted to find the files with the Python extension without grepping, we simply leave out the -exec part:

```
$ find . -name '*.py'
./tmp/config.py
./conf.py
./my_project/hello.py
./guess/guess.py
./with.py
./rand.py
```

1.3.2 Unix shell scripting

> Those who don't understand Unix are condemned to reinvent it, poorly.
>
> —Henry Spencer

Redirecting

You can always write the output of any command to a file by redirecting, i.e. using the '>' character:

```
$ awk '{print $1}' test.txt > output.txt
```

This will create a file called output.txt, overwriting any previous contents, with the output of the 'awk' command.

You can also append to the end of an existing file, by using '>>':

```
$ awk '{print $1}' test.txt >> output.txt
```

Redirecting will allow us to simplify writing our own software. For example, it might not be necessary to open a file for writing in Python, so instead of this:

```
with open('test.txt', 'w') as f:
    for i in xrange(5):
        f.write("%f %f\n" % (0.2, 0.5))
```

...we can simply write this in Python:

```
for i in xrange(5):
    print "%f %f\n" % (0.5, 0.2)
```

...and then run it like this:

```
$ python my_file.py > test.txt
```

This has the added flexibility that we don't have to hard code the output file name.

If necessary, you can also discard the output by redirecting it to the special file /dev/null, which has the sole purpose of consuming and discarding all its input:

```
$ python my_file.py > /dev/null
```

Exercise: rewrite your program that generates the 10,000 functions file to write to standard output.

If you have a program that reads from standard input (stdin), you can have it read a file with a redirection:

```
$ python script.py < myfile.txt
```

Shell scripts

Simple for loops

In most Unix shells including bash you can define for loops. For example, let's say you wanted to run your number generation program three times, and store the output to different files:

```
$ for i in 1 2 3; do python gen.py > functions_${i}.txt ; done
```

This will generate three files named functions_1.txt, functions_2.txt and functions_3.txt.

If we wanted to generate a hundred files, typing in the number would get tedious. We can use "seq" instead:

```
$ for i in $(seq 1 100); do python gen.py > functions_${i}.txt ;␣
↪done
```

This will generate a hundred files. The notation $(...) allows capturing the output of a command within another command. By using curly braces ({}) around the 'i' variable we ensure the variable name gets correctly understood by the shell and not confused with the file name template.

if and branches

The shell built-in command "if" allows branching. There are other built-ins for comparing values against each other. For example:

```
$ grep -q 2345 test.txt ; return_value=$?; if [ $return_value -
↪eq 0 ]; then echo "found"; else echo "not found"; fi
```

This command will output "found" if the string was found in the input file, and "not found" otherwise. (The "-q" switch to grep suppresses output.)

Storing scripts in a file

It's often practical to store scripts to a file. Here's the previous example stored in a file:

```
#!/bin/bash

grep -q 2345 test.txt
return_value=$?
if [ $return_value -eq 0 ]; then
    echo "found"
else
    echo "not found"
fi
```

The script behaves similarly as the one-liner, but the script has one more line: it starts with "#!/bin/bash". This is also called shebang, a character sequence at the beginning of a script indicating which tool should be used to interpret the script (in this case bash).

You can store the above in a file, and then execute it by passing it to bash explicitly:

```
$ bash ./test.sh
found
```

Or you can simply make it executable, in which case it can be directly interpreted using bash:

```
$ chmod +x test.sh
$ ./test.sh
```

(The command "chmod" modifies the access rights to a file, and passing it "+x" means the file is allowed to be executed.)

Process handling

Process handling refers to managing how and when programs (processes) start and end.

Typically, unless overridden by the program, hitting ctrl+c sends SIGTERM (signal to terminate) to the current program. SIGTERM is a signal that tells a program it should terminate, and by default will kill the program. However programs are allowed to install a *signal handler* for SIGTERM so they can perform any necessary cleanup before terminating, for example closing and saving any files that have been modified.

Another useful key combination is ctrl+z which stops the program execution and puts it in the background. This means that you can start a process, for example "less test.txt", then exit the program but keep it running by pressing ctrl+z which will drop you back to the shell. Let's go through an example usage:

```
1 $ cp -i big_file.tgz /mnt
2 ^Z
3 [1]+  Stopped         cp -i big_file.tgz /mnt
4 $ bg
5 [1]+ cp -i big_file.tgz /mnt &
6 $ ls
7 Makefile  dep.rst   ex_js2.rst
8 $
9 [1]+  Done            cp -i big_file.tgz /mnt
```

Let's assume we have a very large file we want to copy somewhere. Copying large files can take time, and cp by default doesn't output anything while copying. We start the copy on line 1.

After waiting for some time, we get bored and want to do something else so we press ctrl+z. This is shown in the terminal with ^Z (line 2). Pressing this key combination will tell us that the copy command has been stopped (line 3), and drops us back in our shell (line 4).

We then issue the command "bg" which means the previous command should run in the *background*, meaning it can run but should not prevent us from using the shell. Issuing this command tells us on line 5 that the copy command continues to run again, pointed out by the & sign at the end of the command.

On line 6 we can then do what we want, e.g. run "ls".

On line 8, we have the prompt again and wait for some time, until we expect the copy command to have finished. We can check if this is indeed the case by hitting enter (doing nothing). Bash uses this opportunity to tell us that the copy operation indeed has finished (line 9).

If you're running a command and you want to start it on the background right away, you can add the & sign to the end of the command:

```
$ cp -i big_file.tgz /mnt &
[1] 23904
$
```

If you have a command running in the background but want to run it on the foreground again, run "fg":

```
$ cp -i big_file.tgz /mnt &
[1] 23904
$ fg
cp -i big_file.tgz /mnt
$
```

If you want to see which commands you have running in the background in the current terminal, run "ps":

```
$ ps
  PID TTY          TIME CMD
 5898 pts/8    00:00:01 bash
23904 pts/8    00:00:00 cp
23905 pts/8    00:00:00 ps
```

If you want to send a SIGTERM signal to another process than what's currently running in the foreground, you can use the "kill" command with the PID (process ID) of the process you want to kill, for example:

```
$ cp -i big_file.tgz /mnt &
[1] 23904
$ ps
  PID TTY          TIME CMD
 5898 pts/8    00:00:01 bash
23904 pts/8    00:00:00 cp
23905 pts/8    00:00:00 ps
$ kill 23904
[1]+  Terminated      cp -i big_file.tgz /mnt
$
```

Note that bash tells you the PID of the newly started process when you start it on the background using &.

Because a program can install a signal handler for SIGTERM, it's possible that sending SIGTERM to a program won't kill it. To force kill a program you need to send the signal SIGKILL:

```
$ cp -i big_file.tgz /mnt &
[1] 23937
$ kill -KILL 23937
$
[1]+  Killed          cp -i big_file.tgz /mnt
$
```

Exercise: Start "less" to browse a file, hit ctrl+z to move it to the background, then run "fg" to bring it to foreground again.

Cron

Cron is a software in Unix-like operating systems which allows the user to configure running a command at given time intervals.

For example, running the command "ls > out.txt" in the home directory once per day, i.e. to store the listing of the files in the home directory in a file, can be done using cron. To do this, one would run the command "crontab -e", which would open the *cron table* in the user's default editor.

The cron table is a file where each row describes what command to run periodically, and how often. E.g.:

```
15 3 * * * ls > out.txt
```

This line would cause cron to run the command at 3:15 AM every day. The columns on the table are minutes, hours, day of month (1-31), month (1-12) and day of week (0-6 where 0 is Sunday and 6 is Saturday). The asterisk ("*") is a placeholder meaning "every". If you want to use cron in your system, you need to ensure it is running (e.g. by running "ps aux | grep crond"; "ps" lists the processes running in the system and crond means *the cron daemon*; daemon being a program that runs in the background). If cron is not running, you can find out how to start it from the documentation of your operating system.

1.3.3 Regular expressions

> Some people, when confronted with a problem, think "I know, I'll use regular expressions." Now they have two problems.
>
> —Jamie Zawinski

A lot can be said about regular expressions. I'll stick to the essentials, bare minimum in this section.

Regular expressions are an extension to the usual search and replace. For example, you might want to find any line in a file that ends with the digit 9:

```
$ grep "9$" test.txt | head
-8.687820 -6.930905 -8.731439
-6.532205 -8.706914 1.642039
3.052381 2.971625 -0.620359
5.722527 -7.593573 -8.653239
[...]
```

'grep' by default assumes the search string provided to it is a regular expression. The string "9$" consists of two characters: 9 and $. $ is called an anchor character: it designates the end of the line. Hence, searching for "9$" means that grep will output all lines where 9 is the last character in the line.

A more complex example is wanting to search any negative numbers in the file between -1.0 and -1.3:

```
$ grep "\-1\.[012][0-9]*" test.txt | head
0.094081 -6.537027 -1.189798
4.145320 -1.276905 -6.513201
-1.240556 -2.562810 -8.189995
-1.114494 -4.974068 -5.414513
[...]
```

This command outputs any line in which a number between -1.0 and -1.3 was found. Let's go through the regular expression "\-1\.[012][0-9]*" piece by piece:

The characters "\-" mean "match the minus character". We need a backslash before the minus character because otherwise grep would confuse it with a switch. The backslash is the escape character; in this case it means "treat the following character as the literal minus character".

1 means we search for a 1.

The characters "\." mean the period character, i.e '.'. This needs to be escaped using backslash because in regular expressions, the period character is short hand for "any character". However in this case we mean the actual period character, hence the backslash.

[012] means that after the period character we search for either a 0, 1 or 2.

[0-9] means that after the previous character (0, 1 or 2) we search for any digit.

* means that the previous search must be repeated as often as possible, i.e. for any digits until some other character is found.

Hence, the regular expression "\-1\.[012][0-9]*" means "search for a string that starts with a minus character, has a 1, followed by a period, followed by either 0, 1 or 2, followed by zero or more digits".

It may become more obvious if we pass the switch "-o" to grep, which means that only the matching strings are output, not the full line of a match:

```
grep -o "\-1\.[012][0-9]*" test.txt | head
-1.189798
-1.276905
-1.240556
-1.114494
[...]
```

Now, grep only outputs the strings that were matched, i.e. the numbers between -1.0 and -1.3.

As implausible as it may sound, experienced programmers are often able to derive a correct regular expression for a certain use case with ease, though sometimes, especially with more complex expressions, some debugging may be needed. This comes with practice; an experienced programmer often uses regular expressions several times per day.

Regular expressions aren't limited to grep, but are available in most programming languages as well as other Unix tools such as sed. To get a refresher on sed, you might, for example, use sed to search and replace the string "123" with "456":

```
$ sed -e 's/123/456/g' test.txt > new_file.txt
```

Now, let's say you had a more advanced use case, for example replacing any negative number with 0.0. This can be achieved using regular expressions with 'sed':

```
$ sed -e 's/-[0-9.]*/0.0/g' test.txt
7.269553 3.427526 6.633603
1.980206 0.0 0.0
0.0 0.0 0.0
0.0 0.0 0.0
0.0 6.908667 4.418877
[...]
```

Let's go through this piece by piece.

- 's/-[0-9,]*/0.0/g' - four components, delimited by '/'. The first one, 's' means search and replace.

The second component is -[0-9.]*:

- - First find a minus character
- [0-9.] Then find any character that is a number (0-9), or a period. Square brackets denote "any of".
- * Repeat the previous as many times as possible. Hence, of the string "-1.234 2.000", the part "-1.234" would be matched because it starts with a minus character, followed by several digits and a period. After reaching the space character the search terminates.

The third component is 0.0: Whatever was matched in the search will be replaced by this.

The fourth component is 'g' again, i.e. apply this search as many times as possible for each line. This means that for example for line "-1.234 -2.000 1.23" the both matching instances will be replaced (both "-1.234" and "-2.000" will be replaced by "0.0").

Exercise: Using your generated file of 10,000 functions, write a 'sed' command to replace all digits after the decimal point with a 0. For example, the line "1.980206 -3.655827 -2.629755" should become "1.0 -3.0 -2.0".

The man page for GNU grep includes a good reference on regular expressions, although this might not be available on non-GNU systems like some BSDs.

GNU? BSD? What's going on?

Unix has a long and complex history. To make it short, BSD (Berkeley Software Distribution, originating from the University of California, Berkeley) is a family of Unix implementations nowadays consisting of a few operating systems including OpenBSD and macOS. The BSD operating systems have the typical Unix tools such as grep implemented and documented. GNU (GNU's Not Unix - implying GNU doesn't contain any original Unix code) is *another* implementation of Unix and hence *also* has typical Unix tools such as grep implemented and documented - but implemented and documented separately and hence slightly differently. While Unix has been standardised, such that one can expect tools such as grep generally behave similarly across various Unix implementations, the different implementations can include additional features in their implementations that others might not have. Or indeed include a reference on regular expressions in their grep man page.

Linux distributions are the most common operating systems that include GNU tools.

Exercise: Look up a regular expression reference to see what character classes and expressions are available.

1.4 Using libraries in Python

1.4.1 Creating a simple web page

Now that we have written some Python code, let's see what we can do by *leveraging* existing libraries.

To do this we'll come up with a goal. Let's imagine we have the following use case:

- We have a computer which is connected to speakers and can hence produce audio
- We'd like this computer to play *internet radio*
- Furthermore, we'd like to stop or start the playback using a smartphone

In other words, we have a computer serving as a very simple media centre, and we want to turn the music on or off without having to get up from the couch. How would we accomplish this?

We'll go through the following steps:

- Setting up the computer for serving web pages - by installing *external libraries*
- Putting together a simple web page with the stop/start buttons
- Setting up the computer for playing music from a command line
- Figuring out how to control the command line from Python
- Putting it all together, i.e. connecting the buttons to the command line music player

External libraries in Python

Because writing all the code needed to serve a web page is a lot of work, we want to install an external library that takes care of most of this for us. In this chapter we'll be using *Flask* - a micro-framework for Python that allows relatively easy creation of web applications.

Python has a tool called *pip* which can download and install libraries. You can find out if you already have pip by running "pip" in the terminal. Most Unix systems include pip as part of the Python installation. If you don't have it, please consult the documentation of pip and your operating system online on how to install it.

Flask has fairly straightforward installation instructions; at the time of writing, running "pip install Flask" might be enough.

Exercise: Look up the web page for Flask, the Python micro-framework.

There are several ways to install external libraries in Python. One very convenient way is to use *virtualenv*, or *virtual environment*: this tool allows you to install libraries without having to install them system-wide, potentially greatly simplifying installation.

Virtualenv is software that can be downloaded from the virtualenv web page. There are several ways to install it; at the time of writing, running "pip install virtualenv" might be enough.

Exercise: Look up the web page for virtualenv. Install it.

Once you have virtualenv installed, you need to create a virtual environment and activate it. Once you've activated it, changes to Python libraries such as installing new ones will only affect the virtual environment. This means that installing libraries might be easier, but in order to use them you'll need to have activated the virtual environment.

At the time of writing, the command "virtualenv myve" creates a virtual environment to directory "myve". This directory will be created as a subdirectory to the current working directory. After creating the virtual environment, it can be activated by running "source bin/activate" in the "myve" directory.

Exercise: Create a virtual environment and activate it. Look up instructions from the virtualenv web page if you get stuck. Install Flask in your virtual environment.

Let's test Flask to ensure you've installed it correctly. At the time of writing, it should be enough to create the following Python file:

```
from flask import Flask
app = Flask(__name__)

```

(continues on next page)

(continued from previous page)

```
@app.route("/")
def hello():
    return "Hello World!"
```

...and run "FLASK_APP=hello.py flask run" (where hello.py is the Python file that was just created). After this, directing your browser to "http://localhost:5000/" should display the text "Hello World!"

Exercise: Test Flask to ensure you've installed it correctly. If you get stuck, consult the documentation on the Flask web page.

Now that we have Flask installed and can serve web pages, we can put together a simple page, though at this stage it won't do anything.

HTML

We'll go more into details around HTML is later in this book. For now, suffice to say, HTML defines what will be shown to the user visiting a web page. We'll create a very simple page with two buttons labelled "Start" and "Stop", and nothing else.

As per Flask documentation, in order to display an HTML page it must reside in a subdirectory called "templates".

Exercise: Create this subdirectory in the directory where your hello.py is by running "mkdir templates".

We can now add an HTML file in this directory. We'll later tell Flask to send this HTML file to anyone visiting our site.

Here's a sample HTML file:

```
<!DOCTYPE html>
<html lang="en">
    <meta charset="UTF-8">
    <meta name="viewport" content="width=device-width">
    <title>Radio</title>
    <form method="post">
        <input type="submit" name="submit" value="Start"><br />
    </form>
</html>
```

Let's go through this line by line:

- Line 1 indicates to the browser which HTML version is used.
- Line 2 *opens* the *html tag*. This tag is closed on line 9.
- Line 3 defines the file encoding. We'll talk about encodings more later in this book.
- Line 4 makes the page more readable on smartphones, as required by our use case.
- Line 5 sets the page title.
- Lines 6-8 define our *form*: a button. By having a form (with POST method) the browser can submit information about button presses to our Python code.
- Line 7 creates a button with the text "Start". The "<br />" marks a line break; this causes any following items to be below the button.
- Line 8 ends our form.

Exercise: Type (don't copy-paste) the above HTML file to a file. Save the file as "radio.html" in the "templates" directory.

We can now ask Flask to display this HTML page. As per the Flask documentation, the following code should do the trick:

```
from flask import Flask, render_template, request
app = Flask(__name__)

@app.route("/", methods=['POST', 'GET'])
def hello():
    return render_template('radio.html')
```

This has a few changes compared to the "Hello world" page:

- We import a few more identifiers from the "flask" package, namely "render_template" and "request".
- We've added another parameter "methods=['POST', 'GET']" to the *decorator* of our function.
- Instead of returning "Hello world", we return the return value of the render_template() function, and pass this function the file name "radio.html".

Exercise: Modify your hello.py or create a new Python file with the above contents. Open your page in your browser. You should be able to see one button labelled “Start”. Clicking it shouldn’t do anything.

We now have one button - but we wanted two.

Exercise: Add a button labelled “Stop” below the first button.

Now, you should be able to access the page from your local computer - but if you tried from another computer (or a smartphone), you might see the access will be denied. This is because by default Flask only allows connections from the local computer as in debugging mode, any Python code could be executed. Assuming you can trust the computers in your network, as per Flask documentation, you can enable Flask to allow connections from all public IPs by adding the parameter “–host=0.0.0.0” to your “flask run” command.

Exercise: If you have another computer or a smartphone available in the same network as your development computer and trust the computers in your network, restart Flask such that it allows connections from your other device. Find out the IP address of your development computer (e.g. by running “ifconfig” on Linux; see your system documentation). (The IP address you need may be the one from your local network, i.e. starting with e.g. 10.0.* or 192.168.*.) Connect to your web page from your other device.

Now that we’re able to display a web page with buttons that don’t do anything, let’s see how we can make the buttons work.

1.4.2 Making our web page work

So we have the buttons, and we have some Python code that doesn't really do much. We can improve things by writing some Python code that reacts to the button presses by starting or stopping an mp3 stream replay. To be able to do this, we should first understand how we can start or stop an mp3 stream replay on the command line.

Streaming mp3 files on the command line

In order to stream mp3 files on the command line, we need two things:

- An mp3 stream
- An mp3 player

For the first one you can try to find a local, interesting radio station who provide an HTTP link to an mp3 stream. If you're out of luck, you can also use one I found: the Norwegian public broadcasting company provides exactly this kinds of links for their radio stations, and some stations are also allowed to be heard and played from anywhere in the world. Here's one such a link: http://lyd.nrk.no/nrk_radio_p1_trondelag_mp3_h

If you try accessing this link from your browser, and have the audio replay set up, you may be able to hear some Norwegian local radio.

Now that we have an mp3 stream, how about the player? There are several mp3 players for various Unix systems that are able to download and replay an mp3 stream via HTTP. Here's an incomplete list:

- mpg123 (or mpg321)
- mplayer
- cvlc
- ffmpeg

Typically, one could use one of these to replay an mp3 stream by passing the URL as the first parameter, e.g.:

```
$ mpg123 http://lyd.nrk.no/nrk_radio_p1_trondelag_mp3_h
```

You can stop the replay by sending the signal SIGTERM i.e. signal 15, to the replayer, e.g. by hitting ctrl+c on most systems.

However, some may not be able to read the mp3 stream via HTTP. If provided with the data, they could still be able to replay the mp3 though. Tools like "curl" come into rescue here:

```
$ curl http://lyd.nrk.no/nrk_radio_p1_trondelag_mp3_h | mpg123 -
```

What we have here is a nice use of the Unix pipe: Curl is a program that can download files over the network e.g. using the HTTP protocol. We output the curl output to a pipe, such that on the other side the data is received by our mp3 player. The dash ("-") at the end is the input "file" for the player; the dash generally means "standard input", i.e. the output of curl in our case. This causes curl to download the stream, and the player to replay it.

Exercise: Install one of the above, or some other suitable mp3 player on your system. Replay the mp3 stream from the command line. Install curl if necessary.

Now that we're able to start and stop the playback on the command line, we can try to hook up our HTML buttons to these actions. But how can we use the command line from Python?

Python subprocess

Python provides a module called "subprocess" which allows us to run shell commands from Python. Here's a simple example:

```
import subprocess

subprocess.call(['ls', '-l'])
```

This would run the command "ls -l" from Python and write the output to stdout.

There's a lot that can be written about subprocess.

Exercise: Look up the reference for "subprocess" online, or by running "help(subprocess)" in the Python interpreter.

However, our use case is fairly simple: we want to be able to start an mp3 player in the background, and kill it.

As per the subprocess documentation, a special optional parameter called "shell" exists. If set to true, the command will be interpreted by our shell. This can simplify our code when we want our command to run in the background, and can also be used for redirecting the command output. (In a real software project, as per the subprocess documentation, it might be better to refrain from using "shell=True" and instead use the subprocess methods for running commands in the background or capturing command output.)

Using "shell=True" also implies that providing the command as a list of parameters to subprocess.call() is no longer necessary. This means that if we wanted to e.g. run "ls -l" and redirect the output to a file called "out.txt", we could write this:

```
subprocess.call('ls -l > out.txt', shell=True)
```

In order to start a command and keep it running in the background, we can add an ampersand ("&") at the end of the command. For example, to start the mp3 player mpg123 and keep it running in the background:

```
subprocess.call('mpg123 http://lyd.nrk.no/nrk_radio_p1_trondelag_
↪mp3_h &', shell=True)
```

We can use a Unix command to send a signal to a process to end it. For example, most Unix systems have a command "killall" which will send a signal (by default SIGTERM) to all processes with a given name. For example, the command "killall mpg123" will stop all mpg123 processes in the system (that the current user is permitted to stop). If killall is not available, another possible command to use is "pkill" which for this use case is equivalent with "killall".

Exercise: Look up the man page of either "killall" or "pkill".

Exercise: Try starting your mp3 player on one terminal. Kill it from another terminal using e.g. "killall".

We now know how to start and stop the player in Python. How will we know under which conditions our code to start and stop should be run?

Controlling playback in Flask

When we press the button "Start" or "Stop" on our HTML page, our Python code gets executed. This is done by Flask.

In our Python code, we can find out whether a button has been pressed or whether the user simply entered the page, and if a button was pressed, which button it was.

If a user simply opens the page, the browser sends a "GET" request. If a button was pressed, a "POST" request is sent instead. We can check whether a POST request was sent in our Python code with the following if statement:

```
if request.method == 'POST':
```

This is because our form in HTML states the method to use is POST.

We can find out which button the user pressed using e.g. the following if statement:

```
if request.form['submit'] == 'Start':
```

This line would evaluate to True if the button labelled "Start" was pressed. We know this because our HTML knows this. (The variable "request.form['submit']" is set to what we wrote in the "value" attribute for each button in our HTML.)

For example, the following would print "Start pressed" whenever the user pressed the "Start" button, and would in any case render the HTML we wrote:

```
def hello():
    if request.method == 'POST':
        if request.form['submit'] == 'Start':
            print "Start pressed"
    return render_template('radio.html')
```

Exercise: Add code to your Python function such that if the "Stop" button was pressed, kill all existing music playing processes. The function should return "render_template('radio.html')" in any case (i.e. whether a GET or POST request was received.) Try your function out. If no music players were found, you should see a message along the lines of "mpg123: no process found".

Exercise: Add code to your Python function such that if the “Start” button was pressed, kill all existing music playing processes (in case any exist) and start a new one.

If everything worked out well, congratulations! You now have a music player controllable over a web page.

CHAPTER TWO

STAGE 1

We're now done with the first few chapters. This stage introduces some fun concepts in theory, JavaScript, and slightly more in-depth topics with help of C and Python.

2.1 Further Unix tools

2.1.1 Version control

Have you ever had the feeling that you want to make large scale changes to your code, but are afraid of breaking something? Has the thought crossed your mind that you could copy your source file or files to another directory, so that you have a backup in case something goes wrong?

If so then that's perfectly normal. You might, however, imagine that if you were to work on a project for a longer time, say, several weeks, the number of backup directories would become difficult to have an overview of, and if you actually had to revert some changes from the past, it might be difficult to remember which directory contained which changes.

Version control systems (VCS) have been implemented to help solve these issues, as well as help developers collaborate on the same source code.

Version control systems have a long history, and I won't go through all of that. Suffice to say, there are lots of different version control systems, and many developers have their own personal favourite.

This book will introduce the reader to one of the most useful ones, named git. Git was originally developed in 2005 by Linus Torvalds for the Linux kernel development, and has since become one of the most widely used version control systems worldwide.

Git has several upsides, and a significant one is how it scales: it's very practical to use in hobby projects of individual developers, but is also being used to version control some of the world's largest source code repositories.

There is lots that can be learned about git; this book will cover the basic fundamentals.

Creating a git repository

Let's assume you have a directory which is otherwise empty except a file you've written, hello.py, which contains "print 'hello world'". Let's turn this directory into a git repository:

```
$ git init
Initialized empty Git repository in /home/antti/book/my_project/.
↪git/
```

Git has now initialised an empty repository. What this means in practice is that git has generated a new hidden directory called .git which we can see by running the command "ls -la":

```
$ ls -la
total 16
drwxr-xr-x 3 antti users 4096 Feb  9 00:30 .
drwxr-xr-x 8 antti users 4096 Feb  9 00:30 ..
drwxr-xr-x 7 antti users 4096 Feb  9 00:30 .git
-rw-r--r-- 1 antti users   20 Feb  9 00:30 hello.py
```

What we want to do next is store the file hello.py in the git repository. After that it'll be version controlled. We can do this by running the following:

```
$ git add hello.py
```

This adds "hello.py" to *the staging area* which is an area describing what will be committed next. We can then run "git status" to see the current status:

```
$ git status
On branch master

Initial commit

Changes to be committed:
  (use "git rm --cached <file>..." to unstage)

    new file:   hello.py
```

What this means is that if we were to commit our changes, i.e. create a new version, the new version would include a new file, namely hello.py. We can furthermore see the contents of the new commit by running "git diff –staged".

Let's create our commit:

```
$ git commit -m "initial commit"
[master (root-commit) b279b4f] initial commit
 1 file changed, 1 insertion(+)
 create mode 100644 hello.py
```

The "-m" switch to git commit allows the user to enter the commit message, which should include a short description about what the commit is about. Since this is our initial commit, we label it as such.

After running the command, git tells us it's created a new commit with the new file included. What happens behind the scenes is that git stores the necessary information about your file in the .git directory, such that it can be indexed and retrieved again when needed.

If we wanted to see the status of our repository now, we can run "git status" again:

```
$ git status
On branch master
nothing to commit, working tree clean
```

This means that the latest version git has stored matches the contents of our files (in this case, hello.py).

Further commits

Let's now assume we want to make a change to our hello.py, by appending "print 'hello world'" to it:

```
$ echo "print 'hello world'" >> hello.py
```

Now that we've modified our file, we can check status again:

```
$ git status
On branch master
Changes not staged for commit:
  (use "git add <file>..." to update what will be committed)
  (use "git checkout -- <file>..." to discard changes in working␣
↪directory)
```

(continues on next page)

(continued from previous page)

```
    modified:   hello.py

no changes added to commit (use "git add" and/or "git commit -a")
```

The status now tells us that we've modified our file, and that the modifications aren't included in any version controlled by git.

We can view the changes we've made by running "git diff":

```
$ git diff
diff --git a/hello.py b/hello.py
index a968078..01283b8 100644
--- a/hello.py
+++ b/hello.py
@@ -1 +1,2 @@
 print 'hello world'
+print 'hello world'
```

The output suggests that there's been a new line added to the end of hello.py.

We can now commit this change:

```
$ git add hello.py
$ git commit -m "add printing hello world again"
[master 43130e1] add printing hello world again
 1 file changed, 1 insertion(+)
```

Now we already have two commits. We can see the commit log by running "git log":

```
$ git log
commit 43130e10f89232f5ce542c4d864ff78e0a171796
Author: Antti Salonen <ajsalonen@gmail.com>
Date:   Fri Feb 9 00:42:07 2018 +0100

    add printing hello world again

commit b279b4fb109844ab0337bc906897f6e48a3c18cf
Author: Antti Salonen <ajsalonen@gmail.com>
Date:   Fri Feb 9 00:35:05 2018 +0100
```

(continues on next page)

(continued from previous page)

```
    initial commit
```

The log will show the summary of each commit as well as the *commit hash*, which uniquely identifies each commit.

git reset

Now comes the interesting part: let's say we want to go back to the previous version, before we added the second "print 'hello world'" to the end of hello.py. One way to do this is the following:

```
$ git reset --hard b279b4f
HEAD is now at b279b4f initial commit
```

The command asks git to reset the state of the current working tree to the commit b279b4f (the first few characters of the commit hash we're interested in). Git does this, and as part of that, replaces our hello.py with the old version:

```
$ cat hello.py
print 'hello world'
```

If we look at the log, we see the previous commit is no longer there:

```
$ git log
commit b279b4fb109844ab0337bc906897f6e48a3c18cf
Author: Antti Salonen <ajsalonen@gmail.com>
Date:   Fri Feb 9 00:35:05 2018 +0100

    initial commit
```

If we wanted to get our changes back, we can, because we noted the commit hash:

```
$ git reset --hard 43130e10
HEAD is now at 43130e1 add printing hello world again
$ cat hello.py
```

(continues on next page)

(continued from previous page)

```
print 'hello world'
print 'hello world'
```

This was a very short introduction to git. There will be more covered in this book later; you can also check the built in documentation for git by running "git –help" or the help for specific commands, for example "git status –help".

Exercise: Create a git repository and repeat the above commands yourself.

Exercise: Use git to version control all your previous and future software development projects.

2.1.2 Working with other git repositories

We've learned how to create a git repository and commit changes to it. Git allows collaboration between different people by having the functionality to *push* commits to and *pull* commits from another repository. (Git is a *distributed* version control system, which means that each repository is equal; there is no server-client relationship like with some other version control systems such as Subversion.)

Let's practice this a bit. We created a repository the last time by running "git init" in a directory. We can *clone* that directory by running "git clone", e.g.:

```
$ mkdir my_clone
$ cd my_clone
$ git clone ../my_project
Cloning into 'my_project'...
done.
$ ls
my_project
$ cd my_project
$ git log
commit 43130e10f89232f5ce542c4d864ff78e0a171796
Author: Antti Salonen <ajsalonen@gmail.com>
Date:   Fri Feb 9 00:42:07 2018 +0100

    add printing hello world again

commit b279b4fb109844ab0337bc906897f6e48a3c18cf
Author: Antti Salonen <ajsalonen@gmail.com>
Date:   Fri Feb 9 00:35:05 2018 +0100

    initial commit
```

What happened here is that by running "git clone" git creates an identical copy of the existing repository. It's not very interesting on your own machine but you can also tell git to clone a remote repository, i.e. over the Internet.

Collaboration

Now, let's make a change in our clone:

```
$ echo "print 'hello world'" >> hello.py
$ git commit hello.py -m "add third print"
[master bc6ef9e] add third print
 1 file changed, 1 insertion(+)
```

We now have one more commit in our clone than in our original repository.

The typical flow, e.g. when working with a repository in GitHub or generally a central repository, is to push the change to the *origin*, i.e. to the repository that was used for creating the clone:

```
$ git push origin master
```

Here, we tell git to push the changes to the *master branch* on the origin. Branches generally speaking allow you to have different developments in different branches, and the master branch is the default branch. You can try the command above but because we work with local repositories, git doesn't by default allow pushing to it.

What we could do would be to change the directory back to the origin repository and run "git pull ../my_clone/my_project" which would fetch and merge the changes from the clone back to the original repository.

Branches

Let's create, add and commit a new file with some more interesting contents:

```
with open('test.txt', 'w') as f:
    for i in xrange(5):
        f.write("%f %f\n" % (0.2, 0.5))
```

This simple Python script generates a new file with some numbers in it.

Now, let's assume we're developing this script together with another developer. We think the values that the script outputs above should be changed. At the same time, the other developer thinks the script should output three values instead of two. Let's simulate this.

We both make our changes locally in different *branches* which are branched from master. In the end both branches should have made some changes to this file:

- The first branch should be called "values" and change the values being written to a file
- The second branch should be called "three" and write three values in the file instead of two

Let's then merge the two branches in master. As there's no obvious way to merge the two branches we'll end up in conflict which we'll have to resolve manually. Apart from this example of working in a team and making conflicting changes, this could also happen if we want to pick different changes from different versions to create a new version. While we'll do this work on local branches, in general the principle is the same when working with remote code, e.g. code from other people.

Let's then create a new branch where we want to change the values that are being saved in the file such that they're 0.0 and 1.0:

```
$ git branch values
$ git checkout values
Switched to branch 'values'
```

What we did here was create a new branch "values", then checked it out, meaning we changed the current branch to it. We can check which branch we're in by running "git branch":

```
$ git branch
  master
* values
```

Now, let's modify the file. By running "git diff" before adding the changes to the staging area or committing them we can see changes in the current checkout:

```
$ git diff
diff --git a/with.py b/with.py
index f61db97..d63b0bf 100644
--- a/with.py
+++ b/with.py
```

(continues on next page)

(continued from previous page)

```
@@ -1,3 +1,3 @@
 with open('test.txt', 'w') as f:
     for i in xrange(5):
-        f.write("%f %f\n" % (0.2, 0.5))
+        f.write("%f %f\n" % (0.0, 1.0))
```

Here, git shows us the changes we've made. We can now commit the changes.

What our repository now looks like is this:

```
$ git log --graph --decorate --pretty=oneline --abbrev-commit --
↪all
* 4cf7d38 (HEAD -> values) change values to be 0 and 1
* 91abbc4 (master) add with
* bc6ef9e add third print
* 43130e1 add printing hello world again
* b279b4f initial commit
```

This means:

- We have the latest commit which is the current working directory state (HEAD) and the head of the "values" branch which has the commit with hash 4cf7d38 where we changed the values to be 0 and 1
- The head of the "master" branch is 91abbc4 where we added the original with.py

You can change between branches by using "git checkout":

```
$ git checkout master
Switched to branch 'master'
$ grep write with.py
        f.write("%f %f\n" % (0.2, 0.5))
$ git checkout values
Switched to branch 'values'
$ grep write with.py
        f.write("%f %f\n" % (0.0, 1.0))
```

Merging and conflicts

Let's then simulate the other developer and create the branch "three" off "master" and create a commit there:

```
$ git checkout master
Switched to branch 'master'
$ git branch three
$ git checkout three
Switched to branch 'three'
$ vim with.py
$ git diff
diff --git a/with.py b/with.py
index f61db97..444a55f 100644
--- a/with.py
+++ b/with.py
@@ -1,3 +1,3 @@
 with open('test.txt', 'w') as f:
     for i in xrange(5):
-        f.write("%f %f\n" % (0.2, 0.5))
+        f.write("%f %f %f\n" % (0.2, 0.5, 0.8))
$ git commit -m "write out three values" with.py
[three dd6c856] write out three values
 1 file changed, 1 insertion(+), 1 deletion(-)
```

Now, let's see where we are:

```
$ git log --graph --decorate --pretty=oneline --abbrev-commit --
↪all
* 4cf7d38 (values) change values to be 0 and 1
| * dd6c856 (HEAD -> three) write out three values
|/
* 91abbc4 (master) add with
* bc6ef9e add third print
* 43130e1 add printing hello world again
* b279b4f initial commit
```

- "values" is still where it is - one commit ahead of master, namely 4cf7d38
- "master" is still where it is - but now it has two branches ahead of it

- HEAD, our current checkout, is at the head of "three", which is a new commit, dd6c856

Now, let's try to switch to the master branch and start with *merging* the changes from "values" to it:

```
$ git checkout master
Switched to branch 'master'
$ git merge values
Updating 91abbc4..4cf7d38
Fast-forward
 with.py | 2 +-
 1 file changed, 1 insertion(+), 1 deletion(-)
```

Here, we run "git merge" to merge two branches. ("git pull" does "git fetch", i.e. downloading the status of a remote repository, followed by "git merge", i.e. merging the status of the remote repository with ours.) It works out well and git modifies our with.py to include the changes from "values". We can check the status using "git log":

```
$ git log --graph --decorate --pretty=oneline --abbrev-commit --
↪all
* 4cf7d38 (HEAD -> master, values) change values to be 0 and 1
| * dd6c856 (three) write out three values
|/
* 91abbc4 add with
* bc6ef9e add third print
* 43130e1 add printing hello world again
* b279b4f initial commit
```

Here, our current state (HEAD) is the head of master, which is also the head of values, and three is a separate branch that doesn't have commit 4cf7d38. It does however have the commit dd6c856. Now, let's try to merge "three" to master as well:

```
$ git merge three
Auto-merging with.py
CONFLICT (content): Merge conflict in with.py
Automatic merge failed; fix conflicts and then commit the result.
```

Now, because we've modified the same location in the same file in two different commits which we try to merge, git doesn't know how to merge these automatically and tells us to fix it ourselves. Let's now take a look at with.py:

```
$ cat with.py
with open('test.txt', 'w') as f:
    for i in xrange(5):
<<<<<<< HEAD
        f.write("%f %f\n" % (0.0, 1.0))
=======
        f.write("%f %f %f\n" % (0.2, 0.5, 0.8))
>>>>>>> three
```

What this tells us is:

- In HEAD, we have code writing out 0.0 and 1.0
- In the other branch (three), we have code writing out 0.2, 0.5, 0.8

We can check the status using "git status":

```
$ git status
On branch master
You have unmerged paths.
  (fix conflicts and run "git commit")
  (use "git merge --abort" to abort the merge)

Unmerged paths:
  (use "git add <file>..." to mark resolution)

        both modified:   with.py

no changes added to commit (use "git add" and/or "git commit -a")
```

We'll then have to fix the code manually, e.g. by deciding we want to output values 0.0, 0.5 and 1.0:

```
$ vim with.py
$ git add with.py
$ git status
On branch master
All conflicts fixed but you are still merging.
  (use "git commit" to conclude merge)
```

(continues on next page)

(continued from previous page)

```
Changes to be committed:

    modified:   with.py

$ git diff --staged
diff --git a/with.py b/with.py
index d63b0bf..ae90c0d 100644
--- a/with.py
+++ b/with.py
@@ -1,3 +1,3 @@
 with open('test.txt', 'w') as f:
     for i in xrange(5):
-        f.write("%f %f\n" % (0.0, 1.0))
+        f.write("%f %f %f\n" % (0.0, 0.5, 1.0)
```

...and commit:

```
$ git commit -m "merged"
[master ab7a9a6] merged with
$ git log --graph --decorate --pretty=oneline --abbrev-commit --
↪all
*   ab7a9a6 (HEAD -> master) merged with
|\
| * dd6c856 (three) write out three values
* | 4cf7d38 (values) change values to be 0 and 1
|/
* 91abbc4 add with
* bc6ef9e add third print
* 43130e1 add printing hello world again
* b279b4f initial commit
```

Now, we see git visualise our repository again:

- The branch "values" has commit 4cf7d38
- The branch "three" has commit dd6c856
- The branch "master", which is also our current working directory (HEAD), we have a commit that merges both threads

In our case, we had a conflict between two local branches, but the process is the same if there are remote branches involved.

Note that in most cases, when two commits have changes in the same files, git is still usually able to merge them without issues. Conflicts only arise when no obvious automatic merge is possible.

In general, there are many different workflows one can use with git, but typically, when working with other people, one fetches and merges the code from others with “git pull”, has to resolve any merge conflicts if any arise, and push any local commits with “git push”.

2.1.3 Some related Unix tools

Hashing

You may have wondered what the hashes are about that git uses.

In general, a hash function takes any data as input and creates a hash value of the data. You can try this yourself by e.g. running the following command on Unix:

```
$ sha1sum with.py
4f2fb68a29c3a1f9978be115a1798371a57e9ae9  with.py
```

Here, we run the command sha1sum which calculates the SHA-1 hash of the file with.py. If you don't have sha1sum you may try e.g. md5sum (or possibly md5 on Mac). Hash functions can have the following properties:

- Changing a file insignificantly (e.g. by adding one byte) may significantly change the hash (e.g. result in a completely different hash)
- The hash function may be *cryptographically secure* - i.e. it is difficult or impossible to modify the input data such that the resulting hash would still be the same

In general, if you know the hash of a file, you can calculate the hash to check whether the file has been modified or corrupted. git uses hashes to uniquely identify commits and to protect against data corruption.

Exercise: Look up the definition of SHA-1 hash function online. You can e.g. find an implementation in pseudocode.

diff and patch

"git diff" gives a practical output of a difference between a file before and after a change:

```
$ git diff
diff --git a/with.py b/with.py
index f61db97..d63b0bf 100644
--- a/with.py
+++ b/with.py
```

(continues on next page)

(continued from previous page)

```
@@ -1,3 +1,3 @@
 with open('test.txt', 'w') as f:
     for i in xrange(5):
-        f.write("%f %f\n" % (0.2, 0.5))
+        f.write("%f %f\n" % (0.0, 1.0))
```

In general, you can *diff* any two files by running the utility "diff". Conventionally the switch "-u" is used to display the output in *unified form*, which is also the default git uses:

```
$ diff -u with2.py with.py
--- with2.py        2018-03-25 22:34:47.530840487 +0200
+++ with.py 2018-03-25 22:05:25.477035716 +0200
@@ -1,3 +1,3 @@
 with open('test.txt', 'w') as f:
     for i in xrange(5):
-        f.write("%f %f\n" % (0.0, 1.0)
+        f.write("%f %f %f\n" % (0.0, 0.5, 1.0)
```

What can be useful is redirecting diff output to a file. There's another utility called *patch* which takes the output from diff to actually make changes to a file, i.e. patch them. Let's say someone sent us the above diff output and we had our file with.py which we wanted to patch:

```
$ patch -p0 < with.diff
patching file with.py
```

Here, "patch" will modify our with.py according to the diff.

2.1.4 Vim

> I've seen [visual] editors like that, but I don't feel a need for them. I don't want to see the state of the file when I'm editing.
>
> —Ken Thompson

In general, the editor is an important part of the *edit-compile-run* cycle. The editor should make you, the developer, as efficient when reading and writing code as possible. While any editor is enough to get started so that you can read and write files, some editors have capabilities that improve productivity and reduce tediousness of editing code.

There are a few classical editors and while there's no shame in using another or a simpler editor (even nano), in this book we'll deep dive to one of the more advanced ones: vim.

In general, in order to install vim, I'll refer you to your OS. If on Linux, you should be able to install vim using your package manager, if it's not already installed. On Mac and Windows you should be able to find a way to install it after searching online.

After you've installed vim, you can start it in Unix shell by running e.g.:

```
$ vim file.txt
```

This opens the file called "file.txt" in vim. If the file doesn't exist, vim opens an empty buffer which, if saved, will be saved as file.txt.

Vim is a modal editor. This means it has *modes*. When starting vim, it is in *normal mode*. You can always get to this mode by hitting the Escape key (ESC) three times. Go ahead, try it out.

The second mode is the *command line mode*. You can enter this mode from the normal mode by pressing colon (:) (without hitting enter afterwards). You should then see a colon at the bottom of the screen.

In command line mode, you can enter several commands. For exit, you can quit vim by typing ":q" followed by enter (or ":q<Enter>"). Try it out. Enter vim again.

Another useful command is ":w", for writing, i.e. saving a file. Try running ":w<Enter>". This should save file.txt. As we didn't enter any contents to the file, it'll be empty.

You can also combine commands. For example, the command ":wq" will save and quit vim.

The third mode is the *insert mode*. This allows you to actually type text in the file. One way to enter this mode from the normal mode is by pressing "i". Now, anything you type will be added in the buffer. You can exit the insert mode by pressing the Escape key.

For example, if you were to type "iHello.<ESC>", you'd enter the insert mode, add the text "Hello." in the file, then go back to the normal mode. Try this out. Save your file with ":w". If you want to be sure, quit vim and run "cat file.txt" to see the file contents. Enter vim again.

Now you have the basics of how to use vim for general file editing. So far, there isn't much that makes vim much better than any other editor.

Some more commands

There are some more commands that are helpful when editing text. These commands are all run from the normal mode. For example, the command "Y" will copy the current line. That is, if you are in the normal mode (which you can reach by pressing ESC), then press the keys for capital Y (shift+y), you've copied the current line. You can then paste this line after the current line by pressing "p". Try this out. You should then have the line "Hello." twice.

You can repeat commands multiple times by entering a number before the command. Try, in the normal mode, after you've copied the line using "Y", to type "10p". This should add ten lines with the text "Hello." in them.

You can undo with the command "u". You can re-do (undo the undo) by pressing ctrl+r. Try this out a few times. You can undo until the point where you started vim, and re-do until the last command.

Let's modify one of our "Hello." lines. You can use the arrow keys to move around the file (or also the h, j, k and l keys). The command "x" will remove the character under the cursor. Try it out. You can also type e.g. "3x" to remove the three next characters.

You can remove a whole line using the command “dd”. (This cuts the line such that you can paste it again.) You can remove the next e.g. three lines with “3dd”. Try it out. Paste them again with “P”. (Capital “P” pastes before the cursor, small “p” pastes after the cursor.) The text from the cursor to the end of the line can be removed with “D”.

You can navigate in the file with arrow keys, but there are shortcuts. Typing “gg” moves the cursor to the top of the file. Typing “G” moves the cursor to the end of the file. “$” moves the cursor to the end of the current line. “^” moves the cursor to the beginning of the current line.

Move the cursor to the top of the file with “gg”. You can delete e.g. the next 50 lines of the file by running “50dd”. Run this to empty the file.

2.1.5 Programming with vim

In order to use vim for programming, it's usually a good idea to configure vim accordingly. Vim can be configured by entering commands in the file "~/.vimrc", i.e. the hidden file called .vimrc in your $HOME directory. Let's open this file in vim:

```
$ vim ~/.vimrc
```

Depending on how vim is installed, it might already have some commands. What happens is vim automatically runs all the commands listed in the ~/.vimrc file in the command line mode when vim is started. For example, this line in ~/.vimrc:

```
set hlsearch          " Highlight search results
```

...means that when vim is started, it automatically runs ":set hlsearch", which enables highlighting search results. (The quote character " in .vimrc denotes a comment until the end of the line.)

I recommend you add at least the following lines to your .vimrc file:

```
syntax on                  " Syntax highlighting
set background=dark        " Vim colours for dark background
set showcmd                " Show (partial) command in status␣
↪line.
set showmatch              " Show matching brackets.
set incsearch              " Incremental search
set history=1000           " History of ":" commands remembered
set hlsearch               " Highlight search results
set autoread               " Automatically read file after it's␣
↪been modified elsewhere
set hidden                 " Hide buffers when they are abandoned
filetype on                " detect filetypes
filetype indent on         " indent depending on file type

autocmd FileType *.c,*.cpp set cindent   " c indent
autocmd FileType *.py      set nocindent " no c indent for python

" python specific
autocmd BufNewFile,BufRead *.py set tabstop=4     " tabstop 4
```

(continues on next page)

(continued from previous page)

```
autocmd BufNewFile,BufRead *.py set softtabstop=4 " spaces in tab
autocmd BufNewFile,BufRead *.py set shiftwidth=4
autocmd BufNewFile,BufRead *.py set smarttab      " tab inserts␣
↪spaces
autocmd BufNewFile,BufRead *.py set expandtab     " tabs␣
↪expanded to spaces
autocmd BufNewFile,BufRead *.py set smartindent   " autoindent
```

The first block sets a bunch of useful vim settings. The second one enables C indenting for .c and .cpp files (you may add move file extensions here depending on languages you use), and disables C indenting for python. The third block ensures only spaces are ever added in Python programs, not tabs, as mixing the two will break Python programs.

Note that if you copy text outside vim and want to paste it in vim, enter the insert mode in vim first by pressing "i", then paste. Otherwise you'll be entering the text in normal mode, causing odd things to happen. Save your changes in .vimrc.

Windows in vim

You can get a description of what each setting does using the ":help" command. For example, try running ":help hlsearch". This opens another *window* in vim with the help on hlsearch. You can browse the window as you normally would. If you want move between windows, first press "ctrl+w", then either arrow down or up to move to either the lower or upper window respectively. Move back and forth a couple of times.

To close the window you're currently in, run ":q".

Let's run the command ":help hlsearch" again. The command line mode (":") supports history. This means you can type ":", then press arrow up a couple of times, and you should see your previous ":help hlsearch" command. Press enter to run this again.

If you have multiple windows open and want to quit all of them, i.e. quit vim, you can run ":qa" (quit all). If you had changes in one of the files you hadn't yet saved, vim will warn you. You can save all unsaved changes by running ":wa". You can quit all without saving your changes by running ":qa!".

Multiple files in vim

You can open multiple files in vim. For example, if you run "vim file.txt file2.txt", you'll open two buffers, one for each file. You can list all open buffers using the ":ls" command. Try it out.

You can switch between the buffers with the ":b" command. For example, ":b1" opens the first buffer. ":b2" opens the second buffer, and so on. Make some changes in the second buffer ("file2.txt"), then change back to the first buffer. If you have "set hidden" in your .vimrc as per above, you should be able to change between buffers without having to save the file in between.

You can always change to the previous buffer, whichever it was, by running ":b#". Try this out. If you run ":ls", you can see which buffer is the previous one (it's marked with a #). Files with unsaved changes are marked with a +. You can save all changes with ":wa".

Typing code in vim

Let's quit vim and open a file "hello.c". Let's go to insert mode using "i" and then type (not copy paste) the following:

```
#include <stdio.h>

int main(void)
{
	printf("hello world\n");
}
```

Exit the insert mode by pressing ESC and save your file using ":w". Vim should have taken care of indentation for you.

Typically, as part of the edit-compile-run cycle, you'd have vim running on one terminal window or tab, and have another window or tab for compiling and running the program. After you've saved the file, you could try compiling and running it e.g. by running "gcc -Wall -o hello hello.c && ./hello".

Alternatively, vim allows you to run shell commands from within vim. E.g. ":!ls" will run "ls" in the shell. You could also type e.g. ":!gcc hello.c && ./a.out" to compile and run your program. Vim will then display the output of your command.

In C, it's optional for the main function to return a value. Let's add a line in our program for this. You could enter the insert mode by pressing "i", then navigating to the end of the printf line, then pressing enter and typing the new line, but vim provides a shortcut for this. The command "o" will automatically create a new line under the current one and enter the insert mode. Try this: move the cursor to the line with the printf statement, then, while in normal mode, press "o", type "return 0;", go back to normal mode by pressing ESC and save with ":w".

Search and replace

Let's say we want to replace word "hello" in our program with "hullo". The following command achieves this: ":%s/hello/hullo/g". Let's go through this one by one:

- ":": We enter the command line mode
- "%": We want the search-and-replace to run for the whole file, not only the current line
- "s": search and replace
- "/hello": search for "hello"
- "/hullo": replace with "hullo"
- "g": replace all occurrences on each line, not only the first one

You can also simply search. If you want to e.g. search for printf, type, while in normal mode, "/printf". This will move the cursor to printf and also highlight the word. To get to the next search match, use the command "n". To get to the previous match, use "N".

Another very useful command is "*". This searches for the word currently under the cursor. If you e.g. have a variable, you can use this to highlight and go to all places where the variable is used.

Code modifications

Let's now duplicate our printf statement by typing "Y" and "P" in the normal mode. We should now have two statements. They both print "hullo world". Let's change one of them back to "hello" manually. Originally, I assume your cursor is at the "p" of the word "printf". To change "hullo" to "hello", we could simply go to insert mode with "i", move to the correct position with the arrow keys, use backspace to remove the "u", and add "e", but vim provides a few shortcuts here.

First, we can move forwards one word at a time by pressing "w" in normal mode. Move forwards a few times. You can move backwards one word at a time with "b". Normally, special symbols like parentheses ("(" and ")") break words, such that you'll need to press "w" a few times (or run e.g. "7w") to go through one printf statement. You can also use capital letters ("W" and "B") which only understand spaces to break words. Use "w" to get to the "h" in "hullo".

You can then move the cursor one character to the right using the arrow keys and press "s" which does both "x" and "i", i.e. removes the current character and goes to insert mode. You can then press "e" to insert "e" and ESC to go back to normal mode.

Another very useful command is ".". Pressing the dot character re-does whichever command you ran. For example, the previous command replaced the character currently under the cursor with "e". Move the cursor around, and press ".". This will replace the character under the cursor with "e".

Indentation

You can shift a line to the left or right by "<<" or ">>" respectively. Try it out.

The command "==" will indent the line correctly based on the line or lines above it.

Now, for a test, let's mess up the indentation and fix it. First, using "<<" and ">>", have the braces ("{" and "}") stick out to the right. Have the printf statements be indented differently.

Then, type "gg=G" to correctly indent the whole file. You may recall that "gg" goes to the top of the file, "=" indents correctly, and "G" denotes the end of the file.

Working with braces

If you have the cursor on top of a start or end of any kind of parenthesis ("(", "[", "{", either opening or closing), pressing "%" will jump to either the closing or opening of the parenthesis. You can use e.g. the command "di(" to delete all text within the "(" parenthesis the cursor is at. (Similarly you can delete a word with "dw", or e.g. delete the next three words with "d3w".) Another useful command is "c", for changing text. Running "cc" will remove the current line and go to insert mode. "cw" will remove the current word and go to insert mode. Running "ci(" will remove the text within parenthesis and go to insert mode. Similarly, running "ci"" (that is, ci followed by quote) will remove the text within quotes (") and go to insert mode.

Combining the above, if you e.g. move the cursor to an opening brace, running "=%" will indent everything within the braces.

Visual mode

Vim also has a visual mode which allows you to select parts of the file and apply operations to it. You can enter the visual mode by pressing "v". Try entering the visual mode, then moving the cursor a few lines up or down, and then pressing "=". This will indent the selected lines correctly.

This concludes our introduction to vim, and should cover a good portion of the functionality to improve productivity.

Exercise: Use vim in your future software development.

2.2 Background on programming languages and algorithms

2.2.1 Typing

> If someone claims to have the perfect programming language, he is either a fool or a salesman or both.
>
> —Bjarne Stroustrup

There are a few concepts around programming languages that help pick up a new language.

Most programming languages come with a more or less sophisticated type systems. The type system defines how the types of variables and functions are used and interpreted.

A common example is the following expression:

```
4 + "2"
```

What is the result of this expression? The following provides an overview:

Language	Output
JavaScript	42
Java	42
Perl	6
Lua	6
Python	TypeError: unsupported operand type(s) for +: 'int' and 'str'
Haskell	Error: No instance for (Num [Char]) arising from a use of '+'
Ruby	String can't be coerced into Fixnum (TypeError)
C	134514105 (undefined behaviour)
C++	garbage (undefined behaviour)

We see four different kinds of answers:

- JavaScript and Java implicitly convert the number 4 into a string, then appends 2, resulting in "42"

- Perl and Lua implicitly convert the string “2” into a number, then add 4, resulting in 6
- Python, Haskell and Ruby throw an error
- C and C++ interpret the addition as pointer arithmetic, accessing memory after the statically allocated string “2”, resulting in undefined behaviour

Another example is about defining a simple function (pseudocode):

```
f(x):
    return 2 * x
```

If we were to define this function in C, it could look for example like this:

```
int f(int x)
{
    return 2 * x;
}
```

This function explicitly defines the input and output types as integers; using other types such as a string when calling this function will issue a compiler warning.

If we were to define this function in JavaScript, it would look like this:

```
function f(x) {
    return 2 * x;
}
```

I.e. no variable types explicitly defined. If we were to use Python, it would look like this:

```
def f(x):
    return 2 * x
```

While in Haskell the definition would look like this:

```
f x = 2 * x
```

Or in Java:

```
public static int f(int x) {
    return 2 * x;
}
```

What if we called these functions with a number? A string? The following table summarises the results when passing different values to the function:

Language	5 (number)	"5" (string)	"abc" (string)
C	10	garbage	garbage
JavaScript	10	10	"NaN" ("not a number")
Python	10	"55"	"abcabc"
Java	10	Compile error	Compile error
Haskell	10	Compile error	Compile error

We see the result makes sense when inputting a number for all languages. When inputting "5" as string, C interprets this as a pointer and undefined behaviour ensues. JavaScript implicitly converts the string to a number, which works when the string is indeed a number but returns "NaN" otherwise. When passing a string to the function in Python, Python interprets the multiplication as a multiplication of the string, hence duplicating the string. Haskell and Java refuse to work with the string input.

The above can be summarised by categorising the language type systems by how dynamic the typing is (static vs. dynamic), and the strength (strong vs. weak).

Static vs. dynamic typing

C, Haskell and Java are statically typed languages: the types of all variables must be defined at compilation time. For C and Java, the types must in most cases be explicitly stated, like we saw in the function definitions above. Haskell typically infers the types at compile time.

JavaScript and Python are dynamically typed languages: the types of variables may change depending on context. For example, the variable "x" in the function above may be a string or an integer, depending on the caller.

Strong vs. weak typing

C and JavaScript are weakly typed languages: the types of the variables aren't fixed but may be implicitly converted to other types depending on the context. For example, passing a string as an int will cause implicit conversion of the string to an int.

Python and Haskell are strongly typed languages: the types of variables are fixed and will not implicitly change, such that any type conversions must be explicit by the programmer.

It should be pointed out that while, based on the above, Java and Haskell are both strongly typed, some languages are more strongly typed than others. In our 4 + "2" example we saw that Haskell returned an error while Java returned "42". In this case, Java *implicitly converted* the type of the expression 4 to a string in order to avoid a compile error and return a string instead. Hence it can be argued that while Java is also a strongly typed language, Haskell is even more strongly typed.

Having this overview of the different type systems helps picking up and understanding new languages.

Duck typing

The combination of strong, dynamic typing is also often called "duck typing". This is based on the notion that "if it walks like a duck and it quacks like a duck, then it is a duck". Let's take a look at our Python function definition again:

```
def f(x):
    return 2 * x
```

The operation to multiply with an int (2 *) is defined for both integers and strings. For integers, the traditional multiplication is performed, while for strings the string is duplicated. From the point of view of the function, it makes no difference which type is passed to the function, as long as it can be multiplied by 2, hence duck typing. As we shall see, this becomes more interesting when writing your own data types.

Exercise: Write Python code that, when executed, prints the asterisk 50 times, i.e. "**". (One line of code.)

Interpreted and compiled languages

Typically (but not always), statically typed languages are compiled languages and dynamically typed languages are interpreted. There are pros and cons to both. The following attempts to summarise this somewhat.

Catching errors

Compilation can catch errors that wouldn't be caught in interpreted programs until the code with the error was executed. For example, accidentally attempting to assign a string value to an int will be a compiler error. With an interpreted language, the error typically won't be raised until the code is ran.

Possible program space

Because compilation and type checking necessarily eliminates some programs which in theory would be sound, the programmer can write programs in dynamically typed languages that aren't possible in statically typed languages. Consider the following example (Python code):

```
def func(which_type, which_value):
    if which_type == 'str':
        return which_value + 'a'
    elif which_type == 'int':
        return which_value + 5
    else:
        return None

# the following parameters are hard coded here but could e.g. be read from a file instead
print func('str', 'foo')
print func('int', 42)
```

The function 'func' returns either a string, an integer or None depending on the input parameter. The program can be run and it'll work perfectly fine, but if one attempts to write a similar program in a statically typed language then one must circumvent the type checking because the types for both the second input parameter and the return value are dynamic, that is, determined at runtime. While for many languages it's possible to circumvent the type checking, in practice the easiest solution in a statically typed language would be to avoid this kind of a construct altogether and reshape the program such that it won't be necessary.

Note: a more idiomatic way to accomplish this in Python would be to use the information about the type of a variable directly. I.e. running "isinstance(which_value, str)" will return True if the variable "which_value" is of type string.

Exercise: Rewrite the above code such that the function "func" only takes one parameter - which_value - and the operation performed on it depends on the output of "isinstance".

In general, there's no clear right or wrong around which kind of typing is the best, and typically arguments around this topic arise the same way normal people would argue about which car make, film, political party or religion is the best. While I attempt to stay objective, the following does include my subjective opinion where necessary - caveat emptor.

Often, for short and simple programs or programs that are easy to test, dynamic typing doesn't hurt, and dynamically typed languages often help implement the program faster. For larger programs that are more difficult to break to smaller pieces that can be executed in isolation, static typing often ends up being a big productivity boost as a large class of errors are trivially caught by the compiler, as opposed to discovering issues at runtime.

In addition to typing, there are other considerations about which language to use when; compiled languages have typically much better performance than dynamically typed languages which, depending on the requirements, may or may not rule out dynamically typed languages; languages with memory safety may be preferred to avoid any security issues or other memory handling related bugs; some platforms, especially embedded systems, may only have a C compiler or an assembler available.

2.2.2 Big O notation

> If you don't know anything about computers, just remember that they are machines that do exactly what you tell them but often surprise you in the result.
>
> —Richard Dawkins

An algorithm is, succinctly put, a piece of code (or logic) which solves a class of problems.

When discussing algorithms, it's handy to understand what big O notation is.

To put it short (possibly oversimplified), the big O notation is a notation to express the run time of an algorithm or a function in terms of the input size.

Maybe it's easiest to go through some examples.

Constant time

Let's assume we have a C array with five integers in it.

```
int my_array[5];
/* define values in the array */
```

If you wanted to access, say, the third element of the array, conceptually this can be done in *constant time* - meaning that the time it takes to read the value of the variable is independent of the index:

```
int val = my_array[2]; /* whether we access the third or the␣
↪fourth element, the run time is the same */
```

Linear time

Now, let's assume we want to check whether the number 42 is included in the array:

```
#include <stdio.h>

int find_in_array(const int *arr, int num_elems, int num_to_find)
{
    for(int i = 0; i < num_elems; i++) {
        if(arr[i] == num_to_find) {
            return 1;
        }
    }
    return 0;
}

int main(void)
{
    int my_array[5] = { 3, 7, 5, 1, 8 };
    int found = find_in_array(my_array, 5, 42);
    if(found) {
        printf("Found it!\n");
    } else {
        printf("Not found\n");
    }
}
```

Here, we have a for loop that goes through the whole array (in the worst case). If our array had 10 elements, it would need twice the time (conceptually speaking). Hence, the run time is *linear* to the size of the array.

Decay to pointer

You had an array, then you passed it to a function, and the function parameter is a pointer! What's going on?

In C, while array in general is not the same thing as a pointer, the two are sometimes interchangeable. In C, arrays are always passed by reference to a function, which means that the array is not automatically copied for the function (like a single int would be), but instead *a pointer* is passed to the function, whereby the pointer points to the first element in the array. Hence the array will *decay* into a pointer.

What do you mean "conceptually?"

You may remember that a CPU has instructions (like ADD, CMP etc.) which operate on data. Typically, the CPU has a few *registers* available for storing this data, each register typically being able to hold a *word*, i.e. the natural unit of data for the CPU, e.g. 32 bits. In addition, the computer (or mobile phone, or a car, or whatever) also has RAM for storing more data.

When you declare an array of, say, five elements, the array is allocated in RAM, and whenever the CPU wants to do anything with any of the values in the array (e.g. compare the value of an element with another value like in our search), it has to fetch the value from the memory. What happens in practice for such a small array is that all of it will be fetched in a *cache* - an extra small memory which is faster for the CPU to access than RAM (but not as fast as registers). The cache is part of a *cache hierarchy* - register, level 1 (L1) cache, L2 cache, L3 cache and finally RAM.

Using data in a register or fetching data from the L1 cache typically takes one CPU cycle (one cycle being the time it takes for the CPU *clock signal* to oscillate once between low and high). Fetching data from the L2 cache can take perhaps 10-15 cycles. Fetching data from RAM could take perhaps 200 cycles, or 200 times as long as fetching data from the L1 cache. If fetching data from the L1 cache is like getting a glass of water from the kitchen (one minute), fetching data from RAM is like going shopping for groceries and then cooking and eating dinner (three hours and 20 minutes).

Because it's silly to go shopping and cooking every time you need to eat or drink something, if the computer needs to go to RAM, it typically fetches a bunch of stuff from there that it thinks it needs later on, like the next few bytes beyond the one address it needs. Hence, if you define an array of five elements, and later look up the first one but the data isn't cached but in RAM, the computer will bring the whole array to the L2 (and L1) cache. However, if you have an array with a million elements (if we assume 32 bits or 4 bytes per integer, that would be 4 megabytes) and randomly access elements in the array then you might need to go to RAM several times, or not, depending on your access pattern. However, *conceptually* the accesses are still in linear time.

In terms of big O notation, constant time is annotated O(1). Linear time, i.e. run time depends directly on the size of the array (n) is annotated O(n).

Exercise: Try to implement the above algorithm of checking if an element is in an array without copy-pasting the code or looking at it.

Quadratic run time

Furthermore, let's assume we want to sort the array. We can invent a simple sorting algorithm for this:

```
#include <stdio.h>

void sort_array(int *arr, int num_elems)
{
    for(int j = 0; j < num_elems; j++) {
        int smallest_index = j;
        for(int i = j + 1; i < num_elems; i++) {
            if(arr[i] < arr[smallest_index]) {
                smallest_index = i;
            }
        }
        int tmp = arr[j];
        arr[j] = arr[smallest_index];
        arr[smallest_index] = tmp;
    }
}

int main(void)
{
    int my_array[5] = { 3, 7, 5, 1, 8 };
    sort_array(my_array, 5);
    for(int i = 0; i < 5; i++) {
        printf("%d\n", my_array[i]);
    }
}
```

This got a bit interesting so let's go through this line by line.

- Line 5: We define the *outer* for loop that goes through all elements, indexed with j.
- Line 6: We define a variable to store the index of the smallest number so far, initialised to j.
- Line 7: We define the *inner* for loop that goes through all elements from j + 1 until the end.
- Line 8-10: If the value at position i (which is bound to be "to the right" of j, if we imagine the array to be a row of boxes extending to the right) is smaller than the value at position smallest_index (which was initialised to j) then we note this index as the index with the smallest number in the rest of the array.
- Line 12-14: We finally *swap* the value at j with the smallest value we found. We swap by copying the value at j to a temporary variable, then putting the smallest value to j'th element, and finally putting the temporary value to where the smallest value was.

Here's an "animation" of how this algorithm would work, for an array of size 5. Each row represents one iteration. The first five columns are the elements in the array:

a0	a1	a2	a3	a4	j	i	Comment
3	7	5	1	8	0	1	i points to 7. Smallest index is 0.
3	7	5	1	8	0	2	i points to 5. Smallest index is 0.
3	7	5	1	8	0	3	i points to 1. Smallest index is set to 3 (1 < 3).
3	7	5	1	8	0	4	Inner loop finished. We swap 0th element (3) with the 3rd element (1).
1	7	5	3	8	1	2	i points to 5. Smallest index is set to 2 (5 < 7).
1	7	5	3	8	1	3	i points to 3. Smallest index is set to 3 (3 < 5).
1	7	5	3	8	1	4	Inner loop finished. We swap the 1st element (7) with the 3rd element (3).
1	3	5	7	8	2	3	i points to 7. Smallest index is 2.
1	3	5	7	8	2	4	Inner loop finished. We swap the 2nd element with itself (no change).
1	3	5	7	8	3	4	Inner loop finished. No change.
1	3	5	7	8	4	4	Inner loop not started because i would start at 5 - sort is done.

This sorting algorithm is called *selection sort* and it's one of the simpler ones.

What's the run time of this algorithm? We saw it has two for loops, and the number of iterations of both is only dependent (and linear to) the array size. Hence, the run time is *quadratic* to n - in terms of big O notation, $O(n^2)$. For every new element in the array we'll have to run the inner loop *and* the outer loop once more. If n = 10, we have 9 * 8 = 72 iterations. If n = 100, we have 99 * 98 = 9702 iterations.

Exercise: Try to implement the above algorithm of sorting an array without copy-pasting the code or looking at it.

Logarithmic run time

With a quadratic run time, the run time grows exponentially as the number of elements grows, which is pretty bad. The opposite of exponential is *logarithmic*, where the run time grows relatively slowly: in order to double the run time, you need to grow the number of elements exponentially. This is annotated O(log n). An example is searching for a person in a phone book:

you could pick a page in the middle, see if the person is alphabetically before or after the page you picked, and pick a page in the middle of either the section before or after your page - with each lookup, you halve the number of pages you need to look at.

O(n log n)

The final common run time class is O(n log n) - logarithmic run time multiplied with a linear run time. This means the run time is generally dominated by the linear part as the logarithmic run time grows relatively slowly. O(n log n) is also been proven to be the fastest possible run time class for a generic sorting algorithm.

Fast sorting algorithms

I won't go through the implementation of a fast sorting algorithm here. Interested readers can look them up online. Suffice to say, there are two popular fast sorting algorithms: *quicksort* and *mergesort*.

Quicksort works by picking one element at random, moving smaller elements than the selected one to its left and larger ones to its right and recursively sorting the elements on the left and on the right: for all the elements on the left, you pick one element at random, then move smaller elements than the selected one to its left and larger ones to its right and recursively sort the elements on the left and on the right. At some point you only have one or zero elements to consider and have thus sorted that part of the array. While quicksort has $O(n^2)$ run time in the worst case, it's O(n log n) in the typical case.

Merge sort divides the original array into sub-arrays of one element each (hence trivially sorted), and then works backwards by merging each sub-array, sorting the resulting array in the process. Merge sort has O(n log n) run time.

Typically it's rare for a programmer to have to implement a sort algorithm, especially a fast one. All main programming languages (even C) provide sorting as part of the standard library. For example, Python:

```
>>> my_array = [3, 7, 5, 1, 8]
>>> my_array.sort()
>>> my_array
[1, 3, 5, 7, 8]
```

(Python uses "Timsort" as its sorting algorithm, which is merge sort when n is large and insertion sort when n is small.) In C, one would do:

```
#include <stdio.h>
#include <stdlib.h>

int comparison(const void *a, const void *b)
{
    return *(int *)a - *(int *)b;
}

int main(void)
{
    int my_array[5] = { 3, 7, 5, 1, 8 };
    qsort(my_array, 5, sizeof(int), comparison);
    for(int i = 0; i < 5; i++) {
        printf("%d\n", my_array[i]);
    }
}
```

For qsort() in C, one has to define a *callback function* - a function that qsort() calls to get information on what the ordering between the elements should be, as well as the *size of* each element in the array. We'll touch more on these constructs later.

Exercise: There are lots of nice visualisations on how sorting algorithms work, for example on Wikipedia. Check out one or two.

2.2.3 Array, stack, queue

For reasons that will soon become apparent, it's useful to have a basic understanding of data structures. This section will cover arrays, stacks and queues.

Arrays

We've already used *arrays* in C: Array is a data structure which contains multiple elements of data, such that each element uses the same amount of memory and they're allocated contiguously:

```
+---+---+---+
| 1 | 2 | 3 |
+---+---+---+
```

As you can possibly imagine, accessing an element in an array is fast (O(1)) because you can calculate the address of an element using the following formula:

```
address(element_index) = base_address + element_index * element_
↪size
```

However, if you wanted to insert an element in an array, you have to move all elements after the new element one slot to the right, making inserting a relatively complex (O(n)) operation. Similarly, were one to ask "do I have value x in the array", one would have to traverse the whole array, making this an O(n) operation as well.

You can define an array in C with the following syntax (for example, an array with 5 ints):

```
int my_array[5];
```

Lists in Python are technically also arrays but each elements holds a pointer to arbitrary data, such that in Python, each element in a list can be of different type.

Stack

Typically the memory layout for a stack is the same as for an array but the usage pattern is different.

You can imagine stack as an array where you only have visibility over the last element in the array: you can read it, pop it (redefine "last element" as one to the left), and push an element (redefine "last element" as one to the right, and set its value).

Stack is also called "LIFO" - last in, first out. Here's an example "animation" of using a stack:

```
+---+---+---+
| 1 | 2 | x | # push(3)
+---+---+---+
      ^ end of stack

+---+---+---+
| 1 | 2 | 3 | # pop() - returns 3
+---+---+---+
          ^ end of stack

+---+---+---+
| 1 | 2 | 3 |
+---+---+---+
      ^ end of stack
```

- Initially, in this example, we have two elements in the stack (1 and 2). In total our array has three elements, such that the stack can't hold any more. If we try to push any more in the stack then we get a *stack overflow*. ('x' denotes unknown memory.) The caret ("^") represents a pointer to the end of stack.
- We then push 3 in the stack, meaning we set the value of the third element to 3 and note that the end of the stack is now on the third element.
- We then pop an element from the stack, meaning we set the end of the stack to the second element. The 3 is still in the memory but not treated as part of the stack.

I've heard of stack overflow before

In computers (mobile phones, what have you) there's normally another, implicit stack: whenever you declare a variable in C, it's typically put in *the stack*, which is memory allocated by the compiler for the program run time for things like local variables. Also, when you call a function, the function parameters as well as the return address are typically put in the stack.

An issue arises when you overflow *this stack* - it typically has a fixed amount of memory allocated to it, for example eight megabytes, and if you have very large local variables (for example an array with tens of millions of elements) or very deep recursion (millions of recursive function calls) then your program will overflow the stack, the operating system will notice this and kill your application. Apart from having your application crash, stack overflows can be security holes and therefore used to hack into systems.

Queue

Queue is similar to stack but the opposite. It typically also has the same memory layout as an array but with a different usage pattern.

You can imagine queue as an array where you only have visibility over the first element in the array: you can read it, pop it (redefine "first element" as one to the right), and push an element (redefine the last element as one to the right, and set its value).

Queue is also called "FIFO" - first in, first out. Here's an example "animation" of using a queue:

```
+---+---+---+---+---+
| 1 | 2 | x | x | x | # push(3)
+---+---+---+---+---+
  ^   ^ end of queue
  start of queue

+---+---+---+---+---+
| 1 | 2 | 3 | x | x | # pop() - returns 1
+---+---+---+---+---+
  ^       ^ end of queue
  start of queue

+---+---+---+---+---+
| 1 | 2 | 3 | x | x |
+---+---+---+---+---+
      ^   ^ end of queue
      start of queue
```

- Initially, in this example, we have two elements in the queue (1 and 2). In total our array has five elements, such that we can't push more than five elements in the queue ever without reallocating.
- We then push 3 in the queue, meaning we set the value of the third element to 3 and note that the end of the queue is now on the third element.
- We then pop an element from the queue, meaning we set the beginning of the queue to the second element. The 1 is still in the memory but not treated as part of the queue.

More buffers

A ring buffer is similar to a queue but, in case the buffer allocated to the queue is full, a new element replaces the oldest element in the queue, such that the oldest element is *overwritten*. This can be useful to e.g. keep track of the last N integers, or pointers, or any other data.

A double-ended queue, or *deque*, is, like the name suggests, a queue where one can append or remove elements at either end of the queue. This can often be implemented as a kind of a ring buffer.

2.3 JavaScript

2.3.1 Guessing game in JS

Let's write a guessing game. This game is fairly simple: the computer thinks of a number between 1 and 25, and the user needs to guess what it is. The user can make a guess, and depending on the guess, the computer may tell the user either "my number is smaller", "my number is bigger" or "correct number!"

Moreover, let's write this such that it's run in the browser. It should look something like this:

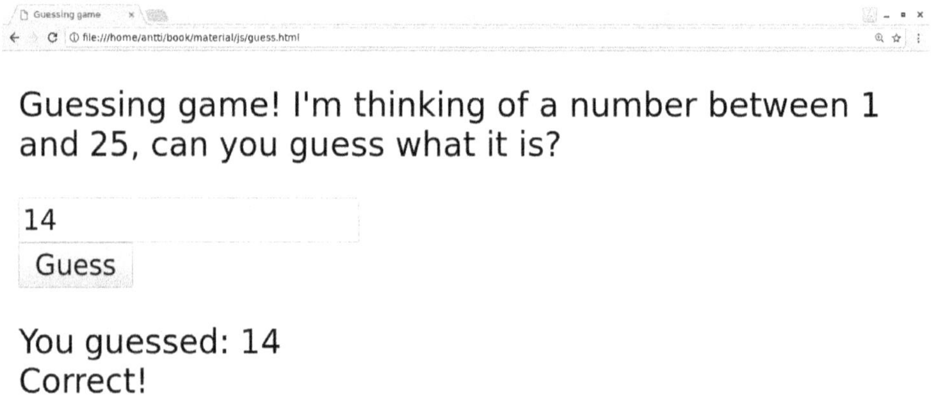
Guessing game
file:///home/antti/book/material/js/guess.html
Guessing game! I'm thinking of a number between 1 and 25, can you guess what it is?
14
Guess
You guessed: 14
Correct!

Now, in order to do this we're going to need JavaScript and HTML.

Disclaimer: This book introduces the basics of JavaScript and HTML but does specifically *not* include the modern best practices around web development. There are several reasons for this, one being that the best practices on web development are still under relatively rapid change, but the material in this book should be enough for the reader to gain a high level understanding of JavaScript and HTML and put together some interactive web pages.

The development environment will work like this: create a file with an extension .html and open it in your text editor. After you've made changes to your file, you can open it in your browser. For example, on Linux, if your file is called hello.html, you can open it in Firefox by running "firefox hello.html" in your terminal. When you make changes to the file, refresh the tab in your browser. If you're running some other system you'll need to find out how to open a local HTML file. On some systems, e.g. Linux, you can use the "file://" scheme, such that e.g. "file:///home/antti/hello.html" would be the URL to an HTML file in the user's directory.

What happens here is that the browser will read in the contents of your file and interpret it. The browser has an engine for reading and rendering HTML, such that if you for example describe, in your HTML, that a part of text should be displayed red, the browser will know to render that text red. Similarly the browser has a JavaScript interpreter built in, and will execute the JavaScript code embedded in the HTML file.

Let's start breaking down this task by creating the most basic HTML and JavaScript. Here's an HTML file:

```
1  <!DOCTYPE html>
2  <html lang="en">
3      <head>
4          <meta charset="UTF-8">
5          <title>Guessing game</title>
6      </head>
7      <body>
8          <p>some text</p>
9      </body>
10 </html>
```

You can type this code into a file and open it in your browser. You should see a plain web page with a text "some text". Some lines of the code aren't important to us right now but let's go through some of it:

- Line 2: we open the "html" *tag*. This is closed on line 10.
- Lines 3-6 are our "head" section which includes, among others, the title for our page
- Lines 7-9 are our "body" section
- Line 8 is our paragraph (denoted with "<p>"). This paragraph has the text "some text".

Here's one of the most basic "programs" that utilises JS and HTML:

```
1  <!DOCTYPE html>
2  <html lang="en">
3      <head>
4          <meta charset="UTF-8">
5          <title>Page</title>
6          <script>
7  function myfunc() {
8      document.getElementById("paragraph").innerHTML = "new text"
9  }
10         </script>
11     </head>
12
13     <body>
14         <p id="paragraph">old text</p><br/>
15         <input type="button" onclick="myfunc()" value="Press me">
16     </body>
17 </html>
```

Let's go through this in detail:

- Lines 6-10: We've introduced a new section within our "head" section: the "script" section which holds our JavaScript code.
- Line 14: We've added an *id* to our paragraph (simply named "paragraph").
- Line 15: We've added a *button* using the tag "<input>" with an attribute 'type="button"'. The button has a text "Press me". Once pressed, it will call the *JavaScript function* "myfunc".

Our JavaScript code consists of one function definition. The JavaScript function "myfunc" has one line: it retrieves the element "paragraph" from the page, and changes its member variable "innerHTML" value to "new text". The element "paragraph" is our paragraph, and its member variable "innerHTML" is the text within that paragraph. Hence, the JavaScript function changes the contents of the paragraph.

If you run this in your browser, you should see a text "old text" and a button. If you press the button, the text is replaced with "new text".

What happens here is that the paragraph has an ID, and the button has a JavaScript function associated with it. When pressing the button, the browser executes the JavaScript code which changes the text.

To be clear, with JavaScript we can change the HTML, i.e. what the user sees, based on logic (code). Our JavaScript code can *read* user input by reading the values stored in the *Document Object Model* (DOM), e.g. by reading the variable of a text field using document.getElementById("guess").value. Similarly our JavaScript code can *write* to the DOM, i.e. modify what the user sees e.g. by changing the value of a variable such as document.getElementById("paragraph").innerHTML. By reading user input from DOM and making changes to DOM, we can build interactive web pages.

In general, HTML describes the content, i.e. what is shown to the user, while JavaScript describes the logic, i.e. what happens.

Let's put together one more example to capture the other bits and pieces we need for our game:

```
<!DOCTYPE html>
<html lang="en">
    <head>
        <meta charset="UTF-8">
        <title>Page</title>
        <script>
var value = Math.random() * 20;
var value_rounded = Math.floor(value);

function myfunc() {
    var str = "Values: " + value + "; rounded: " + value_rounded;
    if(value_rounded > 10) {
        str += "; rounded value is larger than 10.";
    } else if(value_rounded > 5) {
        str += "; rounded value is between 5 and 10.";
    } else {
        str += "; rounded value is smaller than or equal to 5.";
    }
    str += " Text in text box: " + document.getElementById("guess
↪").value;
    document.getElementById("paragraph").innerHTML = str
}
        </script>
    </head>

    <body>
```

(continues on next page)

(continued from previous page)

```
26          <form>
27              <input type="text" id="guess" value=""> <br/>
28              <input type="button" onclick="myfunc()" value="Press␣
↪me">
29          </form>
30          <p id="paragraph"></p>
31      </body>
32  </html>
```

The code in this example isn't very useful as a whole but includes different snippets which are needed for our guessing game:

- Line 7: The function Math.random() is called which returns a random floating point number between 0 and 1. This is furthermore multiplied by 20 to get a number between 0 and 20. This line also demonstrates use of variables in JavaScript. The variable is defined outside the function, such that the random number is only generated once, at page load.
- Line 8: The function Math.floor() is called to round the number down to an integer. The result is a number between 0 and 19.
- Line 11: Different strings and variables can be *concatenated*, or put together, using the "+" operator.
- Lines 12-18: JavaScript also supports branches.
- Line 19: We can obtain the value of an element in DOM and store it in a variable. We can append to an existing string using the "+=" operator.
- Line 22: In HTML, we can use the "<input>" tag with attribute 'type="text"' to create a *text box*. The user can type text in it. We read the contents of this text box in our JavaScript code on line 14.

Exercise: What does the above page do? Try it out. Try reloading the page.

Now we have everything we need to put our game together. What we'll need is:

1. Some JS logic to generate the random number which is the number the computer "thinks" of, and which the user is expected to guess.

Note that you'll need to have this code *outside* any of your functions, such that the number is generated only once per page load.

2. A text field where to input what the guess is
3. A button indicating we'd like to make a guess
4. More JS logic to check the guess against the number the computer is thinking of
5. Changing the text in the paragraph to indicate whether our guess is correct, too low, or too high

You may need to debug JavaScript, for example if you make a typo, causing your program to not run correctly. How to debug JavaScript depends on your browser. For example with Chrome, you can hit F12 to bring up the developer information panel. This shows any JavaScript errors, for example.

Exercise: Implement the guessing game where the computer thinks of a number and the player needs to guess which number it is. The JavaScript code should give hints to the player whether the guess is too small, too large, or correct.

Exercise: Have the program count the number of guesses, and display the total number at the end.

2.3.2 JavaScript meets algorithms

Try to play the guessing game a few times.

What is the best strategy to win the game in the least number of guesses? Have a think before reading further.

You may have noticed that the best strategy is to guess at the middle point of the available range, that is, 12 or 13 when the maximum number is 25, and then on the middle point of the available range again depending on the answer, so either 6 if the number is smaller or 19 if the number is larger. This method will in general arrive at the right answer in the minimum number of guesses.

In terms of big O notation, the performance of such an algorithm would be O(log n), i.e. doubling the problem space will cause one more iteration. Think about it: if the maximum number was 50, the first guess should be 25, after which we know the number is either below 25 or between 26 and 50, such that the range is the same as if the original maximum had been 25.

This algorithm is called "binary search" because it searches for an answer, and splits the search space in half with each lookup. It's one of the most important concepts in computer science.

What we'll write next is a binary search algorithm to solve the game for us. Let's add a button that whenever it's pressed, it'll make an ideal guess (without looking up the correct answer!), such that we can skip playing the game and hit the button enough times to have the function find the correct number for us.

In more detail, what should happen is that pressing the new button will call a function which will need to decide what to guess, enter that number in the field, press the button to make a guess, and read and understand the text saying whether the number was too small, too big or correct.

Here are the building blocks for this to get you started:

```
var my_guess = /* TODO */;
document.getElementById("guess").value = my_guess;
document.getElementById("guess_button").click();
var answer = document.getElementById("paragraph").innerHTML;
if(answer.search("smaller") != -1) {
```

(continues on next page)

(continued from previous page)

```
6       /* TODO */
7   }
```

The above snippet demonstrates the following:

- On line 2, the value of element called "guess" - this should be our text box where the user inputs their guess - is set to be whatever the value of "my_guess" is
- On line 3, a button with the ID "guess_button" is clicked
- On line 4, the text indicating the answer is read from a DOM element called "paragraph" and stored in a variable
- On line 5, the search string is searched for the text "smaller". -1 will indicate the string was not found.

Exercise: What does the search() function as used on line 5 actually return, and what exactly can you pass to it as a parameter? Find the reference for the function online. What is the type of the variable "answer" in the snippet above?

The above, combined with your knowledge from the previous section, should be enough to put the general infrastructure in place for our button. What's still required is the actual logic. I can share some hints:

- You will need to track the upper and lower limit of the range where the correct number might reside
- As these will need to be stored between button clicks (one click will only guess once), they need to be stored outside the function
- The upper and lower limit are needed to define the value to guess, and are influenced by the answer string

Exercise: Implement this button that plays the number guessing game.

Exercise: Once you've implemented this button, you might want to experiment with increasing the maximum number from 25 to something larger, for example 5000. See if your algorithm still finds the correct number with a small number of guesses. Make sure you define the maximum number only once in the source code such that there's no worry of your different functions going out of sync.

Calling a JavaScript function at page load

A quick search online reveals a way to do this:

```
function init() {
    /* my code goes here */
}
window.onload = init;
```

That is, we define a function which we want to be called at page load time, and install it as a *callback* function in the member function "onload" in the global object "window". (We'll get to the concepts of callback functions, member functions and objects in more detail later.)

Exercise: The original image of the game included a text "I'm thinking of a number between 1 and 25," but after the previous exercise, this might not be true anymore. Modify this string based on the variable you have that holds the maximum value. For this you'll need to run JavaScript at the page loading phase.

Exercise: Assuming the maximum number is 5000, what is the maximum number of guesses the algorithm will need in order to find the correct number? Hint: the algorithm has O(log n) complexity.

Note that the JavaScript code is executed in the browser. This means that if you were to load a public web page with, for example, such a game, you can modify the HTML your browser renders to add a new button, and the JavaScript your browser executes to solve the game. It may be difficult to identify and understand the correct JavaScript in order to do this, depending on the web page, but as the JavaScript execution and HTML are in the end controlled by the browser, in general there's nothing stopping any web page visitors from making their own additions to the code they execute.

2.4 Intermediate C

> [C has] the power of assembly language and the convenience of ... assembly language.
>
> —Dennis Ritchie

We've now had our first touch with C. Let's go a bit deeper.

When writing C, it sometimes helps to think about the memory layout, and what the CPU actually does. If you consider that C is practically a thin layer abstracting the CPU, it may start to feel more logical.

2.4.1 Records

In our previous code we worked with functions and quadratic equations. A quadratic equation was represented by three floating point values a, b and c. Let's write a function that returns the value of a quadratic function at a given point x:

```
float function_value(float a, float b, float c, float x)
{
    return a * (x * x) + b * x + c;
}
```

Seems straightforward enough. Now, let's imagine we need to find out the difference between two quadratic functions at a given point x. Let's write this function:

```
float difference_between_functions(float a1, float b1, float c1,␣
↪float a2, float b2, float c2, float x)
{
    float val1 = function_value(a1, b1, c1, x);
    float val2 = function_value(a2, b2, c2, x);
    return val2 - val1;
}
```

This seems a bit unwieldy: The function takes seven parameters in total, and it's easy to make a mistake somewhere. Surely we can do better?

In C (and in fact most programming languages) it's possible to combine values in *records* or composite data types. See below:

```
struct quadratic_function {
    float a;
    float b;
    float c;
};
```

If we wanted to declare such a struct and define its values, we can do simply:

```
struct quadratic_function f;
f.a = 1.0f;
f.b = 2.0f;
f.c = 3.0f;
```

...and use f.a, f.b and f.c as we want. (The above code would need to reside within a function as mandated by C.)

We can now also redefine the function that calculates the value at a given point:

```
float function_value(const struct quadratic_function *f, float x)
{
    return f->a * (x * x) + f->b * x + f->c;
}
```

We've made a few changes:

- The parameters a, b and c are now replaced by (or contained in) f, a struct
- f is passed in as a const pointer, not a value

About passing a variable to a function as a pointer: By default, in C, whenever a variable is passed to a function it's passed *by value* which means a copy of the variable is made for the function (allocated in the stack), and the copy is discarded when the function returns. It often makes sense to pass a pointer to a function instead, i.e. *by reference,* because then the data the function has access to is the original data.

In this case, it makes very little difference except that it saves an unnecessary copy of a few bytes.

About the keyword const: this means we treat the variable f as a constant within the function, and if we wanted to modify the data pointed to by f, i.e. its fields a, b or c, the compiler would issue an error. This is helpful for us as the function implementors to ensure we don't modify data we don't want to modify, and helpful to the caller of the function to know that the function shouldn't modify the input data.

Because f is a pointer, the syntax for accessing the fields of the struct is different: the operator -> is used instead of dot (.).

Now, defining the function difference_between_functions can be much clearer:

```
float difference_between_functions(const struct quadratic_
↪function *f1, const struct quadratic_function *f2, float x)
{
    float val1 = function_value(f1, x);
    float val2 = function_value(f2, x);
    return val2 - val1;
}
```

Exercise: The derivative of a quadratic function $ax^2 + bx + c$ is $2ax + b$. Write a function that calculates the derivative for a quadratic function at a given point x and call it, with the input data passed as a pointer to a struct.

What is a struct

Our example struct consists of three integers. As C is relatively close to the actual hardware, we can reason about what this struct looks like in practice. In general, the amount of memory used by an integer in C is implementation defined but for the purpose of this section we can assume it's 4 bytes (32 bits). Defining a structure like this typically means the data will be packed well, such that 12 bytes will be required for one allocation of struct my_datatype and the layout will only contain the memory required for a, b and c, nothing more. (Mixing different data types of different sizes may cause padding memory to be added by the C compiler, depending on the hardware constraints.)

You can find out what the size of a data type is in C by using the "sizeof" operator:

```
printf("%lu\n", sizeof(struct quadratic_function));
```

In this sense, defining structures in C mostly serves to combine various data into one unit, simplifying code and aiding in having the necessary memory available and allocated.

2.4.2 C and the stack

We touched on stack briefly before. This section goes a bit more in depth on this. Arguably, if you understand the stack then you will also understand pointers and C memory management in general.

You may remember that a CPU doesn't really have a concept of variables; it has memory accesses and registers. What happens, then, when we e.g. define an int in our C code, and use it? The value for each variable is stored either in a register or in RAM where it has a specific address, or a specific offset from an address. The C compiler reads our C code, sees that we e.g. define a variable, picks a register or a memory address for this variable and generates CPU instructions that use the variable.

The stack is a chunk of memory (buffer) that the compiler allocates for your program when the program is started. It's used for all your variables and function calls. You can imagine the stack as a stack of papers where, whenever you declare a variable, or call a function, a sheet of paper is added on top. Each variable is a sheet of paper, and the data written on the paper is the value of the variable. Whenever a variable exits the scope or the function call is over, the related sheets of paper are taken out of the stack again.

Let's imagine we have a toy program:

```
#include <stdio.h>

int main(void)
{
	int a = 3;
	int b = 4;
	int x = a + b;
	printf("%d\n", x);
}
```

This code effectively generates a stack that looks like this when main is entered:

```
| Address    | Contents |
| 0x50000008 | ?        |
| 0x50000004 | 4        |
| 0x50000000 | 3        |
```

What we have here is our stack with three entries: The first one (from the bottom) resides in address 0x50000000 and has been set to 3, i.e. it represents our variable "a". The second one is our variable "b" and the third is our variable "x". (The specific number 0x50000000 is in reality OS and CPU dependent and often arbitrary; we use 0x50000000 here for illustration purposes.)

What's the 0x

0x denotes *hexadecimal numbers*. They're just like regular (decimal) numbers, but we include letters a-f for numbers 10-15.

If we, for example, take the number 3. In hex, we write this 0x3, i.e. simply add 0x in the front to denote a hex number. In binary, this is 0b11. Recall that binary can only have 0 or 1, hence, when we add 1 and 1, we "overflow" and have to add another digit, hence 0b10. When we add 1 again to get 3, in binary this is 0b11.

If we then consider the number 13: in hex, this is 0xd. In binary, this is 0b1101. The reason we call it "13" is because when we added 1 to 9, the decimal system "overflowed" and we had to add another digit. Hex didn't have this issue so it's 0xd.

Finally, if we consider the number 238: in hex, this is 0xee. Because the number is larger than 16, we had to overflow and hence have another digit in our hex number. However it's still less than 256 (0x100) so only two hex digits are required.

Why do we do this? Well, you might recall that as computers generally are built using digital logic, they use binary numbers a lot, and they also often use round numbers for the *memory layout* as well as *memory boundaries*. Hence a program *memory space* could e.g. start at the address 0x50000000. In binary this is 0b01010000000000000000000000000000 (32 bits). In decimal this is 83886080 but because that's generally a less round number than plain 0x50000000, we use hex instead.

Tip: You can easily convert between hex, binary and decimal in the Python interpreter. You can start it by running "python2"; e.g. running "hex(30)" will print the number 30 in hex, "bin(30)" will print it in binary, and running e.g. 0xee or 0b11 will convert hex or binary to decimal.

Because we just entered main and the addition hadn't been executed yet, "x" contains undefined data. After the main function has been executed, our stack looks like this:

```
| Address    | Contents |
| 0x50000008 | 7        |
| 0x50000004 | 4        |
| 0x50000000 | 3        |
```

Function calls

I wrote the stack is also used for functions. Let's have another example:

```
#include <stdio.h>

int double_input(int i)
{
        return i * 2;
}

int main(void)
{
        int a = 3;
        int b;
        b = double_input(a);
        printf("%d\n", b);
}
```

Here, we define a function and call it. At the beginning of main, the stack looks like this:

```
| Address    | Contents |
| 0x50000004 | ?        |
| 0x50000000 | 3        |
```

Fairly unspectacular. However, when main calls the function "double_input" and we enter that function, the stack looks like this:

```
| Address    | Contents   |
| 0x5000000c | 3          |
| 0x50000008 | 0x12345678 |
| 0x50000004 | ?          |
| 0x50000000 | 3          |
```

We now have two new entries in our stack. The top one (0x5000000c) is our variable "i" which has been assigned the value 3 - a copy of our variable a. The third one (0x50000008) contains the *return address of our function call* - it's an *address in the code of main* where the code execution should return to once the function call returns. This is something that's added by the compiler to ensure the program runs correctly.

Pointers

Now, let's have some pointers.

```
1  #include <stdio.h>
2
3  int main(void)
4  {
5          int a = 3;
6          int *b;
7          b = &a;
8          *b = 4;
9          printf("%p\n", b);
10         printf("%d\n", *b);
11 }
```

Let's go through this line by line.

- Line 5: We declare a normal int and assign 3 to it.
- Line 6: We declare a pointer to an int.
- Line 7: We assign the pointer the *address of* "a", i.e. make the pointer point to "a".
- Line 8: We assign the *pointed value* of "b", i.e. "a" to 4.
- Line 9: We print out the value of "b", i.e. the address that "b" points to (just for fun).
- Line 10: We print out the value that "b" points to, i.e. "a".

How does the stack look like for this at the end of main? Can you guess?

```
| Address    | Contents   |
| 0x50000004 | 0x50000000 |
| 0x50000000 | 4          |
```

We declare two variables so we have two entries in our stack. The first one (from the bottom) is "a". The second one is our pointer, whereby its value is the address of "a", i.e. 0x50000000.

Exercise: Run the program yourself and check what the value of "b" is on your computer. (Probably something more difficult to read than 0x50000004. The number of hex digits in your output is a clue as to whether you're running on a 32-bit or a 64-bit CPU.)

Let's then mix pointers and functions:

```
#include <stdio.h>

void double_input(int *i)
{
        *i = *i * 2;
}

int main(void)
{
        int a = 3;
        double_input(&a);
        printf("%d\n", a);
}
```

The function "double_input" takes an int pointer and doubles the value of the integer that the pointer points to. Let's look at the stack when we enter that function:

```
| Address    | Contents   |
| 0x50000008 | 0x50000000 |
| 0x50000004 | 0x12345678 |
| 0x50000000 | 3          |
```

We've declared two variables ("int a" and "int *i"), and "i" was assigned to the address of "a" as the function was called.

The function assigns a value to the address pointed to by "i", namely the value of the address itself multiplied by two, such that the value in address 0x50000000 becomes 6.

2.4.3 Arrays and the stack

Arrays

Arrays are blocks of memory allocated in stack.

```
#include <stdio.h>
#include <string.h>

int main(void)
{
        int my_array[5];
        memset(my_array, 0x00, sizeof(my_array));
        my_array[0] = 3;
        my_array[1] = 2;
        printf("%d\n", my_array[1]);
}
```

Here, at the end of main, our stack looks like this:

```
| Address    | Contents    |
| 0x50000010 | 0           |
| 0x5000000c | 0           |
| 0x50000008 | 0           |
| 0x50000004 | 2           |
| 0x50000000 | 3           |
```

In other words, each integer in the array is available in the stack.

Arrays and functions

When passing an array to a function, the array is not copied like a pointer or an integer, but instead a *pointer* to the first element is passed. The array is said to *decay* to a pointer:

```
#include <stdio.h>
#include <string.h>

void func(int *array, int len)
{
        for(int i = 0; i < len; i++) {
```

(continues on next page)

(continued from previous page)

```
7                 *array = *array * 2;
8                 array++;
9         }
10 }
11
12 int main(void)
13 {
14         int my_array[5];
15         memset(my_array, 0x00, sizeof(my_array));
16         my_array[0] = 3;
17         my_array[1] = 2;
18         func(my_array, 5);
19         printf("%d\n", my_array[1]);
20 }
```

When entering the function "func", our stack looks like this:

```
| Address    | Contents   |
| 0x50000020 | 0          |
| 0x5000001c | 5          |
| 0x50000018 | 0x50000000 |
| 0x50000014 | 0x12345678 |
| 0x50000010 | 0          |
| 0x5000000c | 0          |
| 0x50000008 | 0          |
| 0x50000004 | 2          |
| 0x50000000 | 3          |
```

That is, our array is located from 0x50000000 to 0x50000010. We then have the return address due to our function call, a pointer pointing to the first element (variable "int *array"), the variable "len" which has value 5, and our index variable "i" with value 0. (Remember, each variable we define must have its location in the stack.)

What happens in the function "func"? The interesting part is the contents of the loop. On line 7, we double the value of the number pointed to by the pointer. We then increment *the pointer itself*, i.e. *the address pointed to* by one. Because the pointer is a pointer to int, incrementing the pointer by one effectively makes the pointer point to the next int. This means that after we've iterated through the loop once, our stack looks like this:

```
| Address    | Contents   |
| 0x50000020 | 1          |
| 0x5000001c | 5          |
| 0x50000018 | 0x50000004 |
| 0x50000014 | 0x12345678 |
| 0x50000010 | 0          |
| 0x5000000c | 0          |
| 0x50000008 | 0          |
| 0x50000004 | 2          |
| 0x50000000 | 6          |
```

In other words, we've doubled the value at 0x50000000, added 4 (the size of an int in our example) to the pointer at 0x50000014, and added 1 to "i".

Now, after the function has completed and the execution returns to main, our stack looks like this:

```
| Address    | Contents   |
| 0x50000010 | 0          |
| 0x5000000c | 0          |
| 0x50000008 | 0          |
| 0x50000004 | 4          |
| 0x50000000 | 6          |
```

That is, the top addresses are no longer "officially" part of the stack and the values in our array have all been doubled.

If you're wondering what happens to the memory above the stack when a function call returns, the answer is probably nothing. What the compiler instructs the CPU to do when returning from a function is simply to decrement the *stack pointer* - a pointer that points to the top of the stack, which is needed when adding new data in the stack. The code to manage the stack pointer is added automatically by the compiler.

Stack overflow

Typically, the compiler allocates a chunk of memory for the stack at the beginning of the program execution. The memory is typically eight megabytes. This means that you could possibly - although the behaviour is undefined, meaning the compiler can generate any code - access memory in stack that's been allocated but not defined. We can try this out:

```
#include <stdio.h>

int main(void)
{
        int a = 4;
        int *b;
        b = &a;
        int *c;
        c = b + 2;
        printf("%d\n", *c);
}
```

What happens here is that we first define a variable "a", then a pointer that holds the address of that variable ("b"), and finally a pointer that accesses the memory after "b". At the end of the program our stack could look like this:

Address	Contents
0x50000010	?
0x5000000c	?
0x50000008	0x5000000c
0x50000004	0x50000000
0x50000000	4

That is, "a" has value 4 and "b" has the address of "a" as value, but "c" points to an address in the stack where the contents are unknown. Now, because the behaviour of this program is undefined, the program could output anything, and the output could depend e.g. on the compiler optimisation flags.

Undefined behaviour

Undefined behaviour is a concept that mainly only exists in C and C++ and refers to behaviour which according to the language standard isn't defined. The language specifications in these cases explicitly allow the compiler to do anything. What compilers could do is insert code that would crash your program, or possibly send data over a network or reboot the system. What the compilers typically insert is the "expected" code - e.g. if you read from a variable or a buffer where the contents are undefined, the compiler will insert code to read from it anyway, such that you might get *stale* data - for example, the value of a variable that doesn't exist anymore. In general, bugs involving undefined behaviour are unpleasant to work with, such that it's recommended to avoid undefined behaviour where possible.

If you do use more than eight megabytes of stack, for example by allocating a very large array, then this is typically caught by the operating system, causing it to send the SIGTERM signal to your program, effectively killing it. This is called stack overflow.

2.4.4 Dynamic memory allocation

You might ask yourself any of the following questions:

- The stack can hold up to eight megabytes. What if I need more memory?
- What if I want to allocate memory in a function and have the caller use it?
- What if I want to allocate memory where I don't know how long I'll be needing it?
- What if I want to allocate memory where the exact amount of memory I need isn't known until runtime?

The answer to all of these is *dynamic memory allocation.*

The C standard library provides two functions for this: "malloc" and "free". The function "malloc" (memory allocation) allocates memory, which can then be freed using the function "free". Here's a simple example:

```
#include <stdio.h>
#include <stdlib.h>
#include <string.h>
#include <assert.h>

int main(void)
{
        int *a = (int *)malloc(20 * sizeof(int));
        assert(a);
        memset(a, 0x00, 20 * sizeof(int));
        a[0] = 3;
        *(a + 1) = 4;
        int *b = a;
        b += 2;
        *b = 5;
        printf("%d\n", a[2]);
        free(a);
}
```

Let's first go through this line by line:

- Line 8: We call "malloc" to allocate memory for 20 integers (80 bytes if our int is four bytes). We *cast* the type of the "malloc" return value from void pointer to int pointer. This is because "malloc" in general returns a void pointer, which means any pointer, because "malloc" isn't specific to any type. We'll go a bit deeper around casting later.
- Line 9: We *assert* the return value of "malloc" is non-zero. If "malloc" fails, it will return a NULL pointer, and in this case our assertion would fail, meaning our program would crash itself. This is to ensure our memory allocation succeeded. (In practice there should be no problem allocating 80 bytes.)
- Line 10: We set all of the allocated memory to 0.
- Line 11: We set the first element in our array to 3.
- Line 12: We set the second element in our array to 4. The syntax is different but the semantics here is equivalent to what was used in line 11.
- Line 13: We define a variable "b" which has the same value as "a".
- Line 14: We increment the value of "b" by two (that is, eight bytes, assuming our int is four bytes). It now points to the third element in our array.
- Line 15: We set the value pointed to by "b" to 5.
- Line 17: We free the memory we allocated.

At the end of the main function, our stack will look something like this:

```
| Address    | Contents   |
| 0x50000004 | 0x23456788 |
| 0x50000000 | 0x23456780 |
```

That is, we have two variables, "a" and "b", whereby "a" points to the address of the first byte of the memory we allocated (and freed) and "b" points to an address eight bytes after. The function "malloc", when allocating memory, will, with the help of the operating system, retrieve and provide the address to a block of memory somewhere in RAM, such that the address may look random but will *not* be in the stack. It is said that the memory is in this case allocated in the *heap*.

Exercise: Allocate some memory using "malloc". Print out the address of the memory returned using printf("%p\n", pointer). Compare against the address of a variable you have in stack. Run your program multiple times. Do the addresses change?

Dynamic memory allocation gotchas

There are a few things that could go wrong with dynamic memory allocations, providing job security for programmers for years to come.

Use after free: As we saw in our program above, the variable "a", which contained the address of memory allocated in heap stayed unchanged after freeing the memory. In principle there's nothing preventing the programmer from accidentally reading the memory after freeing it, or writing to it. Reading it and then using the value, for example, in an "if" statement, will cause the code to randomly either branch into the "if" statement or not. Writing to it will possibly mess up some other memory in your program, e.g. accidentally changing some unrelated variable. This is all nasty.

One way to prevent this is to always reset your pointers after freeing the memory that was pointed to. E.g.:

```
int *a = malloc(...);
free(a);
a = NULL;
```

By setting "a" to NULL, which is a special pointer value roughly meaning "invalid", if we now try to either read the value pointed to by it, or write to it, the program will immediately crash. (Actually reading or writing to NULL is undefined behaviour, but in practice compilers seem to do us a favour and crash.) This makes it more obvious what has gone wrong.

Double free: You may accidentally free memory pointed to by a pointer after it's already been freed. This will possibly free some other memory that you're still using, or otherwise generally corrupt your memory. Again, resetting pointers to NULL after "free" helps as calling "free" for a NULL pointer is defined to do nothing.

Memory leaks: You may have a pointer to memory, then point the pointer somewhere else but not free the memory. The memory is now inaccessible but still allocated to your program. If you do this often enough, or if your program runs long enough, it will soak up a significant amount of memory and will need to be restarted.

In general, it's sometimes not clear from using a function what the semantics for memory ownership are. Let's say you call a function from a library which returns a pointer. Should you call "free" on that pointer when you're done with it, or not? This is typically (hopefully) described in the documentation for the function.

2.4.5 C and strings

> The most effective debugging tool is still careful thought, coupled with judiciously placed print statements.
>
> —Brian Kernighan

This section goes in depth around strings (and buffers in general) in C.

C string handling

Before we continue with C, there are a couple of building blocks regarding string handling that you should know about. Let's first cover through some basics about strings in C.

C doesn't really have strings. What it has are buffers (allocation of continuous memory), chars or characters (one byte, representing one ASCII character, meaning English letters, numbers or other symbols) and pointers. Mixing these conceptually results in something like a string. See the below diagram which is a continuous buffer i.e. array with eight slots, each holding one byte (character):

```
+-----+-----+-----+-----+-----+------+---+---+
| 'H' | 'e' | 'l' | 'l' | 'o' | '\0' | ? | ? |
+-----+-----+-----+-----+-----+------+---+---+
```

Digression: what is ASCII?

ASCII is the name of a mapping (encoding) between numbers and characters. ASCII defines that, for example, the letter 'H' is equivalent to the number 72, and vice versa. The letter 'h' (lower case) is equivalent to 104. ASCII also includes non-printable characters, e.g. line feed ("\n") which is equivalent to number 10, or null ("\0") which is equivalent to number 0. You can find the full encoding online. If you need non-English characters then other encodings exist, such as UTF-8, in which case a character may require more than one byte.

This is a buffer with eight slots containing the string "Hello". The sixth slot is a 0, or '\0', which indicates the end of a string. The value of this is in fact

0 but this has two representations: 0 (the number) or '\0' (character). The last two slots are *undefined* and reading them results in *undefined behaviour* like crashing, garbage, nothing, or anything.

You can create such a buffer by e.g. doing the following:

```
1 char my_array[8];
2 sprintf(my_array, "Hello");
```

- Line 1: We allocate the buffer in stack.
- Line 2: We write the string "Hello" to the buffer.

In general, however, you may write something into a buffer where you don't know the length of the string in advance. What you'll need to do in any case is allocate a buffer large enough for your needs, but in addition it's always best practice to *clear* the memory in advance, to avoid undefined behaviour. You must also ensure you don't write *past the end* of the buffer because this will typically overwrite some of your other variables, probably crashing your program and also possibly creating a security hole. It's typically better to do this:

```
1 char my_array[8];
2 memset(my_array, 0x00, sizeof(my_array)); /* sizeof(my_array) will return 8 */
3 snprintf(my_array, 8, "Hello");
```

- Line 1: We allocate the buffer in stack.
- Line 2: We clear the buffer, such that all the values in the buffer are 0. This way, as long as we keep the last character to 0 in the buffer (remember 0 indicates end of a string), we shouldn't be either reading or writing past the end of our buffer. (You will need to #include <string.h> to declare memset().)
- Line 3: We write the string "Hello" to the buffer using *snprintf*, which takes as a parameter the maximum number of bytes to write. We tell it to write maximum eight characters such that the last one will always be 0.

Now, while array in general is not the same thing as a pointer, for strings the two are sometimes interchangeable. For example, let's assume you want to pass your array as a parameter to another function. You can't because arrays are always passed by reference in C. This means that the array will *decay* into a pointer:

```
void my_function(const char *str, int len) {
    /* sizeof(str) will NOT give an answer as to how long the buffer is */
    snprintf(str, len, "Hello");
}

int main(void) {
    char my_array[8];
    memset(my_array, 0x00, sizeof(my_array)); /* sizeof(my_array) returns 8 */
    my_function(my_array, sizeof(my_array));
}
```

Here, "my_function" cannot by itself know how long the string (character buffer) pointed to by "str" is, and must take a second parameter "len" which must have this information. The "sizeof" operator only tells the size of the array (in bytes) at the site where the array is allocated, not where only a pointer is available.

Pointer arithmetic and substrings

Let's say we want to modify the array by a character. We can do this:

```
char my_array[8];
memset(my_array, 0x00, sizeof(my_array));
snprintf(my_array, 8, "Hello");
my_array[0] = 'J'; /* my_array is now "Jello"; */
my_array[4] = 'y'; /* my_array is now "Jelly"; */
```

How would we do this if we only had a char pointer, not the array itself? We can use *pointer arithmetic*:

```
void my_function(char *str) {
    *str = 'J';
    *(str + 4) = 'y';
    /* or equivalently: str[4] = 'y';          */
    /* or equivalently: str += 4; *str = 'y'; */
```

(continues on next page)

(continued from previous page)

```
}

int main(void) {
    char my_array[8];
    memset(my_array, 0x00, sizeof(my_array));
    snprintf(my_array, 8, "Hello");
    my_function(my_array);
}
```

By *dereferencing* the pointer "str" with * we can access individual characters in the buffer, and also assign to them.

By adding a number n to a pointer the resulting pointer points to data n elements after the first element, and by dereferencing it we can also assign to it.

As a diagram it looks like this:

```
+-----+-----+-----+-----+-----+------+---+---+
| 'H' | 'e' | 'l' | 'l' | 'o' | '\0' | ? | ? |
+-----+-----+-----+-----+-----+------+---+---+
.  ^                       ^
. str                     str + 4
```

If one were to pass a char pointer to my_function which pointed to less than five bytes of allocated memory, *my_function* would cause undefined behaviour.

As my_function modifies "str", the parameter can't have the const qualifier.

Digression: debugging

Let's assume you try to run your program, and it crashes. What's going on?

There are a few ways to find out. In the worst case, you simply get a segmentation fault, i.e. tried to access memory your program didn't have access to. There are a few ways to debug this:

1. Code inspection and hardening - going through the code and adding useful *assertions* where necessary.

2. Debug printf - inserting printf calls to various places in your code, seeing which one gets executed, allowing you to pinpoint the line that is the cause for the crash.

3. Using a *debugger* to show the root cause of the crash and the state of the program at the time of crash.

Assertions seem like going through in more detail. For example, if you have an int variable named "foo", and you assume it should always be between 0 and 5, you can use this code (after #including <assert.h>):

```
assert(foo >= 0 && foo <= 5);
```

Now, what happens is the program will always check, when executing the statement, whether your statement is true and if not, will immediately crash the program. This is helpful for detecting cases where your assumptions were wrong.

Finally, *debuggers* are programs which execute your program in a controlled environment with the ability to track and stop the program execution when necessary. One potentially useful debugger is *gdb* (or its clang counterpart, *lldb*). There are many ways to use it but one way is to get a *backtrace* of the function calls leading to the crash, i.e. all the function calls in the stack at the time the crash occurred. This can be achieved by following these steps:

- Compile the program with "-g3" to get include debug data in the program which will be used by the debugger e.g. to display line numbers
- Possibly do not compile with optimisations, i.e. do not compile with "-O2" as this may cause the debugger output to be very different
- Instead of running the application with simply "./program abc", run "gdb –args ./program abc". This will launch gdb (assuming it's installed)
- gdb will display a prompt, allowing you to enter commands. Simply enter the command "r" (for "run") and hit enter. This will run the program.
- If the program crashes, gdb will let you know and also show the line that caused the crash. With the command "bt" ("backtrace") you can see the function stack leading up to the call.
- You can exit gdb with "q".

Here's an example gdb session:

```
Reading symbols from ./segv...done.
(gdb) r
Starting program: ./segv 10 10000

Program received signal SIGSEGV, Segmentation fault.
0x00400825 in run (size=10, loop_size=10000) at segv.c:9
9           array[i] = i + array[i - 1];
(gdb) bt
#0  0x00400825 in run (size=10, loop_size=10000) at segv.c:9
#1  0x004008c1 in main (argc=3, argv=0x7fffe7d8) at segv.c:18
(gdb)
```

Here we can see the program crashed at line segv.c:9, in function "run", which was entered from function "main" at segv.c:18.

Debuggers can do a lot more, e.g. set breakpoints, display variable names, and more.

Exercise: Write a function that will determine the length of a string. You can detect the end of a string by comparing a character in a string against 0, or '\0': if it is 0 then it denotes the end of the string. (This exercise exists for educational purposes; the C standard library includes functions "strlen" and "strnlen" for this.)

Exercise: Write a function to count the number of occurrences of the character 'a' in a given input string.

Exercise: Extend your function from the previous exercise such that the character to count occurrences for is given as an additional input parameter.

String comparisons

You can check if two strings are the same by using the "strncmp" function:

```
char *a;
char *b;
/* set a and b somehow */
if(!strncmp(a, b, 20)) {
```

(continues on next page)

(continued from previous page)

```
    printf("a and b are the same (at least the first 20␣
↪characters).\n");
}
```

(You'll need to #include <string.h> for strncmp as well as most of the other string utility functions, including memset().)

If you want to compare only parts of a string, strncmp can do this too. Let's say you have a buffer, and you know its first letters are "HTTP/1.1 " but you want to know whether they are followed by the letters "200". You can do e.g.:

```
char *input_string = ... ;
if(!strncmp(input_string + 9, "200", 3)) {
    printf("The status code is 200.\n");
}
```

What happens here is that we use pointer arithmetic to skip the first nine characters ("HTTP/1.1 "), then compare the next three (and only three) characters with the string "200". strncmp() returns 0 if the strings matched for the given number of characters.

Another option would be to copy the relevant substring to its own buffer (assuming we don't want to modify the input string):

```
char *input_string = ... ;
char buf[4];
buf[3] = '\0'; /* ensure string termination */
strncpy(buf, input_string + 9, 3);
if(!strncmp(buf, "200", 3)) {
    printf("The status code is 200.\n");
}
```

The function "strncpy" copies n bytes from a source buffer to a destination buffer.

Since it's only three characters were checking, we could also check them manually:

```
char *input_string = ... ;
if(*(input_string + 9)  == '2' &&
```

(continues on next page)

(continued from previous page)

```
    *(input_string + 10) == '0' &&
    *(input_string + 11) == '0') {
    printf("The status code is 200.\n");
}
```

Another potentially useful function is strtok(). Here's an example of its usage:

```
char *str = "this is a string.\n";
char *p = strtok(str, " "); // p now points to "this"
p = strtok(NULL, " ");      // p now points to "is"
p = strtok(NULL, " ");      // p now points to "a"
```

Finally, the functions "strcat" and "strncat" append a string to an existing string:

```
char buf[256];
memset(buf, 0x00, sizeof(buf));
strncat(buf, "hello ", 255);
strncat(buf, "world\n", 249);
printf("%s", buf);
```

Exercise: Let's assume you have 50 words with five letters each and you append each word to a buffer using strncat, one after another. (The buffer is assumed to be large enough.) In terms of big O notation, what's the run time of this algorithm? In order to know where to append to, strncat() iterates through the destination buffer to find the end of the string every time it is called.

2.4.6 Writing a toy web server

After having used Flask a bit, you might have wondered "what's actually happening?"

In essence, Flask receives HTTP requests from the browser over the network, and sends HTML data back to the browser which then displays it. But we should dig a bit further here. In fact, let's write a simple HTTP server ourselves; a program that will communicate with the browser over the network and send HTML files to it.

OSI model

The OSI model is a way to structure the network activity in these kinds of situations. There are total seven layers which make up the model:

Layer	Name	Protocol used in our case
7	Application layer	HTTP
6	Presentation layer	•
5	Session layer	•
4	Transport layer	TCP
3	Network layer	IP
2	Data link layer	Wifi or Ethernet, depending on your network configuration
1	Physical layer	E.g. DSL, depending on your network configuration

The layers 1 and 2 are set up depending on your network configuration.

The layers 3 and 4 are implemented by your OS; Windows, Mac and Linux implement the TCP/IP stack in the kernel.

The layers 5, 6 and 7 are all summarised by HTTP. When we ran Flask, we ran its built-in HTTP server.

Now, we've used OS functions before: When we open a file in C, we call the open() or fopen() functions, which end up calling kernel functions. The kernel functions typically interact with the actual hardware; in case of opening a file, the kernel functions would read data from the physical hard drive in the computer. Similarly, when writing a HTTP server, "all" we need to do is call the relevant kernel functions that trigger TCP/IP communications. Let's try this out.

BSD sockets API

The API for accessing the TCP/IP stack is called the BSD sockets API. (BSD stands for "Berkeley Software Distribution"; the API originates from the University of California, Berkeley.) Here's a simple example using it:

```c
#include <sys/types.h>
#include <sys/socket.h>
#include <netinet/in.h>
#include <arpa/inet.h>
#include <stdio.h>
#include <stdlib.h>
#include <string.h>
#include <unistd.h>

void handle_client(int fd);

int main(void)
{
        struct sockaddr_in sa;
        memset(&sa, 0, sizeof sa);
        sa.sin_family = AF_INET;
        sa.sin_port = htons(1234);
        sa.sin_addr.s_addr = htonl(INADDR_ANY);

        int server_fd = socket(PF_INET, SOCK_STREAM, IPPROTO_
↪TCP);
        if (server_fd == -1) {
                perror("cannot create socket");
                exit(1);
        }

```

(continues on next page)

(continued from previous page)

```
26          if (bind(server_fd, (struct sockaddr *)&sa, sizeof sa)␣
    ↪== -1) {
27                  perror("bind failed");
28                  close(server_fd);
29                  return 1;
30          }
31
32          if (listen(server_fd, 5) == -1) {
33                  perror("listen failed");
34                  close(server_fd);
35                  return 1;
36          }
37
38          for (;;) {
39                  int client_fd = accept(server_fd, NULL, NULL);
40
41                  if (client_fd < 0) {
42                          perror("accept failed");
43                          close(server_fd);
44                          return 1;
45                  }
46
47                  handle_client(client_fd);
48
49                  if (shutdown(client_fd, SHUT_RDWR) == -1) {
50                          perror("shutdown failed");
51                  }
52                  close(client_fd);
53          }
54
55          close(server_fd);
56          return 0;
57  }
```

Let's walk through this step by step:

- Line 14: We define a variable with the type struct sockaddr_in. This is a type that's defined as part of the BSD sockets API.
- Line 15: We clear all the memory allocated for this variable using the standard C library memset() function.

- Lines 16-18: We set some values in that struct, which basically mean that we want to open the TCP/IP port 1234.
- Line 20: We use the first function of the BSD sockets API: socket(). This function should return a socket, i.e. something we can use for communications.
- Lines 21-24: We check the value of our server socket. -1 means something went wrong. In this case we output an error string with perror() and stop the program execution.
- Lines 26-36: We use the API to configure our server socket such that it listens to incoming connections, i.e. as a server. It listens to TCP port 1234 and will allow up to five connections to line up.
- Line 38: We run a for-loop which initialises nothing, has no condition for termination, and does nothing on each iteration. In other words, an infinite loop.
- Line 39: We call accept(), another BSD sockets API function. This function call will block, i.e. our program execution will not proceed, until someone connects to the server. Once a client has connected, accept() will return the *client socket* which we can use for communicating with the client.
- Line 47: We call the function handle_server() which is a function that we will need to write ourselves. This defines what the server actually does.

Digression: type casting

Line 26 is also interesting because we perform a *type cast* here. The line without the type cast would look like this:

```
if (bind(server_fd, &sa, sizeof sa) == -1) {
```

That is, we simply pass the address of our struct sockaddr_in to the bind() function. If we were to try this then we would get a compiler warning, turned error if the "-Werror" switch is used:

```
sock1.c: In function 'main'
sock1.c:26:22: error: passing argument 2 of 'bind' from␣
↪incompatible pointer type [-Werror=incompatible-pointer-
↪types]
  if (bind(server_fd, &sa, sizeof sa) == -1) {
                      ^
In file included from sock1.c:2:0:
/usr/include/sys/socket.h:123:12: note: expected 'const␣
↪struct sockaddr *' but argument is of type 'struct␣
↪sockaddr_in *'
```

What the error tells us is that the function bind() expects a pointer to *struct sockaddr* but we pass it a pointer to *struct sockaddr_in*. Because of the way the API is specified (in the case of IP communication it actually required *struct sockaddr_in* despite what the function declaration says), we cast the type to *struct sockaddr*. Type casting basically means telling the compiler "please pretend this variable has a different type than what it actually has". Having this possibility in C makes C a weakly typed language.

perror?

Most if not all standard C library functions, when they fail, return -1 and set a *global* variable called "errno" (error number). The user is expected to check if the return value is -1 and, if so, the variable errno can be used to obtain more information about the error. What the function perror() does is simply write out a textual description of this variable.

The code listing above can be compiled e.g. with the following:

```
$ gcc -Wall -Werror -o sock1 sock1.c && ./sock1
/tmp/ccf2I2NV.o: In function `main'
sock1.c:(.text.startup+0x73): undefined reference to `handle_
↪client'
collect2: error: ld returned 1 exit status
```

Compilation succeeds but linking fails because the function "handle_client" isn't defined. If we implement that function correctly then we have a simple web server.

Exercise: Check out a man page of one of the BSD sockets API, for example by running "man shutdown".

Reading from a socket

Here's a short and simple implementation of the handle_client function:

```
#include <stdio.h>
#include <string.h>
#include <unistd.h>

void handle_client(int fd)
{
	for(;;) {
		char buf[1024];
		memset(buf, 0x00, sizeof(buf));
		int ret = read(fd, buf, 1023);
		if(ret == 0) {
			return;
		}
		if(ret == -1) {
			perror("read");
			return;
		}
		printf("%s\n", buf);
	}
}
```

This function reads up to 1,023 bytes at once from the client socket and prints them out to stdout.

Because we now have a server which listens to connections to port 1234, we can try connecting to it using a web browser. We should then see what the web browser sends our program.

Exercise: Put together all the above server code and connect to 127.0.0.1:1234 with your browser. 127.0.0.1 means localhost, meaning the computer you're running.

HTTP

After doing the above exercise you should see a nice set of text that the web browser has sent our program. On my setup, the first two lines are these:

```
GET / HTTP/1.1
Host: 127.0.0.1:1234
```

The first line means that the browser would like to retrieve any data from the address / using the HTTP 1.1 protocol. The second line means that from the browser's point of view, it's connecting to 127.0.0.1:1234.

The full HTTP 1.1 protocol is described in RFCs 7230-7237. RFCs (Request for Comments) are documents maintained by W3C (World Wide Web Consortium).

Exercise: Look up RFC 7230 online. Don't read all of it, but try to get an overview of the HTTP 1.1 architecture. Especially note the example message exchange for a GET request.

Now that you've seen RFC 7230, you can probably tell that a simple server response has a few lines of text, beginning with a line such as "HTTP/1.1 200 OK", with the actual data for the user at the end.

Refresher on C string handling

Here's a snippet that puts some of the C string handling together:

```
const char *my_str = "HTTP/1.1 200 OK\r\n"
                     "Date: Mon, 27 Jul 2009 12:28:53 GMT\r\n";

int ret = strncmp(my_str, "HTTP/1.1", 8);
if(ret == 0) {
    printf("my_str begins with \"HTTP/1.1\"\n");
}
int my_string_len = strlen(my_str);
if(my_string_len > 14) {
        ret = strncmp(my_str + 9, "200", 3);
        if(ret == 0) {
            printf("my_str has the characters \"200\" nine characters after the start.\n");
```

(continues on next page)

(continued from previous page)

```
13         }
14 }
15 int value = 42;
16 char buf[8];
17 memset(buf, 0x00, sizeof(buf));
18 sprintf(buf, "%d", value);
```

Let's see what we have...

- Lines 1-2: In C, you can declare strings over multiple lines. The literal quotes will be simply concatenated at compile time. Also note the character sequence \r\n which means CRLF, or "carriage return, line feed".
- Line 4: The function strncmp() checks whether two strings are the same.
- Line 8: The function strlen() determines the length of a string.
- Line 9: Check that we won't be reading past the end of a string to avoid undefined behaviour or creating security holes.
- Line 10: By adding a number to a pointer (string), you can effectively start reading from a later point in a string.
- Lines 15-18: For turning an integer value to a string (character buffer), allocate a buffer large enough, clear it using memset() and finally use the sprintf() function to write the integer value as the contents of the buffer.

With the above knowledge it should be possible to finish the next exercise. You may also find it interesting to take a look at the various man pages of the different functions.

Exercise: Modify the function handle_client to check if the client connecting appears to make a HTTP 1.1 GET request. In this case, respond with a valid HTTP 1.1 200 response, replying with a short message such as "Hello world". Make sure you set the Content-Length part of the response correctly. Connect to your server using your web browser to ensure you send the correct data. You can write data to the client by using the write() function, e.g. 'write(fd, "hello", 5);'. The first parameter to write() is the client socket. The second parameter must point to the buffer of data you wish to send. The third parameter describes the number of bytes you wish to send. You can also write data piece by piece, by calling write() multiple times.

As you can now see, the browser will be able to render your text, which means you have the beginnings of a web server. To make things more interesting, let's have another exercise.

Exercise: Create two HTML pages, with the first one linking to the second. (You can create a link in HTML by using the <a> tag; for example, the following creates a link to a page called two.html: <a href="two.html">link</a>.) For the request to /, serve the first HTML page by reading its contents to a buffer and then sending the buffer contents as part of the response. Again, make sure you set the Content-Length part of the response correctly. You can read file contents into a buffer by using the fread() function - e.g. fread(buf, 1, 1024, fp); it will return the number of bytes read which you can use to determine the size of the file. Parse the request path in detail, such that you'll be able to serve the second page when the browser requests it. Note: in order to have the browser display HTML properly, you'll need to set the Content-Type field to text/html.

At this stage our implementation doesn't respect the whole specification, but it's able to serve some web pages. If you made it here, congratulations.

2.4.7 Security

In the section "Writing a toy web server", I warned about potential security holes when writing C. Let's take a look at the following code, which attempts to copy a string represented by a char pointer to a 20-element char array:

```
char *str = /* ... */; /* some string which is somehow dependent␣
↪on user input */
char buf[20];
strcpy(buf, str);
```

This code is a potential security hole. Can you spot why?

What happens if the string is longer than 20 characters? The function strcpy() will copy past the end of the 20-element array, overwriting something else. Technically, according to the C language standard, the behaviour is undefined, meaning that anything can happen. In practice, some data in the stack will be overwritten, like another variable, or the address to return to when the function returns. The attacker needs to construct a suitable input to modify the variables such that some code that the attacker wants to execute will get executed, typically leading to the attacker gaining full access to the system. The attacker can then e.g. read any passwords, credit card numbers or any other sensitive data available on the system.

This is possible in C and some other languages like C++ because of lack of *memory safety*; memory can be accidentally read or written. It's a good reason to consider using another language for the task at hand, if possible.

Exercise: Take a look at your HTTP server code and see if you can spot any security issues.

2.5 More programming concepts using Python

2.5.1 More data structures

Previously we had a section on arrays. Recall that arrays are a continuous block of memory and have fast random access but slow insertion. This section goes through some more interesting data structures.

Linked lists

Linked lists solve the problem of inserting an element in the middle. They're constructed such that each element in a list holds the data as well as a pointer to the next cell in the list, whereby each cell is individually allocated.

```
+--------+---+        +--------+---+        +--------+---+
| data 1 | -+----->| data 2 | -+----->| data 3 | x |
+--------+---+        +--------+---+        +--------+---+
.       ^
.    Head
```

In this illustration, each element has two fields, the first one holding the payload data and the second holding a pointer to the next element. The "head" pointer points to the beginning of the list. The last element will have the "next" pointer point to NULL (denoted by "x" in the diagram above), signalling the end of the list. If one were now to add an element in the list, this can be done by changing the "next" pointer of the previous cell in the list to point to the new element and the "next" pointer of the new element to the cell that was previously pointed to by the previous cell.

In practice, due to the overhead of allocating memory for individual cells and the performance issues caused by memory fragmentation and poor cache locality, linked lists rarely show any performance benefit over arrays.

Apart from *singly linked lists* like above, there are also *doubly linked lists*, where each element not only has a pointer to the next element but also to the previous one. These allow traversing in both directions in the list for the extra cost of storing a pointer, and maintaining this on element insertion and deletion.

Sets

A set is a data structure that can hold different values of data and efficiently answer the question whether a value is contained in the set or not. A typical way to achieve this is to implement a *balanced binary tree,* i.e. a tree structure which can be traversed top-down when doing basic operations such as looking up or inserting data.

```
.             -------------
Root node --> | 4 | . | . |
.             ------|---|--
.                   |   |
.        ------------  -------------
.        | 1 | x | . |  | 5 | x | x |
.        ----------|--  -------------
.                  |
.        -------------
.        | 3 | x | x |
.        -------------
.
```

Here, the root node is the entry point to the tree. Each node has payload data as well as two pointers, one to the left and one to the right. The pointer to the left points to a node where the payload data is less than in the current node. The pointer to the right points to a node where the payload data is more than in the current node. In this example set we have stored number 1, 3, 4 and 5. If one were now to ask, "do we have number 3 stored in the set", a function answering this would do the following:

1. Root node value is 4, which is more than 3, so enter the left node (as it is not NULL).
2. Our next node value is 1, which is less than 3, so enter the right node (as it is not NULL).
3. Our next node value is 3, which is the value we were looking for, so the function can return *true.*

If we were to ask whether the number 6 is in the set, the function would do the following:

1. Root node value is 4, which is less than 6, so enter the right node (as it is not NULL).

2. Our next node value is 5, which is less than 6, but the right node pointer is NULL, hence the value 6 is not included, so the function must return *false*.

Inserting a number is trickier but, similarly to lookup, can be performed in O(log n) time. (To support efficient insertion, a *self balancing binary search tree* such as a red-black tree is required.)

C doesn't have built in support for sets (although C++ does). In Python, sets can be defined and used in the following manner:

```
>>> my_set = set()
>>> my_set.add(1)
>>> my_set.add(3)
>>> my_set.add(4)
>>> my_set.add(5)
>>> 3 in my_set
True
>>> 6 in my_set
False
```

Exercise: Look up the definition of a red-black tree online.

Dictionaries

Dictionary, also called a *hash map*, is similar to a set but has a *value* associated with each *key* stored in the map, with the key playing the same role as the payload data did for sets.

Hence it can have a similar internal structure to a set, but with another pointer in each cell indicating the value for the key.

Apart from a binary search tree, another way to implement dictionaries is to use a *hash function* to hash the data, i.e. generate an index (or *bucket*) for each data point and use this index to retrieve the data. For example, if we have keys 1, 3, 4 and 5 in our dictionary, we could *hash* these to indices 0, 1, 2 and 3 of an array. Now, when the user asks for the value for the key 1, we access our array at index 0 and return the corresponding data.

(As an aside, technically, as sets are very similar to dictionaries - the only difference being that sets don't have a value associated with each key - sets can also be implemented using a hash function instead of a binary search tree.)

In practice, the *hash function*, i.e. the function which generates this mapping from keys to indices, isn't perfect (unless all keys are predefined) and there will need to be more indices in the array than keys, and two or more keys may use the same index, requiring the implementation to handle this case (*hash collision*), for example by storing a linked list for each index, with each element in the linked list corresponding to one key-value pair. These complexities lead to the worst case insertion (where all indices have to be regenerated) to have O(n) runtime. Search can also have O(n) worst case runtime in the case where all keys end up in a single index, such that the search degenerates to a search in a linked list.

C doesn't have built in support for dictionaries (although C++ does). In Python, dictionaries can be defined and used in the following manner:

```
>>> my_dict = dict()
>>> my_dict['a'] = 1
>>> my_dict['b'] = 2
>>> 'a' in my_dict
True
>>> my_dict['a']
1
>>> my_dict.get('c', -1) # for get(), the last parameter is the␣
↪default if the key is not found
-1
>>> del my_dict['b']
>>> 'b' in my_dict
False
>>> try:
...     print my_dict['d']
... except KeyError:
...     print 'not found'
...
not found
```

(This example also demonstrates Python exception handling and the Pythonic EAFP ("easier to ask for forgiveness than permission") principle as well as exceptions: it's typically cleaner code to try to access a key in a dictionary and handle the error if the key is not found than check beforehand whether the key is in a dictionary and only access it if it is.)

Priority queues

A priority queue is a data type where each element added to it has a priority (e.g. an integer), and retrieving the element with the highest priority is typically a fast operation. It supports adding elements with a given priority and removing the element with the highest priority. Priority queues are often implemented as *heaps*, which are a kind of a tree data structure (often a binary tree) with the element with the highest value as the root of the tree.

Summary

Finally, here's a summary table of the performance of the different operations:

Data type	Access	Insertion
Array	O(1)	O(n)
Linked list	O(n)	O(1)
Set or a dictionary (implemented using a binary search tree)	O(log n)	O(log n)
Set or a dictionary (implemented using hashing)	O(1) on average (O(n) in the worst case)	O(1) on average (O(n) in the worst case)
Priority queue (implemented using a binary tree)	O(1) (only for the highest priority element)	O(log n)

2.5.2 Object oriented programming

Object oriented programming is fairly common in Python, and we've used it pretty much from the beginning. See for example this code:

```
with open('test.txt', 'w') as f:
    for i in xrange(5):
        f.write("%f %f\n" % (0.2, 0.5))
```

Here, "f" is a file object and "write" is a *member function* of the file class.

In general, in many languages including Python, if you call a function such that the function syntactically appears to "belong" to a variable, like with "f.write()", then you're probably calling a member function of a class.

Defining your own data types

In Python, data types are defined using the "class" keyword:

```
1  class A(object):
2      def __init__(self, foo):
3          self.foo = foo
4  
5      def add_one(self):
6          self.foo += 1
7  
8      def call_me(self):
9          print 'A called - my foo is: ' + str(self.foo)
10 
11 obj = A(42)
12 
13 obj.call_me()
14 obj.add_one()
15 obj.call_me()
```

Let's go through this line by line:

- Line 1: We define a *class* named A. At a high level, a class is a data type, describing data types and functions common to the class.
- Line 2: We define the *init function*, or *constructor*: a function that will be automatically called when an object of this class is created.

- Line 3: The constructor will create a *member variable* named foo - a variable that's contained within the object.
- Line 5-6: We define a *member function* - a function that's part of a class.
- Line 8-9: This member function produces some output and also uses the member variable value.
- Line 11: We create (or *instantiate*) one object of class A. Class A has a constructor that requires one parameter: we pass in 42.
- Line 13: We call the member function "call_me" for class A.
- Line 14: We call the member function "add_one" for class A.
- Line 15: We call the member function "call_me" for class A.

Executing this will output:

```
$ python2 cl1.py
A called - my foo is: 42
A called - my foo is: 43
```

Duck typing revisited

Here's a bit larger example:

```
class A(object):
    def __init__(self, foo):
        self.foo = foo

    def add_one(self):
        self.foo += 1

    def call_me(self):
        print 'A called - my foo is: ' + str(self.foo)

class B(object):
    def call_me(self):
        print 'B called'

my_objects = [A(42), B()]
```

(continues on next page)

(continued from previous page)

```
16
17 for o in my_objects:
18     o.call_me()
```

Let's go through this line by line:

- Lines 1-10: As in the example above.
- Line 11: We define another class named B.
- Line 12-13: We define a member function for class B - with the same name as we did for class A.
- Line 15: We define a list with two elements, and create (or *instantiate*) one object of each class; one of class A, one of class B. Class A has a constructor that requires one parameter: we pass in 42.
- Line 17: We iterate through our list.
- Line 18: We call the member function "call_me" for each element in the list, i.e. once for our object of class A, once for our object of class B.

Executing this will output:

```
$ python2 cl.py
A called - my foo is: 42
B called
```

We see an example of duck typing here: while classes A and B technically have nothing to do with each other, they do share the same *interface*, namely calling the function "call_me". We also see that the classes in Python are more powerful than the structs in C: in Python we can combine multiple variables in one object, but in addition we can have member functions and use these to define an interface on interacting with the data.

2.5.3 JSON

JSON stands for JavaScript Object Notation but is used a lot outside JavaScript.

It's a data format for storing any basic data, is fairly simple and is often used for exchanging data between different programs (often implemented in different programming languages) or more generally storing the output of a program.

Here's a simple JSON file:

```
{
    "key": "value"
}
```

This JSON file contains one key named "key" which has the value "value". JSON can store objects (collections of key-value pairs) like above, numbers, strings and lists. Here's a more complex JSON file:

```
{
     "my_list": [
         1,
         2,
         3,
         4
     ],
     "alphabet": {
         "a": 1,
         "b": 2,
         "c": 3
     }
}
```

Here we have an object with two keys: my_list and alphabet. The item my_list is a list with four numbers as elements. The item alphabet is an object with three key-value pairs. Because objects and lists can include lists or other objects, JSON is very flexible and can support arbitrarily complex data. The top level item in JSON must be either an object or a list. In professional settings, it's not uncommon to work with JSON files with thousands of entries.

One of the main strengths about JSON is that pretty much all main languages have support for reading and writing JSON. Here's an example Python code to read and use the above JSON file:

```
import json

with open('data.json', 'r') as f:
    data = json.load(f)
print len(data['my_list'])
print data['alphabet']['c']
```

The above will print 4 and 3 (the length of the list and the value for key 'c' respectively). Here's an example JavaScript code to read and use the same JSON file:

```
var parsed = JSON.parse(data);
console.log(parsed['my_list'].len);
console.log(parsed['alphabet']['c']);
```

Here's an example Python code to generate this JSON file:

```
import json

data = dict()
data['my_list'] = [1, 2, 3, 4]
data['my_alphabet'] = {'a': 1, 'b': 2, 'c': 3}
print json.dumps(data, indent=4)
```

Or in JavaScript:

```
var data = {};
data.my_list = [1, 2, 3, 4];
data.alphabet = {'a': 1, 'b': 2, 'c': 3};
console.log(JSON.stringify(data));
```

JSON vs. delimiter separated data

In our code where we read in the 10,000 quadratic equations we used delimiter separated data (delimiter being the space character in our case). In other words, our data looked like this:

```
7.269553 3.427526 6.633603
1.980206 -3.655827 -2.629755
-8.687820 -6.930905 -8.731439
-0.608791 -8.126272 -8.652504
[...]
```

This is fine for many cases but it has some pros and cons when compared to JSON, namely:

- Delimiter separated data is easier to work on with standard Unix tools than JSON
- JSON provides more flexibility in terms of nesting data or variable length lists
- If no JSON library is available, parsing delimiter separated data is usually easier

If we were to store this data in JSON, we could use for example:

```
[
    {
        'a': 7.269553,
        'b': 3.427526,
        'c': 6.633603
    },
    {
        'a': 1.980206,
        'b': -3.655827,
        'c': -2.629755
    },
    ...
]
```

That is, a list of objects, whereby each object has the keys a, b and c. If we wanted to parse and use this in Python we could e.g. do this:

```
import json

with open('data.json', 'r') as f:
    data = json.load(f)    # data is now a list with 10,000␣
↪elements
```

(continues on next page)

(continued from previous page)

```
print len(data) # would print 10000 for 10,000 objects in the␣
↪list
for equation in data:
    print equation['a'], equation['b'], equation['c'] # prints␣
↪out the values for each equation
```

Another way to store the same data would be:

```
[
    [7.269553, 3.427526, 6.633603],
    [1.980206, -3.655827, -2.629755],
    ...
]
```

That is, a list of lists, whereby each inner list always has three entries. We could then use this data in Python e.g. like this:

```
import json

with open('data.json', 'r') as f:
    data = json.load(f)     # data is now a list with 10,000␣
↪elements
print len(data) # would print 10000 for 10,000 elements in the␣
↪list
for equation in data: # equation is a list of three floats
    print equation[0], equation[1], equation[2] # prints out the␣
↪values for each equation
```

Whichever way the data is structured is mostly a matter of personal preference, though the latter in some ways has less room for error as there are no keys to type.

Exercise: Rewrite the Python program that generates 10,000 quadratic equations to generate JSON instead. You can simply put your data in a list, which you'd then need to write out using json.dumps(my_list, indent=4). You can initialise a list e.g. by stating my_list = list(), and append to a list using my_list.append(item). You can also create a dictionary e.g. by stating my_dict = dict(), and setting a value by stating my_dict['key'] = value.

Exercise: Modify your Python program that reads in 10,000 quadratic equations to read from your JSON file instead.

2.5.4 More useful Python constructs

To demonstrate some of these constructs, let's start by loading some data to work on. As before, let's work on the 10,000 quadratic equations we defined before, and load this data from JSON.

```
data = json.load(open('/dev/stdin', 'r'))
```

We read the JSON data from stdin, meaning that we can define the input file on the command line like this:

```
$ python2 useful.py < test.json
```

In the following, we assume the data is stored in a list of lists, i.e.:

```
[
   [
      6.44887349885013,
      -6.80408794830961,
      5.87205564819696
   ],
   [
      0.839489029433732,
      -8.86306739443021,
      -1.69246328305772
...
```

List comprehensions

List comprehensions are a shorthand notation for doing things with lists. They spare you at times from having to write tedious for loops.

```
bs = [l[1] for l in data]
```

This line fetches the second column of our data, i.e. all the 'b' values for our quadratic equations (hence the variable name, 'b's). What it means is:

> "For each data point (l) in our input list (data), take the second element."

```
print "Number of b's: " + str(len(bs)) # prints 10,000
```

The variable bs is a list of 10,000 numbers. With "len(bs)" we can obtain the length of the list. (With "str()" we can convert data to a string for output purposes.)

We can now calculate the average of all 'b's:

```
b_avg = sum(bs) / float(len(bs))
```

(We need to convert the denominator to float to ensure the result is also float.)

In other words, while for delimiter separated data we could write a one-liner in awk to calculate the average, for JSON we'll need to write about three lines of Python. On the other hand JSON is in general more powerful than delimiter separated data.

Slices

```
first_hundred = data[:100] # len(first_hundred) is 100
```

Here, with "[:100]" we say "*slice* the list such that only the first hundred elements are included".

You can also slice the end of the list by using negative index.

Sorting

Python has sorting built in:

```
print sorted(data, reverse=True)[:3]
```

This line introduces a few concepts:

- By calling the function sorted(data), we can obtain a sorted copy of the data.
- sorted() takes an *optional parameter* "reverse" which we set to True. This means that the returned list will be sorted in descending order instead of ascending.

Useful built in functions

"sum" sums up all the numbers in a list:

```
sum_of_all_numbers = sum([sum(l) for l in data])
```

"all" returns True if all values are True in a list, and False otherwise. ("any" return True if any element in a list is True.)

```
def all_numbers_in_list_are_above_zero(l):
    return all([n > 0 for n in l])
```

List comprehensions also support *filtering*, i.e. applying a function to only include certain elements in the resulting list:

```
above_zero_equations = [f for f in data if all_numbers_in_list_
↪above_zero(f)]
```

Exercise: For your data set, find the quadratic equations where the sum of its values (a, b and c) is the highest.

Exercise: For your data set, find the quadratic equations where the sum of its values (a, b and c) is the highest *and* all values a, b and c are negative.

Tuples

Tuples in Python are quite similar to lists, but the size of a tuple is fixed. This means that while you can remove or add elements to a list in Python, this isn't possible with tuples, making tuples a nice way to implicitly document a fixed nature of some of your data.

Tuples can be created using parentheses:

```
my_tuple = ('a', 1)
```

They can be accessed like you access lists:

```
my_tuple[0] # returns 'a'
my_tuple[1] # returns 1
```

They can be used like any other variable, e.g. added in lists:

```
my_list = [('a', 1), ('b', 2)]
print my_list[1][0] # first element of the second element in the␣
↪list, i.e. 'b'
```

A fun function is “zip” - which zips two given lists to one list of tuples:

```
list1 = ['a', 'b', 'c']
list2 = [1, 2, 3]

zipped_list = zip(list1, list2)
print zipped_list # prints [('a', 1), ('b', 2), ('c', 3)]
```

2.5.5 Callbacks and anonymous functions

This section explains some concepts that will be needed later.

Functions as first order values

The concept of functions as first order values means that variables can have functions as values like any other type. Code speaks more than a thousand words so let's take a look at an example:

```
my_list = [3, 4, 5]
my_functions = [min, max, sum]

for function in my_functions:
    print function(my_list)
```

This snippet defines two lists. The first one looks typical but the second has three functions in it: "min", "max" and "sum". All of these functions can take a list of numbers as input; they'll return the smallest, largest and sum of the list respectively.

Exercise: What do you think this code will print? Try it out.

Callback

A callback, put shortly, is a function that will be called back. It follows the Hollywood principle - "don't call us, we will call you". Let's take another look at our at our example of sorting a list in Python.

Sorting in Python

Recall that we can read in our data of 10,000 functions to a list of lists, such that we have a list with 10,000 entries, each a list of three elements, e.g. [[6.44, -6.80, 5.87], ...]. We can sort this list to get the first three elements like this:

```
print sorted(data)[:3]
```

However, what if we wanted to sort by the third element in the inner lists, i.e. by the value "c" in the functions? The function "sorted" supports this by allowing us to supply a *callback* function which will be called for each element, such that the return value of the function defines the ordering of the resulting list. Let's show the code:

```
def my_callback(values):
    # values is a function, i.e. list with three elements
    return values[2]

print sorted(data, key=my_callback)[:3]
```

What happens here is that we define a function called "my_callback" which returns the third value in a list. That's a fairly boring function, but we provide this function as a *callback* to the sorted() function, namely as the "key" parameter. As sorted() calls the key function for each element and uses that to define the ordering, we end up with the resulting list being sorted by the third value in the functions, i.e. the value "c".

Sorting in C

In the section "Big O notation" we touched upon sorting in C using the built in "qsort" function. Here's the code again:

```
#include <stdio.h>
#include <stdlib.h>

int comparison(const void *a, const void *b)
{
    return *(int *)a - *(int *)b;
}

int main(void)
{
    int my_array[5] = { 3, 7, 5, 1, 8 };
    qsort(my_array, 5, sizeof(int), comparison);
    for(int i = 0; i < 5; i++) {
        printf("%d\n", my_array[i]);
    }
}
```

Now, what happens here is the following:

- Line 4: We define a function which we use as our callback. It takes two parameters (const void pointers, i.e. pointers to any unknown data) and returns an int, whereby the two input parameters are the values to compare and the return value should describe how to sort them, such that negative value means the first parameter should be before the second.
- Line 6: We cast the void pointers to int pointers (as we know our data is ints) and subtract a from b such that if a is less than b, it will be before b in the result.
- Line 12: We call the qsort() standard library function which takes a *pointer to a function* as the fourth parameter. Pointer to a function is how a callback function is defined and used in C.

Callbacks in JavaScript

We already had an example when we defined a function to call at the page load phase:

```
function init() {
    /* my code goes here */
}
window.onload = init;
```

Here, our function "init" is defined as the callback function for the object "window".

Anonymous functions

In some languages including Python and JavaScript, we can define functions *anonymously*, meaning we don't have to really define a function with a name, but merely a function without one. Going back to our Python example about providing a callback function as the "key" parameter, we wrote a function to return the third element of a list but this function is actually very simple. We can shorten our code by doing the following:

```
print sorted(data, key=lambda l: l[2])[:3]
```

In Python, *lambda* is a key word for defining an anonymous function: instead of using “key=my_callback”, we set “key” to a lambda function, which is otherwise defined like a regular function but we skip the “return” keyword. This will have the same behaviour as our earlier example where we defined a named function as the callback.

2.5.6 Functional programming

> The most powerful programming language is Lisp. If you don't know Lisp (or its variant, Scheme), you don't appreciate what a powerful language is. Once you learn Lisp you will see what is missing in most other languages.
>
> —Richard Stallman

The programming languages we've used so far are all *imperative*; they're based on the mental model of a computer executing instructions in a series, from a list, from the top, one by one. This is furthermore based on the mathematical model of a *Turing machine*, described by Alan Turing; a machine that points to an element on a memory tape and has instructions to move on the tape and modify elements on it.

There are several programming paradigms other than imperative, but one of interest for us is *functional programming*. We won't go to details and actually program in a functional programming language in this book, but there are some aspects you should know about. (Again, as this section is about different programming languages, several programmers will disagree with the contents.)

Functional programming is based on *lambda calculus*, a formal system described by Alonzo Church in the 1930s. It was later hypothesised that the work by Turing and Church is actually equivalent; that is, a Turing machine can be formally translated to lambda calculus and vice versa.

The first functional programming language was Lisp, described in 1958 by John McCarthy. At the time, one of the most common imperative languages was Fortran. To get a high level understanding on how the languages look like, here's an example snippet from both:

Lisp:

```
(if (> b 3) (println "b is bigger than 3"))
```

Fortran:

```
IF (NB.GT.3) THEN
  PRINT *, 'B is larger than 3.'
```

(continues on next page)

(continued from previous page)

```
END IF
```

Fortran was originally mainly used when entering code to computers using punch cards, while Lisp was originally described in a research paper but it was later discovered that an interpreter for this originally theoretical language could be implemented. So they have very different backgrounds and approaches but Lisp had some features that were at the time not available for other languages, including:

- Dynamic typing
- Recursion
- if-then-else
- Anonymous functions
- First class functions
- Dynamic memory allocation
- Macros i.e. running code at compile time
- Garbage collection, i.e. memory is freed automatically when it's not used anymore

There's been a trend since the 1960's and continuing that mainstream (imperative) languages are slowly adopting features that Lisp and functional programming in general have pioneered. This is mostly because there are less limitations around computer hardware, and the focus is shifting to increasing programmer productivity and ergonomics. Indeed Python and JavaScript as well as several other languages such as Java have incorporated one or more of the above list either as best practices, or as integral parts of the language.

This section is mostly concerned with providing examples around best practices in Python which can often be applied for other languages as well, as a means to reduce the number of bugs, reduce typing, and make code easier to understand.

Map and reduce

Map and reduce are the most primitive operations to apply to lists (or arrays). As much of the power of computers and software development lies in the fact that once an operation has been described in code, it can easily be applied thousands or millions of times, it's important to understand how to extend basic logic to be applied multiple times.

"Map" relates to the general concept of applying a function that processes data over a list. For example, let's have a simple function named "process" that tells how many digits are there in an integer, which would, for example, return 1 when given 5 as input, or 2 for 15, or 3 for 115.

Exercise: Implement the described function. (You can convert from string to integer using the int() function.)

This function takes a value of type "int" and returns a value of type "int". Now, we can pass a value to this function and receive the answer. If we had a list of numbers, and wanted to have a list of results of this function, we could do:

```
inp = [5, 15, 115]
out = list()
for i in inp:
    out.append(process(i))
```

However, with a list comprehension, we can reduce the amount of code and simply use:

```
inp = [5, 15, 115]
out = [process(i) for i in inp]
```

Either way, this process of applying a function over a list is called *map*.

A related operation is *reduce*, where we also apply a function to multiple elements of a list but the result is a single value that's accumulated over each element, not a list. For example, our function could be a simple addition:

```
def add(x, y):
    return x + y
```

Now, our input could e.g. be [1, 2, 3, 4]. In order to *reduce* this we want to apply the function "add" continuously, and also define the initialisation value, in this case 0:

```
inp = [1, 2, 3, 4]
out = 0
for i in inp:
    out = add(out, inp)
```

Note: "add" was here implemented for demonstration purposes. In actual code you'd rather just use the '+' operator directly. However, if you do want to pass addition as a function you could either use a lambda function, or import operator and pass operator.add.

There's no list comprehension for this pattern. However, there's a special case of reduction, namely filtering, or creating a new list with only values that fulfil a given condition. For example, if we wanted to only keep numbers less than 3:

```
inp = [1, 2, 3, 4]
out = [i for i in inp if i < 3]
```

Finally, map and filter can be combined, e.g.:

```
inp = [5, 15, 115]
out = [process(i) for i if i < 100]
```

This snippet returns a list with two elements, with the function "process" called for both of them.

Exercise: Write a list comprehension that returns a list of elements that have less than three digits in them. For the example input of [5, 15, 115] it should return [5, 15].

Now, while the examples here are in Python, the concepts of map, reduce and filter apply to several languages, both static and dynamic.

CHAPTER

THREE

STAGE 1.5

Now that we've seen a bit of algorithms, JavaScript, C and Python, let's see if we can step it up a notch. We'll start with our first somewhat larger project. We'll then continue with looking at some binary data before introducing strongly, statically typed programming languages with a related larger project.

3.1 Web development with Python and JavaScript

In this chapter we'll turn our guessing game from a single HTML page to a simple web app. Our goal is to have a *high score table* for the guessing game: the page should store and track the number of guesses for different players, and show which players have finished the game in the smallest number of guesses.

We'll learn about the following topics:

- HTML table generation
- JSON; which we'll need to transfer data between backend and frontend
- Setting up a simple NoSQL database
- AJAX; data transfer between backend and frontend in practice
- Putting everything together

What we'll end up is a two-page guessing game as well as a simple algorithm to play it for us, with a high score list displayed on the page and stored in a database. The high score list could look e.g. like this:

Position	Date	User	Guesses
1	2018-02-14 22:00:47.418645	ai	5
2	2018-02-14 22:01:14.371682	User	6
3	2018-02-14 22:00:35.543943	ai	6
4	2018-02-14 22:00:45.238895	ai	7
5	2018-02-14 22:00:51.128031	ai	8

It doesn't sound like much but includes some software development fundamentals.

Again, this book does *not* cover modern web development practices. However, the following sections will help the reader understand some concepts related to web development such as the difference around frontend (client) and backend (server) and using a database in the backend.

3.1.1 HTML tables

In our program, we'll need an HTML table which we'll use to show the high score list to the user.

HTML tables are a fairly straightforward concept. Here's one:

```
1     <table id="hiscore" border="1">
2         <tr>
3             <td>Position</td>
4             <td>Date</td>
5             <td>User</td>
6             <td>Guesses</td>
7         </tr>
8         <tr>
9             <td>1</td>
10            <td></td>
11            <td></td>
12            <td></td>
13        </tr>
14        <tr>
15            <td>2</td>
16            <td></td>
17            <td></td>
18            <td></td>
19        </tr>
20    </table>
```

- Line 1: We start the table with the <table> tag. We assign it an ID and request it to be rendered with a border.
- Line 2: We start defining a row for the table using the <tr> (table row) tag.
- Line 3: We define a cell using the <td> (table data) tag. The contents are simply text in this case but can in general be any HTML.

In order to modify tables in JavaScript, we can do the following:

```
table = document.getElementById("hiscore");
for(var i = 1; i < 3; i++) {
    table.rows[i].cells.item(1).innerHTML = "2017-02-15";
}
```

- Line 1: We obtain a reference to the table
- Line 2: We iterate over two table rows using a for loop, skipping the header (both rows and cells, and JavaScript arrays in general, are 0-indexed, meaning the arrays start at 0)
- Line 3: We set the contents of the second cell of the i'th row to "2017-02-15".

Exercise: Add a HTML table in your guessing game web page as a placeholder for the high score list. You can set the values for the first row in the table (i.e. the header) but leave the other cells empty for now.

3.1.2 Redis

Redis is a NoSQL database that we'll use for storing the data for our high score list.

Let's do the following:

- Download Redis source, compile it and run it - it, like most databases, runs as a server, which means we'll just leave it running in a terminal
- Install a Python client to Redis and test it
- Figure out how to use Redis with some examples

What is a database?

In general, database is a program that allows other programs to perform data operations. The typical data operations are CRUD:

- Create, i.e. add some data in the database
- Read, i.e. fetch some data from the database
- Update, i.e. modify some existing data in the database
- Delete, i.e. remove some data from the database

So in essence, a database needs the following:

- Some storage, typically as a file or files on a hard disk, where it stores the data in some format it deems best
- Some interface for other programs to interact with it

The interface is typically, though not always, a TCP/IP socket, such that a program can connect to it over web (or from the same machine as the database is running on), and then send commands and data to the database, and receive data.

In some cases, like our programs that worked with 10,000 quadratic equation definitions, as databases can be used to store data persistently, a database can be used instead of storing data in a file. The program would then read the data from the database instead of a file.

SQL vs. NoSQL

SQL is a wide-spread class of databases. There are several SQL databases, for example the open source MySQL and PostgreSQL as well as Microsoft SQL. The main common characteristics is that the interface to them is defined by the SQL language which standardises many of the common database operations. SQL databases are also relational, meaning that relationships between data can be explicitly described. Typically, the data tables, i.e. the format in which the data can be stored, must also be defined explicitly, and will to some extent be verified by the database.

NoSQL databases generally mean any database that don't have SQL as the interface for performing database operations, however the term is often used for a certain type of databases which often aren't relational and don't expect the user to define the tables beforehand.

There have been a lot of discussions about pros and cons of SQL and NoSQL. The following is mostly my opinion which, like many hot topics in software development, won't be shared by most other developers - caveat emptor. In general, SQL, forcing the user to structure the data formats beforehand, is suitable when the user benefits from the database ensuring the user is doing the right thing. In other words, if you have or will have lots of code working with the database, it's beneficial to use an SQL database because the database will help you do the right thing. On the other hand, for simpler projects with little code touching the data, it can be more effective to use a NoSQL database as it's often faster to set up and use. As this project is about introducing the concepts around web development and the amount of code is relatively little, we'll use a NoSQL database. We'll be using an SQL database later on.

Setting up Redis

Redis is one of the more popular NoSQL databases: it's relatively simple and small (about 16,000 lines of C), and easy to set up. It's a key-value database, meaning the user can store data simply by defining the key and the value, and read data using the key. In the simplest case, both key and value are strings so one can e.g. store the value "bar" with the key "foo", and then retrieve the value "bar" by querying for key "foo".

While Redis could be installed a more traditional way (e.g. package manager on Linux), we can use this as an opportunity to compile other people's code from source.

If you go to the Redis website, you'll see a download link and some instructions on how to set Redis up. At the time of writing these are the instructions:

```
1 $ wget http://download.redis.io/releases/redis-4.0.8.tar.gz
2 $ tar xzf redis-4.0.8.tar.gz
3 $ cd redis-4.0.8
4 $ make
```

This introduces us some important concepts:

- Line 1: We use wget to download a tarball (file with a .tar.gz ending). wget is a tool for downloading files from the web (similar to curl), and tar is a common way in Unix to package several files into one for easier handling.
- Line 2: We extract the contents of the tarball. tar takes three switches:
  - 'x' means "extract"
  - 'z' means "decompress gzipped data" - the file extension .tar.gz implies the files have been packaged using tar, and compressed using gzip
  - 'f' means read from a given file
- Line 3: We then change directory to the directory that was extracted. The convention is that when extracting a tarball, it should only create one directory with the name of the tarball as not to mix up with files in the current directory.
- Line 4: We run "make", which is a standard Unix tool for compiling code. What it does is software specific; make as such only executes what's been defined in the Makefile. In case of Redis, the Makefile starts compiling a bunch of C code.

Running these commands should result in your system compiling Redis and all its dependencies. If something goes wrong then your C compiler might not be correctly set up.

Software versioning

The Redis package downloaded in the example was version 4.0.8. The typical convention is that the number '4' in this version denotes the *major* version number, '0' is the *minor* version number and '8' is the *patch level* version number. As Redis is software we'll write software to work against and hence has an API, it's important to note which version is being used. When we use Redis we assume that the documentation matches its behaviour - but this might change in future Redis versions. Typically, in new versions which only have the patch level changed, e.g. 4.0.9, all changes made will be *backwards compatible* - that means, all the code that was written against 4.0.8 will work for 4.0.9. This is typically also the case for minor versions, but a major version change can be expected to introduced changes that *break* backwards compatibility. That means, if we were to update our Redis server years later, it might end up e.g. as version 6.0.0, and if changes that break backwards compatibility were introduced and we tried running our old code with that version we'd get errors.

Code that's ended up not working due to software it's dependent on having moved on to break backwards compatibility is said to have *bitrot*. Somewhat related, code that has been written over a longer time without consideration over maintainability or proper structure is said to have *organically grown*. Code for which the execution flow is hard to follow due to various branches and lack of structure is called *spaghetti code*.

As per the documentation, once the compilation is done, you can then start the Redis server by running "src/redis-server". This is the binary that resulted from the compilation. You should then see a bunch of text running through, ending with something along the following lines:

```
16870:M 13 Feb 23:32:25.161 * DB loaded from disk: 0.000 seconds
16870:M 13 Feb 23:32:25.161 * Ready to accept connections
```

Redis should now be running and accepting TCP/IP connections. You can leave it running as we try to connect to it using Python.

Exercise: Download, compile and start Redis. Feel free to take a look at the code while you're at it.

Python Redis client

The main Python Redis client can be found online (at the time of writing, in GitHub). There are a few ways you could install this, but pip is probably the most straightforward:

```
pip install redis
```

Exercise: Install the Python Redis client.

It's probably best to install it in your virtualenv, but you may want to install it system wide (with sudo) instead.

If the installation was successful, you should now be able to connect to your Redis server and store and fetch some data by running the following:

```
$ python2
Python 2.7.13 (default, Dec 21 2016, 07:16:46)
[GCC 6.2.1 20160830] on linux2
Type "help", "copyright", "credits" or "license" for more␣
↪information.
>>> import redis
>>> r = redis.StrictRedis(host='localhost', port=6379, db=0)
>>> r.set('foo', 'bar')
True
>>> r.get('foo')
'bar'
```

If you get an error when importing redis, the client isn't installed correctly. If you get an error when connecting, the Redis server isn't running.

If you were able to import and connect, the line "r.set('foo', 'bar')" sets the value for key "foo" to "bar", and the line "r.get('foo')" retrieves the value for key 'foo'.

Exercise: Try out your Python Redis client.

Now, we should be all set to go.

Using Redis

There are several ways to store data in Redis. While Redis can store simple string key-value pairs, it can do more, for example lists and sets. The best way depends on how you access and modify the data, but for getting a bit familiar with Redis we can envision the following exercises.

Exercise: Write a Python program to read in your JSON file with 10,000 quadratic equations, and store it as a value, as a string, in Redis. The key isn't very important for this exercise.

Exercise: In your Python program that reads 10,000 quadratic equations from a file, add functionality to read the data from the Redis database instead. You'll need to parse the JSON string.

3.1.3 High level architecture

In this section we'll discuss the high level architecture for our web app.

Let's begin with the requirements. Remember that what we wanted to do was have a high score list for our guessing game. We'll have two HTML pages. The first one is the entry point for the user and allows them to enter their name as well as the maximum number that the computer will think of. This information will be used in the second page for the actual guessing game which will also include the high score table.

Here is an illustration of what we want to achieve:

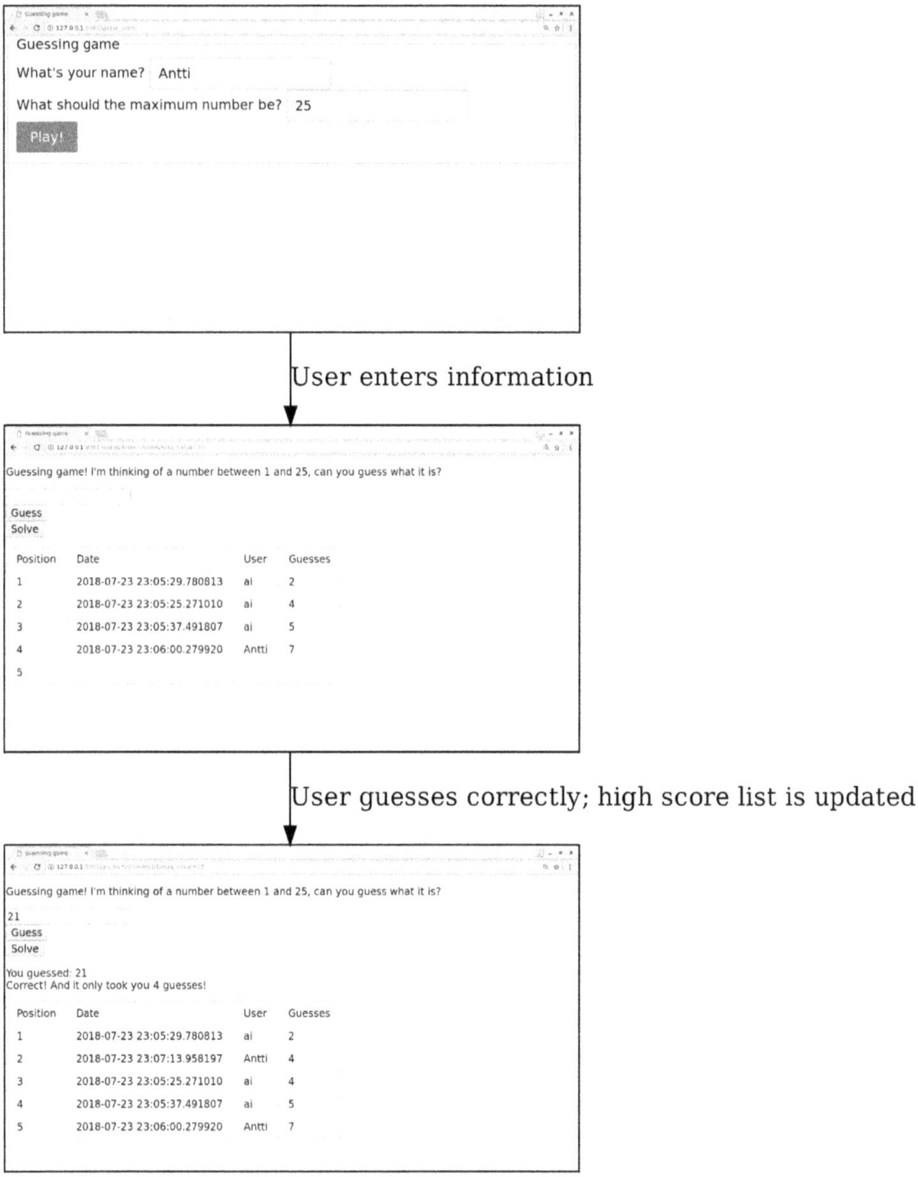

In order to do this, we need to have a database which stores the high scores. In order to have and use the database, we need to have some *server side* code. This means we get to pull up Flask, our web micro-framework again, as it has the capability of running a web server which we need going forwards.

Exercise: Move your guessing game HTML to be served by Flask. To do this, as per Flask documentation, you need to 1) create a directory named "templates" and move your HTML file there; 2) Set up a Flask "hello world" program such that there's a URL which serves your HTML file (using render_template()); and 3) Start Flask and try it out to ensure everything is set up correctly.

Terminology wise, the code that will be executed by the browser, i.e. our JavaScript code, is the *front end*. The code that will be executed on the server, i.e. our Python code, is the *back end*.

We have the following constraints:

- The client (browser) displays HTML and executes JavaScript
- The server has direct access to the database while the client does not

These constraints have implications for the overall architecture. The following is a *sequence diagram* and displays, at a high level, the interactions between different components over time.

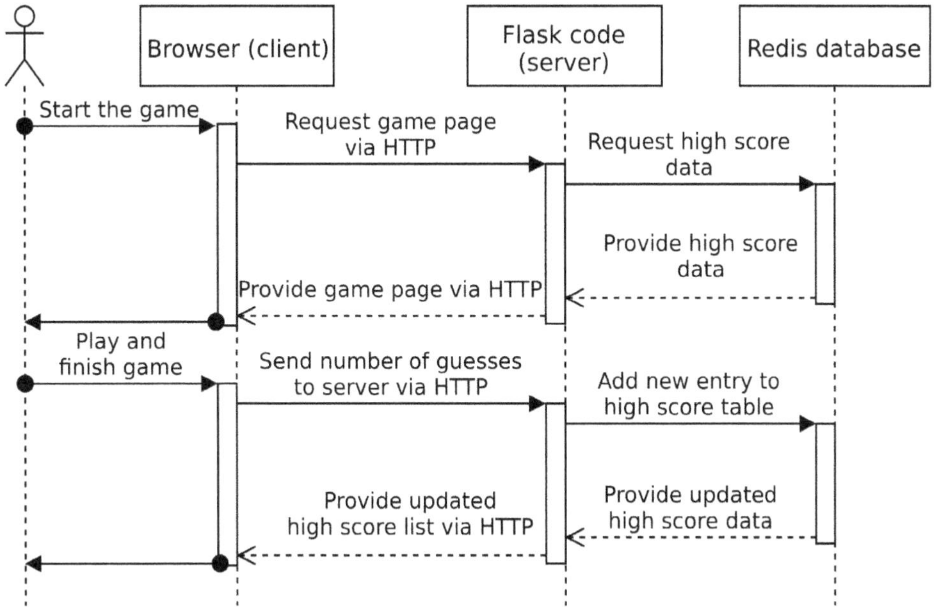

Here, the time is on the Y axis and advances from top to bottom. The user wants to play the game, and as a result their browser will contact our server. Our server will want to provide a HTML page with the necessary information including the high score list. To do this, our server code will contact the database, retrieve the necessary data, and use this data to generate the proper HTML. Once the user has guessed the correct number, the browser will tell this to the server which will update the database and also the client with the new high score list.

In terms of communication, we hence have the following:

- Once the user has guessed the correct number, as we want to store this in the database, the client will need to send this information to the server
- In order to update the high score table on the page, the server will need to send the information about the high score list to the client
- The above should happen without having to refresh or reload the page

In the next section we'll investigate how we can implement the communication between the client and the server.

3.1.4 AJAX

AJAX stands for Asynchronous JavaScript and XmlHttpRequest which is quite a mouthful. Before we go through what it is, let's explain why we need it.

From a high level software architecture point of view, this is how the flow is expected to work:

1. User opens the relevant URL in his or her browser and has some means to enter his or her name on the page
2. Our web server serves the HTML and JavaScript that is our guessing game
3. The user plays the game happily in the browser, executing JavaScript, without the server being aware
4. Once the user guesses the right answer, JavaScript sends the number of guesses and the player name to the server
5. The server stores the number of guesses and the player name in the database
6. The server fetches the high score list from the database, and sends it to the client (JavaScript)
7. The client displays the high score list

Seems simple, doesn't it?

Apart from entering the name, we've already covered steps 1-3 and to some extent step 5. In this section we'll cover steps 4 and 6. They're basically what AJAX is about: being able to communicate and exchange data between our JavaScript code and our server code.

A note on security: As we've seen, we're not really in control of the JavaScript code - a user can replace the JavaScript code with whatever code they prefer. In this sense, were we to use this architecture in a real program, a user could easily replace the data sent to the server and fake their way to the top of the high score list. For educational purposes we assume we can trust the user in this case, but were one serious about such a game and offering it for the public, the game logic would have to be done on the server side, such that the correct number would be generated on the server and each guess would need to be sent to the server.

Asynchronous execution

Asynchronous JavaScript and XmlHttpRequest. Asynchronous means that the code is not run synchronously. So far all our code has run synchronously. For example here:

```
1 var x = 3;
2 x += 5;
3 document.getElementById("foo").value = x;
```

Line 1 is executed before line 2, which is executed before line 3. Asynchronous execution changes this. Instead we have something like this (not real JavaScript code):

```
1 var request = new ServerRequest();
2 request.callback = function () {
3     document.getElementById("foo").value = request.response;
4 }
5 request.send();
```

What happens here is:

- Line 1: We create a new variable which is of type ServerRequest
- Lines 2-4: We define the *callback* - a function which will be called later, but not now
- Line 5: We send the request to the server (via HTTP)

After the request is sent to the server, the server (our Python code) will handle it and send something back (via HTTP). As this goes over the network it can take several milliseconds or even longer depending on what the server does. Once the server has sent the reply, the browser will receive it and its JavaScript interpreter will call the function that was defined in lines 2-4 with the data from the server. In this case, the HTML element with ID "foo" will have its value changed, i.e. the result from the server is visible to the user.

What makes this asynchronous is that we define code which isn't run synchronously with the execution flow otherwise.

XmlHttpRequest

XmlHttpRequest is an API that allows asynchronous communication with the server. It's now standardised across browsers such that all major browsers provide this API, allowing us as JavaScript programmers to send and receive data from the server via HTTP. It's called XmlHttpRequest (probably) because it was originally mainly used to send and receive XML data, but in general it can be used to transfer any data. Specifically, we'll be using it to transfer JSON.

> **XML and JSON**
>
> You might wonder, what is this XML that I keep hearing about. XML (Extensible Markup Language) is a markup language that shares many similarities with HTML. Here's an example XML document:
>
> ```
> <?xml version="1.0" encoding="UTF-8"?>
> <start_tag>
>     <second_tag attribute="value">
>         second tag body
>     </second_tag>
> </start_tag>
> ```
>
> In general, you can define all the values (tag names, attribute keys and values, the contents in the body of a tag) as you wish. In this sense XML can be used to transfer generic data between two programs or components. For this use case XML is very similar to JSON. We're focusing on JSON in this book instead of XML because it's generally simpler to work with, and seems to be at least as common as XML if not more.

Here's an example of XmlHttpRequest in practice - JavaScript code that requests some data from the server:

```
var xhr = new XMLHttpRequest();
xhr.open('GET', 'file.html', true);
xhr.onreadystatechange = function () {
    if (xhr.readyState == XMLHttpRequest.DONE && xhr.status == 200) {
        console.log("Data received: " + xhr.responseText);
```

(continues on next page)

(continued from previous page)

```
6     }
7 };
8 xhr.send(null);
```

Let's go through this line by line:

- Line 1: We create a new object of type XMLHttpRequest which is an API for getting data from the server
- Line 2: We specify that we want to send a GET request (as opposed to POST), namely the URL "file.html"
- Line 3: We define the callback function which will be called when the server has its response. The syntax used here creates an *anonymous function* - a function that doesn't have a name but is defined. It's practical because we can define the function inline as opposed to defining it somewhere else and referencing it here, and it's also necessary as we can use variables in it that are in scope in this example (namely "xhr") that wouldn't be in scope if we defined it as a named function.
- Line 4: We check the state of the request. We want it to be DONE and have the status code 200 (which means "OK" in HTTP).
- Line 5: If this condition is satisfied then we write text in the console, including the response text from the server. This can be anything - plain text, JSON, XML, binary data - whatever the server is programmed to send.
- Line 8: We send the request to the server.

This example doesn't do anything with the data besides showing it in the log, but the data could be used to manipulate DOM, i.e. to change the HTML presented to the user. Let's try this out ourselves.

Exercise: Implement the above AJAX request. You'll need the following:

1. Create a new HTML file which has nothing but a button which calls a JavaScript function (<input type=”button” onclick=”my_function()” value=”Button to GET data”>), and a JavaScript function which does nothing more but the code from the block above.
2. Add a function in your Python code to serve this new HTML page using Flask (render_template()).

3. Add another function in your Python code to serve the URL that the AJAX request will request. In the example above, that URL is "file.html". Note that the URL doesn't need to have a file extension. That function should return a string, like "Hello world!"

4. Run your Python code using Flask. Navigate to the HTML page that has the button. Open the JavaScript console in the browser developer menu. Click the button. You should see the text from the Python server code in the console.

GET vs. POST

To summarise, GET and POST are both two "verbs" in HTTP - commands the client sends to the server. What are the differences?

- GET typically has no data attached to it from the client, except for the URL - it's meant to say "I want to download a page or a file"
- POST can have data - any kind of data - attached to it - it's meant to say "I want to upload data to the server"

The rule of thumb is that if you're only reading information from the server - but not changing anything in the server - you should use GET. You should use POST if the action results in changing something on the server, for example adding data in the database.

The example above requests something from the server. We can also send data to the server by using the HTTP command POST. Here's an example of sending a block of JSON:

```
var xhr = new XMLHttpRequest();
xhr.open('POST', 'file.html', true);
xhr.onreadystatechange = function () {
    if (xhr.readyState == XMLHttpRequest.DONE && xhr.status == 200) {
        console.log("Data received: " + xhr.responseText);
    }
};
xhr.setRequestHeader("Content-type", "application/json");
xhr.send(JSON.stringify({'my_number': 42}));
```

This looks very similar to the GET request above. The differences are:

- Line 2: We use 'POST' as the first parameter as opposed to 'GET'
- Line 8: We have a new function call, namely setRequestHeader(). This sets the type of data we're sending to JSON. We need this so that the server can handle the incoming data properly.
- Line 9: We include the data we wish to send as a parameter to send(). We use JSON.stringify to convert JSON to a string. The server will need to parse the JSON when receiving the data.

Once the client POSTs some new data to the server, how can the server use it? The following illustrates some concepts:

```
1 @app.route("/guess/finished", methods=['POST'])
2 def finished():
3     data = request.get_json()
4     print data['my_number'] # prints the number
5     return json.dumps(data)
```

This introduces a few new concepts:

- Line 1: We want the URL /guess/finished to handle POST requests. We need to tell this to Flask explicitly by using the "methods" optional parameter in the @app.route decorator.
- Line 3: As per Flask documentation, Flask provides the globally accessible object called "request" which includes all data associated with the request. More specifically, it allows us to access the POST data the user sent. If the user sent JSON, it's available to us using the get_json() member function.
- Line 4: As the JSON data has been parsed by the get_json() function, it's available to us in Python dictionary form.
- Line 5: We use the json.dumps() function to convert the dictionary to a string. We'll then return this string to the client which will be available in the xhr.responseText variable. (We need to import json first.)

Exercise: Add the above POST request in your HTML page, and the code in your server side to handle the incoming data. The server should return the same JSON data back but with the number multiplied by 2, e.g. if the client sends "{'my_number': 42}" to the server then the server should send back "{'my_number': 84}".

3.1.5 Gluing AJAX and Redis together

After the exercises in the previous section we're starting to have some pieces we can put together. Let's start with a couple more exercises.

Exercise: Modify your guessing game such that when the number was guessed correctly, send the number of guesses to the server in JSON. You don't yet need to handle this data on the server side.

Exercise: Connect to the Redis server in your Python module. Note that the code in the Python module will be executed automatically when you start Flask. This means you can connect to the Redis server in your top level Python code (e.g. with "r = redis.StrictRedis(host='localhost', port=6379, db=0)"), without having to define a function for this.

Now, let's see if we can store the number of guesses in the Redis database. Here's something to get you started:

```
1 @app.route("/guess/finished", methods=['POST'])
2 def finished():
3     data = request.get_json()
4     print data['guesses'] # prints the number of guesses
5     curr_date = str(datetime.datetime.now())
6     our_string_to_store = json.dumps({'guesses': 42})
7     r.lpush("25", our_string_to_store)
8     return 'abc'
```

This introduces a few new concepts:

- Line 5: We can query the current system time by calling the function "datetime.datetime.now()" (after importing datetime). Furthermore we can convert it (and almost any other data type including numbers) to a string by calling the str() function.
- Line 7: Here, we insert data in the Redis database whereby the connection is represented by the "r" object. We use the member function "lpush" which ensures the value in the key-value pair is a list. More specifically, it:
  - Takes two parameters, the key and a value
  - Creates a new list if the key didn't yet exist, such that the value is a new list with a single element, namely the value

    - Appends the value to the end of the existing list if the key existed

- Line 8: We return a string which will be available in JSON in the xhr.responseText variable.

Here, we also implicitly defined the *database schema* for our data: the key is the maximum number that the computer could think of, as a string. For now it's hard coded to 25 but we'll make it configurable later. The value is a list whereby each element in a list describes a finished game. Each finished game should be represented in JSON, such that the JSON has a field describing the number of guesses required in the game as well as the timestamp when the game was finished. We'll expand on this later.

Note that there are different ways the schema could be defined for this use case - this is one of the simplest ways but in general, schemas can be defined in significantly different ways, depending on the use case, amount of data and any performance requirements.

Exercise: When your server receives the number of guesses from JavaScript, store this in the Redis database.

Here are some hints:

- If you need to purge the database, call r.flushdb(). This will erase all data in the database.
- You may want to write a small script or a URL handler to check the contents of the database to ensure you're adding the correct data. You may alternatively want to use the Redis command line interface for this.

This should result in two relevant URLs that we serve in our Python code:

- The guessing game itself: an HTML page with the relevant JavaScript that allows the user to play the game
- The URL that receives the number of guesses and is called by our AJAX request

We should now be able to store something resembling a high score list in a database, but we're still lacking the possibility for the user to enter his or her name, configuring the maximum number the computer thinks of and understanding how exactly turn the contents of a key in a database to a correctly sorted high score list. This will be the scope for the next sections.

3.1.6 The page for starting a new game

We should have a "start new game" page for our guessing game. The purpose of this page is to capture the player user name and the maximum number that the computer will think of.

How could we go about this? Let's define the use case first:

1. The user will enter a page where he or she will have to enter a name and a maximum number. The page should have a button "Play" that takes the user to the guessing game.
2. In the guessing game page, the maximum number the computer will think of will need to be determined by what the user entered.
3. Once the user has guessed the correct number, the user name and the maximum number will be stored alongside the number of guesses in the database.

What are the challenges around implementing this? It's often helpful to think about the interfaces, i.e. data exchanges between different components, including pages as well as the server and the client. We should also note that we need a mechanism to transfer the data (user name and maximum number) from the first page to the second. One way to do this is to encode the relevant information in the URL by using the *query string*. This means that the URL for the guessing game could look e.g. like this:

"http://127.0.0.1:8081/guess/?user=Antti&max_value=25"

Here, the part after the question mark ("?") is the query string. It has two parameters, namely "user" and "max_value" with values "Antti" and "25" respectively. *HTML forms* can be used to generate the query string.

Once we have the user name and the maximum value provided to our guessing game, we need to use this information. There are (at least) two possibilities how we could do this:

1. We could modify our server code to generate the guessing game HTML differently based on user input.
2. We could modify our JavaScript code in the guessing game to read the user parameters from the URL, and modify our HTML accordingly.

It doesn't seem to make a huge difference which way we go, but let's pick the first alternative. (The second one involves using regular expressions in JavaScript to parse the parameters from the URL.)

The following sequence diagram illustrates the communication flow.

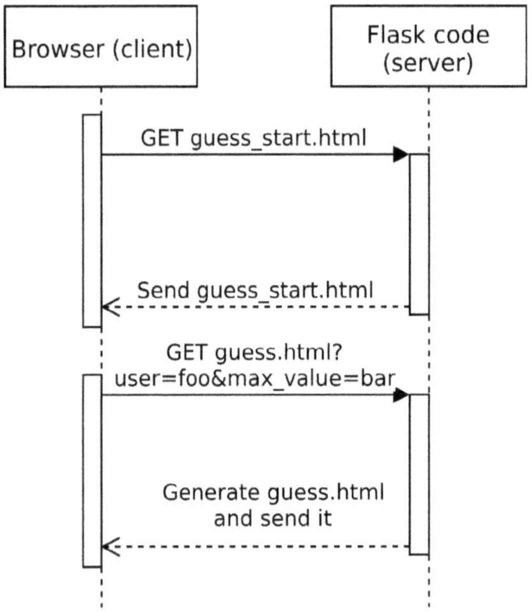

To break this down in tasks:

1. We need to write the HTML for the "start new game" page. This page should have an HTML form for capturing user input, and pressing the button to submit the form should lead the user to the guessing game page.
2. We need to update our server code to serve this new "start new game" HTML page for some URL.
3. We need to handle any possible GET parameters in our server code such that they'll be used when generating the guessing game page.
4. We need to modify our guessing game HTML and JS such that it reads the user name and maximum number from parameters provided by the server code.
5. We need to modify our JS code that uploads data in the database to include the user name and the maximum number.

Let's do this then.

HTML forms

HTML forms are a fairly simple way to get simple data from a user. Here's an example:

```
1  <!DOCTYPE html>
2  <html lang="en">
3      <head>
4          <meta charset="UTF-8">
5          <title>Guessing game</title>
6      </head>
7      <body>
8          <form action="/guess/" method="get">
9              What's your name? <input type="text" name="user"␣
   ↪value="User"> <br/>
10             <input type="submit" value="Play!"> <br/>
11         </form>
12     </body>
13 </html>
```

- Line 8: We define the form. It has two attributes: *action* and *method*. Action tells the browser which page should be fetched when the form was submitted. Method tells the browser whether it should GET or POST.
- Line 9: We create a text box with a default value ("User") and name ("user"), the contents of which will be sent to the server. As GET will be used, they will be sent in the URL.
- Line 10: We use the <input> tag to define the button pressing which will submit the form.

Exercise: Add this HTML to your templates directory. Add a text box such that the user can also input the maximum number.

Exercise: Add a new Flask function to serve your HTML using render_template().

Using templates

So what we have now is a page that has a form, which, when filled and submitted, will fetch our guessing game page, and send the parameters from the form to the server as part of the URL when fetching the guessing game page. (If you try this out you should see the parameters encoded in the URL.) However, the guessing game page doesn't use these parameters. Let's fix this.

Earlier we decided to handle this using *templates*: Flask provides an easy way to define variables in our HTML files such that the server can *generate* the HTML page differently depending on the parameters. This is documented thoroughly on the Flask web site but let's see how it would look in our URL handler function:

```
1 @app.route("/guess/", methods=['GET'])
2 def guess():
3     user = request.args.get('user', 'User')
4     return render_template('guess.html', user=user)
```

What Flask provides us is a globally available object named "request" which contains any GET parameters. We use this on line 3. It has the member variable "args" which has the member function "get" which takes two parameters: the name of the GET parameter, and a default value should the parameter not exist.

On line 4, we pass this parameter to the HTML generation function. In order to use the parameter, we need to modify our HTML file. Check this out:

```
<p id="intro">
Hello {{ user }}! This is the guessing game! I'm thinking of a number between 1 and 25, can you guess what it is?
</p>
```

Here, we use the parameter "user" using double curly braces ('{{' and '}}'). What happens is Flask will generate HTML based on this template, i.e. replace "{{ user }}" with the value from our Python code, and serve the generated HTML to the browser.

Exercise: Handle both user name and maximum number parameters in your Flask code and guessing game HTML. For the maximum number, you can have Flask insert it in your JavaScript code by doing e.g. "var overall_max_value = {{ max_value }};". Also store the user name as a JavaScript variable for later use.

Uploading more JSON data

Now we should have everything in place such that the maximum number depends on the user input, and the user name is available for our JavaScript. Let's add this information in the database when the user has correctly guessed the number. We should currently have something like this in our JavaScript code:

```
xhr.send(JSON.stringify({'my_number': 42}));
```

...with the number of guesses sent instead of 'my_number'. Can you find out how to add the user name and the maximum number of guesses here?

Exercise: Include the user name and the maximum number of guesses in the JSON to be sent to the server.

There's one more step we need to do before the correct data is added in the database. From before we should have a line like this on the Python handler when the correct number is guessed and JS POSTs the result:

```
r.lpush("25", json.dumps({'guesses': 42}))
```

...with the value being a JSON string containing the number of guesses and the current date and time, as a string. Let's improve on this.

Exercise: Modify your data insertion code such that the key is the maximum number, and the value JSON includes the user name.

Now we should have almost everything in place, except the user doesn't have visibility over previous scores. Let's fix this in the next section.

3.1.7 Generating the high score table

We should now have the following:

- The user can play the game and data over previous games is stored in the database, and we have an empty table as a placeholder for the high score table

What we're missing is updating the high score table both on starting the new game, and when the player has guessed the correct number.

Let's connect the dots. Here's how our high level architecture should look like:

- On page load, the JavaScript code requests the high score data from the server using AJAX.
- In Python, we have a handler that replies to this request by fetching data from the database and uses this data to generate and send back a suitable JSON that can be used for the high score table.
- In JavaScript, in the AJAX callback function, we receive this data, and write and call a function that takes this data as the input parameter and inserts it in the HTML high score table.
- Once the player has guessed the correct number, the server shall provide updated high score data to the client which the client shall use to update values in the high score table again.

The following sequence diagram illustrates the flow in more detail.

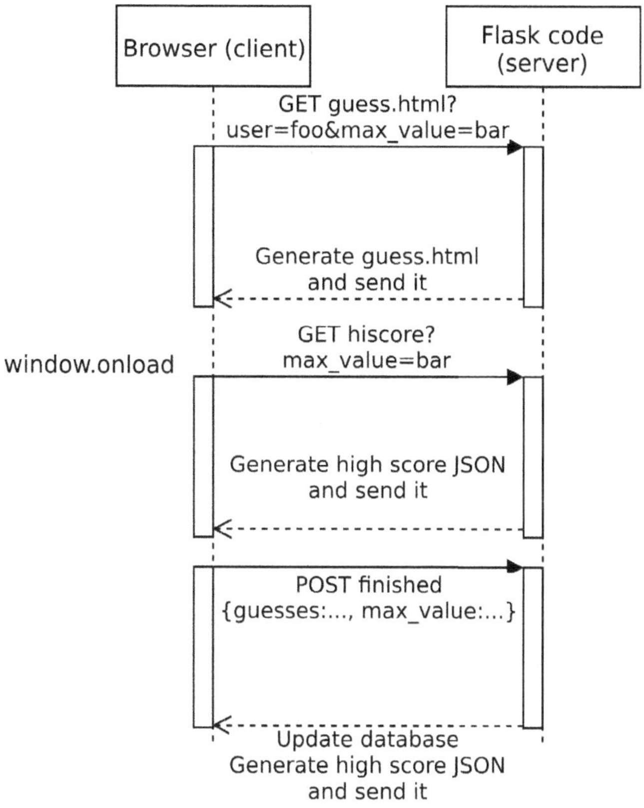

You might wonder, why have the JavaScript code request data from the server at page load time instead of generating the high score table as part of the template on the server? While this is certainly a feasible approach, the good thing about having the JavaScript generate the high score table at page load is that as we want to have JavaScript code to update the high score table at the end of the game anyway, we can reuse that code at page load and hence have only one piece of code update the high score table instead of two.

Actually updating the high score table

You may remember from the section "JavaScript meets algorithms" how to call a JavaScript function at page load. If not, the hint is that you assign the member function "onload" in the global object "window" as your callback function.

Let's install a function called update_hiscore() as the function that will be called at page load time, and implement it.

First of all, we need to send an XMLHttpRequest to the server. We should use GET as we're only asking the server for data. However we'll need to supply a parameter to the server, namely *which* high score table we want - as the high score table should be different based on the maximum number the computer can think of. As we've learnt, with GET we can only pass parameters as part of the URL, so let's do that. The URL should look something like "hiscore?max_value=25" - in this example, we'd fetch the page "hiscore" from the server, with "max_value" as the GET parameter, with 25 as its value.

Exercise: Implement the update_hiscore() function. It should do nothing else but send an XMLHttpRequest to the server, asking for the high score data, for the maximum number that the user is currently using in his or her game. You can concatenate a number to a JavaScript string with the '+' operator, e.g. "hiscore?max_value=" + my_variable. The handler for the data that is received from the server should do nothing else but call a function "display_hiscore()" (which we haven't defined yet), passing the response text to this function. For testing purposes you'll want to add a Flask handler for this URL, but for now it can return only a test string.

Providing the necessary data server side

We now have the client asking for high score data, but the server not providing any. Let's fix that next.

We might already have some Flask handler that will be called when the client requests for high score data. (If not, then add that now.) What we'll need to do in that function is:

- Fetch the relevant data from the database
- Parse the JSON we've stored
- Sort the data and pick the top five entries
- Serialise this data in JSON
- Send it to the client

You may recall we decided that in our database schema, the key is the maximum number and the value is a list, with each entry in the list representing one finished game. In order to fetch data from Redis where the value is a list, according to Redis Python client documentation, we can use the "lrange" function:

```
stored_data = r.lrange(key, 0, -1)
```

The "lrange" function takes three parameters: the key, start index and end index, which, if negatively indexed, counts from the end. In other words, passing 0 and -1 as the indices we fetch the full list. The variable "stored_data" now holds a list of strings, each string being JSON data.

Exercise: In your handler function, read all the data for the relevant key in a variable. You need to use "request.get.args()" to get the GET parameter.

We can parse a string which should be well formatted JSON data by using the "json.loads()" function:

```
parsed_data = json.loads(element)
```

Exercise: Parse all the JSON strings in the list such that you have the data available in Python dictionaries. You should be able to e.g. access the number of guesses field. Ideally you'd parse the strings by using a list comprehension.

Now that we have the data available, we need to sort it by the number of guesses and send the data to the client (by converting it to JSON using (json.dumps() and "return"ing it in our Flask handler function).

Exercise: Sort the data based on the number of guesses, from lowest to highest. Pass the optional argument "key" to the list.sort() or sorted() function. As the key, pass a function (anonymous or named) which return the field in the dictionary that is the number of guesses. Serialise the first five elements of that list into a JSON string and return the string to the client.

Handling the high score data on the client

On the client side, we have a function that requests the high score data from the server, and calls a callback function when this data is available, passing the data to the function.

The data that this function receives should be the JSON string that we programmed the server to send in the previous section. (You can use console.log() to verify.)

Now, what we should do is take that data and put it in our HTML table.

We already saw some JavaScript code before to change a cell in an HTML table:

```
table = document.getElementById("hiscore");
for(var i = 1; i < 3; i++) {
    table.rows[i].cells.item(1).innerHTML = "2017-02-15";
}
```

We've also seen how to parse a JSON string into a JavaScript dictionary:

```
var parsed = JSON.parse(data);
```

Then, it seems what we need to do is take the data from our dictionary, iterate over it in a loop and add the data in the relevant cells in our HTML table, cell by cell.

Exercise: Fill in the high score table. Make sure you don't overwrite the header row in the table - add one to your index where necessary. If you're sending more entries in your server code than you have space for in your table, you can use the function "Math.min(a, b)" to limit the number of iterations in your for loop.

Updating the high score table at game end

It would be nice to update the high score table once the game has finished. It seems all we need to do is call the update_hiscore() function at the right time. This would work but seems a bit ugly:

- At game end, the client POSTs the game result to the server
- The server replies with... nothing in particular
- The client immediately after GETs the updated high score data

It seems more elegant if we, when the client POSTs the game result, reply with the new high score data, and have the client use this to update the high score list - no additional GET necessary. So let's do this instead.

Exercise: In your server code, in your POST handler, have the POST handler return the JSON string the same way your GET handler does when the high score data is being requested. Instead of copying code, move any common code to a function and call that function from different places instead.

Exercise: In your client code, when POSTing the game result, have the handler call display_hiscore() the same way you do when GETting high score data at page load.

Congratulations! Our odyssey of turning our guessing game to a simple web app is now done.

3.1.8 Some more tips and tricks

Our simple web app is now fully functional. This page includes some tips related to it.

Using our new API outside the browser

As we wrote a new GET handler in Flask to send the high score data, we created an API for the high score that can also be used outside the browser. To demonstrate this, you can e.g. run the following command in your shell:

```
$ curl -s localhost:5000/guess/hiscore?max_value=25
```

(The "-s" switch reduces the output of curl such that only the response from the server is output. You may need to change the URL and the parameter to match your code.)

If you run this, you should get a JSON string back representing your high score list. This is practical because you can do all kinds of things with this API, such as:

- Write a script that gets the JSON files for all max_values, and display statistics over:
  - Which max_values have been played and which haven't
  - Who are the most active (or best) users of the game
  - How do the high score lists evolve over time
- Visualise the high score list in some other way, e.g. as a 3D scene
- Fetch the high score list periodically and automatically email an alert when the list has changed

It's often beneficial to expose such an API for reasons like this.

CSS, or making web pages prettier

CSS (Cascading Style Sheets) is a standard for defining how web pages look like. It's typically used together with HTML and JS; HTML controls the layout, JS defines the logic and CSS defines the looks. As this book isn't a web design book we won't go to the details on CSS but here's an overview:

- You create a .css file which describes e.g. what colour or fonts different tags should use, for example headings or paragraphs. CSS looks something like this:

```
body {
    background-color: #ff0000;
    color: #00ff00;
}
```

(Colours are defined from 0 to 255 for red, green and blue separately, in hex notation, i.e. ff stands for 255. In other words, the above sets the background colour to strong red and the text colour to strong green.)

- You can also define a *class*: a style that applies to multiple elements.
- Once you've defined your CSS file you reference it in your HTML by including something like the following tag in your head section:

```
<link href="my_file.css" rel="stylesheet">
```

- If your CSS defines styles for a class, then you need to define which class your element uses. For example:

```
<table id="hiscore" border="1" class="my-table-style">
```

For those with little eye for design, there are several CSS libraries available online that can be used and downloaded by your web page such that you don't have to specify the style yourself. After searching online for a while you might find some. One of the popular ones is Pure.

Exercise: Find the Pure CSS website.

Pure CSS modules

If you take a look at the usage section on Pure, you'll find the URL you can use to reference in your HTML such that when opening your page, the browser will download the Pure CSS modules in addition and use those if you define any of your elements to use the Pure styles. At the time of writing, the Pure page instructs you to do this:

```
<link rel="stylesheet" href="https://unpkg.com/purecss@1.0.0/
↪build/pure-min.css" integrity="sha384-
↪nn4HPE8lTHyVtfCBi5yW9d20FjT8BJwUXyWZT9InLYax14RDjBj46LmSztkmNP9w
↪" crossorigin="anonymous">
```

This includes the URL to the Pure css file (at unpkg.com) as well as a hash of the file to ensure the file hasn't been modified by a malicious party.

Once we have this css defined, we can set the class of some of our elements such that they use Pure. As per Pure documentation, you can define the class for your high score table using the following:

```
<table id="hiscore" border="1" class="pure-table">
```

That is, you can otherwise keep it the same but include the "class" attribute to refer to "pure-table".

Exercise: Modify your HTML to use Pure. You can start with the table, but if you're interested you can also modify the form in your page for starting the new game to use Pure. You'll need to use a couple of extra HTML tags to use all of Pure's features.

Accessing your page from other devices

By default Flask only accepts connections from the computer Flask itself is running on. As per Flask documentation you can override this by passing the –host parameter to Flask, e.g.:

```
$ FLASK_APP=guess.py flask run --host=0.0.0.0
```

This will allow connections from all devices in your network. (If you've enabled Flask debugger and don't trust all users in your network or expose your computer to the Internet directly then don't run this as in debug mode Flask allows users to execute code on your computer directly.)

In order to connect to your page from another device, you'll need to know the IP address where to connect. How to find this out is operating system dependent; on Linux, for example, you can typically run either "ifconfig" or "netcfg". You'll typically have multiple IP addresses (at least 127.0.0.1 and one more if you're connected to Internet) - pick one that makes sense for your network.

Exercise: Connect to your page from another device. Look up online how to find out your IP address if necessary. By default Flask serves your pages at port 5000 so you'll need to include that in your URL.

3.2 Working with binary data in C

3.2.1 PNG files

PNG (Portable Network Graphics) is a common file format for storing image data. Let's write a parser to parse some parts of PNG files in C. This will help teach us the following concepts:

- Working with binary data
- Data driven programming in C - or, how to structure C programs nicely

On the side, we'll learn about the following smaller but important C concepts:

- C macros
- Command line options
- The switch-case statement
- typedef

We'll end up with a program that can parse some parts of a PNG file and display what it parsed. The program will be around 150 lines of code. The reader should ideally be able to finish the exercises within 40 hours.

Introduction to PNG

PNG file format is described online at e.g. Wikipedia but also at the RFC (Request for Comments) 2083 which describes the format in detail. In a nutshell:

- PNG starts with a *signature*, a sequence of bytes which can be used to identify a file as a PNG file
- The signature is followed by multiple *chunks*, whereby each chunk contains different kind of information about the file, including the actual image data
- Each chunk is identified by four characters and includes, apart from the identifier, the length, the actual data, and the *CRC*, or *cyclic redun-*

dancy check - a checksum used to ensure the contents of the buffer are valid

Exercise: Look up RFC 2083 online. You'll be needing it later.

The signature is eight bytes long and contains the following values, in hex format:

89	50	4E	47	0D	0A	1A	0A

In ASCII, the bytes 2-4 (starting from 1) are "PNG"; bytes 5-6 are "\r\n" (CRLF) and byte 8 is "\n".

Let's write a program that loads a given input file to a buffer. For this, we'll allocate a buffer of 16 megabytes. If the user attempts to open a larger file, we exit. This is naive but works well enough for our purposes.

```
#include <stdio.h>
#include <stdlib.h>
#include <string.h>

#define MAX_SIZE (16 * 1024 * 1024)

int main(int argc, char **argv)
{
        if(argc != 2) {
                printf("Usage: %s <png file>\n", argv[0]);
                return 1;
        }
        char *buf = (char *)malloc(MAX_SIZE);
        if(!buf) {
                fprintf(stderr, "Couldn't allocate memory\n");
                return 1;
        }
        FILE *f = fopen(argv[1], "r");
        if(!f) {
                perror("fopen");
                free(buf);
                return 1;
        }
        int size = fread(buf, 1, MAX_SIZE, f);
        fclose(f);
```

(continues on next page)

(continued from previous page)

```
26          free(buf);
27          return 0;
28  }
```

Let's go through this line by line:

- Line 5: We define a *macro* that contains the maximum size of the file we can open (16 MB). Because we need this value in several places, it's best to define it in one place to keep the uses in sync.
- Line 9-13: We check the command line arguments. In C, we can either define the main function to take no parameters (void) or "int argc, char **argv". If we use the latter, the variable "argc" contains the number of arguments and the variable "argv" the arguments themselves. If argc is 1, then the only argument (found at argv[0]) is the program name itself. We want to accept one additional argument so we ensure "argc" is 2.
- Line 18: We open the given file.
- Line 24: We read the whole file into our buffer.

Now, that program doesn't do very much so let's change that. We can, after opening and reading in the file, add a function call to a new function "check_header", which receives our buffer as the input parameter:

```
void validate(int val, const char *msg)
{
    if(!val) {
        fprintf(stderr, "Invalid file: %s\n", msg);
        exit(1);
    }
}

void check_header(const char *buf)
{
    validate((unsigned char)buf[0] == 0x89, "header byte 1");
    validate((unsigned char)buf[1] == 'P',  "header byte 2");
}
```

Here, our function "check_header" calls "validate" twice, for the first two bytes in the buffer. The function "validate", defined above, checks if the condition is true, and if not, prints out an error and exits the program.

Digression: what is "unsigned"?

In C, there are several integer data types; e.g. char (one byte), int (one word, e.g. 4 bytes, but depends on the system), *long* (system dependent but at least 4 bytes) and others. In addition, each data type can either be *signed* or *unsigned*. Signed means they can have a minus sign, i.e. can be negative. Typically, as some space e.g. one bit is used for the sign, the unsigned data can have a larger range. For example, a signed char has a range of at least from -127 to 127 while an unsigned char has a range from at least 0 to 255.

In the above, the byte values in the PNG header can be more than 127, e.g. the value 0x89 is 137 in decimal, hence the cast to unsigned char.

Digression: stderr

The function "validate" prints out the error using *fprintf*, which is similar to printf but allows defining the output file for writing. We define the output to go to *stderr*, or "standard error", which is very similar to standard in but is another file. The main use case is redirecting: if we were to direct the output of our program to a file, what gets written to stderr actually gets written out in the terminal, not in the output file. E.g:

```
$ ./png file.c > out.txt
Invalid file: header byte 1
$ cat out.txt
$
```

If you want to redirect stderr, you can use "2>", e.g. "./png file.c > out.txt 2> stderr.txt".

The function call 'printf("abc\n");' is equivalent to 'fprintf(stdout, "abc\n");'.

Exercise: Expand the program to check for all eight bytes of the header. Find a PNG file to test your program on.

You can download a sample PNG file from the book web page - a screenshot from another chapter.

You'll need to use either this exact image or another image with the same chunks for later exercises in this part of the book.

Now we have a program that checks, for a given input file, whether it has the correct PNG signature or not. Let's see if we can expand it to read all the headers in a PNG file. You may have read from the RFC or Wikipedia that after the signature, the series of chunks begins, with each chunk having the following format:

Length	Chunk type	Chunk data	CRC
4 bytes	4 bytes	*length* bytes	4 bytes

In other words, each chunk starts with four bytes indicating the length of the chunk data in bytes, followed by the chunk type (4 bytes), the chunk data (arbitrary length), and finally the CRC which is 4 bytes and can be used to check the data for correctness.

Now, let's see if we can parse this. Let's add the following code after we've checked the header:

```
int pos = 8;
while(1) { /* FIXME: infinite loop */
    char lenbuf[4];
    memcpy(lenbuf, buf + pos, 4);
    int len = get_big_endian(lenbuf);
    char chunkbuf[5];
    /* TODO: fill chunkbuf */
    printf("chunk: %s - len: %d (%d)\n", chunkbuf, len, size -␣
↪(pos + len + 12));
    /* TODO: increment pos correctly */
}
```

The code is a bit incomplete but a nice skeleton to start with:

- We define the variable "pos" which refers to our position in the full buffer.
- We then loop over all the chunks in the file (and more).

- We first copy the bytes designating the length of the buffer to a 4-byte buffer.
- We then convert that to an integer using the function "get_big_endian" (to be defined).
- We fill in the chunkbuf, i.e. a buffer containing the name of the chunk. We allocate a buffer of five bytes for this for convenience - the four bytes which are the chunk name are all ASCII so by allocating five bytes and finishing the buffer with a zero we can treat the buffer as a string and pass it to printf directly.
- We then call printf telling us which chunk we've found, what the length of the chunk is, and how much of the file is still left after this chunk.

Before we fill in the blanks, let's go to the details around "get_big_endian".

Endianness, and bit level operations

You may have noticed from the RFC or other sources that some values in the PNG file are stored as *big endian*. What does this mean? Let's first have a refresher on binary numbers. Imagine we have the number 135,200 and we want to store this. The number 135,200 is in decimal - in binary it is (using the Python interpreter to check):

```
>>> bin(135200)
'0b100001000000100000'
```

In other words - each of the four bytes in binary and hex:

00000000	00000010	00010000	00100000
0x00	0x02	0x10	0x20

The first byte has no bits set. Each of the other bytes has one bit set each.

Now, the way the table is here is in *big endian* - the most significant byte is the first one from the left, i.e. the bytes are ordered from the big end.

This means that in our buffer, if the length was 135,200 bytes, we'd have the following contents:

buf[pos + 0]	buf[pos + 1]	buf[pos + 2]	buf[pos + 3]
0x00	0x02	0x10	0x20

Now the question is, how would we convert these four bytes (char values) to an integer containing the value 135,200. This is the purpose of the function "get_big_endian".

To make it short, here's the function definition:

```
int get_big_endian(const char *buf)
{
    return ((unsigned char)buf[0] << 24) |
           ((unsigned char)buf[1] << 16) |
           ((unsigned char)buf[2] << 8)  |
            (unsigned char)buf[3];
}
```

This introduces two new operators: *bit shifting* and *bitwise or*.

Bit shifting shifts bits within a variable. Let's assume we the following code:

```
int x = 4;
x = x << 1;
printf("%d\n", x); // prints "8"
```

Here, "x" originally had the value 4, or "00000100" in binary (skipping some 0's at the front). We then *shift the bits to the left* by one on the second line, ending up with "00001000", or 8. This is bit shifting.

Bitwise or then:

```
int x = 3;
int y = 6;
int z = x | y;
printf("%d\n", z); // prints "7"
```

Here we "or" the bits of x and y, bitwise:

x	00000011
y	00000110
x | y	00000111

...and 00000111 is 7.

Where does that leave us with get_big_endian? Let's take another look:

```
return ((unsigned char)buf[0] << 24) |
       ((unsigned char)buf[1] << 16) |
       ((unsigned char)buf[2] << 8)  |
        (unsigned char)buf[3];
```

We take the first byte, shift its value by 24 bits to the left. We take the second byte, shift its value by 16 bits to the left, and 'or' the two. We take the third byte, shift its value 8 bits to the left, and 'or' the three. We take the fourth byte and 'or' it with the rest. Hence constructing the representation of an int from the four bytes.

Now we have everything to fill the gaps in our loop to go through all the chunks in a PNG file.

Exercise: Implement the missing bits. Terminate the loop when you reach the end of the file, as identified by the "size" variable. Increment pos by the chunk header size plus the length. Initialise the chunk string appropriately. Your program should output something like this (for guess1.png):

```
chunk: IHDR - len: 13 (15154)
chunk: bKGD - len: 6 (15136)
chunk: pHYs - len: 9 (15115)
chunk: tIME - len: 7 (15096)
chunk: iTXt - len: 29 (15055)
chunk: IDAT - len: 8192 (6851)
chunk: IDAT - len: 6827 (12)
chunk: IEND - len: 0 (0)
```

3.2.2 Finishing our simple PNG parser

We're now able to do some preliminary parsing of a PNG file, but we're still lacking the parsing of the actual blocks.

We won't parse all blocks - most notably, we won't parse the actual image data - but we can get some information out of some of the other blocks. For example, the header block (IHDR), the background colour block (bKGD) and last modification block (tIME) give us some good cases for practising our programming skills. For such blocks, we can set the goal of simply printing out the contents to stdout.

Data driven programming

Now, we have code to tell when we've stumbled upon a block, we know how long a block is in bytes, and we know where to find the contents of the block. What we could do is simply check the type of the block and then have some logic to react to it, i.e.:

```
printf("chunk: %s - len: %d (%d)\n", chunkbuf, len, size - (pos␣
↪+ len + 12));
if(!strcmp(chunkbuf, "IHDR")) {
    printf("Image width: ...");
    /* more printfs */
} else if(!strcmp(chunkbuf, "tIME")) {
    printf("Year: ...");
    /* more printfs */
} else if(...) /* and so on */
```

However, this is an excellent use case to simplify the logic (i.e. reduce the number of if's) and try *data driven programming*, where we capture the different functionality in *tables*, or arrays with an ID and a function pointer designating what to do.

What we want to have is the following:

1. We'll have one function for each type of chunk
2. We'll create an array of structs, whereby each struct has a string (const char pointer) which is the type of the chunk, and a function pointer pointing to the function that handles the chunk

3. We'll have a for loop looping through this array instead of the if-else if chain, calling the relevant function for each found block

Let's illustrate this.

Typedefs

First of all, when working with function pointers in C, it's often practical to define the type of the function in a *typedef*. This is mainly because the syntax of declaring function pointers in C can be seen as a bit complex, and with a typedef we can capture this complexity in one place. What typedef does is simply assign another name to a type. In our case, our type is a function pointer.

We want a separate function for each type of chunk, and our typedef should describe the type for such a function. Our function should return nothing (void), and it should take a const pointer to an input buffer plus its length as parameters. Here's an example declaration of such a function:

```
void time_handler(const char *buf, int len);
```

A typedef for function pointers that could point to such functions would be:

```
typedef void (*handler_ptr)(const char *buf, int len);
```

Now, when we want to have a variable which points to a function, we can use "handler_ptr" as the type for that variable. In fact, let's do just that, and declare such a variable as part of a struct:

```
struct handler {
    const char  *type;
    handler_ptr func;
};
```

Here we have a struct with a const char pointer and a function pointer.

Now we can define a global variable which is an array of such structs. While generally global variables aren't great, our array will be constant and as such not lead to confusing code even though it's global:

```
const struct handler handlers[] = {
    { "IHDR", header_handler },
    { "tIME", time_handler },
    { NULL,   NULL }
};
```

Here we have an array of total three structs, such that the const char pointer identifies the type of the chunk and the second variable in the struct refers to a function to call for that chunk. We have the last value only contain NULL pointers to mark the end of the array which will be useful soon.

We can now define each function - they can be empty for now:

```
void header_handler(const char *buf, int len)
{
}

/* repeat for time_handler */
```

Finally, we can add the loop in our main function to call each function:

```
1 for(int i = 0; handlers[i].type != NULL; i++) {
2     if(!strcmp(chunkbuf, handlers[i].type)) {
3         handlers[i].func(buf + pos + 8, len);
4         break;
5     }
6 }
```

Let's go through this line by line:

- Line 1: We loop through our array. The terminating condition checks for NULL value for the type: if the type pointer is NULL, we know we've reached the end of the array and terminate the loop. This is a convention we've agreed to by ourselves.
- Line 2: We check if the current element in the array matches the chunk type we've found in the file.
- Line 3: We call the function pointer pointed to by the struct in the array, and pass it the data from the file.
- Line 4: As we've found the correct handler and called it, we can terminate the loop.

Exercise: Put all of the above together. Your handlers don't need to do anything with the data yet but your code will need to compile.

Parsing the chunks

We can now implement our first chunk handler - the handler for the header. We simply need to validate the input to ensure we're not reading past the end of the buffer, then call "printf" for the relevant data as per the file format specification. The chunk handler can start like this:

```
void header_handler(const char *buf, int len)
{
    validate(len == 13, "header must be 13 bytes");
    printf("Width:              %d\n", get_big_endian(buf));
    printf("Height:             %d\n", get_big_endian(buf + 4));
    printf("Bit depth:          %d\n", (unsigned char)buf[8]);
    ...
}
```

Exercise: Finish the header handler. Look up from the spec what the contents of the header are expected to be.

We can then proceed to the time handler (type "tIME"). If you check the spec you'll see that it has a field with two bytes. If it was one, we could simply cast to unsigned char. If it was four, we could use our "get_big_endian" function. Since it's two, we need another function to parse it correctly.

Exercise: Implement the time handler. Read in the year using a function "get_2_byte_big_endian" which you need to define yourself. It should work the same as "get_big_endian" but only read in two bytes.

Exercise: Add another handler to handle the "pHYs" block. Look up from the spec what the format is.

Finally, for this section, we'll need to implement the background colour handler. This is interesting because, if you look at the spec, you'll see that how to parse it depends on the colour type which was defined in the header. This means that we'll have to store the colour type in a variable in the header handler and have it accessible for the background colour handler.

While we could in theory use a global variable for this, such generally leads to confusing code, and we can do better. A nice way to go about this is to add another parameter to the handler functions which is shared among all functions. Generally it's best to define a struct for all the data you need to thread through the functions, e.g.:

```
struct png_data {
    int color_type;
};
```

Now, we need to change the function pointer typedef to include a pointer to "struct png_data", and add this parameter to all the handler functions. We can then define a variable of this type in main, clear its memory, and pass a pointer to it to the handler function being called.

Once we have this, we can set the "color_type" variable in the header handler, and read its value in the background colour handler. (As we'll pass a pointer to the struct to the functions, we can access it with the -> syntax, e.g. png->color_type.)

Exercise: Add the background colour handler function to your program. Depending on the file, it should print either the palette index, grey colour value or the red, green and blue background colour values.

Slight digression: switch-case

You may have implemented the background colour handler using something like this:

```
if(png->color_type == 3) {
    ...
}
else if(png->color_type == 0 || png->color_type == 4) {
    ...
} ...
else {
    printf("unknown color type\n");
}
```

This works, but C provides another way to implement this kind of a pattern, namely the *switch-case* syntax. The above could be translated to switch-case like this:

```
switch(png->color_type) {
    case 3:
        /* code here */
        break;

    case 0:
    case 4:
        /* code here */
        break;

    /* more cases here */

    default:
        printf("Unknown background color type\n");
        break;
}
```

In other words, we can define the points to jump to depending on the input variable value. We'll need to add break statements at the end of each case as otherwise the execution would continue to the next case. The "default" case is jumped to if no other case matched.

Exercise: Rewrite your background colour handler to use switch-case.

One thing we didn't discuss here was checking the CRC to ensure the data hasn't been corrupted. However, RFC 2083 includes C code to calculate the CRC which we can reuse.

Exercise: Copy the code from RFC 2083 to your program. Using the sample code, calculate the CRC of each block and compare it to the CRC stored in the file (they should match). Note that the CRC needs to be calculated over the data field *and* the chunk type field. You may need to make some modifications to the sample code to account for const and different signs.

After these exercises, for the sample image, the output should be something like this:

```
chunk: IHDR - len: 13 (15154)
Width:              732
Height:             150
Bit depth:          8
Color type:         6
Compression method: 0
Filter method:      0
Interlace method:   0
CRC correct: 1
chunk: bKGD - len: 6 (15136)
R: 255
G: 255
B: 255
CRC correct: 1
chunk: pHYs - len: 9 (15115)
pixels/unit, x: 2835
pixels/unit, y: 2835
unit:           1
CRC correct: 1
chunk: tIME - len: 7 (15096)
Year:   2018
Month:  2
Day:    4
Hour:   22
Minute: 44
Second: 30
CRC correct: 1
chunk: iTXt - len: 29 (15055)
CRC correct: 1
chunk: IDAT - len: 8192 (6851)
CRC correct: 1
chunk: IDAT - len: 6827 (12)
CRC correct: 1
chunk: IEND - len: 0 (0)
CRC correct: 1
```

Congratulations, you now have your own simple (partial) PNG file parser.

3.3 Strongly, statically typed languages

This chapter introduces some strongly, statically typed languages but before we get to those, we need to understand how the languages we've so far used actually behave.

3.3.1 Under the hood

We've now used a couple of languages and gotten some meaningful output out of them, but we haven't really gone into the details of how exactly do they tell the CPU what to do.

In general, as we know, the CPU executes instructions, one after the other. If we program in a language such as C, our compiler typically takes our code and turns it into a listing of CPU instructions.

What's new is that you can ask the compiler to output the *assembly code* into a file for inspection. Let's do just that. In the section "C and the stack", we had an example program:

```
#include <stdio.h>

int main(void)
{
        int a = 3;
        int b = 4;
        int x = a + b;
        printf("%d\n", x);
}
```

Now, typically (i.e. for gcc and clang), you can instruct the compiler to generate assembly by passing the "-S" flag. The assembly code is then generated in the file specified with the "-o" flag. E.g.:

```
$ clang -Wall -S -o st1.s st1.c
```

Exercise: Run the above and inspect the resulting assembly code.

The assembly code is specific to the CPU ISA (instruction set architecture). At time of writing the main CPU ISA families are x86 (which is used in most desktop, laptop and server computers) and ARM (which is used in most mobile devices such as smart phones). Chances are you ran the compiler on an x86 computer.

If you take a look at the assembly code, you see a lot of code that's always necessary in order to set up a program to execute. In general, code that's always required for setup without being heavily dependent on the rest of the program is called *boilerplate*. In our case, we should focus on the assembly code generated from lines 4-8 as those are the most relevant lines in our program.

When I run the above command (using clang 3.9.1 on Linux x86-64), and inspect the output, I see what's listed below (only including the call to "printf" and a few instructions before):

```
1   subq     $16, %rsp
2   movabsq $.L.str, %rdi
3   movl     $3, -4(%rbp)
4   movl     $4, -8(%rbp)
5   movl     -4(%rbp), %eax
6   addl     -8(%rbp), %eax
7   movl     %eax, -12(%rbp)
8   movl     -12(%rbp), %esi
9   movb     $0, %al
10  callq    printf
```

While we won't go into details of the x86 assembly, for the purposes of attempting to get a basic understanding of what's happening let's go through this instruction by instruction:

- Line 1: we subtract 16 from the *stack pointer* - i.e. move the stack pointer by four integers i.e. allocate four integers in the stack
- Line 2: $.L.str is our static string, "%d\n". We move this in the rdi register which is used by printf.
- Line 3: We move the fixed value 3 to the address rbp - 4. rbp is the stack base pointer. This means we set a value in the stack to 3.
- Line 4: We set the next value in the stack to 4.
- Line 5: We move the value from address rbp - 4 to the register eax. Register eax can be used for basic arithmetic functions such as addition.

- Line 6: We add the value from address rbp - 8 with the value stored in the register eax, such that the resulting value is stored in eax. In other words, 3 + 4.
- Line 7: We move the value from eax to rbp - 12, i.e. from the register into the stack.
- Line 8: We move the value from rbp - 12 to esi, which is a register also used by printf. printf uses the value from rdi as the first parameter ("%d\n") and the value from esi as the second parameter (x).
- Line 9: We set the value of the register al to 0. al is used to describe the number of vector registers used, which in this case is 0.
- Line 10: We call the function printf.

Many commands for a simple operation! If you think some of the moves aren't necessary, you're right. In fact, as we compiled the program without any *compiler optimisation flags*, it outputs fairly naive assembly code. We can pass the argument "-O2" to the compiler, which means it should apply most common, yet not too aggressive optimisations. Let's do this:

```
$ clang -Wall -S -O2 -o st1.s st1.c
```

If we then inspect the assembly, it looks different:

```
1       movl    $.L.str, %edi
2       movl    $7, %esi
3       xorl    %eax, %eax
4       callq   printf
```

This seems shorter:

- Line 1: As before, we move the static string to the register edi.
- Line 2: We move the value 7 to the register esi. The compiler inferred the calculation and calculated the result during compilation.
- Line 3: We reset the register eax. xorl applies the "xor" (exclusive or) operation. Applying "xor" with the same value on both sides results in 0. The compiler does this because it's the fastest way to also clear the register al, which is used to describe the number of vector registers used.
- Line 4: We call the function printf.

Now, in general it's not very common for developers to have to read or write assembly. It's still good to understand what happens when compiling a program, and helps understand the principle of virtual machines.

3.3.2 Virtual machines

In the previous section we discussed the assembly language. Many languages, including C and C++, are typically compiled to a machine specific assembly code before the program can be executed. Which prompts the question, what do other languages do.

Python

Python is an interpreted language. This, however, doesn't mean that the interpreter looks at each character in the code while the program is being executed; instead, the interpreter compiles the code to *bytecode* - a code similar to assembly, which is then interpreted by the interpreter. You may see files with the suffix .pyc after running some Python code - these contain the bytecode.

The standard Python implementation also provides a library for inspecting the resulting bytecode. Take a look at this example:

```
import dis

def func(a, b):
    return a + b

dis.dis(func)
```

What happens here is we define a trivial function, then use the built in module "dis" to display the disassembly of this function. You can also use this module in the Python interpreter.

The program outputs this:

```
4           0 LOAD_FAST                0 (a)
            3 LOAD_FAST                1 (b)
            6 BINARY_ADD
            7 RETURN_VALUE
```

The first two lines load two values, a and b, and the third one adds the two.

If you recall the x86-64 assembly, this is somewhat similar, but arguably simplified. Which is kind of the point: it's relatively fast for the Python interpreter to interpret the bytecode, but it's still independent of the machine, such that Python code can in general be run on any platform that can run the Python interpreter. Hence such interpreters are also called *virtual machines* - they run a program which isn't compiled for a certain platform and is hence platform independent.

Speaking of the Python interpreter, it's also a good idea to take a look at the Python implementation to get a better understanding of how it works.

Exercise: Find the source code of the main Python implementation online. (This is also called "cpython", as in, the C implementation of Python.) Make sure you pick the source code of the 2.7 branch, not the Python 3 code. You may either download a package with all the source code, or browse the code as it's stored in version control, though downloading the whole code might be easier for searching (find and grep). See if you can find the function which interprets the command BINARY_ADD.

Other virtual machines

JavaScript is implemented by each browser, and several implementations are actually virtual machines which compile JavaScript to bytecode and interpret this at run time. However, many of the main implementations actually compile JavaScript code directly to machine code before the code is run for better performance; so called *JIT* or just-in-time compilation.

Java is generally not compiled into machine code but to bytecode executed by *JVM*, or Java Virtual Machine. JIT is also used with JVM.

Similar to JVM, .NET from Microsoft contains a virtual machine (called *CLR* or Common Language Runtime) which executes .NET bytecode and uses JIT for improved performance.

As virtual machines generally only take the specific bytecode as the program input, and the bytecode generally is not strictly tied to a higher level language, it's often possible to implement a compiler for another language which outputs bytecode which can then be interpreted by the virtual machine. There are several languages that are not Java but can execute on the JVM, such as Clojure (which is a dialect of Lisp) and Scala. Similarly, there are several languages that can run on the .NET virtual machine such as C# and Visual Basic .NET. There are also implementations of Python that compile Python to JVM and CLR bytecode.

3.3.3 The case for statically, strongly typed languages

> There are only two kinds of languages: the ones people complain about and the ones nobody uses.
>
> —Bjarne Stroustrup

We've so far mostly used three languages:

- JavaScript: a dynamically, weakly typed language
- C: a statically, weakly typed language
- Python: a dynamically, strongly typed language

Let's see what alternatives we have for a statically, strongly typed language.

Disclaimer: different programming languages are another topic that can get fairly religious among programmers. While I attempt to remain objective, 90% of programmers will probably disagree with at least some of the contents of this section. That is their right.

This section attempts to summarise different programming languages by identifying their most important traits. The languages have vast differences but the scope of this section is not to capture all of them, but instead only serve as an introduction. We will make a deeper dive to some of the languages later.

All the languages here are statically, strongly typed as well as imperative, such that it shouldn't be very difficult for the reader to implement FizzBuzz for any of the languages after seeing the "Hello world" program and possibly a search or two online on syntax. To make things more interesting we'll also, for each language, quote two programs for relatively common operations:

- Splitting a string by a space, with the goal to be able to access and print out each word separately.
- A separate function which filters numbers less than zero from a list (or an array)

For the second operation, the implementation should be implemented generically, i.e. for any different numeric types, if possible, in each language.

This may be helpful in illustrating the different concepts between languages.

Exercise: Implement both of the above operations in one of the languages (C, Python or JavaScript). Note that example implementations will be listed below. If you pick C, you may want to use the function "realloc". If you pick JavaScript, you may want to look up the reference for the JavaScript array class first.

To prepare, here's how to split a string in C, Python and JavaScript:

C:

```
#include <stdio.h>
#include <string.h>
#include <assert.h>

int main(void)
{
# define MAX_WORDS 20

    char *str = "this is a string.\n";
    char str_buf[256];
    memset(str_buf, 0x00, sizeof(str_buf));
    strncpy(str_buf, str, 255);
    int indices[MAX_WORDS];
    int next_index = 1;
    memset(indices, -1, sizeof(indices) / sizeof(int));
    indices[0] = 0;
    int len = strlen(str);
    for(int i = 0; i < len; i++) {
        if(str_buf[i] == '\0') {
            break;
        }
        if(str_buf[i] == ' ') {
            indices[next_index++] = i + 1;
            str_buf[i] = '\0';
            assert(next_index < MAX_WORDS);
        }
    }

    const int num_words = next_index;
```

(continues on next page)

(continued from previous page)

```

    /* printing out each word */
    for(int i = 0; i < num_words; i++) {
        printf("%s\n", &str_buf[indices[i]]);
    }
}
```

(Compile and run e.g. using "gcc -Wall -O2 -o str str.c && ./str".)

Some explanation to the above: we create a buffer where we store a copy of the original string, with each space replaced with a string terminator ('\0'). We index into the buffer in order to access the individual words. In order to do this, we create an array with MAX_WORDS (20) elements, each one including the index (position) of the word.

Python:

```
string = "this is a string.\n";
for word in string.split(' '):
    print word
```

JavaScript:

```
var str = "this is a string.\n";
var res = str.split(" ");
for(var i = 0; i < res.length; i++) {
    console.log(res[i]);
}
```

Here's the program to filter numbers less than zero in C, Python and JavaScript:

```
#include <stdio.h>
#include <stdlib.h>
#include <string.h>

/* filt: filter out positive numbers from an int array
 * Input parameters:
 *   arr: pointer to array with numbers
 *   len: number of elements in arr
 *
```

(continues on next page)

(continued from previous page)

```
 * Output parameters:
 *   return value: pointer to a newly allocated array with only
 *                 negative numbers
 *   end_len: number of elements in return value
 *
 * Return value may be NULL if no memory available.
 * Otherwise, caller must free() the return value after use.
 */
int *filt(int *arr, int len, int *end_len)
{
        // first allocate memory large enough to hold the
        // whole array in case this is needed
        int *res = (int *)malloc(sizeof(int) * len);
        if(!res) {
                perror("malloc");
                return NULL;
        }
        memset(res, 0x00, sizeof(int) * len);

        // end_len serves as our index so we know where to
        // put the next number
        *end_len = 0;

        for(int i = 0; i < len; i++) {
                if(*arr < 0) {
                        res[*end_len] = *arr;
                        (*end_len)++;
                }
                arr++;
        }

        // resize the size of the output buffer
        int *new_res = (int *)realloc(res, sizeof(int) * *end_
→len);
        if(!new_res) {
                perror("realloc");
                free(res);
                return NULL;
        }
        return new_res;
```

(continues on next page)

(continued from previous page)

```
}

int main(void)
{
        int inp[8] = {3, -1, 4, -2, 5, -3, 6, -4};
        int end_len;
        int *res = filt(inp, 8, &end_len);
        if(!res) {
                return 1;
        }
        for(int i = 0; i < end_len; i++) {
                printf("%d\n", res[i]);
        }
        free(res);
        return 0;
}
```

(This uses "realloc" for re-allocating existing memory.)

Python:

```
def filt(arr):
        return [n for n in arr if n < 0]
inp = [3, -1, 4, -2, 5, -3, 6, -4]
print filt(inp)
```

JavaScript:

```
var inp = [3, -1, 4, -2, 5, -3, 6, -4];
function filt(arr) {
    var out = arr.filter(function(n) {
        return n < 0;
    });
    return out;
}
console.log(filt(inp));
```

(We use the built-in array class member function "filter" and pass it an anonymous function as the callback that defines what to filter on.)

What's new

What could statically, strongly typed languages improve on compared to the above?

Python and JavaScript are fairly concise but, when compared to C, have some characteristics that can be perceived as disadvantages:

- The performance of Python and JavaScript is generally not as good as C and much of this is due to dynamic typing, although there are optimisations that can be done to alleviate this (for example *JIT*, or just-in-time compilation, where parts of a program can be compiled during execution after the runtime has collected data on which type is typically associated with each variable)
- There's arguably more room for error with dynamic typing; errors that could be caught before running the program may cause a run time error during execution

On the other hand, C has some characteristics that can be perceived as disadvantages compared to Python and JavaScript:

- C is fairly verbose; based on the number of lines already there's arguably more effort required in C to achieve the same behaviour
- C is not memory safe, opening the possibility of nasty memory related bugs and security holes
- C is not as strongly typed as Python, such that some bugs in the code could go undetected which would raise a (run time) error in Python
- While we haven't discussed C projects with multiple files in detail, in general the system in C with header files and source files, with the header files being included in source files using the #include preprocessor directive (which practically automatically copy-pastes the header file in the source file) introduces some drawbacks that ideally can be improved upon

Generic functions

Another point to note is that because types have to be explicitly defined in C, it is generally not possible to implement some *generic* functions in C without eliminating type safety. A classic example is a function to return the maximum value of two values:

```
int max_int(int a, int b)
{
    if(a > b)
        return a;
    return b;
}

int max_float(float a, float b)
{
    if(a > b)
        return a;
    return b;
}

/* repeat for all types for which you want to find the maximum */
```

Typically, in C, this particular case would be handled with a *macro*:

```
#define max(a, b) ((a) > (b) ? (a) : (b))

int x = 5;
int y = 4;
int res = max(x, y);
```

(The *ternary operator* ?: returns the term before the : if the term before the ? is true and the term after the : otherwise.)

However, macros provide no type safety, such that it's e.g. possible to mix the types of "a" and "b" in the above without warning. (Macros also have other issues; if, for example, an expression with side effects such as "x++" was passed to the above "max" macro, then x could be incremented twice.)

Other languages may attempt to improve on the above points. It should be noted that there is no silver bullet, i.e. even with static, strong typing it can be argued that no language is categorically better than all other languages.

3.3.4 Established languages

> Java is C++ without the guns, knives, and clubs.
>
> —James Gosling

C++

C++ started in the 80s as an addition of features to C. Since then it has accumulated an impressive set of features. It's still mostly backwards compatible to C - such that most C can be compiled with a C++ compiler with little changes - but has a lot of features that C doesn't have.

Some things that C++ "fixes" comparing to C are:

- Automatic code execution when a variable leaves the scope: We saw in our BSD socket handling code that we had to call close() and sometimes shutdown() whenever we saw something go wrong. This is easily forgotten or neglected, causing resource leaks (in this case file descriptors but can also be e.g. memory). C++ uses the concept of classes to enable automatic cleanup when necessary. This also enables *smart pointers* - pointers with *reference counting* such that no manual memory management is necessary, and instead the pointers should know themselves when the memory pointed to can be freed.
- Arrays: In C, the programmer has to keep track of the length of an array (or pointer to an array) manually - it's not automatically associated with the array. C++ has array data types which include the length, greatly simplifying the code.
- Generic programming: In C, if one were to e.g. implement a function to return the larger of two numbers, it's necessary to implement the function for all numeric data types, e.g. float, int, etc. even when the body of the function is the same. C++ solves this using *templates*.
- Extended standard library: E.g. the max() function but also several string handling functions are included in the C++ standard library. Furthermore, data structures such as linked lists, sets and dictionaries (maps) are included.

Things that C++ hasn't (completely) fixed include:

- Memory safety: While it's possible to write safe C++, it still allows things like pointer arithmetic and manual memory management for backwards compatibility reasons.
- Module system: It's still necessary to have a header file (.h) for declaring the functions and data types and the source file (.cpp) for function definitions.

Hello world program:

```
#include <iostream>

int main()
{
    std::cout << "Hello world" << std::endl;
}
```

In C++, instead of calling printf() with its inherent lack of type safety (as the format string can be dynamic, it's in general not possible for the compiler to check that the format string matches the types that are provided as extra parameters, or indeed that the number of extra parameters is correct), the C++ standard library provides an object called std::cout which has *overloaded* the "<<" operator (left shift) to mean writing to it.

Split string:

```
#include <iostream>
#include <vector>
#include <sstream>
#include <iterator>
#include <algorithm>
#include <string>

int main()
{
    std::string s("this is a string.\n");
    std::vector<std::string> res;
    std::istringstream iss(s);
    std::copy(std::istream_iterator<std::string>(iss),
          std::istream_iterator<std::string>(),
          std::back_inserter(res));

```

(continues on next page)

(continued from previous page)

```
17      for(const auto& w : res) {
18          std::cout << w << "\n";
19      }
20  }
```

- Line 1-6: Necessary includes.
- Line 10: Our input string.
- Line 11: Our *vector* (dynamic array) to hold the result (individual words).
- Line 12: Input stream, a class that holds the string, but as a stream.
- Line 13-15: We copy the data from the stream to our vector. When reading the stream, it returns words one at a time, which are inserted into our vector using the class std::back_inserter.
- Line 17-19: Writing out each word.

This can be compiled and run e.g. with the following command: g++ –std=c++11 -Wall -O2 -o str str.cpp && ./str

Filtering numbers less than zero:

```
#include <iostream>
#include <vector>
#include <sstream>
#include <iterator>
#include <algorithm>
#include <string>

template<typename T>
auto filt(const std::vector<T>& arr)
{
        std::vector<T> res;
        std::copy_if(arr.begin(),
                     arr.end(),
                     std::back_inserter(res),
                     [](T i) { return i < 0; });
        return res;
}

```

(continues on next page)

(continued from previous page)

```
19 int main()
20 {
21     std::vector<int> inp = {3, -1, 4, -2, 5, -3, 6, -4};
22     auto res = filt(inp);
23     for(const auto& i : res) {
24         std::cout << i << "\n";
25     }
26 }
```

Due to how C++ works, we have to define the function that does the actual work before we define main. Let's go through main first.

- Line 21: We define our input, a vector of integers.
- Line 22: We call our processing function. We don't need to type the type of the variable but use "auto" instead, meaning the compiler can deduce it for us. In this case, the type is std::vector<int>.
- Line 8-17: Our processing function implementation.
- Line 8: We define a *template* for our function. This means that the type named "T" will be replaced by whatever the called used to call the function. In this case, int. This way our function only needs to be implemented once for all numeric types including floating point numbers.
- Line 9: We define the signature of our function such that the input is a *reference to* a std::vector which holds elements of type "T" (in our case, int). Reference is created using the "&" symbol. It's very similar to a pointer in C, but it is more restricted. For example it must always be defined to refer to a variable, and it cannot be set to NULL. The output of our function is "auto", i.e. automatically derived, but in our case std::vector<int>.
- Line 11: We define our variable which we'll return in the end.
- Line 12-14: We use C++ standard template library functions to describe copying values from one vector (array) to another.
- Line 15: Here, we define a *lambda* function that takes "T i" (in our case, "int i") as a parameter, and returns true if i is less than 0. This is used as the predicate for our copying function.

C++ is a fairly large language, both from syntax and the standard template library. I'd expect most C++ programmers to spend a significant portion of their programming time perusing the various language and library references.

Java

Java is a language introduced in mid-90s and has a strong notion of *object oriented programming*. Compared to C++, Java:

- Generally has memory safety - no manually managed memory, or pointers
- Uses *garbage collection* - instead of relying on the programmer to free memory that's not used, Java periodically checks whether memory is still in use or not and if not, will mark it as free
- Has an improved module system - with no need to define header files

Java has also been evolving and the newer versions of the language include some features that haven't been part of Java before, such as lambda functions and generic functions.

Splitting a string in Java:

```
1 class Split {
2     public static void main(String[] args) {
3         String str = "This is a string.\n";
4         String[] words = str.split(" ");
5         for(String s : words) {
6             System.out.println(s);
7         }
8     }
9 }
```

You can compile and run this e.g. by running "javac split.java && java Split". (You'll need to have the Java framework installed.)

Let's see what we have:

- Line 1: We put all our code in *class* Split. All Java code must reside in a class. The class name will specify what the output file will be (here Split.class) which is needed when executing the program ("java Split").

- Line 4: We call the member function (or "method" in Java terminology) "split" of the class String which returns an array of Strings.
- Line 5: We define a for loop where we iterate over the array, printing out each word in stdout.

As you can see, the Java code is for this example not very different from Python or JavaScript.

Filtering numbers in an array:

```
1  import java.util.Arrays;
2  
3  class Filt {
4          public static void main(String[] args) {
5                  int[] d = {3, -1, 4, -2, 5, -3, 6, -4};
6                  int[] d2 = filt(d);
7                  for(int v : d2) {
8                          System.out.println(v);
9                  }
10         }
11 
12         public static int[] filt(int[] arr) {
13                 return Arrays.stream(arr).filter(x -> x < 0).
   ↪toArray();
14         }
15 }
```

- Line 5: We define our array.
- Line 6: We call our method which does the filtering.
- Line 13: We convert the array into a *stream* using the "stream" method, then use the "filter" method which takes a lambda function as a callback to specify which values we want to keep. Finally we convert the stream back into an array using the "toArray" method and return the result.
- Lines 7-9: We iterate over our resulting array, printing out the values.

Note that this function only works with integers, not e.g. with floating point numbers unlike C++. The reason is that the templating system in C++

simply replaces the type T with the used type, i.e. int in our case, such that were we to e.g. use a float, the comparison with literal zero (0) would still work. However, the generics system in Java doesn't allow this.

C#

C# is a language by Microsoft which is similar to Java and runs on a virtual machine called CLR (Common Language Runtime) which is part of a framework called .NET.

Although there are many differences between C# and Java, on a grand scale they're fairly similar, such that e.g. differences between C++ and Java or C++ and C# are relatively larger. Like Java, C# has memory safety, garbage collection and a proper module system.

The main implementation of C# (compiler and the CLR runtime) is available from Microsoft for Windows, Mac and Linux. Alternative implementations exist such as Mono.

Here's a program to split strings in C#:

```
using System;

public class Split {
    public static void Main(string[] args) {
        string str = "This is a string.\n";
        string[] words = str.Split(' ');
        foreach(var s in words) {
            Console.WriteLine(s);
        }
    }
}
```

There are a few subtle differences between C# and Java:

- In C#, we need to use the "using" directive in order to access the console (stdout)
- In C#, Main is capitalised but string isn't
- In C#, the method "split" takes a character as a parameter while in Java it takes a regular expression; also, in C# the method name is capitalised (technically speaking, the C# Split method takes a character

array as a parameter with the single character implicitly converted to an array)

- In C#, the for loop is somewhat different. The main difference is that we don't need to define the type of the variable we use for iterating, but can use simple "var" instead, which automatically infers the correct type.
- Instead of System.out.println in Java, C# has Console.WriteLine().

Overall many of the differences here are cosmetic.

Filtering elements in a list in C#:

```
using System;
using System.Linq;

public class Filt {
    public static void Main(string[] args) {
        int[] d = {3, -1, 4, -2, 5, -3, 6, -4};
        int[] d2 = filt(d);
        foreach(var v in d2) {
            Console.WriteLine(v);
        }
    }

    public static int[] filt(int[] arr) {
        return arr.Where(x => x < 0).ToArray();
    }
}
```

This is again fairly similar to Java, with the main difference being that the syntax for the actual filter operation is somewhat different.

3.3.5 Newer languages

> Within C++, there is a much smaller and cleaner language struggling to get out.
>
> —Bjarne Stroustrup

The previous section covered languages that are relatively established, with C++ originating from the 80s and Java and C# from mid-90s and early 2000s respectively. This section covers some of the languages which are a bit newer and hence somewhat less common, though still interesting. I should also point out that there are in fact hundreds if not thousands of new programming languages created in the past couple of decades so this section only covers a couple of hand picked ones, however there are several others that are widely used, to some extent more widely used than the selection here, and also arguably more different from other languages covered in this book.

Go

Go is a language created by Google and originally launched in 2009. Its standard implementation compiles to machine code and it aims to be an improvement over C, with memory safety and garbage collection included, among other features.

Splitting a string in Go:

```
package main

import (
        "fmt"
        "strings"
)

func main() {
        s := "This is a string.\n"
        s2 := strings.Split(s, " ")
        for _, word := range s2 {
                fmt.Println(word)
```

(continues on next page)

(continued from previous page)

```
13          }
14  }
```

This looks a bit different to e.g. C# and Java:

- Line 3-6: We define the list of modules to import, namely "strings" and "fmt"
- Line 9: We define our string, assigning to it with the := operator
- Line 10: We split our string by calling the function "Split" from the strings module
- Line 11: We iterate over our string array using a for loop and the *range* keyword. What range does is provide an iterator for the loop, with two variables in each iteration, namely the index and the element itself. We capture the element in the "word" variable and ignore the index by denoting it with an underscore ("_").
- Line 12: We use the "fmt" module to print out each word to stdout

If the Go compiler is installed, this can be compiled and run using "go run split.go".

Filtering elements from an array in Go:

```
package main

import (
        "fmt"
)

func main() {
    d := []int {3, -1, 4, -2, 5, -3, 6, -4}
    d2 := filt(d)
        for _, v := range d2 {
                fmt.Println(v)
        }
}

func filt(arr []int) (ret []int) {
    for _, i := range arr {
```

(continues on next page)

(continued from previous page)

```
17          if i < 0 {
18              ret = append(ret, i)
19          }
20      }
21      return
22  }
```

- Line 9: We call our function filt which does the work.
- Line 15: The function implementation begins. It takes one parameter called "arr" which is an array of integers. Its return value is called "ret" and is also an array of integers.
- Line 16-20: We define a simple for loop for adding the relevant numbers in the return value. The function "append" appends an element to an array, and returns the array with the element appended.

Go doesn't support defining generic functions so this function only works for integers.

Swift

Swift is a language announced by Apple in 2014. It's also compiled to machine code and is designed as the main language for writing applications for Mac and other Apple devices.

Splitting a string in Swift:

```
import Foundation

let str = "this is a string.\n"
let s2  = str.components(separatedBy: " ")

for word in s2 {
    print(word)
}
```

Swift infers the types of the variables in this example.

Filtering elements from an array in Swift:

```
1  import Foundation
2
3  func filt<T: BinaryInteger>(arr: [T]) -> [T] {
4      return arr.filter { $0 < 0 }
5  }
6
7  let d = [3, -1, 4, -2, 5, -3, 6, -4]
8  let d2 = filt(arr: d)
9
10 for i in d2 {
11     print(i)
12 }
```

This seems interesting:

- Line 3: We define our filtering function. It takes an array of T as input, and returns an array of T as output. Swift allows use of generics here such that we can define T to be of generic type *BinaryInteger*, which means any kind of integer, but not e.g. floating point. This means our function can be used for different kinds of integer numbers but not for any numbers.
- Line 4: Function body. We use the filter function with a lambda function as the predicate. The special variable $0 is the element in the array passed to the lambda function.

Swift infers the types of our arrays (d and d2) but the types needed to be explicitly defined for the function definition.

Rust

Rust is another fairly recent language, being announced by Mozilla in 2010. It's intended to be an improvement over C++ with good performance and improved memory safety.

Splitting a string in Rust:

```
fn main() {
    let str = "this is a string.\n";
    let s2 = str.split(" ");
    for word in s2 {
```

(continues on next page)

(continued from previous page)

```
        println!("{}", word);
    }
}
```

Rust infers the types of our variables in this program.

Filtering elements from an array in Rust:

```
1  extern crate num;
2  use num::Num;
3  
4  fn main() {
5      let d = [3, -1, 4, -2, 5, -3, 6, -4];
6      let d2 = filt(&d);
7      for i in d2 {
8          println!("{}", i);
9      }
10 }
11 
12 fn filt<T: Num + PartialOrd + Copy>(arr: &[T]) -> Vec<T> {
13     arr.into_iter().filter(|&&i| i < T::zero()).cloned().
   ↪collect()
14 }
```

Again, this seems interesting:

- Line 5: We define our input data. This is an array of integers (specifically 32-bit integers), whereby the type is inferred by Rust.
- Line 6: We call our function. We pass a reference of "d" to the function.
- Line 12: We define our function. The parameter called "arr" is a reference to an array of T's. It returns a vector (dynamically allocated array) of T's. T is a generic type parameter but the function mandates it must implement the Num, PartialOrd and Copy *traits*, meaning it must be numeric, sortable and copyable.
- Line 13: We first convert our input variable, an array, to iterable using "into_iter", which is required by the next step. We then filter on it using the built in "filter" function. We pass an anonymous function as the predicate, whereby we call the variable passed to the predicate

"i". We need to use "&&i" instead of plain "i" to copy "i" for comparison with T::zero(), which is a generic function representing a generic zero. Finally we clone the resulting array which is required for turning it into a vector, which is done by collect().

The type system and generics in Rust allows us to write the function such that it works for all numeric types.

To summarise, Rust allows fairly direct control over allocation and its type system is extensive, however some work is required from the developer to take advantage of all Rust features.

Exercise: Out of the six new languages described in this and the previous section, pick one that seems to appeal to you the most, and one that seems to appeal to you the least.

Exercise: For both of the two languages you picked, implement Fizz Buzz and the exercise of finding the largest root for a few quadratic equations. Note that for most of the languages you don't necessarily have to install the compiler on your computer; there are several web pages that provide an interactive code editor and compiler for testing out a language. Try searching for e.g. "rust online" or "rust playground".

3.4 Learning C++ using Sudoku

3.4.1 Introduction to Sudoku

In this part of the book we'll learn some new programming concepts using Sudoku, a Japanese game.

We'll learn about the following concepts:

- Using a statically, strongly typed language to solve a problem
- Some bits around algorithms, namely search and constraint propagation, i.e. some classical AI
- Recursion

What is Sudoku? Sudoku is a game with a grid of 9x9 numbers, whereby each cell in the grid can have a number between 1 and 9. Some cells are pre-filled and the goal of the game is to fill all the cells, such that each cell contains a number that is not already used by any of its peers. The peers of a cell are the cells either on the same horizontal line, on the same vertical line, or within the same 3x3 grid. The cells that are peers of each other, i.e. on the same horizontal or vertical line or within the same 3x3 grid are called a *unit*.

Here's an example Sudoku puzzle:

```
1..|42.|...
...|..6|...
...|...|...
---+---+---
.51|.4.|.87
..3|.5.|.61
...|3..|..5
---+---+---
28.|..7|..4
...|...|5..
6.5|.18|.2.
```

Now, what we're going to write is a program that, given any Sudoku puzzle, will solve it.

In order to be able to write such a program, we must first be capable of understanding the problem, i.e. understanding what our program should do. To gain this understanding it's helpful to try to solve the Sudoku puzzle manually first. Then, "all" we need to do is replicate this logic in code.

Exercise: Try to solve the above Sudoku puzzle. (No need to actually solve it.)

Now, when trying to solve the puzzle, you probably came up with one common strategy: try and see if a cell only has one possible value because its peers rule all other values out, and in this case, fill the cell with this value.

Another common strategy is to see if a number has been ruled out for all cells in a unit except one. In this case it must be the correct number for that cell.

If you fill a cell with a value, then this rules out that value of its peers, meaning you can again check those peers if they only have one possible value.

At some point you may have seen that it's not possible to progress using these strategies: all open cells may all have more than one possible value. What you could try then is guess: pick one of the possible values, assume it's the correct one and see if you end up with the solution for the Sudoku.

While there are several more strategies to solve a Sudoku puzzle, these two, combined with the guessing, are enough for our purposes.

Our program will have the following parts:

- Reading in a Sudoku puzzle from a file
- Checking if a cell has only one possible value, and if so, set it
- If a value was set in a cell, see if this causes some other cell to only have one possible value (also called *constraint propagation* - whereby constraints propagate to create further constraints)
- Guess, or search: assume a value is correct for a cell, then propagate the constraint and search further until a solution is found, or guess another value if the previous guess turned out to be wrong (also called *backtracking*)
- Checking we solved the puzzle, and printing out the solution

You can use any programming language but the snippets in the book necessary for writing the program will be in C++. Should you choose to use another language you'll need to find out the relevant snippets yourself. It's been demonstrated this problem can be solved in about 20 lines of Python, though I'd recommend using a statically typed language for the sole reason of gaining more experience using one. The solution for the problem in this book is about 300 lines of C++.

I'd also like to credit Peter Norvig for writing an excellent article about this problem which is the foundation for this part of the book. You may want to look it up online after completing the exercises.

Sudoku and classes

As mentioned we'll be using C++ to solve this. We'll also use some object oriented concepts to see how these can be used for such a problem.

Generally speaking, it's often useful to first identify the main data structures and how they relate to each other. In this case, we can see there are following structures:

- The puzzle itself - either in solved or unsolved state
- Cells - whereby each cell can be represented by which value it has, or better, could have

On relations, we can see the puzzle contains multiple cells, namely 9x9=81.

In the spirit of object oriented programming, we can construct objects for these two structures.

In C++, the syntax for declaring a class is the following:

```
1 class Counter {
2     public:
3         Counter(int my_value); // constructor
4         int get_value() const; // getter function
5         void increment();
6 
7     private:
8         int value;
9 };
```

Let's go through this line by line:

- Line 1: We use the keyword *class* to define a class. This is similar to "struct" - indeed, almost equivalent.

- Line 2: We use the keyword *public* to denote functions (and possibly variables) that can be called from code that is not part of the class. This specifies the *interface* of the class.
- Line 3: We declare a function with the same name as our class, and without a return value. This function is called the *constructor* and is called whenever an object of this class is *instantiated*, i.e. whenever a variable of this type is defined. In this case, the constructor takes one int as a parameter.
- Line 4: We define a *getter function* - a function which has the simple function of returning some variable for which direct access is not allowed from the outside. We denote this function with the keyword *const* at the end - this means that the function does not modify the object (i.e. the variable of this type).
- Line 5: We define a function that modifies the object somehow. In this case, we'd expect the function to increment the value of the internal int by one.
- Line 7: We use the keyword *private* to denote functions and variables that are part of the class but not accessible from code outside the class.
- Line 8: We declare an int as the internal data for this class.

Now, the above defines the interface for the class as well as its (hidden) data. We still need to define the member functions. This can be done as follows:

```
Counter::Counter(int my_value)
      : value(my_value)
{
}

int Counter::get_value() const
{
    return value;
}

void Counter::increment()
{
    value++;
```

(continues on next page)

(continued from previous page)

```
14 }
```

In other words:

- Line 1-4: We define the constructor. We first copy-paste the declaration and add "Counter::" in front of the function name. Second line demonstrates the syntax for initialising internal variables. The function body itself is empty.
- Line 6-9: We define the function "get_value". We again copy-paste the declaration and add "Counter::" in front of the function name. Instead of a semicolon at the end we have the function body. It's very simple in this case, returning an integer containing the value of the variable "value".
- Line 11-15: We define the function "increment" which simply increments "value" by one.

If we wanted to use this class, we could e.g. do the following:

```
int main()
{
    Counter a(3);
    a.increment();
    std::cout << a.get_value() << "\n";

    Counter b(12);
    std::cout << b.get_value() << "\n";
    return 0;
}
```

This would print "4" and "12".

This class is fairly trivial but demonstrates most of the concepts we'll be needing. In terms of usability of this class, it effectively *encapsulates* an integer such that most integer options are not possible, for example subtraction or multiplication. It could be used e.g. as a counter for something.

Exercise: Add a "decrement" function to our class. Test it by using it in test code.

3.4.2 Containers for Sudoku

Recall that our main idea to solve Sudoku (constraint propagation) revolves around the idea of checking how many possible values a cell has, and if it has only one possible value, set it.

We then discussed the concept of a cell - which may either have a value, or at least we should know which values it could and could not have.

After our discussion around classes we now almost have enough to implement a class "Cell", which represents a cell and the value it has or could have. Before we implement this, let's consider for a moment how we could achieve this concept of potential values.

If we know which value a cell has, it's no different from an integer. However, if it can have multiple values, then it can effectively be represented as a set of multiple integers.

Exercise: What ways or data structures can you think of to store this information?

We've talked about arrays before, but arrays generally have a fixed size. We could, however, e.g. have an array of nine integers, each integer having a value between 1 and 9, or -1 if one or more numbers have been eliminated.

Alternatively we could use a dynamically sized array, and only store the possible values there. If only one value is stored, then we know the value in the cell.

Furthermore, we could use a *set*, i.e. a *binary search tree* which is similar to vector in the sense that it stores values, but with the feature of having a faster time complexity for e.g. lookup functions than a vector (O(log n) vs. O(n)).

The following quickly demonstrates the three approaches in C++, with the example of attempting to find a number 3 in an array as well as checking the size:

```
#include <iostream>
#include <array>
#include <set>
#include <vector>
#include <algorithm>
```

(continues on next page)

(continued from previous page)

```

int main()
{
	bool found;
	int size;

	// C type array
	int old_type_array[5] = {2, 3, 4, -1, -1};
	found = false;
	for(int i = 0; i < 5; i++) {
		if(old_type_array[i] == 3) {
			found = true;
			break;
		}
	}
	size = 0;
	for(int i = 0; i < 5; i++) {
		if(old_type_array[i] != -1) {
			size++;
		}
	}
	std::cout << "Found: " << found << "; size: " << size << "\n";

	// C++ has a specific array type
	std::array<int, 3> arr;
	arr[0] = 2;
	arr[1] = 3;
	arr[2] = 4;
	found = std::find(arr.begin(), arr.end(), 3) != arr.end();
	size = arr.size();
	std::cout << "Found: " << found << "; size: " << size << "\n";
	// printing all values in the array:
	for(const auto& v : arr) {
		std::cout << v << "\n";
	}

	// C++ vector
```

(continues on next page)

(continued from previous page)

```
        std::vector<int> vec;
        vec.push_back(2);
        vec.push_back(3);
        vec.push_back(4);
        found = std::find(vec.begin(), vec.end(), 3) != vec.
↪end();
        size = vec.size();
        std::cout << "Found: " << found << "; size: " << size <<
↪"\n";
        // vec.clear() would remove all elements in the vector
        // The following line removes element 3 from the vector
        vec.erase(std::remove(vec.begin(), vec.end(), 3), vec.
↪end());
        std::cout << "Size: " << vec.size() << "\n";

        // printing all values in the vector:
        for(const auto& v : vec) {
                std::cout << v << "\n";
        }

        // C++ set
        std::set<int> s;
        s.insert(2);
        s.insert(3);
        s.insert(4);
        found = s.find(3) != s.end();
        size = s.size();
        std::cout << "Found: " << found << "; size: " << size <<
↪"\n";
        // s.clear() would remove all elements in the set
        s.erase(3);
        std::cout << "Size: " << s.size() << "\n";

        // printing all values in the set:
        for(const auto& v : s) {
                std::cout << v << "\n";
        }

        return 0;
}
```

Vector and set also allow initialisation using the {} notation like arrays, but the above demonstrates the functions to add values in them explicitly.

Most of this is possibly rather self explanatory, but it seems two pieces of code are of specific interest:

- Erasing an element in a vector; this is the so-called *erase-remove* idiom which is the (admittedly clunky) way in C++ to remove an element from a vector. It uses std::remove(), a generic function in the C++ standard template library (STL) which takes *iterators* as parameters, which are provided by the standard containers in C++ for iterating over the containers and conceptually are pointers pointing to an element. This is passed to vec.erase() which will then remove the element from the vector. E.g. the first element in a vector or a set can be accessed using "*vec.begin()".
- In the for loops, we use the construct "const auto &v". This means "v should be a reference to a constant variable of automatically inferred type". What referencing ("&") means in practice is that we don't copy the data, possibly saving some CPU cycles. What "const" means is that we promise not to modify the data within the container. Overall this means we simply want to read the contents. If we wanted to, say, modify the element then we should remove "const". If we wanted to construct a copy of the element (e.g. for modifying it but without modifying the element in the container) then we should remove the "&".

So what is this "reference"?

In C++, a reference ("&") to a variable is semantically almost the same as a pointer. The main semantic difference is that a NULL reference isn't allowed while a NULL pointer is. Also, while pointer arithmetic is allowed, "reference arithmetic" is not. Apart from this, a reference is a syntactic shortcut: you don't need to use the address-of operator when passing a reference of a variable to a function, and you don't need to dereference the pointer using "*" when using the variable.

Cell class

Now, we should have everything we need for a Cell class. It should have the following functionality:

- On construction, it should store the numbers from 1 to 9.
- It should be possible to *set* it, i.e. remove all values except one (which is given as a parameter).
- It should be possible to check whether a cell is valid, i.e. whether it has at least one value still available.
- It should be possible to *eliminate* a value, i.e. remove a value if it exists. For convenience, let's have the function "eliminate" return false if the last number in the cell was eliminated and true otherwise.
- It should be possible to ask whether it contains only one number, or multiple.
- It should be possible to retrieve the current values.

More specifically, it should correctly implement an interface as used by this program:

```
#include <iostream>

/* Cell class declaration and definition goes here */

int main()
{
```

(continues on next page)

(continued from previous page)

```
    Cell c1;
    std::cout << c1.count() << "\n";    // outputs "9"
    bool ret = c1.eliminate(7);
    std::cout << c1.count() << "\n";    // outputs "8"
    std::cout << ret << "\n";           // outputs "1" (true)
    c1.set(3);
    std::cout << c1.count() << "\n";    // outputs "1"
    std::cout << c1.valid() << "\n";    // outputs "1" (true)
    std::cout << c1.has_one() << "\n"; // outputs "1" (true)
    auto values = c1.get_values();
    for(const auto& v : values) {
        std::cout << v << "\n";         // outputs "3"
    }
    return 0;
}
```

Here, the return type of the member function get_values() is implementation specific, i.e. it could be e.g. either vector<int> or set<int>. The usage of the variable "values" would stay the same in either case.

Bounds checking

Similar to assertion, and relevant in C++, is *bounds checking*. Normally, when you access an element in an array (with e.g. "a[3]"), there's nothing stopping you from trying to access an element beyond the size of the array, leading to undefined behaviour. At a small (typically negligible these days) runtime cost you can, for the classes std::vector and std::array, have the bounds checked at each access by using e.g. "a.at(3)" instead. Now code will be called that will check whether the element is within the bounds and throw an exception if not, hopefully saving lots of debugging time in the future.

Exercise: Implement the Cell class. You can use any data structure you like although either vector or set should be the easiest ones. Test it with the test code above.

We may need some more member functions for our Cell class later, but we can implement these as we go along.

3.4.3 Sudoku Puzzle class

Now, we can start implementing our Puzzle class. From data point of view, this is nothing else but an array of cells. Let's declare this:

```
class Puzzle {
    public:
        Puzzle();
        bool solved() const;

    private:
        std::array<Cell, 81> cells;
};
```

Exercise: Implement the constructor and the "solved" function. The constructor doesn't need any contents as the array elements will be constructed using the default constructor for Cell, which as per the previous exercise initialises the cell such that all values are possible. The "solved" function will need to check whether all cells have only one number, and only return true in this case. (Initially, it should hence return false.)

Now, we can look into actually constructing an object of class Puzzle by reading a Sudoku puzzle from a file.

As per Norvig, let's define the file format for a Sudoku puzzle such that a number in a file defines the value for a cell, while either a dot (.) or a zero (0) denote an unknown cell, and all characters can be ignored. This means that e.g. the following line is a valid puzzle (courtesy QQWing, an open source Sudoku puzzle generator):

```
1..42.........6.............51.4..87..3.5..61...3....528...7..4..
↪....5..6.5.18.2.
```

The same puzzle could be represented like this:

```
1.. 42. ...
... ..6 ...
... ... ...

.51 .4. .87
..3 .5. .61
... 3.. ..5

28. ..7 ..4
... ... 5..
6.5 .18 .2.
```

Now, let's write the code to read this. In C++, one can read a file to a string with the following snippet (this uses the first parameter given to the program):

```
#include <iostream>
#include <fstream>
#include <string>

int main(int argc, char** argv)
{
    std::ifstream ifs(argv[1]);
    std::string contents((std::istreambuf_iterator<char>(ifs)),
            (std::istreambuf_iterator<char>()));
    return 0;
}
```

Now that we can read file into a string, let's turn this into a puzzle. We want to implement the following:

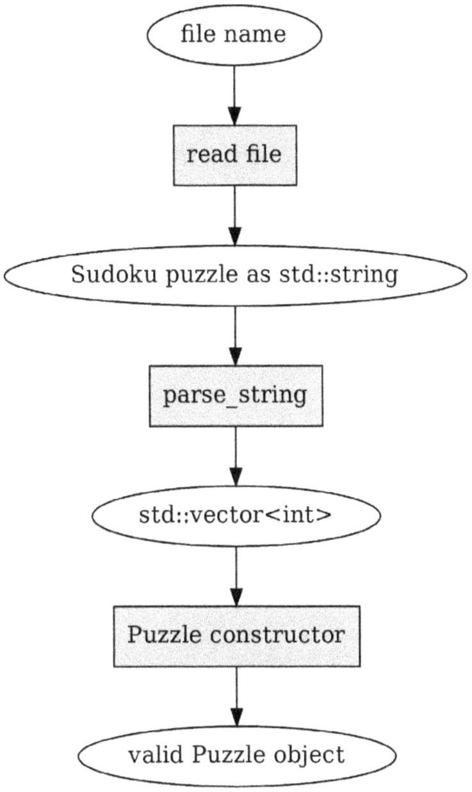

In other words, we want to read the file to an std::string, pass this string to a function called parse_string() (which we still need to write) which shall convert the std::string to a vector of integers. Once we have a vector of integers we'll pass it to our Puzzle constructor which shall use this vector to set the correct values in the member variable of type std::array<Cell, 81>. Phew!

The interfaces for parse_string() and the Puzzle constructor would hence look like the following:

```
int main()
{
    std::string s = /* ... */;
    std::vector<int> values = parse_string(s);
    Puzzle b(values);
    return 0;
}
```

We see here how the Puzzle class constructor shall receive an std::vector<int> as input. Each element in the vector should either be a number between 1 or 9, denoting a pre-filled cell, or something else (like 0) to denote a clear cell. We should also have a function "parse_string" to turn the string to an int vector.

As a skeleton, let's put something together that also introduces character-to-integer conversions in C++, exceptions and reference parameters.

```
1  std::vector<int> parse_string(const std::string& s) {
2      int buf_location = 0;
3      std::vector<int> my_buf;
4      for(auto c : contents) {
5          if(c >= '1' && c <= '9') {
6              my_buf.push_back(c - '0');
7          } else if(c == '.' || c == '0') {
8              /* TODO */
9          }
10         if(buf_location == 81) {
11             /* TODO */
12         }
13     }
14     throw std::runtime_error("Unable to parse");
15 }
```

Let's go through this line by line:

- Line 1: We define the function such that it takes a parameter "const std::string& s". A simpler version to write effectively the same thing would be "string s", however the latter would cause the input string to be copied for the function. With the former version we receive a reference to a constant string instead, saving an unnecessary data copy.
- Line 2: We define a variable to keep track of the current cell we might fill.
- Line 3: We define our return variable.
- Line 4: We iterate over all characters in the string.
- Line 5: We check if the character value is between '1' and '9'. As the character values are based on the ASCII table, meaning they can be treated as numeric values, we can use arithmetic operators (>= and <=) to compare them.

- Line 6: We subtract the ASCII value '0' from "c". This results in the integer value 0 for the character '0', 1 for character '1', 2 for character '2' etc.
- Line 7: We check whether the character is a dot or a zero.
- Line 10: We check whether we've found a symbol for each cell in the puzzle.
- Line 14: If we didn't find enough symbols of interest, then we cannot fill our array of cells any further and *throw an exception*: this effectively ends the current execution of the code and goes up the function call stack until a caller is found who *catches* the exception thrown. As we have no code to catch the exception, this effectively prints the error message on the screen and terminates the program.

Digression: What do you mean, "subtract the ASCII value"?

You may remember from the section "C and strings" that ASCII is a mapping between characters and numbers. Our variable 'c' is a character, but also a number. E.g. the character '3' is equivalent to the number 51 in ASCII. Hence, by subtracting 48 ('0') from 'c' we end up at the number which the ASCII character represents. By pushing the result of this subtraction to the std::vector<int> we implicitly convert the result to an int.

Exercise: Implement the above function. Fill out the correct code for the TODOs such that the return variable is updated correctly and returned. See if you can run it without an exception being thrown with the example input from above.

Now that we're able to parse a string to an int vector, let's turn this int vector to a Puzzle.

Exercise: Rewrite the constructor of the Puzzle class to take an int vector as a parameter, and loop through it to set the contents of the "cells" member variable. Use the "set" member function of the Cell class to set the values.

Displaying puzzles

We're now able to read in a Sudoku puzzle but have no visibility over the contents of the Puzzle class. To remedy this, let's write a function to display the puzzle. Here's the declaration:

```
class Puzzle {
    public:
        ...
        void print() const;
        ...
};
```

That is, a public member function which doesn't modify the object.

Now, we can implement this function by looping through the array of cells, and for each cell, print out something. What we print should have the same number of characters for each cell for proper formatting. The simplest way to do this is to either print out a number if a cell has one, or a placeholder (e.g. a space or a dot) otherwise.

Exercise: Implement this function and test it.

We can now start thinking about the meat of our program: actually implementing the first strategy of constraint propagation. Recall that what we want to do is:

1. For each cell that has only a single value set, eliminate that value from all its peers
2. Since eliminating a value from a cell can cause it to only have a single value set, if this is the case, we should eliminate that value from all its peers

In order to implement this, what we need is:

1. A function to eliminate a value from a cell
2. Identifying what the peers are for a cell
3. A function that calls the above functions, i.e. checks, for all cells, which values can be eliminated

We already implemented 1) when we implemented the Cell class. Let's implement 2) next.

Finding Sudoku peers

Recall that the peers of a cell are the cells that are on either the same horizontal line, on the same vertical line, or in the same 3x3 sub-grid, i.e. in the same *unit* as the cell.

On the interface for our function that finds the peers, it seems like an easy way to encode cell positions could be to use integers which represent the index in our cell array. For example, an integer 0 would mean the first element in our array, or the cell at the very top left in the puzzle. The integer 50 would represent 50 % 9 = 5th column (0-indexed) and 50 / 9 = 5th row, or the bottom right cell in the middle 3x3 sub-grid.

This suggests we have the function declaration:

```
class Puzzle {
    public:
        ...

    private:
        std::vector<int> peers(int index) const;
        ...
};
```

That is, our function takes an integer as a parameter (which cell to find peers for), returns a vector of integers (which cells are the peers), and doesn't modify the data within the Puzzle object. Furthermore our function is *private* as it's not necessary to call this function from outside the class.

Now, here's one way to find the indices to the cells that are in the same vertical line:

```
std::vector<int> Puzzle::peers(int index) const
{
    std::vector<int> ret;

    int column = index % 9;
    for(int i = 0; i < 9; i++) {
        int peer_index = i * 9 + column;
        if(peer_index != index) {
            ret.push_back(peer_index);
        }
```

(continues on next page)

(continued from previous page)

```
11     }
12 
13     return ret;
14 }
```

Let's go through this in detail.

- Line 3: Our return variable.
- Line 5: We calculate *the column* for the given index by dividing by 9 and taking the remainder. This means that e.g. indices 4, 13, 22 etc. all return the same column (4).
- Line 6: We define a loop that goes through nine elements.
- Line 7: We calculate the *peer index* by multiplying the variable "i" by 9 and adding the column. This means that e.g. with index 4 we get 4, 13, 22 etc.
- Line 9: We add the peer index in the return variable.

Now, let's add the missing logic.

Exercise: Add the logic for the horizontal lines and the 3x3 grids in the above function. Try it out.

Digression: static member functions

You may have noticed that our function above not only does not modify the data in the Puzzle object ("cells" array), it doesn't even read it. This means it could actually be a free standing function and doesn't have to be a member function of the Puzzle class. On the other hand, it may be convenient to group functions that are relevant for certain classes together. There's a mechanism for this: *static member functions*. You can declare one by including the keyword "static" at the beginning of the declaration. You'll then need to name the class when calling it. Here's an example:

```
#include <iostream>

class Foo {
    public:
        static void foo();
};

void Foo::foo()
{
    std::cout << "static member function Foo::foo called\n";
}

int main(void)
{
    Foo::foo();
}
```

You mustn't use the keyword "const" to annotate the function const as it's a static function and hence won't be able to access object data anyway.

3.4.4 Propagation and search

We now have the means to eliminate a value from a cell, and to find the peers of a cell. This means we can put everything together and implement the actual propagation function.

Let's put this function together in C++:

```
1  bool Puzzle::propagate(int i)
2  {
3      bool has_only_one = cells[i].has_one();
4      if(has_only_one) {
5          auto value = cells[i].get_one();
6          auto peers = peers(i);
7          for(const auto& peer : peers) {
8              if(cells[peer].has(value)) {
9                  bool still_valid = cells[peer].eliminate(value);
10                 if(!still_valid)
11                     return false;
12                 still_valid = propagate(peer);
13                 if(!still_valid)
14                     return false;
15             }
16         }
17     }
18     return true;
19 }
```

The summary of this function is that we go through each cell, and if it only has one value, we eliminate the value from the peers if they had it. If a peer ends up only having one value, we repeat for that cell. If we invalidate the puzzle with this (which shouldn't happen), we stop.

Now, a couple of notes:

- Line 3: We previously introduced the Cell class member function "has_one". This is used here.
- Line 5: We need an additional function to get the single value (although "get_values" could be used as well).
- Line 6: We call the function "peers" which returns the peers of a cell.
- Line 7: We iterate through all the peers.

- Line 8: We can access the peers in the "cells" array by index "peer", and call the Cell class member function "has" which should return true if the value is possible for the cell. The function is yet to be defined.
- Line 12: We call this function for the peer; recursion. What happens is another function call is pushed to the stack, such that we enter the function "propagate" again but with the variable "i" being set to "peer" for this second call. Once that function call returns then we end up at line 12 again, with "i" at the original value, continuing the original for loop to process the rest of the peers. With recursion, it's important to have a *base case*, i.e. a case where the recursive call will not be made, to avoid infinite loop. Our base cases are either no cells having only one value, or all peers already having a single value.

Recursion is generally equivalent to iteration (e.g. for loops) but can be useful because, like in this case, the stack of variables to use is implicitly stored in the call stack. Were one to replace recursion with iteration in this case, one would need to add another variable to hold the indices where elimination is required.

The following diagram demonstrates how the function uses recursion to propagate the elimination through the cells:

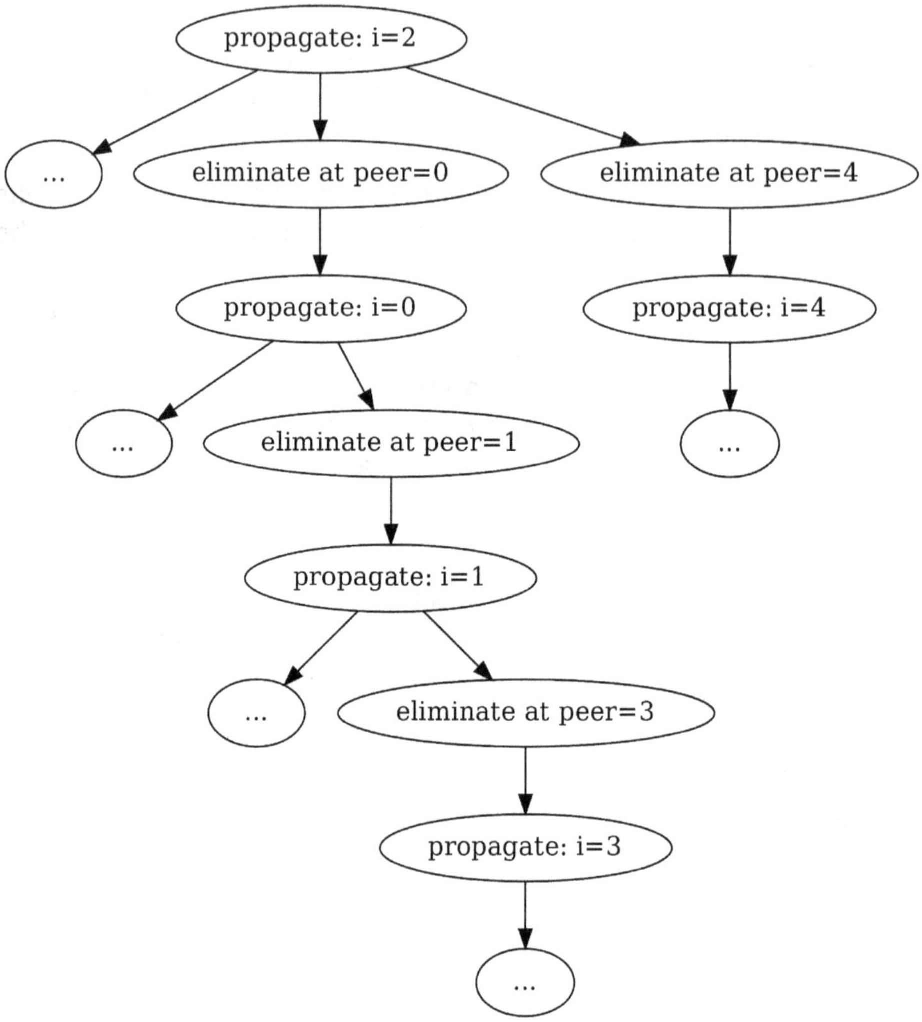

What we have here, after filling out the blanks, is the propagation function, which eliminates numbers from peer cells, and also propagates this if the peer cell ends up with only one value.

Exercise: Implement the “get_one” and “has” member functions for the Cell class.

Exercise: What happens when the user of the Cell class calls “get_one” but the cell has more than one value? What is the cell has no values at all (all numbers eliminated)? What would you expect to happen? Is it possible to improve the has_one/get_one interface to avoid invalid use?

Now, let’s put everything together:

- Parse the Sudoku puzzle from the previous section into a Puzzle object
- Call propagate() whenever you set a value of a cell
- Check if it's already solved using the solved() function
- Print out the puzzle after reading it

If everything works correctly, your program should be able to solve the example Sudoku puzzle just by using constraint propagation alone.

Exercise: Put everything together and see if you can solve the first puzzle. If not, debug.

Now we have enough to solve one easy Sudoku puzzle, but our program won't solve most puzzles, especially not the difficult ones. To test, here's one more difficult puzzle:

```
.7...18......7......6..91.....415.78...6.345........1.56..3....
↪78...6.499...5....
```

Searching

The next puzzle to solve is searching. Recall that we wanted to propagate constraints where possible but at some point we won't be able to progress any further and have to guess (search). How searching should work in principle is this:

- We pick one cell where we make a guess (namely the one with the least possible options to minimise the number of searches)
- We make a copy of the current puzzle and make a guess on this copy (by calling the "set" member function of the cell object)
- We propagate this guess
- If propagation shows we've solved the puzzle, we're done
- If propagation shows we haven't solved the puzzle but can't progress any further, we repeat this (search recursively again on this board)
- If propagation shows we've ended up with an invalid puzzle (wrong guess), we throw out this copy and guess a different number on the

same cell. If we've tried all numbers then we've made a wrong guess at some point before and return from our (recursive) function call.

What we have here is *depth-first search*. It's called depth first because we follow one "path" until we either find the solution, in which case we return this, or a dead end, in which case we try the next path. It's similar to trying to find the exit from a maze by always following the wall on one side; you may have to traverse the maze quite a lot but you'll find the exit eventually (if it exists). This is in contrast to *breadth-width search* which, instead of following one path down, visits each neighbouring node first before progressing further down the graph.

The following diagram illustrates depth-first search by example:

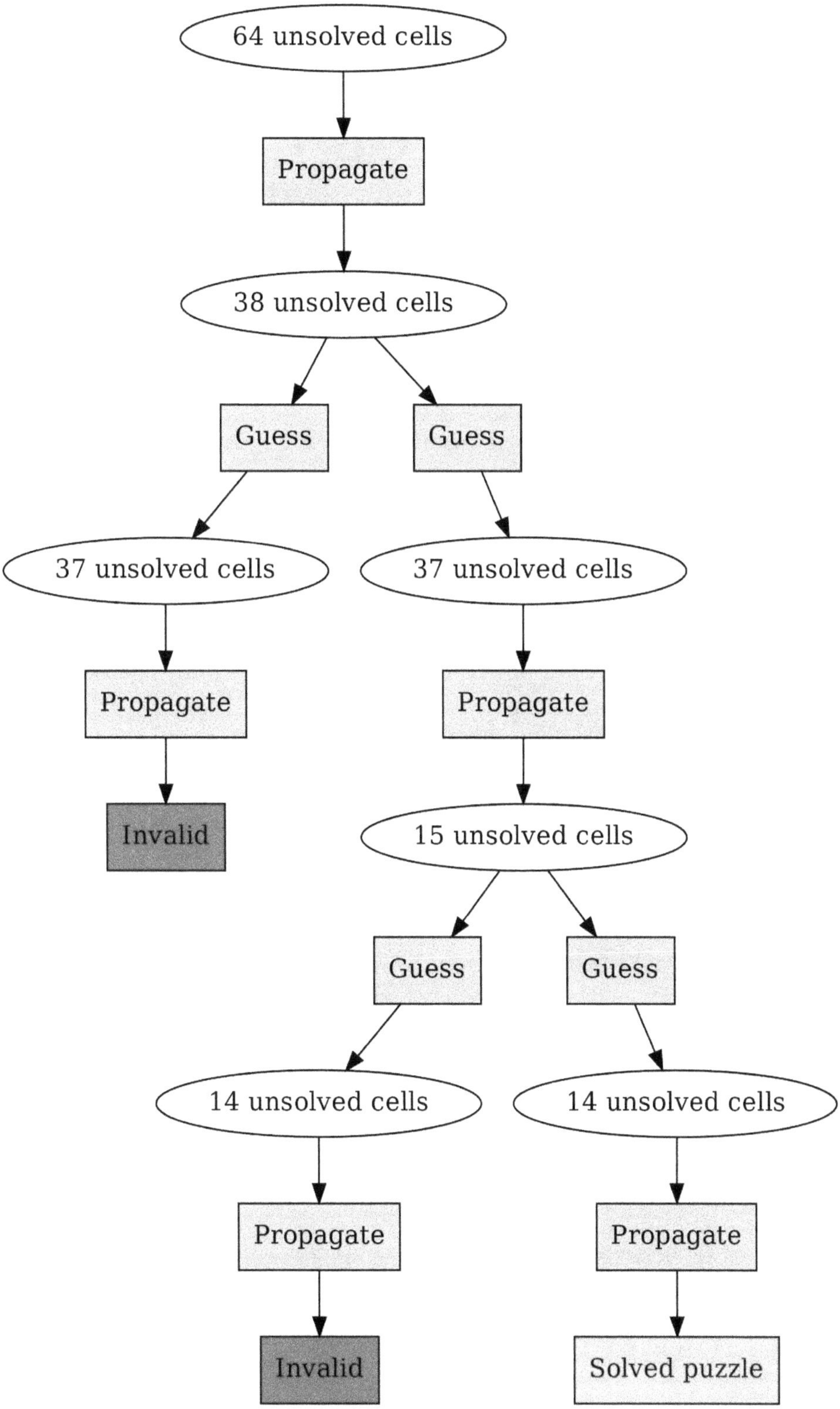
64 unsolved cells
Propagate
38 unsolved cells
Guess
Guess
37 unsolved cells
37 unsolved cells
Propagate
Propagate
Invalid
15 unsolved cells
Guess
Guess
14 unsolved cells
14 unsolved cells
Propagate
Propagate
Invalid
Solved puzzle

Here, we start with 64 unsolved cells. After propagation, we still have 38 so we have to guess. After a guess and a propagation we find we have an invalid puzzle so the guess was wrong. We then make another guess and propagate, leading to 15 unsolved cells. We make a guess and propagate, but find an invalid puzzle again. We backtrack and make another guess, and propagate, which finally leads us to the solved puzzle.

Generally speaking we can agree on the following structure:

- The Puzzle class has a member function "search", which, when called, will return a Puzzle class which is expected to be the solved puzzle
- The "search" member function does the following:
  - Check if this puzzle is solved; if so then return self
  - Check if any of the cells in this puzzle are invalid, i.e. don't have any valid options; if so then return self
  - Find the cell with the smallest number of valid options (but still more than 1)
  - For all the options in the selected cell, make a copy of the puzzle, set a value in the copy, search in the copy; if solution found then return it, else return self

Now, in terms of syntax, there are a couple of useful things to know.

Working with "this"

In C++, "this" is a keyword which means a pointer to the current object. In our case, it allows us to make a copy of our object. Here's an example use:

```
Puzzle Puzzle::search()
{
    if(solved()) {
        return *this;
    } else {
        int cell_index_to_guess = /* ... */
        auto possible_guesses = cells.at(cell_index_to_guess).
↪values();
        for(auto guess : possible_guesses) {
            Puzzle alt = *this;
```

(continues on next page)

(continued from previous page)

```
            alt.set_cell(cell_index_to_guess, guess);
            bool valid = alt.propagate();
            if(valid) {
                alt = alt.search();
                if(alt.solved()) {
                    return alt;
                }
            }
        }
    }
    return *this;
}
```

Here, we define a function named "search" which is a member function of the class Puzzle. It has Puzzle as its return value. We check if this Puzzle is solved, and if so, we return the *dereferenced pointer* to "this", meaning a copy of the Puzzle. If this Puzzle is not solved we call "search" recursively. (Because we set a cell value each time we search, we either find a solution or a dead end.)

Exercise: Finish the above function. Call it from your program. See if you can solve the more difficult Sudoku puzzle.

Solving more Sudoku puzzles

There is a file downloadable at the book web site containing 30 easy Sudoku puzzles, courtesy QQWing, an open source Sudoku puzzle generator.

Exercise: Save the above to a file. Rewrite your program to read each of these, and solve them all one after another. See how long it takes. (On Unix, you can time your program execution by prefixing the command with "time", e.g. "time ls".)

There is a file downloadable at the book web site containing 30 difficult Sudoku puzzles, courtesy QQWing.

Exercise: Solve these puzzles as well. If you get tired of waiting, remember to compile your program with optimisations, that is, with the compiler command line flag "-O2" which can speed up C++ programs significantly.

Constraint propagation with units

We've missed one part of our plan: in the introduction we said that "another common strategy is to see if a number has been ruled out for all cells in a unit except one. In this case it must be the correct number for that cell."

This means that if e.g. we have a row where a cell could have values 2, 3 and 7, but the number 7 was eliminated in all peers, then we can assign the number 7 for this cell.

Exercise: Implement this strategy as part of the propagation function. Note that you may find it necessary to use recursion. See if this strategy speeds up your program execution. You may want to reuse parts of your function to identify peers of a cell, and rewrite it to suit you better.

Now we have a program that can solve all Sudoku puzzles fairly quickly.

Exercise: Look up Peter Norvig's essay on solving Sudoku puzzles online, which served as inspiration for this chapter.

CHAPTER

FOUR

STAGE 2

Our last stage involves some larger projects as well as introducing final, somewhat more advanced topics.

4.1 Larger software

4.1.1 Introduction to larger software

> There are two ways of constructing a software design. One way is to make it so simple that there are obviously no deficiencies. And the other way is to make it so complicated that there are no obvious deficiencies.
>
> —C.A.R. Hoare

We've had and solved a few different smaller software problems. You may wonder, what about real life, professional, large scale software problems. This chapter discusses this in more detail.

Overview

Though not always obvious, the typical flow for software development, and indeed much of engineering in general is:

- Capturing the requirements - understanding what needs to be built
- Capturing the engineering specification - understanding how to build what needs to be built; this typically *breaks down* the problem into *components* or sub-tasks
- Implementing each component and testing them individually
- Integrating all components to the final software and testing it
- Quality assurance, or validation - checking that the end product meets the original requirements

Depending on the software, problem at hand and lots of other factors, all these steps can be followed at e.g. two-week cycles, or multi-year cycles, or anything in between. The terminology also often differs between companies and kinds of software. For example, a web site may have a new request from a user to add new functionality to the website; this may require getting more information from the customer, planning the technical changes to the web site and implementing these, and finally checking whether the result works as intended both from internal and user's point of view. On the other hand, e.g. developing software for a space shuttle may require several years to capture the requirements before planning, implementing, integrating and testing the software.

In this chapter we'll build software from scratch to address a very specific use case: we imagine we're a software company with a contract from a local transport company to improve the public transport bus service. The company has fitted GPS transmitters to the local buses and would like to improve the experience of the passengers waiting for a bus by installing screens on the bus stops which would show which buses are expected to soon arrive at the bus stop, and when.

This is a problem that could potentially require a fairly large amount of software; in our case, as we'll cut some corners, we'll end up with relatively little code. However, it's enough to introduce the general steps of software development and software design.

Specifically, we'll start with having the requirements well captured in advance, which often is not the case. We'll go through breaking down the problem space, and discuss two different ways to actually implement such a software. We'll end up with two implementations for this problem, which sum up to a total of around 600 lines of C++ and 200 lines of Python. The reader will get to write these two implementations as well. The reader should ideally be able to finish the two implementations in about 40 hours.

Requirements

The following is the requirement specification for the software. It's written by our customer. It describes what the expected output of the software is, what the inputs to the software are, and what external constraints the software has.

Requirements

General

The software will need to output a table on a 640x480 screen displaying the buses arriving at the bus stop where the screen is installed, to the best of the knowledge of the software, as specified by its inputs.

The software will run on a computer directly connected to the screen.

The output table will need to have the following rows:

- First row must include the bus stop name as well as the current time
- Rows 2-8 must include the bus route number, the final destination of the bus route, and the expected arrival time of the bus

The expected arrival time must either be derived from the bus schedule (if GPS data is not available) or from the GPS data (if available).

If no GPS data is available, the arrival time must reflect this by prefixing the time with text "ca.".

The bus schedule data must be used directly when displaying the bus arrival time.

The times must be displayed in 24 hour format and contain the hour and the minute.

The routes displayed must be sorted such that the one arriving soonest must be displayed at the top.

The first row text must be in yellow while the other rows must be in white. The background colour must be white.

The table must not have any borders.

This is an example ASCII representation of the table:

```
Park Avenue                 10:00


72  Hill Street             10:04
29  Central Park            10:05
3   Park Street             10:05
6   Manhattan Square        10:09
848 Wall Street             10:11
3   Park Street             10:12
848 Wall Street         ca. 10:17
```

This is an example image representation of the final screen:

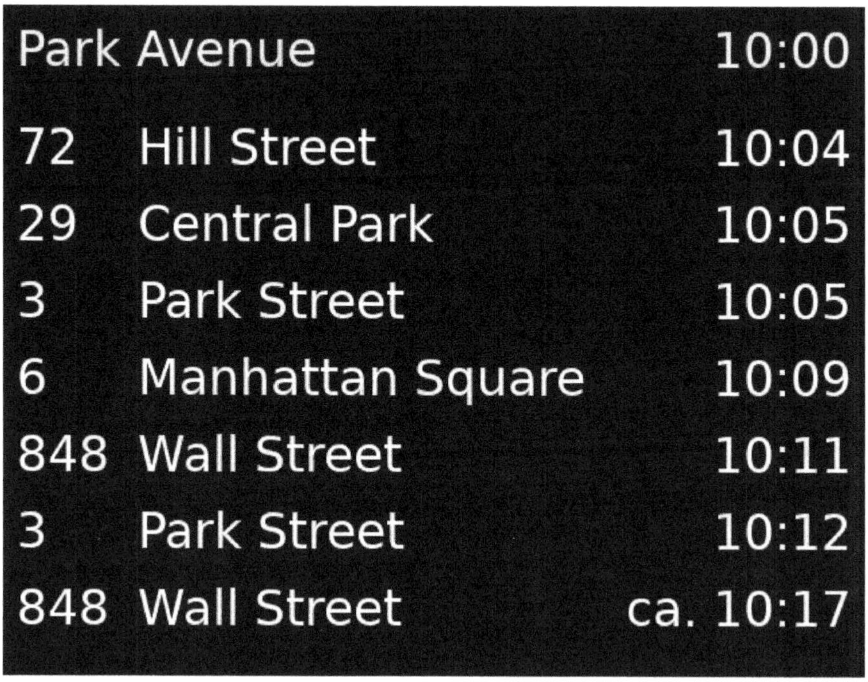

The font to use is Deja Vu Sans.

Inputs

The system will have the following inputs: bus schedule, historical GPS data from previous bus runs, current GPS data from current buses and current bus stop name.

The bus schedule is a file available at “sched.txt”. The file is an ASCII text file with several, unspecified number of lines. Each line has data in the following format:

```
<integer representing the route number> <integer representing the start number> <integer representing the hour of the bus arriving at the stop> <integer representing the minute of the bus arriving at the stop>
e.g.:
3 1 5 6
3 2 5 16
[...]
```

In other words, each line has four integers separated by spaces. The first integer identifies the route. The second is a counter for the bus for this route for each day (start number). The third and fourth integers represent the time the bus is expected to arrive at the stop.

The schedule is the same for all days of the week.

The historical GPS data is a file available at “gps.txt”. The file is an ASCII text file with several, unspecified number of lines. Each line has data in the following format:

```
<integer representing the route number> <floating point␣
↪number representing the time it took for the bus to reach␣
↪the bus stop from this position in minutes> <the distance␣
↪from the measurement position to the bus stop on the X␣
↪axis (west-east axis) in meters> <the distance from the␣
↪measurement position to the bus stop on the Y axis (north-
↪south axis) in meters>
e.g.:
3 10.8713536724 -4003.3505052 -3998.10233076
3 10.7045996484 -3943.15506994 -3938.06461792
[...]
```

In other words, each line has four numbers separated by spaces. The first integer identifies the route. The second is the time it took for the bus to reach the bus stop at the time the data was collected. The third and fourth are the position coordinates relative to the bus stop. They've been normalised such that the unit is in meters as opposed to degrees.

The current bus GPS data is a file available at “gps_raw.txt”. The file is an ASCII text file with several, unspecified number of lines. Each line has data in the following format:

```
<integer representing the route number> <integer␣
↪representing the start number> <the distance from the␣
↪measurement position to the bus stop on the X axis (west-
↪east axis) in meters> <the distance from the measurement␣
↪position to the bus stop on the Y axis (north-south axis)␣
↪in meters> <an integer representing whether the bus has␣
↪already passed this bus stop; 0 meaning no, 2 meaning yes>␣
↪[other possible data to be ignored]
e.g.:
72 21 -1534.20182433 1469.51178823 0 3 5.82836846952
3 30 -200.376943403 -205.032704345 2 -4 -0.345019886326
[...]
```

In other words, each line has at least five numbers separated by spaces. Each line could have more numbers which are not to be used. The first number identifies the route. The second identifies the start number as is used in the schedule file. The third and fourth provide the relative position of the bus to the bus stop as is used in the historical GPS file. The fifth identifies whether the bus has already passed the bus stop.

The current bus GPS data is updated automatically by another process running on the system approximately every 10 seconds. The program must take into account that the current GPS data file may be empty because it's being rewritten. In this case the contents of the previous GPS file must be used.

There may not be GPS data available for all buses approaching the bus stop.

The current bus stop name will be passed to the program as a command line parameter. The program will be started using: './bus <bus stop name>'; e.g. './bus "Park Avenue"'

The algorithm to identify the time to reach the bus stop from GPS data must work as follows:

- The time to reach the bus stop is assumed to be the average time of all the points in the historical data within 100 meters of the current bus position for the route of the bus.

If a bus is marked as having already passed the bus stop in the GPS data, it must not be shown in the final table.

The mapping between the route numbers and the final destinations is the following:

- 3 - Park Street
- 6 - Manhattan Square
- 29 - Central Park
- 72 - Hill Street
- 848 - Wall Street

Constraints

The program will run on a Linux OS on an embedded system with 1GB of RAM and a 800 MHz CPU. The program can store several megabytes of data in the current working directory, for storing any intermediate files. The current working directory will have the font file available as "DejaVuSans.ttf".

It will have access to the files described above using normal file operations.

It has access to a screen with resolution 640x480, 16 bits of colour.

The screen is available through the fbdev Linux subsystem.

The program will need access to current date and time. These are available using normal OS time functions.

Sounds fun, doesn't it?

We won't actually have the hardware to try this out so we'll have to simulate. We'll have a few input files to work with; for output we'll have to write something that displays the view matching the requirements on our development computer, and not need to worry about the actual hardware.

I should note, the overall architecture as described or implied by the above requirements specification could be done differently. For example, the transporting company might not want the software on the bus stops to calculate the estimated bus arrival time; instead this could be done on the central server which would then provide the estimated arrival time to the bus stop software instead of providing the historical and current GPS data.

However, this architecture makes for a somewhat more interesting software design problem.

You can find download links at the web site of this book for input files necessary for testing.

You can download the font file from the Deja Vu fonts web page. You may already have the font available somewhere on your computer.

4.1.2 Breaking software down to components

> Controlling complexity is the essence of computer programming.
>
> —Brian Kernighan

So, we now have the requirements captured to the point where we can start specifying the software, i.e. how to fulfil the requirements.

We have some understanding of the inputs and the outputs of our software: the output is the visual output on the screen. The main inputs, ignoring minor ones such as the name of the bus stop, are the bus schedules, the historical GPS data, and the current GPS data. The first two are fixed while the last one changes every ten seconds or so. How would we go about actually planning how to write this software?

Drawing this as a diagram - we'll start with this:

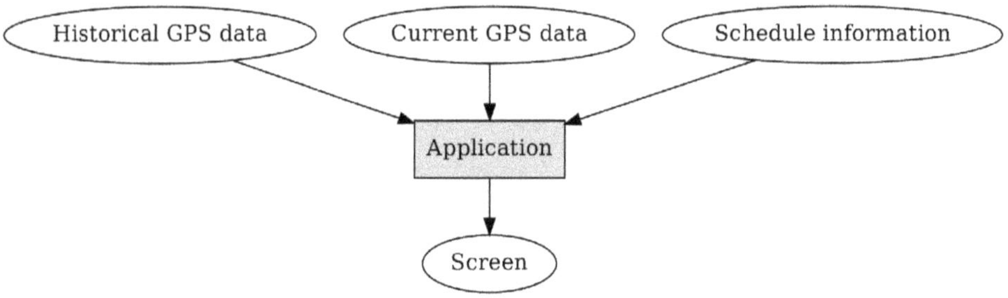

Here, round items represent some or other kind of data, while square, grey boxes represent logic, or software components.

As a thought exercise, we should further assume we have a team of software engineers, e.g. five people assigned to work on this. Ideally all of them would have something useful to do at all times.

Keeping this in mind, one very useful way to decompose software to identify the components is to specify *interfaces* between components, i.e. the inputs and outputs required for each component.

In order to identify the components, we could start e.g. from the end, i.e. the final output, or the output on the screen. The requirement specification gave us an example of this: the first row having the current date and the bus stop name, other rows having the time of arrival, bus route number and destination for each of the upcoming buses. If we treat this as a separate component then we can say the purpose of this component is to display the input data, whereby the input data simply is a few text labels. A few being 23 to be exact - two on the first row, then three on each following row, times seven.

We've now identified our first component:

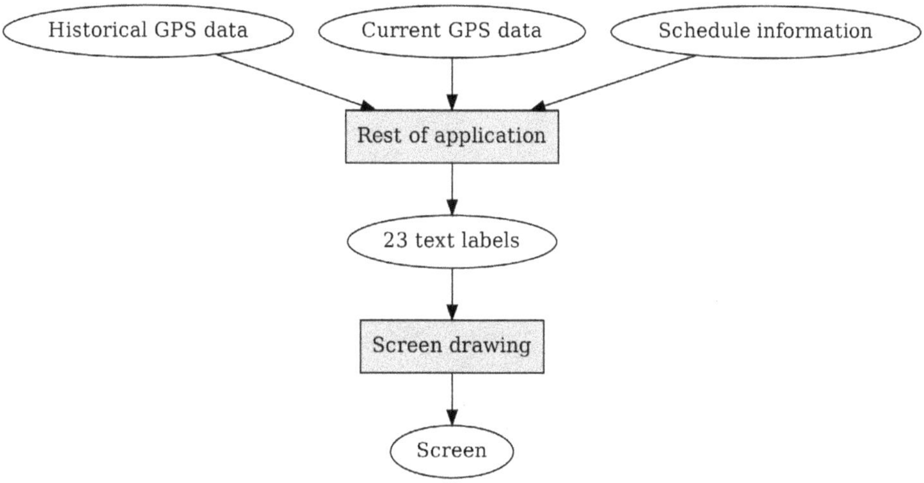

Now, let's find out how to generate these 23 text labels. The first two are relatively trivial in that we don't depend on the main inputs for them. How do we know whether we should use the GPS data or the schedule data? The requirement spec says we should use GPS data when available and schedule data otherwise. It seems just figuring out which data to use or not is worthy of another component. This also implies we could have one component processing the GPS data, and one component processing the schedule data.

So we could have one component that reads in some kind of GPS data and some kind of schedule data, with the goal of outputting 23 text labels. What should the input formats be for this component? The inputs will be generated by the components handling the GPS and the schedule data, and it seems simplest to have a single format for these two. Putting all of this together, we have:

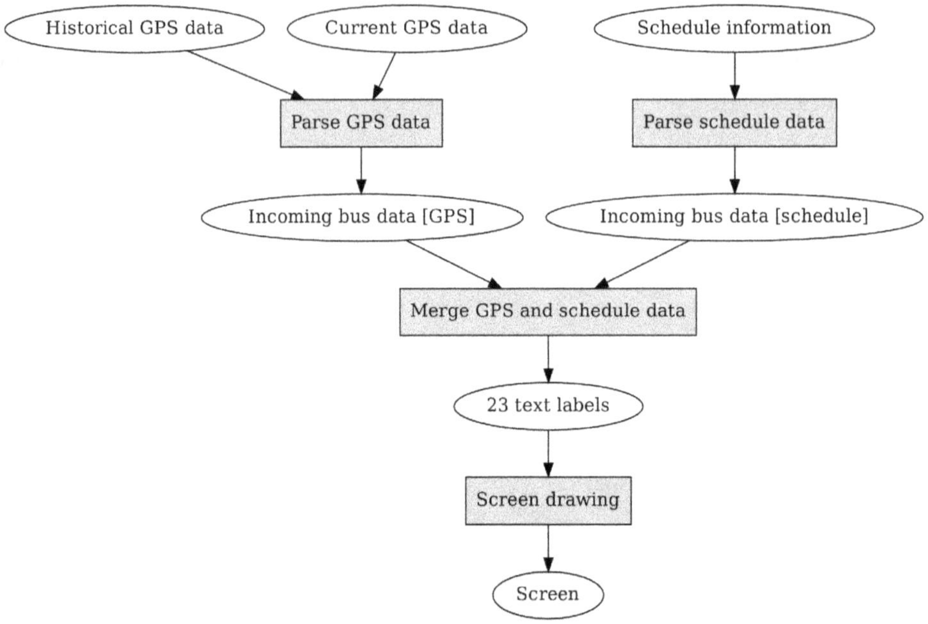

Now, it looks like we've identified our main components. We can then further define the functionality of the components as well as the interfaces. First the components:

- Screen drawing: takes 23 strings as input, with the purpose of drawing these on the screen
- Merge GPS and schedule data: takes two incoming bus data sets as input, finds the seven buses that seem to arrive at the bus stop first, preferring buses with GPS information if available, and generates 23 strings as output which identify the bus route numbers, destinations and the times of arrival. The input data will need to include the start number so we can match GPS entries with schedule entries.
- Parse GPS data: read in the GPS data and calculate the estimated arrival time for each bus for which GPS data exists using the algorithm specified in the requirements (average time in historical data for that location), and output the bus route numbers, start numbers and estimated time of arrival
- Parse schedule data: read in the schedule data and output the bus route numbers, start numbers and planned time of arrival for the next few buses that are next expected at the bus stop

Then the interfaces:

- 23 text labels: 23 strings (trivial, e.g. in an array).
- Incoming bus data (same format for whichever source): for each incoming bus, the route number, the start number, the type of arrival (estimated from GPS data or planned) and the time need to be captured. The data format itself could then be e.g. an array of structs, whereby each struct contains this information.

It's worth pointing out that identifying the components and the interfaces is closer to software design and architecture, and less about actual coding, and hence there is no obvious right or wrong answer - different people will end up with different designs.

Engineering specification

Now, as mentioned before, we will write two different engineering specifications and have two different implementations to fulfil the requirements, for the purpose of understanding the different trade offs between software design decisions.

The first specification will follow the *Unix philosophy*. The Unix philosophy originates from the developers of Unix, including Ken Thompson, Dennis Ritchie and Doug McIlroy, and emphasises minimalist, modular software development. It was later summarised this way:

> This is the Unix philosophy: Write programs that do one thing and do it well. Write programs to work together. Write programs to handle text streams, because that is a universal interface.
>
> —Doug McIlroy

The Unix philosophy has also been summarised as "KISS", or "Keep it simple, stupid". Much has been written about the Unix philosophy but applying it to our problem at hand, we could arrive at the following engineering spec:

Engineering spec 1

The software shall consist of five executables: parse_gps, sched, merge and display to implement the main behaviour and a main executable, bus, to glue them together.

"parse_gps" shall take three parameters: current time, filename identifying the current GPS data (gps_raw.txt) and filename identifying the historical GPS data (gps.txt). It shall output, to stdout, the incoming bus data in the following format:

- Five integers per row
- Several rows (as many as necessary)
- First integer is the bus route number
- Second integer is the start number
- Third is the hour of estimated arrival
- Fourth is the minute of estimated arrival
- Fifth is the identifier for the type: 0 for GPS data, 1 for schedule data, 2 if the bus has already passed the bus stop

For buses that have already passed the bus stop, the time (hour and minute) can be zeroes.

"parse_gps" shall read in the two input files, then, for all buses with current GPS data, calculate the estimated arrival time, and finally print out the incoming and passed buses in the format as specified above.

"sched" shall take two parameters: current time and filename identifying the schedule data (sched.txt). It shall output, to stdout, the incoming bus data in the same format as "parse_gps". It shall find the next 50 buses planned to approach the bus stop and output the data for these.

"merge" shall take four parameters: our bus stop name, current time, and filenames for the output of "parse_gps" and "sched". It shall output, to stdout, 23 lines, each one containing the text for one label, from top to bottom, from left to right, i.e. the bus stop name, current time, then route number, destination and arrival time for the next seven buses.

"display" shall take one parameter: a filename for the output of "merge". It shall output, to a window in a test environment, the bus information as specified in the requirements. It shall read the contents of the input file every ten seconds to update the output view.

"bus" shall take no parameters. It shall run "parse_gps", "sched" and "merge" every ten seconds, such that the final output file is updated. It shall start "display" in the background with the output of "merge" as the input parameter.

This is a fairly high level spec - it doesn't specify the contents of the individual components - but it does specify the interfaces in some detail, and how they should be integrated to run together.

It doesn't specify the programming language for the executables. We'll be using Python for "parse_gps", "sched" and "merge"; C++ for "display" and bash for "bus".

The other engineering spec we'll write is somewhat opposite to the Unix philosophy: it specifies a *monolithic application* - an application where all functionality is integrated into a single executable.

While the engineering spec here won't specify the language to use, we will use C++ for the implementation. However, in general it could be written in almost any language, e.g. Java or C#.

Engineering spec 2

The software shall consist of one executable "bus" with the following input parameters: a string identifying the current bus stop and three filenames for the input files (gps_raw.txt, gps.txt and sched.txt).

It shall, every ten seconds, perform the following tasks:

- Read in the current GPS data
- Generate the data for incoming and passed buses based on the GPS data
- Generate the data for incoming buses based on the schedule data
- Merge the data for incoming buses to generate 23 labels

- Render the 23 labels on the screen

The data flow is the following:

- The data from the input files is parsed to data structures containing the route numbers, start numbers etc. as is available in the input files
- The incoming bus data has the following fields:
  - int route_nr;
  - int start_nr;
  - Time time;
  - Kind kind;
- "Time" is a class containing the fields hour and minute. Kind is an enumeration describing the kind of data, i.e. either GPS, Schedule or Passed.
- The task to merge the data will read in two arrays of incoming bus data (for GPS and scheduled data). The output of the merging shall result in the 23 labels used for rendering.

Here, the main differences to the first spec are that there is only one executable, and hence the incoming bus data does not need to be stored in intermediate files but is instead passed from one component to another in a data structure.

As with design in general, there is no right or wrong answer on which design is better. There are some pros and cons to the two approaches though:

- When separating the functionality to multiple executables, different components can be implemented in different programming languages. This can be a good thing in terms of flexibility but can also create more confusion.
- Having multiple executables involves extra overhead in writing out data to intermediate formats and then parsing it in the next step.
- Having multiple executables can make it easier to test each component in isolation.

In any case, it's important to note that however the functionality is written, the main thing to do is decompose the problem to subproblems, with well defined interfaces, such that the components can be implemented and tested separately. In our case, we have the same overall design in both approaches, also to highlight that the decomposition stays the same independent of the approach on how to write the actual code. If we had a team of engineers working on this, each could mock up some input data and start implementing their component. After each component was seen to work individually, they could then be integrated to the final application.

4.1.3 Drawing to a screen using SDL2

Let's tackle the problem of drawing something on the screen.

The requirement is that an image will be drawn on the screen at the bus stop, which is running an embedded CPU with Linux, with the screen being driven by fbdev (framebuffer device). We don't have to care about these details because we don't have the actual hardware available so we'll have to simulate it. What one can do in this case is write an application that can be run on a desktop computer (or some other device that's easily available), but make it configurable or portable such that if the same code was compiled for the system running at the bus stop, it would use the relevant system interfaces to display the information on the bus stop screen instead. When running the code on our development computer we'll simply create a window and draw in it instead.

Now, depending on the OS you're using (Linux, Mac, Windows), the interface to create a window and draw something on it is different. We'll skip this platform specific bit and instead use a library called *SDL2*, or *Simple DirectMedia Layer 2*, which is a relatively thin library providing one interface for all our window handling and drawing needs. Although SDL2 is common among game developers, it's also fairly widely used with embedded software.

What SDL2 does, in a nutshell, is provide functions that do something like this:

```
void SDL_CreateWindow(int width, int height)
{
#ifdef _WIN32
    /* Windows specific API calls are here */
#elif __linux__
    /* Linux specific API calls are here */
#elif __APPLE__
#ifdef TARGET_OS_MAC
    /* Mac OS specific API calls are here */
#elif TARGET_OS_IPHONE
    /* iPhone specific API calls are here */
#else
#error Unknown Apple target
#endif /* __APPLE__ */
```

(continues on next page)

(continued from previous page)

```
#else
#error Unknown platform
#endif
```

What this exemplifies is the use of the C preprocessor to define what code to compile. The C compiler typically defines the platform specific defines automatically, but it's also possible to set defines either in source code or in the compiler command line. Long story short, the people behind SDL have taken care of this such that we won't have to, and we can simply call the SDL functions. As a bonus, SDL supports Linux fbdev as well (which is a rather primitive interface for displaying graphics on Linux but popular on embedded systems) so our software could theoretically actually work on a bus stop.

Exercise: SDL2 can be downloaded online although your OS may also provide it. In either case, install SDL2 on your computer. One way to do this is to download the source code, extract it and compile it using "./configure && make". You can check out the file INSTALL.txt for more details. The author used SDL2 version 2.0.8.

Although SDL2 is a C library (and hence can be used from C++ directly), many *bindings* to it exist from other language. A binding is a simple wrapper that allows using a library written in one language from another language. E.g. Java bindings for SDL2 exist; this means that there is a Java library available which does nothing more but calls the C SDL2 functions, allowing the use of SDL2 from Java. Typically programming languages only have built in support for calling C functions. This means that if a library was written in e.g. Java and one wanted to call it from Go, this might not be easily possible without first writing a wrapper of the library in C and then calling the C library from Go. The takeaway is that our bus stop program could be written in e.g. Java if we wanted to.

Hello world in SDL2

```
#include <stdio.h>

#include "SDL.h"

```

(continues on next page)

(continued from previous page)

```
5  int main()
6  {
7      if(SDL_Init(SDL_INIT_VIDEO) != 0) {
8          fprintf(stderr, "Could not init SDL: %s\n", SDL_GetError());
9          return 1;
10     }
11     SDL_Window *screen = SDL_CreateWindow("My application",
12             SDL_WINDOWPOS_UNDEFINED,
13             SDL_WINDOWPOS_UNDEFINED,
14             640, 480,
15             0);
16     if(!screen) {
17         fprintf(stderr, "Could not create window\n");
18         return 1;
19     }
20     SDL_Renderer *renderer = SDL_CreateRenderer(screen, -1, SDL_RENDERER_SOFTWARE);
21     if(!renderer) {
22         fprintf(stderr, "Could not create renderer\n");
23         return 1;
24     }
25
26     SDL_SetRenderDrawColor(renderer, 0, 0, 0, 255);
27     SDL_RenderClear(renderer);
28     SDL_RenderPresent(renderer);
29     SDL_Delay(3000);
30
31     SDL_DestroyWindow(screen);
32     SDL_Quit();
33     return 0;
34 }
```

The above program should, when run, create a window with black contents, display it for three seconds, then terminate. It's a test case to ensure the library can be used.

Let's go through this line by line:

- Line 3: We include the header for the SDL library. This ensures we have the relevant SDL functions declared.

- Line 7: We initialise SDL, asking for support to video (i.e. drawing to a screen). We check the return value. If it's unequal to 0, we terminate.
- Lines 11-15: We create a window of size 640x480 with title "My application".
- Line 20: We create a renderer, i.e. something that can draw something to a window. We ask SDL to create a *software* renderer, i.e. something that doesn't use hardware acceleration (GPU) for drawing to the screen.
- Line 26: We set the colour to be used for clearing the screen to be black.
- Line 27: We ask the renderer to clear the screen.
- Line 28: We ask the renderer to *present* the contents. How rendering typically works is that all pixel colours are first set in a memory buffer, and presenting the contents actually interacts with the OS API to draw something on the actual screen. Hence, clearing the screen on line 27 effectively set the contents on the memory buffer.
- Line 29: We pause the execution for three seconds.
- Lines 31-33: We clean up and exit.

Now, let's try to compile and run this application to ensure we're able to use the SDL2 library.

E.g. on Linux, if you have the library installed via package manager, this command should compile the code:

```
g++ -Wall $(sdl2-config --cflags --libs) -o main sdl_hw.cpp
```

Here, $(sdl2-config ...) is a *shell expansion*, i.e. it executes the command within the parenthesis and includes the output in the command line. The contents typically are something along the lines of "-I/usr/include/SDL2 -D_REENTRANT -L/usr/lib -lSDL2". This means:

- -I/usr/include/SDL2: Include the path /usr/include/SDL2 in the path where to search for header files. In other words, when compiling, because we had the line #include "SDL.h" in our source code, the file SDL.h should be found somewhere during compilation. We can point to the directory where SDL.h can be found by using the -I switch.

- -L/usr/lib: Include the path /usr/lib in the path where to search for library files. In other words, when compiling, because we call functions such as SDL_Init(), the function should be compiled somewhere so our program can call it. We can point to the directory where the library containing the compiled code is by using the -L switch.
- -lSDL2. *Link* against the library SDL2. In other words, when linking our program to create the final executable, because we call functions such as SDL_Init(), the compiler needs to know which file includes the compiled functions. On Linux, with the combination of the -L/usr/lib flag above, we tell the compiler that we expect the library to be found at /usr/lib/libSDL2.so.

If we compiled the SDL2 source code ourselves but didn't install it on the system, we could compile the code e.g. using this command:

```
g++ -Wall -ISDL2-2.0.8/include -D_REENTRANT -LSDL2-2.0.8/build/.
↪libs -lSDL2 -o main sdl_hw.cpp
```

This basically does the same thing but tells the compiler to look for the header and library files in local directories instead of the system directories.

Exercise: Compile and run the above program. Try changing the clear colour and running again.

Now, you may wonder what all is there that SDL provides, and what are all the different parameters that the different functions can accept. This is a very valid question and is answered in the SDL *reference*.

Exercise: Look up the SDL documentation for the functions SDL_Init and SDL_CreateRenderer. Find the definitions of the functions in the SDL source code.

SDL and font handling

Now, what we want is display text on a screen using SDL. As nothing is ever as simple as you'd think when programming, SDL doesn't provide drawing text out of the box, but instead there's another library called SDL2_TTF which provides this functionality. How this works in a nutshell is that you initialise SDL2_TTF, then load a font from a .ttf file (the DejaVu Sans font that was referenced in the introduction), then use that font to create an SDL surface which we then convert to an SDL texture which we copy to the screen buffer using the renderer, finally showing the text on the screen when we present the buffer. Confused yet? The following diagram illustrates the data flow.

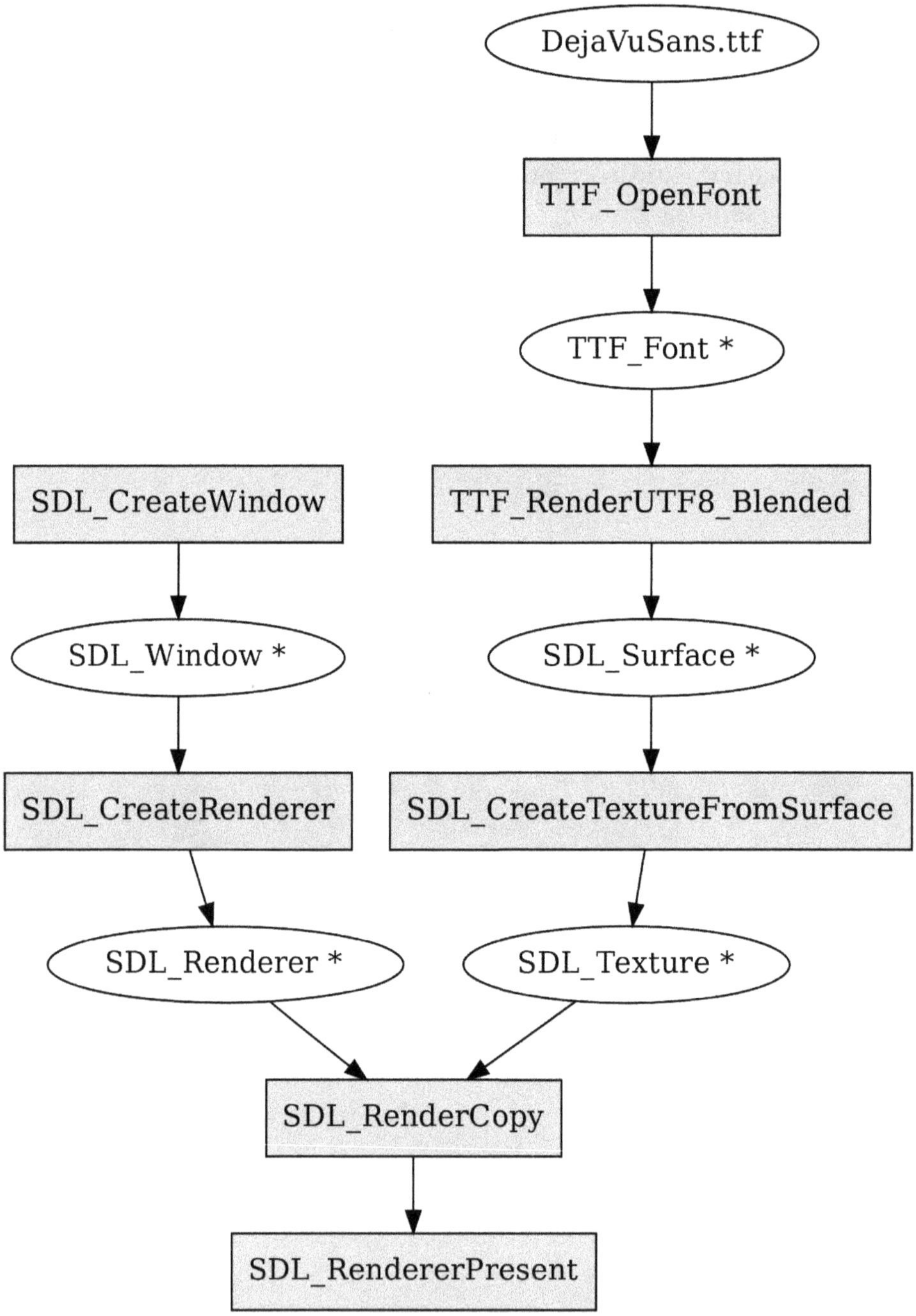

The good news is that we only need to implement this once.

Exercise: Install the SDL2_TTF library. As before, you may either install it using your OS or compile it from source.

Exercise: Look up the documentation for the functions TTF_OpenFont() and TTF_RenderUTF8_Blended().

Here's some code to demonstrate usage of SDL2_TTF together with the SDL2 renderer to draw some text.

```
#include <stdio.h>

#include "SDL.h"
#include "SDL_ttf.h"

int main()
{
    /* TODO: init SDL */
    if(TTF_Init() != 0) {
        fprintf(stderr, "Couldn't init SDL_ttf: %s\n", TTF_GetError());
        return 1;
    }
    TTF_Font *font = TTF_OpenFont("DejaVuSans.ttf", 72);
    if(!font) {
        fprintf(stderr, "Couldn't load font\n");
        return 1;
    }
    /* TODO: create SDL_Window and SDL_Renderer */

    SDL_Color col_white;
    col_white.r = 255;
    col_white.g = 255;
    col_white.b = 255;
    col_white.a = 255;
    SDL_Surface *text = TTF_RenderUTF8_Blended(font, "Hello world", col_white);

    /* TODO: clear the renderer */
    SDL_Texture *texture = SDL_CreateTextureFromSurface(renderer, text);
    SDL_FreeSurface(text);
    text = NULL;
    SDL_Rect dest;
    dest.x = 10;
    dest.y = 10;
```

(continues on next page)

(continued from previous page)

```
    SDL_QueryTexture(texture, NULL, NULL, &dest.w, &dest.h);
    SDL_RenderCopy(renderer, texture, NULL, &dest);
    SDL_DestroyTexture(texture);
    texture = NULL;
    /* TODO: present, delay and clean up both SDL and TTF libraries */

    return 0;
}
```

This code is unfortunately missing some key SDL2 calls. If it was complete, you could compile it with the same command as you compile the previous example, but with the added switch "-LSDL2_ttf" to also link against the SDL2_ttf library containing the TTF_* functions.

Exercise: Fix the TODOs to get a program that displays some text on the screen. It should display "Hello world" in the top left corner. Note that as the example code is, it will search for the font in the current working directory, i.e. where your shell is when you run the program. Make sure your font file can be found.

Now, provided we had the text labels for our bus stop, we should be able to actually display a window that meets the requirements. What we'll do in this section is that we'll have this bit of C++ code which is shared by both implementations of our software; our software following the Unix philosophy will create a text file with the labels which is read by the C++ code to display the correct window while our monolithic C++ application will take the labels as a function parameter and display them. In either case, the SDL code stays the same so we only need to implement that part once.

4.1.4 Drawing the schedule screen using SDL2

We're now able to draw some text on a screen using SDL. Let's expand this so we can draw the bus schedule screen.

As per the requirements and our engineering spec, we need to draw 23 different text labels. We'll want one piece of C++ code to be shared for both implementations but let's start with the simpler one - the Unix way. We have this written in our engineering spec:

- "display" shall take one parameter: a filename for the output of "merge". It shall output, to a window in a test environment, the bus information as specified in the requirements. It shall read the contents of the input file every ten seconds to update the output view.
- "merge" shall [...] output, to stdout, 23 lines, each one containing the text for one label, from top to bottom, from left to right, i.e. the bus stop name, current time, then route number, destination and arrival time for the next seven buses.

So let's adapt our SDL code to read in a text file which has 23 lines, and then display these lines on the final image.

If your existing SDL code is anything close to mine, it's difficult to extend. The exercise solution has all the code in one function, main(), which has about 50 lines of code including several variables declared along the way which we don't really care about but which are necessary for the rendering. Surely we can do better.

Refactoring

Taking existing code and modifying it such that the functionality stays the same but the code is cleaner or easier to maintain is called *refactoring*. Let's refactor our code to start with. First, let's consider how we'd want our code to look for the purpose of the specification of showing 23 different labels based on file contents. Our input is the file name, our output is shown on the screen, and we need a bunch of SDL related variables in between to take care of the displaying.

Generally, a function is a nice way to abstract *stateless* logic - where you have some certain input, causing some certain output, not specifically depending on anything external. A class is a way to capture *state* - such that the member functions of an object also produce some output for a certain input but the output also depends on the state, i.e. the member variables, of the object. Because we need a few variables which are relatively fixed after the initialisation, such as the font handle, let's implement a class that takes care of our task in a clean way.

A good way to start designing such a class is to write *the interface* - the public functions that the class exposes. We want the object creation to only take the filename as input, and we want to update the screen every ten seconds. It seems like one way to design this, then, is to have a constructor and a render member function. We'll also need a *destructor* - a function that's automatically called when the memory the object resides in is freed.

We can also already think about the private member variables for this class. Since we already have a starting point for our work in the previous exercise's main function, we can think of all the variables used in the main function to be private member variables of our class. We'll then end up with the following class declaration:

```
class SDL_Schedule {
    public:
        SDL_Schedule(const std::string& filename);
        ~SDL_Schedule();
        void render();

    private:
        TTF_Font *font;
        SDL_Window *screen;
        SDL_Renderer *renderer;
        SDL_Color col_white;
        SDL_Rect dest;
};
```

In other words, let's refactor our code such that it does what it did before, but such that the old code now resides in a class, whereby the initialisation and the cleanup is captured in the constructor and destructor functions and the actual rendering of the text happens in another member function. This way, when making further changes to actually use the data from the file to decide what to render, future code changes will be easier to make.

Once we have the functions defined then we can have the main function instantiate an object of this class, call the render() function, wait for three seconds, and exit. The main function could have e.g. the following contents:

```
int main(int argc, char** argv)
{
    if(argc != 2) {
        fprintf(stderr, "Usage: %s <filename>\n", argv[0]);
        return 1;
    }
    SDL_Schedule sched(argv[1]);
    sched.render();
    SDL_Delay(3000);

    return 0;
}
```

Here we also parse the command line options. Although we don't yet have any code to read in the file, as per the class interface we'll need to pass the function some string as the filename, so we can just as well go ahead and pass on the actual command line parameter. If we were to compile such a main function to a binary and run the binary with command line options such as e.g.:

```
$ ./main file.txt
```

...then the variable "argc" (argument count) would be 2, and the variable "argv" (argument vector) would be a pointer to an array of two pointers, first one (argv[0]) pointing to a character buffer containing "./main" (null delimited) and the second one (argv[1]) pointing to "file.txt". This way we can access the command line options in our C or C++ code.

Here, then, we check that there was one command line parameter passed to our function, and pass that on to our constructor. We then call the "render" member function, wait for three seconds, and exit the program, which also calls the destructor of our SDL_Schedule class as a side effect.

Exercise: Refactor your existing code to live in a class instead of a function. You need to define the functions mentioned above, i.e. the constructor, the destructor and the render function, and ensure they include the code of your old main function which displayed "Hello world" on the screen. You don't need to read in the file contents at this stage.

This pattern of having a class constructor do all the necessary initialisation to use the object, and the destructor free all acquired resources is called *RAII* (resource acquisition is initialisation), and is a C++ specific pattern for ensuring objects have a valid state. In order to have good error handling in the constructor, it's typically necessary to *throw an exception* in case of an error. This can be done e.g. by stating 'throw std::runtime_error("error")' in your code. You may need to #include <stdexcept> to get std::runtime_error in scope.

Now that we've done some refactoring, we can go ahead and do the rest of the work.

Reading in the labels

A quick online search will reveal a way to parse lines from a file to a std::vector<std::string> in C++:

```
#include <fstream>
#include <sstream>

...

std::ifstream ifs(file);
std::string contents((std::istreambuf_iterator<char>(ifs)),
        (std::istreambuf_iterator<char>()));
std::stringstream ss(contents);
std::string to;
std::vector<std::string> res;
while(std::getline(ss, to, '\n')) {
    res.push_back(to);
}
```

Here, "file" is our input file name. The C++ way includes defining several intermediate variables but the final output we actually care about is stored in the "res" variable.

Exercise: Integrate the above to your program. Store the parameter to your constructor in a member variable. In the render function, read the file contents using the snippet above. For now you don't need to do much with the result though you may want to write it out to stdout. In order to test it, create an input file.

You may also download a sample input file from the book web site.

Now, instead of drawing a single "Hello world" label, let's draw 23 of them.

You'll need to write a loop in your render() function that loops through your std::vector<std::string>.

Instead of passing a static string to TTF_RenderUTF8_Blended, pass in a string that you read from the file. You can convert an std::string to a character buffer by calling the "c_str()" member function, e.g:

```
std::string s("abc");
const char* my_pointer = s.c_str(); // my_pointer now points to
↪"abc"
```

Define another colour, in addition to white; this other colour should be yellow and used for the first row of labels. In your for loop, make the colour depend on the loop variable.

Before, for our "Hello world", we used an SDL_Rect variable to determine the location of the label. We need to do the same thing here. This is the formula to get the correct layout (whereby (0, 0) is the top left corner of the screen):

- The first column should be 10 pixels from the left border of the screen
- The second column should be 100 pixels from the left border
- The third column should be right aligned, such that the text ends 10 pixels from the right border of the screen
- The first row should be 10 pixels from the top of the screen
- The second row should be 80 pixels from the top of the screen
- The following rows should be 55 pixels further down; e.g. the third row should be at 80 + 55 = 135 pixels from the top of the screen
- The font size should be 36

You'll need to define the SDL_Rect variable correctly and pass it to the SDL_RenderCopy() function so that the layout of the labels is correct. You can do this using loops. The right alignment of the text can be done by taking the width of the screen (640 pixels) and subtracting the width of the label which is available after calling the SDL_QueryTexture() function.

Exercise: Add the necessary code in your program as described above to display the 23 labels on the screen. If you made it here, congratulations.

4.1.5 Unix way - sched

We now have a C++ program that can display labels provided in a text file. Let's take another look at our high level architecture:

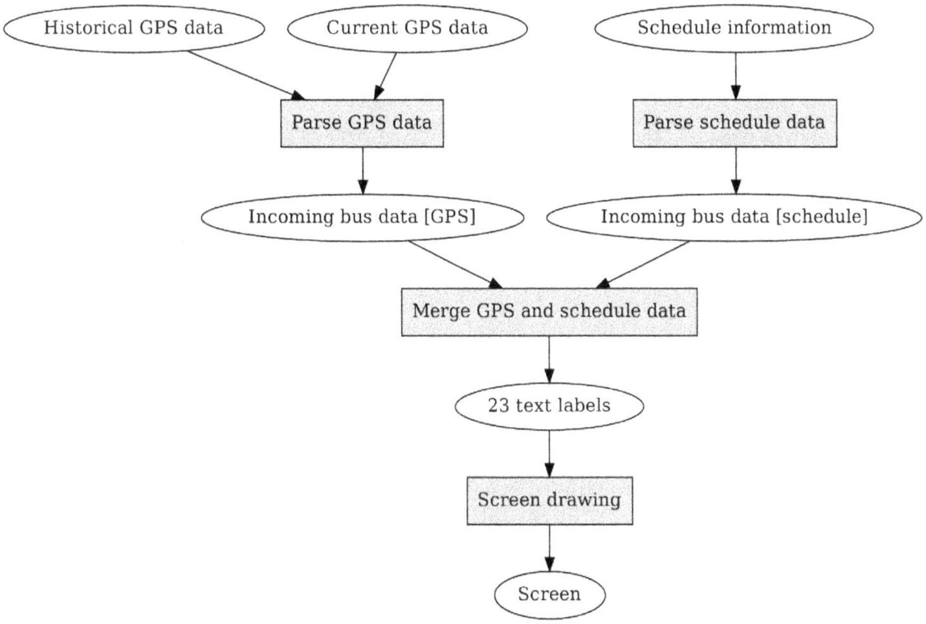

Furthermore, let's implement the Unix way i.e. engineering spec 1 first.

The input to our screen drawing program should be given by a program called "merge". However, "merge" requires incoming bus data which we don't yet have so let's implement the programs to generate this data from the original input i.e. schedule information and GPS data first.

sched

As per the requirements document, the schedule information, which is the input to sched, will look like the following:

```
3 1 5 6
3 2 5 16
```

Here, the numbers are the route number, the start number, and the hour and minute of the bus arrival according to the schedule.

As per our engineering spec, the output of sched should look like the following:

```
3 1 5 6 1
3 2 5 16 1
```

In other words, the output format is exactly the same but with a 1 appended at the end to signal the fact that this data point is from a schedule, which is needed when merging the predictions based on GPS data with the schedule information. The tricky bit about sched is that it should only output the next (up to) 50 buses arriving based on the current time which is also given to the program as a parameter. So if e.g. the time 5:10 was passed to sched, it shouldn't output any buses arriving before 5:10.

We can put together a simple test case so we can see whether our program works as intended.

Exercise: Create a test input file for sched. It should have the input format as above and include e.g. five lines for five buses. The buses should have different arrival times so that if you had a functioning sched and passed a time and your test file to it as input, you could see whether that the buses that according to schedule have already passed wouldn't be included in the output.

Now, let's implement this program and try it out. Here's what our program will need to do:

- Parse command line arguments and note the given time and filename
- For all entries in the given file, filter out the entries that are in the past
- Sort the remaining entries by time and retain the 50 first ones
- For all the entries, print them out to stdout in the given format

Command line arguments

Accessing command line arguments in Python can be done using the sys.argv list:

```
import sys

def main():
    num_args = len(sys.argv)
    print 'we have %d arguments' % num_args
    for arg in sys.argv:
        print arg

if __name__ == '__main__':
    main()
```

Here we introduce a couple of concepts:

- We import 'sys' and use the sys.argv list to access the command line arguments to the script
- We put our code to a function called main. In our toplevel code we check whether the special, built-in variable called __name__ equals '__main__'. If it does, this means the user has executed the program directly as opposed to importing the file from another Python script. Structuring the code like this makes it possible to use as a library which will become useful later. If the program was executed directly we call the main function which does all the real work.

Working with bus schedule entries

One potentially tricky thing is finding out whether an entry is in the past or not. How would you go about it? Have a think.

What we have is two time stamps, both having two integer values (hour and minute). The first one is the current time while the second one is the time stamp of an entry. We need to find out whether the second one is before or after the first one.

Now, because the time of day is circular, a time stamp can be said to always be after another one: it could just be 23 hours and 59 minutes after. We can break this cycle by agreeing e.g. that only the entries 12 hours after the current time are actually considered to be in the future. We should also ensure we handle midnight correctly such that e.g. the time 00:02 is treated as after 23:58; we want the bus schedule display to show buses travelling right after midnight even if it's right before midnight.

We can use this to put together a small test suite:

- First parameter: 06:34; second parameter: 06:40; return value should be 6
- First parameter: 06:40; second parameter: 06:34; return value should be -6

...and so forth. We can formalise this in Python:

```
def test():
    assert diff_time((6, 34), (6, 40)) == 6
    assert diff_time((6, 40), (6, 34)) == 6
    assert diff_time((6, 56), (7, 14)) == 20
    assert diff_time((7, 14), (6, 56)) == -20
    assert diff_time((7, 14), (9, 30)) == 136
    assert diff_time((9, 30), (7, 14)) == -136
    assert diff_time((23, 58), (1, 12)) == 74
    assert diff_time((1, 12), (23, 58)) == -74
```

Here, the function diff_time is our function to implement. It takes two parameters, each being a tuple of two integers. This is a *unit test*: it tests the code of one unit in isolation of others and can be used to ensure that a function performs correctly.

On the implementation of diff_time itself, "all" that it needs to do is take into account that an hour is 60 minutes, and track which time is bigger. It might be useful to think of it such that the timestamp can be converted to a number of minutes passed since midnight, so that e.g. the time 6:00 is represented as 360 (6 * 60) minutes, making the comparison easier.

Exercise: Implement the function diff_time which shall return the number of minutes the second timestamp is ahead of the first timestamp. Use the above test suite to ensure correctness.

In the above, the timestamps were represented simply as tuples. It might be clearer to represent a timestamp using a class instead, such that the class has two member variables, i.e. hour and minute. Feel free to refactor your code to use a class instead if you prefer.

Now that we're able to parse command line arguments and we have the diff_time function, and we have some understanding of sorting and slicing lists in Python as well as printing out values, we can tie everything together. The final program should e.g. behave as the following:

```
$ ./sched.py 5:15 sched_test.txt
3 2 5 16 1
3 3 5 26 1
3 4 5 36 1
3 5 5 46 1
```

That is, the time should be given in hh:mm format, and the output should be written to stdout. Here, the bus arriving at 5:06 is not output despite it being present in sched_test.txt.

As a reminder, here are some building blocks to get you started:

```
1  def main():
2      argument = sys.argv[1]
3      after_split = argument.split(':')
4      hour, minute = after_split
5      hour_as_int = int(hour)
6      entries = list()
7      with open(sys.argv[2], 'r') as f:
8          for line in f:
9              # TODO: parse line here
10             entries.append((route, startnr, time_diff, hour, minute))
11
12     entries.sort(key=lambda (route, startnr, time_diff, hour, minute): time_diff)
13     for (route, startnr, time_diff, hour, minute) in entries[:50]:
14         print route, startnr, 1
```

The above snippet demonstrates the following:

- Argument parsing (lines 2 and 7)
- String parsing (line 3)
- Tuples (lines 4, 10, 13)
- Converting string to int (line 5)
- Reading a file (lines 7 and 8)
- Appending to a list (line 10)
- Sorting using a callback (line 12)

- List slicing (line 13)

Exercise: Tie everything together to read a test schedule file and output the next schedules buses. Once you're done, test with the full sched.txt file that was available for download a couple of sections back.

4.1.6 Unix way - parse_gps

Let's take a look at our software architecture diagram again:

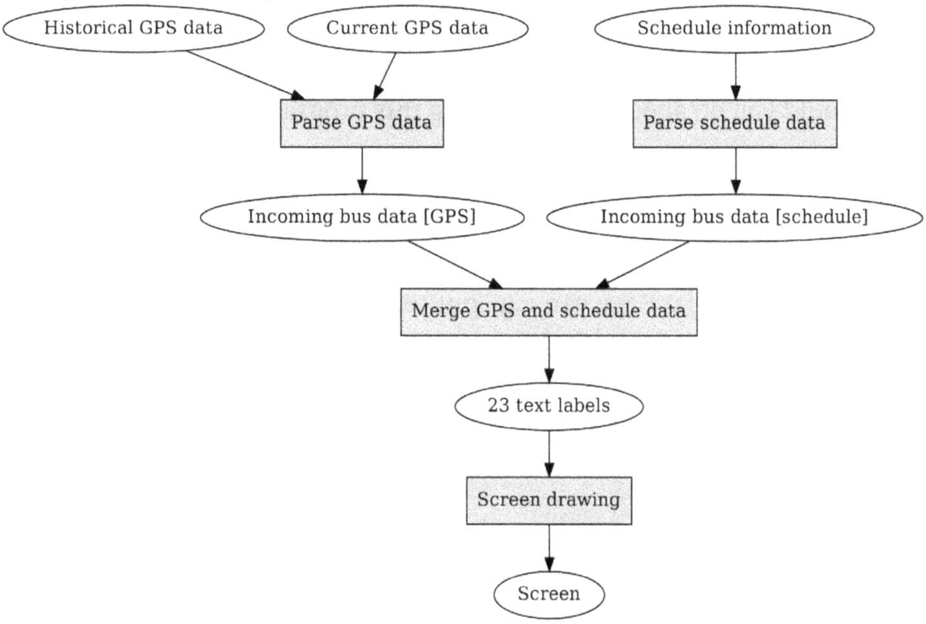

Before we implemented the schedule data parsing and screen drawing boxes. Let's implement the GPS data parsing next.

Parsing the GPS data takes both historical as well as current GPS data as input and outputs a description of buses expected to arrive soon in the same format as sched. The requirements specification gives some input as to how exactly the input format should look like, for both historical and current GPS data:

"[...] Each line has four numbers separated by spaces. The first integer identifies the route. The second is the time it took for the bus to reach the bus stop at the time the data was collected. The third and fourth are the position coordinates relative to the bus stop. They've been normalised such that the unit is in meters as opposed to degrees.

[...] Each line has at least five numbers separated by spaces. [...] The first number identifies the route. The second identifies the start number as is used in the schedule file. The third and fourth provide the relative position of the bus to the bus stop as is used in the historical GPS file. The fifth identifies whether the bus has already passed the bus stop."

The specification furthermore explains the desired logic for predicting the bus arrival time:

"The time to reach the bus stop is assumed to be the average time of all the points in the historical data within 100 meters of the current bus position for the route of the bus."

How would you go about implementing this program? Have a think.

As with sched, let's imagine some testing data, sketch the plan for the software top down and implement it bottom up, i.e. the most detailed part first.

For the historical data, we can e.g. put together just six data points, such that we have two routes with three data points each, at different locations. For example:

```
3 5.5 100.0 100.0
3 6.5 150.0 150.0
3 9.5 500.0 500.0
6 5.5 100.0 100.0
6 6.5 150.0 150.0
6 9.5 500.0 500.0
```

Here, we have mock-up data for bus routes 3 and 6; three data points each. The first column is the bus route number. The last two columns are coordinates indicating the bus position relative to the bus stop (bus stop being at 0, 0). The second column indicates the time, in minutes, it took for the bus to reach our bus stop. As you can see, we've seen buses that are 500 meters out in both X any Y directions to take nine and a half minutes to reach our stop while buses nearer have required less time.

Let's mock up some relevant current GPS data:

```
3 3 120.0 120.0 0
6 3 475.0 475.0 0
5 3 130.0 130.0 0
3 2 320.0 320.0 2
```

Here, we have information about four buses:

- Bus with start number 3 from route 3 is at location (120, 120) and has not yet passed the bus stop. We'd expect our program to see that there are two historical data points which can be used for this bus, as those two data points are for route 3 and within 100 meters of the current location. Considering that according to the requirements, the average time from historical data from data points within 100 meters should be used for estimates, how many minutes should our program estimate this bus to take before arriving at the bus stop?

- Bus with start number 3 from route 6 is at location (125, 125). We have one historical data point that our program is able to use to predict the arrival time.
- Bus from route 5 is included but we have no historical data for this bus.
- Bus with start number 2 from route 3 has already passed the stop.

Exercise: Write down what the expected output for the program would be for this input data. The program will receive some timestamp (hour and minute) as an input parameter; pick some numbers. Check that the output data format matches with the data from sched.

Now, how would we implement software to perform this operation? Again, let's break this down to sub-tasks:

- We need to parse the command line arguments and read in the input data
- We need to loop through the current bus information
- For each current bus, we need to decide what the output should be
  - For a bus that has passed we simply output the fact that the bus has passed
  - We should output the estimated arrival time whenever we have the historical data to be able to calculate the estimation
  - For other buses we won't be able to output anything
- We finally output the results in the required format

Exercise: Put together the skeleton for the program: parse the command line arguments, open the files, read in the information from the files to lists. Feel free to either store a data point (a row in either file) either to a tuple or using a class and member variables. You can convert a string to a floating point value by using e.g. "f = float(s)". You can remove all whitespace (line breaks, spaces etc.) from a string by using the "strip" string member function, e.g. s.strip(). Your program doesn't need to output anything yet.

Now that we have the skeleton in place, we can try to implement the core logic. There are a couple of primitives that our core logic requires, namely calculating an average of a list of numbers and calculating the distance between two coordinates; it might be interesting to implement these first.

Exercise: Implement and test a function to calculate the average of numbers in a list. You can use the built-in function "sum" to sum all the values in a list. Note that you probably want to cast the denominator to a floating point number to ensure the result is also a floating point number.

Exercise: Implement and test a function to calculate the distance between two coordinates. Use the Pythagorean theorem for this: distance = math.sqrt((x_diff ** 2) + (y_diff ** 2)). You need to import math to have access to the sqrt function.

For the most complex part of deciding what the output should be, the pseudocode could look something like this:

```
for bus in current_gps_data:
    if bus.passed:
        # don't try to predict the arrival time but note that
        # we need to include this bus in the output
    else:
        # find historical data points for this route
        historical_data_points =
            [data_point for data_point in historical_data if
                data_point.route_number == bus.route_number]
        # only include data points that are within 100 meters
        # of current position
        close_historical_data_points =
            [point for point in historical_data_points if
            distance(bus.position, point.position) < 100.0]
        bus.estimated_time_from_now = calculate_average(close_
↪historical_data_points)
```

In other words, we need to find the relevant historical data points (matching route number and close enough to the current bus location), and then calculate the average arrival time based on them. Once we have this information we can print it out.

It seems like we're starting to have all the pieces so we can put our program together.

Exercise: Implement the rest of your program. Test it with the mock-up data first. If that passes, see what output you get for the larger test files that were provided.

4.1.7 Unix way - merge

Now we have all pieces of our software except merge. Merge is expected to take the outputs of both sched and parse_gps and produce the input for display. Merge should use the tuple (route number, start number) to match the data from schedules and GPS data; if an entry from a schedule data has the same route number and the same start number as an entry from the GPS data, then we have the GPS data available for this schedule data entry. The output will need to show the estimated bus arrival time where possible and the scheduled bus arrival time otherwise, and sort the buses based on the arrival time, i.e. interleave the estimated and scheduled arrival times as needed. Have a think about how you would design this software.

As before, let's break this down:

- Parse the command line parameters and read in the input data, either to a list of tuples or a list of classes
- Implement the core logic to handle the input data
  - If a bus is scheduled but the GPS data says it's already passed, don't show it
  - If a bus is scheduled and there is no GPS data, include the scheduled time in the output
  - If there is GPS data for a bus, include the estimated time in the output
  - Sort the output by time difference to current time (given as command line parameter)
- Output the final result according to the specified data format

There are a few interesting tidbits that arise during the implementation:

- The output will need to include the actual bus route names. The names for the routes are defined in the requirement specification but we haven't used them in our code before. An easy way to go about this is to define a Python dictionary where the keys are route numbers and values are route names. This way we can easily convert a route number to its name when needed.
- Because we need to sort the output by the arrival time, we'll be needing to calculate the time difference between two time stamps again.

We already implemented this as part of sched. Instead of implementing this again, we can *reuse our old code* by running e.g. "import sched" and then calling the function e.g. "sched.diff_time".

- As part of the implementation, we'll need to ask the question "has a bus with this route number and start number already passed our bus stop?" Such questions can be dealt with by defining a Python set of buses (e.g. route number and start number tuples) e.g. with "my_passed_set = set(l)" where l is our list of buses that have passed the bus stop. One can then check whether a tuple exists in the set by e.g. using "(routenr, startnr) in my_passed_set". This expression will return true if the tuple exists in the set.
- The type of data entry (GPS based data, scheduled data, or passed) is a good candidate for an *enum*. An enum (short for enumeration) is a simple data type which simply assigns a name to a set of constants. In our case, the constant 0 means GPS based data, 1 means scheduled data and 2 means passed data. We can construct an enum in Python using the following syntax:

```
class Kind(object):
    GPS = 0
    Schedule = 1
    Passed = 2
```

Here, we define a class with three class variables. Now, we can simply e.g. type Kind.GPS in our code which means 0. This has the benefit that instead of having code where we have numbers like 0, 1 and 2 littered around, by typing e.g. Kind.Passed instead the code becomes easier to understand when reading it.

- We'll need to output the time stamps in proper time format. Python has support for this; e.g.:

```
print '%02d:%02d' % (hour, minute)
```

This print statement will print two integers with a colon in between, but if either of the integers are less than 10 it will *pad* the output by leading zeroes, such that e.g. the number 5 will be printed as 05.

Now we should have what we need to implement this program.

Exercise: Put together some mock-up data for merge. You can create this by running the sched and parse_gps programs. Modify the inputs of these programs such that you have a good input data set: a bus that is included in the schedule but has already passed; a bus that's included in the schedule but GPS data for a prediction exists as well; a bus that's included in the schedule but no GPS data for it exists.

Exercise: Implement merge as planned.

Gluing everything together

We now have a few programs where we can take inputs, generate outputs, provide these as inputs again etc. Let's put together a simple shell script that we can use to save us from repetitive work, and also to help document the flow. One way to go about this is to copy-paste all the commands you run to a file, add any boilerplate at the top, and then replace any repetitions with variables. You might end up with something like this:

```
1  #!/bin/bash
2
3  set -e
4  set -u
5
6  TIME="05:15"
7  SCHED_OUT=sched_out.txt
8  GPS_OUT=gps_out.txt
9  MERGE_OUT=merge_out.txt
10
11 ./sched.py $TIME sched_test.txt > $SCHED_OUT
12 ./parse_gps.py $TIME current_gps.txt historical_gps.txt > $GPS_
   ↪OUT
13 ./merge.py "My stop" $TIME $GPS_OUT $SCHED_OUT > $MERGE_OUT
14 ./bus $MERGE_OUT
```

Let's go through this line by line:

- Line 1: Shebang
- Lines 3-4: We set some bash settings to make our code safer: set -e causes the script execution to terminate immediately when a command returns with a non-zero exit code. This means that if we have

a bug and a Python script raises an exception, the following commands will not be executed. This is often practical as the following commands may not be sensical if a previous command failed, making it more difficult to spot the actual issue. set -u causes bash to terminate the execution if a variable is used before it is set.

- Lines 6-9: We define some variables that reduce redundancy in our script.
- Lines 11-14: We run our program one after the other, resulting in the display program being run.

Note that this doesn't exactly conform to the requirements specification as it specified only the bus stop is supplied as a parameter, however this is easier to test and should be relatively easy to adapt to fully match the requirements when necessary.

Exercise: Write a shell script or modify the above one to fit your environment so that you can run all your code in one command.

Makefiles

Make is a traditional Unix program that runs commands in a sequence based on whether a file has been updated or not. It's often used to run a compiler to compile source files to an executable after source code changes. It can also run tests or anything else, depending on what you tell it to run. Here, we'll use it to compile our C++ program and run the script we just wrote.

You execute make by running "make" in your shell:

```
$ make
make: *** No targets specified and no makefile found.  Stop.
```

Make looks for a file called "Makefile" in your current directory and executes commands specified in it. As we have no makefile it won't do anything. Let's fix this by writing a makefile:

```
default: bus
	./run.sh

```

(continues on next page)

(continued from previous page)

```
bus: sdl_sched2.cpp
	g++ -Wall -g3 -O2 $(shell sdl2-config --cflags --libs) -lSDL2_ttf -o bus sdl_sched2.cpp
```

Here, we define two *targets*. Normally, defining a target means that a file with the name of the target will be created by running the given command or commands. Our second target is a target called "bus": by running the compiler (g++), a file called bus is created. This is our C++ executable. We also tell Make that the file depends on sdl_sched2.cpp; this is our source file.

A caveat on Makefiles is that the whitespace before the commands *must* be a tab. Spaces are not allowed.

Our first target (the first target is also the default target for Make) is called "default". It depends on the bus executable and simply runs our shell script.

Now, with this makefile, running "make" gives the following:

```
$ make
g++ -Wall -g3 -O2 -I/usr/include/SDL2 -D_REENTRANT -L/usr/lib -lSDL2 -lSDL2_ttf -o bus sdl_sched2.cpp
./run.sh
$
```

In other words, it runs the C++ compiler to generate the executable "bus", followed by running our shell script, provided the compilation succeeds.

Now, if you were to run make again without making changes to the C++ source file, you get this:

```
$ make
./run.sh
$
```

In other words, Make detects that recompiling the C++ file is not necessary and simply runs the script.

If you do want to run the C++ compiler without making changes to the source file, you can either simply save the file, or use the Unix command "touch", e.g. "touch sdl_sched2.cpp". Either action will update the file modification timestamp which Make uses to detect whether the command to generate the target needs to be re-run or not.

Make can be used for lots of things and there's *a lot* more to Make than this short section might suggest; but some important properties of Make were introduced here. The main takeaway is that Make can be used to drive the build and test process.

Exercise: Put together your Makefile to compile your C++ code as well as for running your Python and C++ programs.

4.1.8 Monolithic way - parsing

Now that we're to a large part done with the Unix way, let's shift focus on the monolithic way where we implement the functionality of our three Python programs in one C++ program.

The basic principle of designing the software top down still applies. Let's start with writing down all the things we need to do:

- Parse input files
  - With GPS data, as with the Python version, we'll need to be able to calculate the distance between two points
- Merge the GPS estimates and the scheduled times
  - This includes writing some code to handle timestamps, more specifically, to calculate the difference between timestamps
- Pass on the text labels to the SDL code that actually renders them

It may also make sense to think about what data types we will have. We'll have at least the following:

- Timestamp
- Historical GPS data
- Current GPS data
- Schedule entry
- Arriving bus entry (either estimated via GPS or scheduled)
- Group of text labels

In C++ (and in many other languages) it often makes sense to think of each kind of data type as a class. For example, we could have a class for timestamp, with member variables "hour" and "minute" (both integers), and a function that returns the difference in minutes between two given timestamps.

Exercise: Think about the data types listed above. What data (member variables) would they hold? What operations would exist for them?

Timestamps

We can then go about implementing each of these classes, one by one, along with the relevant logic. For example, for a timestamp, we could come up with the following class definition:

```
class Time {
    public:
        Time();
        Time(int h, int m);
        int hour;
        int minute;
};
```

Here we define the Time class with two public member variables (as they're simple data, there's arguably no need to hide the data by making it private) and two constructors. The first constructor should simply generate a timestamp object with both hour and minute set to 0, and the second constructor should set the hour and minute as given. The functions for this class could be defined e.g. as the following:

```
Time::Time()
    : hour(0),
    minute(0)
{
}

Time::Time(int h, int m)
    : hour(h),
    minute(m)
{
}
```

We now have our (arguably very simple) first class. We already touched upon a function to calculate the difference between two timestamps; while we could have such a function as a member function for the Time class, it's also possible to have this as a free standing function. If we implement it as such, it would have the following declaration:

```
int time_diff(const Time& t1, const Time& t2);
```

In other words, a function that takes two constant Time objects and returns an integer.

Exercise: Implement this function and test it.

Schedule entry

The requirements spec defined the schedule entry to have a route number, a start number and a timestamp. We've identified one task as parsing the schedule information, in other words, reading the relevant file contents and generating a list (std::vector) of schedule entries. For this we need to do the following:

- Declare the schedule entry class
- Write the functionality to convert a text line to a schedule entry class
- Read in a file and call use above mentioned functionality in a loop to generate an std::vector of schedule entries

Let's start with the first one.

Exercise: Declare the schedule entry class. It should have a route number, a start number and a timestamp as member variables. The first two can be integers while we should instantiate a Time object for the last one.

Now, converting a string which contains space delimited numbers to integers is funny business in C++. A quick online search shows us one way to do this:

```
#include <string>
#include <sstream>

void func()
{
    std::string line;
    // TODO: set contents of line appropriately
    std::istringstream iss(line);
    int route_nr;
    int start_nr;
    int hour;
    int minute;
```

(continues on next page)

(continued from previous page)

```
13      if(!(iss >> route_nr >> start_nr >> hour >> minute)) {
14          throw std::runtime_error("Could not parse data");
15      }
16      // TODO: use our integers here
17  }
```

Let's go through this line by line:

- Lines 1-2: include string and sstream (stringstream) which we'll be needing shortly.
- Line 6: the variable line contains our input data.
- Line 8: We convert the data from an std::string to std::istringstream. Istringstream allows reading integers from it fairly easily (using the >> operator).
- Lines 9-12: We define our variables which will hold the integers we'll read in.
- Line 13: We use the >> operator to read in four integers. The operator will return false if something went wrong during parsing (for example, the input data contained letters). In this case, we throw an exception.

How would you get each line from a file in C++? Another online search reveals a way:

```
#include <iostream>
#include <string>
#include <fstream>

void func()
{
    std::ifstream infile("input_file.txt");
    std::string line;
    while(std::getline(infile, line)) {
        // TODO: use line here
    }
}
```

Let's go through this line by line as well:

- Lines 1-3: Import iostream, string and fstream (file stream).
- Line 7: Instantiate an object of type std::ifstream named infile. We pass the file name to its constructor as the parameter. This object represents an input file we can read data from.
- Line 8: Declare an std::string which will hold each line of the file as we read them in.
- Line 9: Use the C++ standard function std::getline() which takes two parameters: the input file stream and an std::string. The contents of the next line will be read from the input stream and stored in the string. The function will return false when the whole file was processed, allowing us to use it in a while loop.

We should now have everything we need in order to read in the schedule data and generate an std::vector of schedule entry objects.

Exercise: Generate an std::vector of schedule entry objects by reading in the schedule data file. Test your code.

While we're in the parsing business, let's go ahead and repeat this for the historical GPS data file.

Exercise: Implement a class to hold the historical data. It will need to have some floats as member variables to hold the time it took the bus to reach the bus stop as well as the X and Y coordinate data. Read in a historical GPS data file to an std::vector of historical data objects.

As per our requirements specification, the only file type we aren't yet able to parse is the current GPS data. This data is interesting because it has the integer representing whether the bus has already passed our bus stop or not (0 if not, 2 if passed). As with our Python code, it seems like a good way to make our code clearer to read if we use an enumeration for this. Enums in C++ can e.g. be defined as the following:

```
enum class Kind {
    GPS,
    Schedule,
    Passed
};
```

This defines a new data type called Kind which is an enumeration: it can only have a value GPS, Schedule, or Passed. (In C, the keyword "class" would have to be left out; it can also be left out in C++ but including it improves type safety by prohibiting implicit conversions between the enum and int, potentially reducing bugs).

You can then define and set a variable of this type e.g. with the following:

```
Kind my_variable = Kind::GPS;
```

You can also convert an integer to Kind. For example:

```
int val = 1;
Kind my_variable = Kind(val);
// my_variable is now Kind::Schedule
```

By default, with our above definition of the data type, the value 0 is converted to Kind::GPS, value 1 to Kind::Schedule, and value 2 to Kind::Passed.

We should now be able to define a class to hold the current GPS data, and parse a file holding such data.

Exercise: Define a class for current GPS data. It should include a member variable of type enum class Kind. Write code to read in a file of current GPS data to generate an std::vector of objects of your class, and test your code.

Now that we're able to parse in all the data we need, it seems that, apart from any necessary glue code, the actual logic we need to implement is reduced to:

- Calculating the estimated arrival times from GPS data
- Reading in the scheduled bus arrivals based on the current time
- Merging the estimated (and already passed) bus arrivals with the scheduled arrivals
- Parsing the command line arguments - including parsing time from a string "hh:mm" to a timestamp
- Converting timestamps to strings of format "hh:mm" for displaying purposes and calling the relevant function to display the labels

We'll address these in the next section.

4.1.9 Monolithic way - scheduled arrivals and GPS data

In the previous section we wrote the code to read in all the necessary data. Now let's use some of it.

We want to write the logic that takes two things as input:

- The scheduled arrivals
- Current time of day

And, like sched in our Python version, outputs the next 50 buses that will be arriving at the bus stop. The output will be merged with the output of the GPS data analysis.

To start, let's define the output data type. We've already defined a few - schedule entries, historical data, current GPS data - but none of them seem to match the requirement of encoding the arrival time, route number, start number and kind, i.e. the fact that this data results from the bus schedule (or indeed arriving or passed bus based on GPS data).

While we could organise this differently, by e.g. using the schedule entry data type, as per our original architecture diagram we can simplify the merging logic by ensuring the data format for both GPS and schedule data is the same. In other words, both GPS and schedule data will output data in the output data type (class), and merge will take this data as input.

Exercise: Write a class that includes the arrival time, route number, start number and kind as member variables.

Filtering

We can now implement a function that finds the next 50 buses that will be arriving according to the bus schedules. It will need to do three things:

- From a list of all scheduled arrivals, filter only those that arrive e.g. in the next 12 hours
- Sort this filtered list by how long it takes for the bus to arrive
- Keep only the first 50 elements of the list (slice)

In Python, this could look e.g. something like the following:

```
l = [entry for entry in l if time_diff(current_time, entry.time) > 0]
l = sorted(l, key=lambda entry: entry.time)
l = l[:50]
```

In C++, we can conceptually do the same, albeit with a bit more typing.

We can filter in C++ by #including <algorithm> and using std::remove_if, e.g.:

```
/* my_array is the input list */
/* curr_time is the current time */
std::remove_if(my_array.begin(), my_array.end(),
        [&](const auto& bi) {
            return time_diff(curr_time, bi.time) < 0;
        });
```

Here, we call the function remove_if with three parameters:

1. The start iterator - beginning of our array (or list, or any collection)
2. The end iterator - end of our array
3. The lambda function which works as the filter. The lambda function itself consists of three elements:

    a) [&] - this tells the compiler which local variables to *capture*, and how. Capturing a variable in a lambda function refers to using a variable that's defined outside the function. In this case we need to capture the curr_time as it's a local variable and used in the lambda function, and we don't wish to copy it but instead refer to it, which is expressed with [&].

    b) (const auto& bi) - this is the parameter to our lambda function. It's the same type as the elements in our array my_array. We can use the keyword "auto" instead of explicitly naming the type.

    c) "return time_diff(curr_time, bi.time) < 0;" - the function body itself. This will result in removing all elements where our function time_diff returns a value less than zero.

Exercise: Look up the C++ reference for std::remove_if.

Alternatively, primitives such as for-loops and vector::push_back() can be used instead.

Exercise: Write the beginning of our sched function - a function that takes the schedule data that was parsed and a timestamp, and returns bus arrivals, namely those arriving next. The result doesn't yet need to be sorted. Run your code.

Sorting

Remember that we want to output the next 50 buses arriving, sorted such that the next to arrive is the first in the output array. We haven't yet sorted data in C++ so let's fix that. Sorting can be done e.g. like this:

```
std::sort(my_array.begin(), my_array.end(),
    [](const auto& b1, const auto& b2) {
        return time_diff(b2.time, b1.time) < 0;
    });
```

Again we provide three parameters: two iterators for the begin and the end, and the lambda function that defines the sorting order. Here, we sort based on the time difference between entries.

Exercise: Look up the C++ reference for std::sort.

Note: std::sort assumes the function parameter describes the order as strict weak ordering. If this is not the case then undefined behaviour will occur. This means that e.g. in the above, if the operator <= was used instead of <, then the code may crash when executed.

Exercise: Include sorting in your sched function.

Slicing

Now, let's tackle the final hurdle of only keeping the first 50 elements of our array (or list). We already touched upon the erase-remove idiom with our Sudoku exercises, and keeping the first elements is similar:

```
if(my_array.size() > 50)
    my_array.erase(my_array.begin() + 50, my_array.end() - 1);
```

Here, we first ensure the iterator my_array.begin() + 50 is valid, and if so, we pass the range of elements we want to remove to std::vector::erase, namely the start and end iterator. If your code uses std::list, the above snippet is still valid but will call std::list::erase instead.

Exercise: Include the code to remove excessive elements from your container in your sched code.

We now have the code in place to find the next buses to arrive at our bus stop, according to the bus schedule.

Handling GPS data

For GPS data, as with our Python code, we need to do the following:

- For all current GPS data, find the relevant historical data points - i.e. data points with the same route and within 100 meters of the current position
- For all the relevant historical data points, calculate the average time it took for the bus to arrive, and use this to calculate the estimated arrival time for the bus
- Sort the current GPS data by the estimated arrival time, and keep the first 20 points
- Output the buses that seem to arrive soon, and additionally the buses that have already passed according to the GPS data

Now, the main new thing is *associating* a time with the GPS data point. We already have a class representing a current GPS data point. We could define a new class that e.g. includes an object of such a class as a member variable, and has the average time based on historical data as another member variable. Another way to do this is to use *tuples*: ad-hoc combinations of multiple data types in one. Here's an example of using tuples in C++):

```
#include <iostream>
#include <tuple>

class C {
    public:
        C(int a, int b) : m_a(a), m_b(b) { }
```

(continues on next page)

(continued from previous page)

```
7            int m_a;
8            int m_b;
9    };
10
11   int main()
12   {
13       std::tuple<C, int> c = std::make_tuple(C(1, 2), 3);
14       std::cout << std::get<0>(c).m_a << "\n"; // prints 1
15       std::cout << std::get<1>(c) << "\n";     // prints 3
16   }
```

Let's see what we have:

- Line 2: We #include <tuple> as is needed when working with tuples
- Lines 4-9: We define a class called C. It has one constructor which takes two parameters, a and b. It also has two member variables, m_a and m_b. They are initialised when the constructor is run. Because it has a constructor defined, it has no *default constructor*, i.e. the two values need to be passed to the constructor whenever an object of class C is instantiated.
- Lines 11-16: We define the main function.
- Line 13: We define our tuple. It's a tuple of C and int. We create it using the std::make_tuple() function, which takes an object of type C and an int as is required from the tuple type definition. We instantiate an object of type C with values 1 and 2.
- Line 14: Using std::get<0> we can access the first element in the tuple, i.e. the value of type C. We can then access its public member variable using ".m_a", hence printing 1.
- Line 15: We can access the second element in the tuple using std::get<1>.

Similarly to any other type, you can have a vector of tuples. This could be defined and used e.g. like this (after #including <vector>):

```
std::vector<std::tuple<C, int>> my_array;
my_array.push_back(std::make_tuple(C(4, 5), 6));
std::cout << std::get<0>(my_array[0]).m_b << "\n"; // prints 5
```

Exercise: Look up the C++ reference for tuple.

Exercise: Implement a function that takes a current GPS data point and the historical GPS data and will return the average time of the historical data points within 100 meters of the current GPS data point, or a sentinel value (e.g. -1.0) if no historical data points within 100 meters were found. Feel free to use dummy data to test your code.

Exercise: Use the above function to capture, for each current GPS data point, what the predicted time until arrival is, or whether the bus has already passed.

Exercise: Sort your resulting data based on the time until estimated arrival. Output the data using the same data type as your code that works with the scheduled arrivals. You can do this by adding the time until estimated arrival with the current time of day. Also include the passed buses in your output.

Digression: parameters and god classes

We've now written a few functions which take several different kinds of data as input and return several kinds of data as output. For example, the above GPS analysis function will need, in addition to the current and historical GPS data, the current time of day, and will return an array of incoming bus data. While it's typically no problem writing such functions, there's another way to organise such code: instead of passing all the data as parameters we can define a class which has all the necessary data as member variables and write the logic as member function or functions. With this scheme, all the functions always have access to the data, making passing or returning data unnecessary.

This has the benefit of potentially simplifying the code, but the downside of breaking code modularity - because all code has access to all data, it may quickly become unclear what each function does and how it depends on other functions without inspecting the code of other functions. Because of this, it's generally better practice to isolate the different functions from each other and not have so called "god classes" - so called because they see and have access to everything. Never the less, in some cases writing a god class may be easier and quicker than splitting all the logic to isolated functions.

4 *Stage 2*

We now have the code to read in all our schedule and GPS data. What's left is merging this data and final touches regarding command line option parsing and label output.

4.1.10 Monolithic way - merging and putting it all together

We now have the logic to create incoming bus data from GPS as well as from the schedules. Let's merge these to the final output that will be shown on the display.

Like in Python, our merging logic could work e.g. the following way:

- Combine the two arrays (vectors) to one
- Find out which buses (route number/start number combinations) have already passed, and for which buses GPS data exists
- From our array, filter out the entries which originate from the schedule where we either have the GPS arrival data or know they have already passed
- Sort the final array

The output data format can be the same as the input data format, i.e. data that tells the route number, assumed arrival time and the kind (scheduled or estimated from GPS data) for each bus. Once we have this data we can create the labels required for the display.

Here are some hints to help you get started:

- You can append one vector at the end of another by using the following code: vec1.insert(vec1.end(), vec2.begin(), vec2.end());
  - The first parameter tells the std::vector::insert() member function where to start appending. The second and third parameters tell from where to where to append.
- In Python we used sets to take note which buses have already passed or we have GPS arrival data on. We can do the same in C++ but as the amount of data is relatively small it should be no problem to use std::vectors for holding this data. Similarly to Python, tuples can be used to identify the buses. You'll need to note both the route number and start number. In other words, the type for the data could be e.g. std::vector<std::tuple<int, int>>.
- We've already seen how to remove (filter) elements from a vector. Finding an element in a vector to use in a predicate can be done like this:

```
return std::find(vec.begin(), vec.end(),
        std::make_tuple(route_nr, start_nr)) != vec.end();
```

This code searches the vector "vec" for a tuple which has the values "route_nr" and "start_nr". std::find returns vec.end() if the element was not found. Hence, e.g. the following code would remove all elements from a vector "vec1" that are included in another vector "vec2":

```
std::remove_if(vec1.begin(), vec1.end(),
        [&](const auto& bi) {
            return std::find(vec2.begin(), vec2.end(),
                    std::make_tuple(bi.route_nr, bi.start_nr)) !=
↪vec2.end();
        });
```

Exercise: Implement the merge function and test it.

Parsing a timestamp

We're starting to have a decent program but it's not yet parsing the command line options (unless you already added it). We'd want to support e.g. the following command line:

```
$ bus "Bus stop name here" gps_raw.txt gps.txt sched.txt 10:23
```

Here, the first parameter is the bus stop name and will only be used as a string to display on the final screen. The next three parameters are input file names. The final one is the current time.

To be precise, according to the spec, the process should only receive only one parameter, namely the bus stop name, but we can make things a bit simpler for us for now. If necessary we can wrap most of this in a shell script if necessary, except for the time stamp. While we could query the current time stamp in our code, for now we can make things simpler (and easier to test) and supply the time as a command line parameter.

One question when implementing the command line parsing might be about parsing a timestamp in format "hh:mm". We need to split this string by the ":" character, similarly to s.split(':') in Python. This can be done in C++ e.g. using the following code:

```
1 const char* time;
2 // FIXME: set time to hold a string in "hh:mm" format here
3 std::string t(time);
4 auto ind = t.find(":");
5 if(ind == std::string::npos)
6     throw std::runtime_error("Could not parse time");
7 int h = std::stoi(t.substr(0, ind));
8 int m = std::stoi(t.substr(ind + 1));
```

Going this line by line:

- Line 3: We convert time from char* to an std::string
- Line 4: Find the index of the character ':'. std::string::find will return std::string::npos if the character was not found.
- Line 7: We find the *substring* within t that holds the hour. The function std::string::substr(a, b) will return a string that includes characters from a to b (a inclusive, b exclusive).
- Line 7: We then convert the string to an int using the built-in function std::stoi (string to int).
- Line 8: We repeat this for minutes, but pass only one parameter to std::string::substr. This causes the function to return all characters from the given index until the end.

Exercise: Look up the reference for the function std::string::substr.

Exercise: Add command line argument parsing to your code. It should receive the current timestamp in "hh:mm" format, the name of the bus stop to display, and three file names for the schedule data, historical and current GPS data respectively. Check the value of argc to ensure you're receiving the correct number of parameters. Exit with an error message and a return value of 1 otherwise.

Displaying the labels

As part of our sections around SDL we put together a program that will display the labels as required, and take a filename as input which must contain the labels to be displayed. While we could generate such a file in our C++

program and then call that program, the cleaner way seems to be to call the existing code directly.

What we need to do for this is:

- Refactor the existing code which displays the screen using SDL. The constructor of the class we wrote previously took the file name as the source for the labels, but for our purposes it would be better if it took an std::array<std::string, 23> as a parameter instead and used the contents of that array directly. We can add another constructor for this purpose.
- Instantiate an object of that class in our C++ program, putting together and passing it an std::array<std::string, 23>
- Call the relevant member function or functions of that object such that the correct visual output is generated

Now, in order to use both our existing SDL code and our new C++ code together, you have a couple of options:

- Copy-paste all the existing SDL code to our new .cpp file
- Expose the existing SDL code in a *header file*, #include that header file in our new .cpp file, and compile and link the two .cpp files to one program

As the first one introduces duplicate code we'll go with the second option.

Header files

A header file in C and C++ typically describes the interface of the functionality implemented in the corresponding .cpp file. This means that it shouldn't have any function definitions but it should declare the functions that are defined in the .c or .cpp file and define the data structures (including classes) that may be used from other files.

In our case, our header for exposing the SDL functionality could look like this:

```
#pragma once

#include <array>
```

(continues on next page)

(continued from previous page)

```
4  #include <string>
5
6  #include "SDL.h"
7  #include "SDL_ttf.h"
8
9  class SDL_Schedule {
10     public:
11         SDL_Schedule(const std::array<std::string, 23>& labels);
12         SDL_Schedule(char* fn);
13         ~SDL_Schedule();
14         void display();
15
16     private:
17         void init();
18
19         TTF_Font* m_font;
20         SDL_Window* m_screen;
21         SDL_Renderer* m_renderer;
22         SDL_Color m_col_white;
23         SDL_Color m_col_yellow;
24         std::string m_labels_filename;
25 };
```

Let's see what we have.

- Line 1: We include a *header guard* which ensures the header file will only be compiled once per compilation unit (typically a .cpp file, plus any headers that were #included). Without "#pragma once", if one were to #include this header file more than once, either directly or indirectly, we'd have declared the class multiple times, leading to compile errors. Another way to define a header guard is to use e.g. "#ifndef MY_HEADER_H" followed by "#define MY_HEADER_H" at the top of the header file and "#endif" at the end of the header file. These are a commonly used way to say "if this random string hasn't yet been defined, define it, then define the rest of the header, end if", i.e. "only include this file once".
- Lines 3-7: We #include the header files that are required for our class definition.

- Lines 9ff: We actually define our class. We don't define any member functions here but only include the definition of the class. The logic is that function definitions can only be defined once per executable program but the data type needs to be visible to any compilation unit that defines variables of that data type.

We should end up with e.g. have the following structure:

- sdl.cpp - this includes the member function definitions of the class SDL_Schedule. It #includes sdl.h. It must not include a main function. If it does then comment it out, or move it to another file.
- sdl.h - this has the SDL_Schedule class definition as per above.
- bus.cpp - this has our other logic, and most importantly, the main function. It #includes sdl.h and defines and uses a variable of type SDL_Schedule.

The following diagram summarises the dependencies.

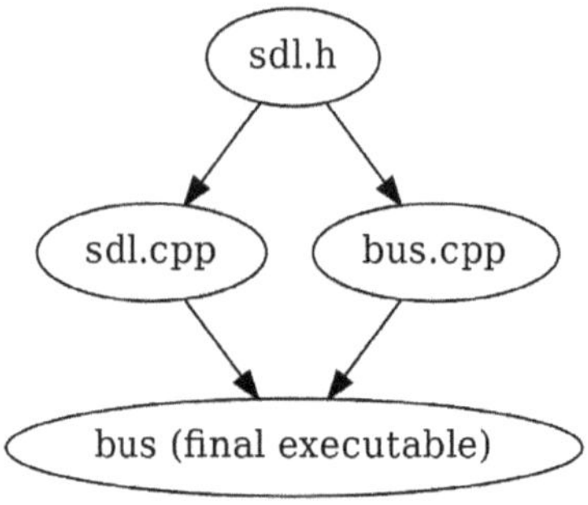

Now, generally in C and C++, source files are compiled to object files (binary files including the machine code instructions that were generated from the input C code), and one or multiple object files can be linked to an executable. When you run e.g.:

```
$ g++ -o hello hello.cpp
```

...what the compiler actually does is implicitly convert all the intermediate steps to one. To explicitly compile an object file and link it to an executable, you'd do:

```
$ g++ -c -o hello.o hello.cpp
$ g++ -o hello hello.o
```

Here, we first instruct the compiler to generate an object file with -c, then ask the compiler to link the final executable (by not specifying -c), passing it the object file as input. (Instead of calling g++, depending on the C++ compiler, one could also call the linker directly, e.g. ld.)

Now, when we have two .cpp files, we have two options:

```
$ g++ -o hello file1.cpp file2.cpp
```

Here, we pass the compiler two .cpp files to compile to a single executable. The compiler compiles each file separately, and finally invokes the linker to link them.

Alternatively we can use:

```
$ g++ -c -o file1.o file1.cpp
$ g++ -c -o file2.o file2.cpp
$ g++ -o hello file1.o file2.o
```

Here, we explicitly compile each .cpp file to an object file by passing -c and finally tell the compiler to link all of them to an executable. The good thing about this method is that is improves the time it takes to compile our program; the former will always compile each .cpp file while with the latter, you can skip compiling the .cpp files that haven't been changed since the last compilation. Makefile rules come in handy here.

#include <header> or #include "header"?

We've seen two ways to include headers: either using the angled brackets or quotes. The difference is in the path the C++ compiler uses to find the header file; for angled brackets, it searches in the system directories which are dependent on the compiler and typically include the libraries installed on the system while the quoted brackets mean the compiler first searches in the local directory before going to the system directories. Typically you should use quotes for the header files in the project you're currently working on, and angled brackets for libraries that aren't included in your current project. SDL2 recommends a bit different approach and suggests the user should always use quotes for including SDL2 headers.

Furthermore, you can specify more directories to search for headers when invoking the compiler. The switch -I followed by a path adds the given path to the list of directories to use when searching for headers. E.g. the SDL2 command sdl2-config –cflags, which we use during compilation, could include e.g. the string "-I/usr/include/SDL2" when expanded, meaning the compiler should look for the headers in that directory.

Compiling and linking our program becomes more interesting when external libraries like SDL2 are used. To make it short, when compiling, the compiler needs to know where to find the header files. When linking, the compiler needs to know where to find the library files. In case of SDL2, we could e.g. use the following:

```
$ g++ -Wall -I/usr/include/SDL2 -c -o file1.o file1.cpp
$ g++ -Wall -I/usr/include/SDL2 -c -o file2.o file2.cpp
$ g++ -L/usr/lib -lSDL2 -lSDL2_ttf -o hello file1.o file2.o
```

Here, we pass the include path to the compiler while compiling using the -I switch, such that the compiler will be able to find the SDL2 header files.

After compilation, we pass the compiler the path where to find libraries using the -L switch, and tell it which libraries to link using the -l switch (in this case, SDL2 and SDL2_ttf).

SDL2 provides us with the helper tool sdl2-config which can generate these for us. sdl2-config –cflags generates the correct -I line (and more) while sdl2-config –libs generates the switches required by the linker. This is the reason we call and expand sdl2-config when we compile our code that uses SDL2.

Exercise: Use our SDL code from our bus logic code. Create a new header file or files as necessary. Compile and run your code. Fill out all the holes so that your code will do everything: parse the input files, generate the labels required for the display and display the labels. Create an std::map to map route numbers to names.

If you made it here, congratulations.

4.2 A fistful of Python exercises

Let's introduce some more concepts that are typical in software development.

4.2.1 Graphs

In this section we'll learn a bit about *graphs*.

A graph is a collection of *nodes* as well as *edges* that connect nodes. There are lots of different kinds of graphs:

- The nodes or edges may have *labels*
- The edges may be *directional* (bidirectional or unidirectional)
- The edges may have a *cost* associated with them

As with the other topics in this book, we only treat graphs in a shallow way. Namely to solve a very precise problem.

Here's an example graph:

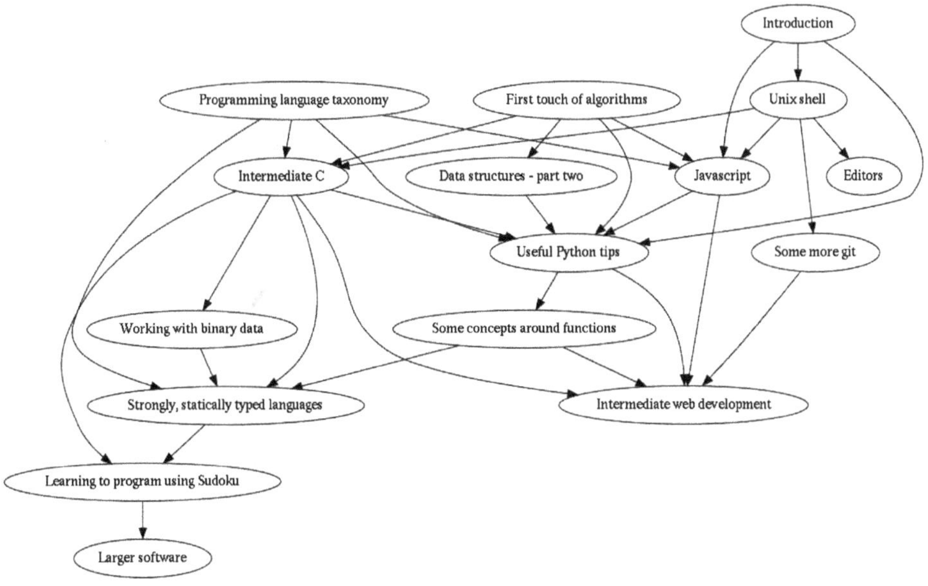

It's a graph showing the dependencies between some of the chapters of this book. For example, the chapter "Unix shell" has "Introduction" as its dependency.

(Apart from describing dependencies between chapters, graphs can be used for describing other kinds of dependencies like in a supply chain. They can also be used to describe other relationships like distances or routes between places, relationships between people etc.)

Now, here's the problem with this graph: it has too many edges. You see, the code that creates the edges for this graph isn't very smart, so it includes some edges that strictly speaking don't need to be there. For example, you see the edge from "Introduction" to "JavaScript"? As "JavaScript" already depends on "Unix shell" which depends on "Introduction", there's no need to have an edge from "Introduction" to "JavaScript". This edge can and should be removed.

We have two parts to this problem: one is finding the algorithm that does what we want it to do, i.e. remove the edges, and the other is putting this algorithm into use to actually generate a graph with unnecessary edges removed.

Can you think of how the algorithm to remove unnecessary edges would work?

One way to think of it is that an edge from A to C should be removed if we find an edge from B to C, where B is dependent on A, either directly or indirectly. That way we "only" need to keep track of which nodes are dependent on which. In pseudocode this could look something like this:

```
for node in nodes:
    for direct_child in node.get_direct_child_nodes():
        for other_child in node.get_direct_child_nodes():
            if other_child.depends_on(direct_child):
                node.remove_edge(other_child)
```

It's probably a good idea to draw the above on paper to get an understanding of how it would work.

Now that we have a very rough description of an algorithm in place, we can consider the question about how we actually would create or modify a graph.

Graphviz and dot

Graphviz is a software suite for working with graphs. Dot is a program which is part of graphviz that produces images of graphs specified in the *dot* language. Here's an example graph described in the dot language:

```
digraph g {
    A -> B;
    A -> C;
    B -> D;
    C -> D;
    D -> E;
    A -> E;
}
```

This file can be fed to the dot program, e.g. like this:

```
$ dot -Tpng < graph.dot > graph.png
```

As you can see, dot takes the output format as a parameter, can read dot files from stdin and output to stdout. The result could look like this:

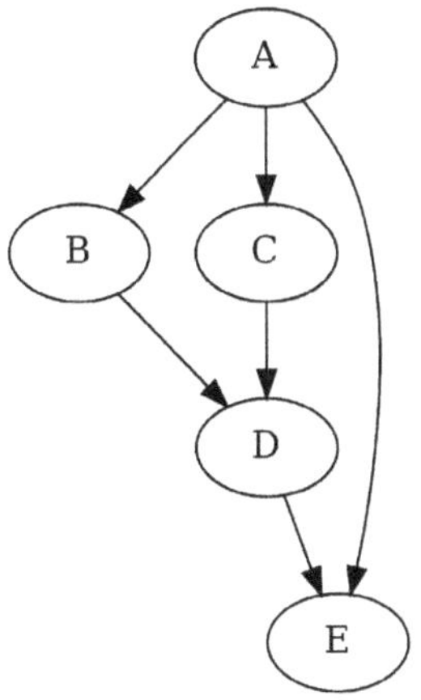

(The edge from A to E is unnecessary.)

Exercise: Install the graphviz suite on your computer. Run the above dot command to make sure you have everything set up correctly. Bonus points if you compile it from source.

As you can see, the dot language is fairly simple, at least in this case, and fairly intuitive.

The source for the graph at the beginning of this section is a bit more complex. It has this kind of structure:

```
digraph dep2 {
    bin_index [label="Working with binary data"];
    design_index [label="Larger software"];
    // ... more nodes ...

    int_c_index -> bin_index;
    ud_index -> design_index;
    ds_index -> ds3_index;
    // ... more edges ...
}
```

The full source can be downloaded at the book web page.

The main difference, apart from having more nodes and edges, is that the nodes have *IDs* associated with them, and each ID has *a label*. This way, the lengthy name that will be displayed for each node is only written once in the dot file, even when a node is referenced multiple times.

Now, what we could do is read in a dot file, *parse* it i.e. understand its contents and store a representation of it in a variable, modify the data structures representing the graph to remove edges we don't want, and finally write out a new dot file with the edges removed which can then be fed to dot for generating a better graph. Sounds good?

How would you go about this problem in practice? Go ahead and give it a try using the dot file from above. The next section will walk you through solving this.

Parsing dot files

There are several ways to approach parsing dot files. We'll introduce and implement two ways as part of this book: the *hacky* way and the *more accurate* way. Here are the pros and cons:

- The "hacky" way is faster to implement
- However, the "hacky" way is designed to only work with dot files that are structurally very similar to the ones above; adding support for more dot features will be very difficult

Conversely, the more accurate way is somewhat more difficult to implement but is closer to a "real" dot parser, such that extending it later will result in more maintainable code. In our case, the hacky way results in about 30 lines of Python code while the more accurate way will be about 150 lines. These numbers include not only parsing but also applying the algorithm to remove unnecessary edges.

The hacky way

The hacky way involves use of regular expressions.

The principle is simple:

- For each line, see if it matches a pattern "(word) -> (word);"
- If not, print out the line (remember, we wanted to end up printing a dot file with the unnecessary edges removed), unless the line is simply a '}' which denotes the end of the dot file
- If it does, note the two words as a link (key and value in a dictionary)

After this "parsing" we'd end up with a dictionary describing all the links. The key of the dictionary would be a string while the value would be a list of strings, i.e. all the edges from a node. We could then do the following:

- Apply our algorithm to remove unnecessary edges - that is, remove the unnecessary entries in our dictionary
- Write out all the edges by simply printing " %s -> %s;" % (word1, word2)
- Print '}' to close the dot file description

That's it, really.

collections.defaultdict

collections.defaultdict is a handy little Python library that can be helpful when creating dictionaries. Without it, the code to append an element to a list which is the value in a dictionary would look e.g. like this:

```
my_dict = dict()
key = 'foo'
value = 'bar'
try:
    my_dict[key].append(value)
except KeyError: # key not in dict
    my_dict[key] = list()
    my_dict[key].append(value)
```

What this code does is add a value to a list in a dictionary, unless the list doesn't exist yet in which case it needs to be created first. collections.defaultdict simplifies this code:

```
import collections

my_dict = collections.defaultdict(list)

key = 'foo'
value = 'bar'
my_dict[key].append(value) # will automatically create a new␣
↪list when needed
```

Regular expressions in Python

In Python, you can check if a regular expression matches a string by using e.g.:

```
import re

regex = re.compile('[0-9]+')
s = '123'
result = re.match(regex, s)
if result:
    print '"s" is a number'
```

You can also *capture* what was matched with parentheses, e.g.:

```
import re

regex = re.compile('[a-z]*([0-9]+)[a-z]+([0-9]+)'))
s = 'abc123def456'
result = re.match(regex, s)
if result:
    print 'The number within "s" is:          ', result.group(1)
    print 'The number at the end of "s" is:', result.group(2)
```

Here, you can define which captured string you want via the parameter to group().

Exercise: Implement this hacky method to "parse" a dot file. You don't need to remove the unnecessary edges yet. Write the output of your program to a file and diff against the original. They should match except possibly for line ordering and whitespace. You can sort the lines in both files alphabetically using the "sort" Unix command for easier comparison. Feel free to reach out to a reference on regular expressions if needed.

Removing unnecessary edges

This process, after searching online, reveals to be called *transitive reduction*.

Exercise: look up transitive reduction online.

We already roughly described an algorithm to remove unnecessary edges in pseudocode. Let's see what we need to do in order to turn it into real code:

- We need to be able to get a list of the direct child nodes of a node. Our dictionary we put together above works well here.
- We need to be able to remove the edge between a node and a child node. Again, this is something we should be able to do with our dictionary (with e.g. my_dict[key].remove(node)).
- We need to be able to tell if node A is either a direct or an indirect child node of node B, i.e. whether node B depends on node A. We don't have this yet.

Let's implement this algorithm: we need to *traverse* the graph to be able to tell whether a node depends on another. There are two major kinds of graph traversals, *depth first search* and *breadth first search*. In this case it doesn't matter which one we pick.

Graph traversal

Let's take a look at the simpler graph from before again:

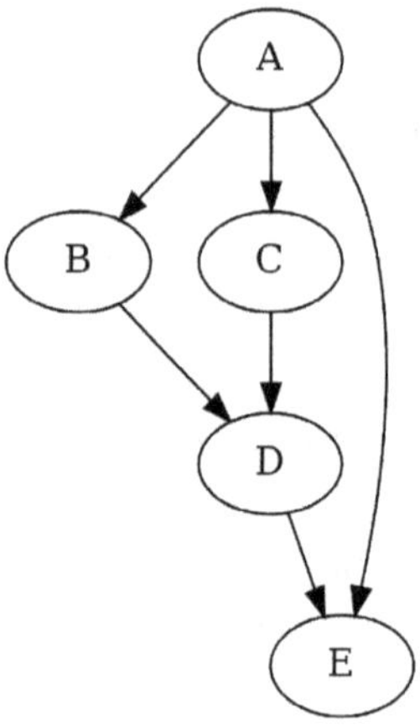

If we were to start our traversal from node A, the depth first traversal, which, as the name says, goes into depth when traversing, would traverse the nodes e.g. in the following order:

A -> B -> D -> E -> C

This is because depth first traversal traverses along the edges of the last visited node first. In other words, depth first traversal maintains a *stack*, such that any edges from newly visited nodes are added at the top of the stack.

If we were to traverse from node A using breadth first traversal, the order would e.g. be the following:

A -> B -> C -> E -> D

This is because breadth first traversal traverses along the edges of the first visited node first. In other words, breadth first traversal maintains a *queue*, such that any edges from newly visited nodes are added at the end of the queue.

In Python, a simple list can function either as a stack or a queue, with the pop() member function being able to return (and remove) either the first or the last element of the list, and the insert() and append() functions being able to add elements either the beginning or the end of the list, though Python also has more specific data structures that can be used such as collections.deque.

Finding out whether node B is either directly or indirectly dependent of node A is then a matter of traversing the graph from node A. If node B is encountered, it depends on node A.

Exercise: Using your dictionary describing the dependencies in a dot graph, write a traversal function to check if a node is a child node of another. You can use either depth first or breadth first search.

You may recall that function calls are also stored in a stack, such that the computer (or virtual machine) knows where to jump to after a function has finished. This correctly implies that we can implement the depth first search recursively, i.e. instead of having our explicit stack we simply call a recursive function that does the search for us.

Exercise: Implement depth first search using recursion.

We should now have all the pieces we need to finish our program.

Exercise: Finish the program to remove unnecessary edges. See the pseudocode above for the principle. Use your traversal function to determine whether a node depends on another.

By the way, the Graphviz suite also includes a tool called "tred" which performs transitive reduction similarly to our code. You can use this to validate the output of your program.

Exercise: Look up the source code for "tred" in the Graphviz source.

4.2.2 Parsing

Now that we have the hacky solution, let's see what a nicer solution would look like.

One problem that our hacky solution had was that it made fairly strict assumptions about the input data. For example, in dot, as the semicolon is the delimiter between statements, it's not necessary for the left hand side and the right hand side of an arrow to be on the same line. That means, e.g. the following file is a valid dot file:

```
digraph dep2 {
    A
->
       B
    ;}
```

If given to dot, it would display a graph showing an arrow from A to B as expected. But our hacky solution would be unable to parse this. Furthermore, it could be fairly non-trivial to improve our solution to work on all dot files with different formatting. For this, proper parsing is necessary.

Grammar

Now, parsing means turning an input (text) stream into a data structure. We did this in our hacky solution, but another attribute of parsing is that the input is parsed according to a certain *formal grammar*. Grammar is often described using the *Backus-Naur form* (BNF). We could define a grammar for the subset of dot files we want to parse using Backus-Naur form by e.g. the following:

```
graph         ::= "digraph" characters '{' statements '}'
statements    ::= '' | statement statements
statement     ::= label | edge
label         ::= characters labelname
labelname     ::= '[' "label" '=' quotedstring ']' ";"
quotedstring  ::= '"' labelstring '"'
labelstring   ::= characters | ' ' labelstring | characters␣
↪labelstring
edge          ::= characters "->" characters ";"
```

(continues on next page)

(continued from previous page)

```
characters    ::= '' | 'a-zA-Z0-9_-' characters
```

This defines the formal grammar for our dot files recursively. For example:

- A graph is parsed when the following is encountered: the string "digraph", followed by characters, followed by the character '{', followed by statements, followed by the character '}'
- Characters is defined either by nothing, or any printable letter from the English alphabet, or a digit, or an underscore or a hyphen ('-'), followed by characters
- Statements is defined either by nothing, or a statement followed by statements
- A statement is defined as either label or edge

...and so forth. (Note that the above strictly speaking isn't valid BNF as for example the regular expression-like definition in characters isn't included in the original BNF definition. Many variations of the original BNF are used in practice.)

Exercise: The Graphviz project also document the full grammar for the dot language. Look it up online.

Lexing

Now that we have our grammar defined, we can almost start writing the actual parsing code. However, if you try this you'll see it's more difficult than you'd expect: there's a lot of *state* to keep track of when going through your input file character by character. For example, if you encounter a quotation mark ("), you need to note that you're now inside a quoted string. If you encounter a character, you need to know whether you're parsing a graph, or the "digraph" word of the graph, or the name of the graph (characters), etc. Writing a parser this way can become cumbersome very quickly.

A way around this is to split one part out and preprocess the input: *lexical analysis* or *lexing* first turns the character-by-character input stream to *lexemes* or *tokens* which are much easier to work with when parsing. In our case, the following could be our tokens:

- The word "digraph"

- characters (an identifier)
- The character '{'
- The symbol "->"
- A quoted string
- Etc.

After the lexical analysis, instead of handing our parser a list of characters, we hand it a list of tokens. Then, our parser needs to check that the input tokens are correct and store the data in the correct data structures as necessary, making this a much easier task.

How would we start? We can first define tokens as an enumeration:

```
class Token(object):
    EQUALS = 0       # the character '='
    DIGRAPH = 1      # the word "digraph"
    IDENTIFIER = 2 # characters
    QUOTE = 3        # quoted string
    OPEN_CURLY = 4 # the character '{'
    # and so forth
```

Now, when reading in a text stream, how would we know whether we've encountered a token? With a regular expression! Furthermore, as we learnt in "PNG files", we can apply *data driven programming* by defining a list which defines a regular expression for each token:

```
tokens = [(re.compile('='), Token.EQUALS),
          (re.compile('[ \n\t]+'), None),
          (re.compile('digraph'), Token.DIGRAPH),
          # and so forth
```

Here, we define a list with the following characteristics:

- The first element in the tuple for each element in the list is a regular expression: this may either match or not.
- The second element in the tuple describes which token the regular expression should generate when it matches. Note that we also parse whitespace but don't associate it with a token. This way we can consume all whitespace out of the way.

Now that we have our tokens defined we can start with the lexical analysis:

```
pos = 0
lexer_output = list()
while pos < len(input_stream):
    for regex, token in tokens:
        # TODO: check for match with regex
```

In the above snippet, we have the input stream as a string which we can slice like a list, we want to output a list of lexemes, and have an integer (pos) to track the current position in the input stream. We can do this:

- Use input_stream[pos:] as the input - that is, the string after cutting out the first pos characters
- Loop through our possible tokens and use re.match() to apply a regular expression to the input
- If we have a match, store both the token and what was matched in lexer_output. We need sto store what was matched so the parser has the necessary information required for parsing later on. You can retrieve what was matched by running result.group() whereby "result" is the return value of re.match().
- After a match we can advance position by the length of what was matched
- If none of the tokens matched we should raise an error

Exercise: Finish and test the lexer. If you prefer you can start with a simpler form of dot files first, i.e. without labels but instead only the "A -> B;" form.

Data structures

Now that we have our lexer output, we could parse it. Overall we'd like to have the following data flow:

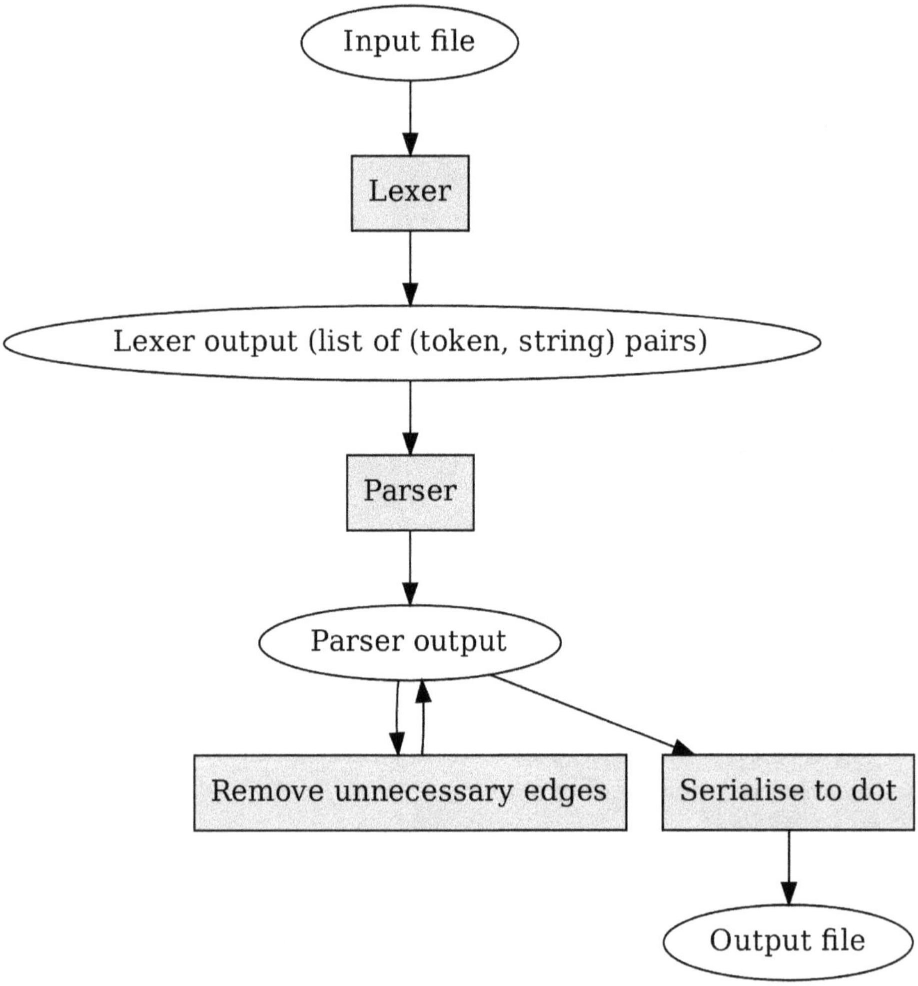

Here, one thing to note is that the parser output format should be something where we can remove unnecessary edges, and use for generating a dot file.

In terms of code, the high level view of using this could be e.g.:

```
lexer_output = lex(input_filename)
p = Parser(lexer_output)
p.parse()
p.graph.simplify()
print p.graph
```

Hence we should store the output of our parsing in data structures and we should define these first. Classes seem like a good way to do this, and our classes should also somewhat reflect the data that we can expect to find in our dot files. This means we can be inspired by our grammar definition when defining our classes. E.g.:

```
class Graph(object):
    def __init__(self, name):
        self.name = name
        self.statements = list()

class Label(object):
    def __init__(self, name, label):
        self.name = name
        self.label = label

# TODO: include other necessary classes such as Edge
```

Exercise: Implement the necessary data structures for storing the parsed data.

Parsing

Now we can finally actually parse our lexer output. We need to write a loop that goes through the list, keeps track of the current *state*, i.e. what's expected, checks the input for validity, and stores the parser output to data structures.

Exercise: Give this a try. Don't worry if it doesn't work; the next section will provide help.

Now, when writing a parser, there are several patterns that come up. For example:

- Getting the next token
- Checking whether the next token is as expected
- Extracting information from a token; for example, a token holding characters may be an identifier which we want to store as the name of a graph

It's often helpful to write helper functions for these. Furthermore, it may clarify the code to have the parser state like how far the parser has progressed by having this state stored as member variables of a class. One could then use the class e.g. like this:

```
p = Parser(lexer_output)
p.parse()
# p.graph would hold the parsed data
```

The parser you wrote at the previous exercise may work but you may be able to make your code cleaner by restructuring it e.g. as follows:

```
class Parser(object):
    def __init__(self, lexer_output):
        self.lex = lexer_output
        self.pos = 0
        self.token = self.lex[self.pos]

    def next(self):
        self.pos += 1
        if self.pos < len(self.lex):
            self.token = self.lex[self.pos]

    def match(self, char):
        if self.token[0] != char:
            raise RuntimeError('Expected "%s", received "%s"' %␣
↪(char, self.token))
        self.next()
```

With this, writing the parser becomes relatively simple as we need to use our primitives to progress through the input, e.g.:

```
def parse(self):
    self.match(Token.DIGRAPH)
    name = self.identifier() # TODO: implement
    self.graph = Graph(name)
    self.match(Token.OPEN_CURLY)
    self.statements()
    self.match(Token.CLOSE_CURLY)

def statements(self):
    while self.token[0] != Token.CLOSE_CURLY:
        name = self.identifier()
```

(continues on next page)

(continued from previous page)

```
        if self.token[0] == Token.OPEN_SQUARE:
            self.match(Token.OPEN_SQUARE)
            self.match(Token.LABEL)
            # TODO: write the rest
        elif self.token[0] == Token.ARROW:
            self.match(Token.ARROW)
            name2 = self.identifier()
            # TODO: write the rest
        else:
            raise RuntimeError('Expected statement, received "%s"
↪' % self.token)
```

Now we can write the rest of the parser.

Exercise: If your parser didn't work after the previous exercise, make it work using the code snippets above. Also try giving it some invalid input.

Now, if all has gone well, we have the contents of the dot file in our data structures and can proceed with the following:

- Remove unnecessary edges using the algorithm from the previous section
- *Serialise* our data structures to a dot file, i.e. write out the contents of our data structures in the proper format

Exercise: Write a member function of the Graph class that removes unnecessary edges and test it.

There are a few ways we could serialise our data. Ideally we'd be able to do this:

```
g = Graph(name)
print g # this statement writes out the graph as a dot file to␣
↪stdout
```

How "print" works in Python is that it calls the member function __str__ of your class, expects a string as an output of that function, and then writes that output to stdout. We can define this function e.g. like this:

```
def Graph(object):
    def __init__(self, name):
```

(continues on next page)

(continued from previous page)

```
        self.name = name
        self.statements = list()

    def __str__(self):
        ret  = 'digraph %s {\n' % name
        for s in statements:
            ret += str(s) + '\n'
        ret += '}'
        return ret
```

Now, all we need to do is define __str__ for all our classes.

Exercise: Serialise your data to a dot file by implementing the necessary __str__ member functions. Tie everything together by lexing and parsing the input dot file, removing unnecessary edges and serialising the output. Check that the output matches the output of the previous section.

Congratulations, you've now written a parser. More specifically, this is a *top down parser* as it parses the top level data first before proceeding to further levels. Even more specifically, this could be a *recursive descent parser* because our grammar is defined in a recursive manner (e.g. characters), though in practice your implementation probably doesn't use recursion as our lexical analysis merged tokens such that no recursion during parsing is necessary.

Parsers are fairly common in that they're part of the implementation of compilers, interpreters including for languages such as Python and JavaScript, HTML renderers, regular expression engines, editors (syntax highlighting and indenting) and more. As such, during this book we've already indirectly used several different parsers.

Another tidbit is that the formal grammar we defined is a *context free grammar* which has an interesting mathematical definition but in practice means, among other things, that one can define the grammar in BNF form. Context free is opposed to *context sensitive grammar* where context matters; tokens before or after a token determine what the token means. For example parsing the C language is context sensitive because e.g. the asterisk ("*") may mean either part of a pointer variable declaration, pointer dereferencing or multiplication depending on context.

A subset of context free grammars is a *regular grammar*. A language described by a regular grammar is called a *regular language*. A concise way to describe a regular language is by using a *regular expression*. In other words, a regular expression like e.g. “[a-z]+” is, like BNF, a way of defining a formal language (in this case one or more lower case letters), and evaluating a regular expression is equivalent to parsing a string with the regular expression as the grammar and returning whether the input conforms to the language or not.

Because regular grammar is a subset of context free grammars, context free grammars generally cannot be parsed using regular expressions, similarly to how context sensitive grammars generally cannot be parsed using context free parsers. (This grammar hierarchy is also known as *Chomsky hierarchy*.)

Exercise: Is it possible to parse HTML with regular expressions?

4.3 SQL and its relationship with online shops

If you've ever shopped for clothes online, you may be familiar with the return form for returning products you don't want to have: you order something, decide for whatever reason you don't want to keep some products, and, along with some piece of paper, send the products you don't want back. The piece of paper may either be a form you fill out yourself or something you receive pre-filled from the online shop and print yourself.

In this section we'll assume the role of an online clothing shop and write some code to generate that return form in PDF format. Our business works like this:

- Our products are all stored in a warehouse which is automated as much as possible to save money and give a competitive advantage, with robots moving products from the massive warehouse to conveyor belts which further transport the products to workers who actually package and send the packages.
- Upon receiving a return package, a worker will look for the return form in the package which will include a *bar code* which the worker will scan. The bar code will contain information about which products were returned such that the worker can then hand the products directly over to a robot for storing in the warehouse.

From customers' point of view, it looks like this:

- When a customer orders something, we send the products to them, and note the order in the database
- When a customer decides to return something, they enter a web page where they can enter which products they want to return, and why. We'll store this information in the database. The customer will then receive a PDF for printing which they'll send to us alongside the products.

This all furthermore implies that we have a database with a bunch of relevant information, like who our customers are, what our products are, who has ordered or returned what etc.

From technical point of view, in this section we'll learn about the following:

- SQL - schemas, adding, modifying and querying data

- Generating a bunch of random test data
- Generating PDFs and barcodes using Python
- Primitive business analytics
- Displaying database contents, filling forms and sending PDFs using Flask (again - but this time without JavaScript)

The whole thing will end up at about 300-400 lines of Python, with a good chunk of it being SQL statements.

4.3.1 Introduction to SQL

As mentioned in section "Redis", SQL is a language for querying databases, and there are several SQL databases which support this language, or their own dialect thereof, for the database operations. There are several reasons to use or not use an SQL database vs. a no-SQL database, but some reasons why we might want to use an SQL database for this kind of an application are:

- The data is relatively heavily *relational* - there are relationships between e.g. products and orders, orders and customers, and returns and orders. SQL has built in support for working with relations.
- SQL typically works with a fixed *database schema*, making it somewhat more robust against errors in the code that operates with the database
- Several SQL databases are *ACID* compliant - ACID standing for "Atomicity", "Consistency", "Isolation" and "Durability" - which means they intend to be robust against errors such as power failures etc.

Generally, when starting from scratch with SQL (or with databases even more generally), the flow is something like the following:

- Decide on the *schema* for your data - what data is it that you want to store? How do you want to store it? What are the relationships between different kinds of data?
- Implement the schema in a database of your choice by creating the necessary *tables* which will hold the data.

- Use your database: add your data in it, query for data, modify and delete data.

We'll be using SQLite in this book which is an SQL database similar to e.g. MySQL, Postgres etc. There are pros and cons to each database but I picked SQLite for this book because:

- The setup is fairly simple. SQLite, as the name implies, is a fairly lightweight database. While most other commonly used SQL databases operate in the server-client mode, i.e. the database administrator (DBA) would set up the database to run on a server computer while the clients (program using the database) would connect to it over the network, SQLite operates *locally*, i.e. the database is simply a file that SQLite will read and write to from our code, and no server process is necessary.
- The core SQL syntax is more or less the same for all SQL databases. While each database has their own features and extensions to SQL, we will focus on the basics (like for everything else in this book) and won't go very much into database specific features.

There are a few ways to use SQLite. It includes a command line program which supports all database operations including creating a new database. For example, after you've installed SQLite, you can run:

```
$ sqlite3 my_db
SQLite version 3.16.2 2017-01-06 16:32:41
Enter ".help" for usage hints.
sqlite> create table my_table(my_number integer);
sqlite> insert into my_table values(5);
sqlite> insert into my_table values(7);
sqlite> select * from my_table;
5
7
sqlite>
```

The above creates a new database called "my_db" with one table called "my_table" which has one column "my_number" which holds integers, and two rows with values 5 and 7. You can then find a file with the name "my_db" which is the database. (You can think of tables a bit like sheets in a spreadsheet program; they have a fixed number of columns, and you can add, remove and query for rows in the table.)

Exercise: Install SQLite and try it out. Bonus points if you compile it from source.

Digression: how is the database file structured?

The database file needs to support fetching, adding, modifying and removing data efficiently. To do this, the database is often saved as a *B-tree*. A B-tree is a special kind of binary tree which allows more than two children per node and is well suited for storing, reading and writing larger blocks of data. You can find the exact specification of the SQLite database file format on the SQLite home page.

Database schemas

Now that we're able to use SQLite let's consider what we need to store there. As our focus is generating the return form PDF, let's take a look at what the expected output could be like:

MyCorp

121

Order number: 148

John Armstrong
493 Ash Lane
15443 Washington D.C.

Return label

Product number	Description	Size	Reason
109	Red Men's Belt	36	1
174	Green Women's T-Shirt	M	4

Reason code	Description
1	Too large
2	Too small
3	Not as expected
4	Other

Don't focus on the details (e.g. the U.S. zip code "15443" is actually in Pennsylvania, not in Washington D.C.) but the objects we want to include are:

- At the top left, the company name and our logo (you can dream something up and draw a logo yourself, like I did)
- Name and address of the customer below the logo
- Bar code which encodes the return number at the top right
- The order number below the bar code
- A text "Return label", and a table of products that are returned: product number, description, size and a reason code
- A table at the bottom describing the reason codes

The idea is that the customer fills in the necessary information about the products to return and the reason for return on our web page, then clicks a link which generates a PDF like the one above.

Now, what would we need to have in the database for generating this? What "objects", or entities do we have, and what data is associated with them?

- There are customers, with a name and an address
- There are products, with a number, a name and a size
- There are orders by customers for certain products
- There are returns of some orders where some products are returned, and a reason associated to each product
- The returns reasons and the associated codes can also be stored in the database

Some of this is straightforward but we're making a few decisions here, e.g.:

- We assume a product is associated with a size, i.e. the same piece of clothing with a different size has a different product number. This is for simplicity's sake but could be designed differently.
- We assume that if a customer orders some product multiple times but returns some of them, each item is listed on a separate row on the PDF. That means we don't need to have a "quantity" column in our PDF, nor in our returns table in the database.

To identify each customer, product, order etc. we use *identifiers*, or *primary keys*. E.g. customer number 12345 will refer to a certain specific customer.

We can now specify our first table. Let's call it "customers". This SQL statement will create a new table:

```
CREATE TABLE customers(id INTEGER PRIMARY KEY,
                       name TEXT,
                       address TEXT,
                       zipcode TEXT,
                       city TEXT);
```

This means the following:

- We CREATE a new TABLE which is called "customers"
- It has five fields: "id", "name", "address", "zipcode" and "city"
- The field "id" is an integer, and a primary key. SQLite will be able to generate this automatically, and will do so in an autoincrement fashion, i.e. the first customer added will have id 1, second will be id 2 etc.
- The other fields are all text

One note is that the SQL keywords such as "create" and "table" can be written either upper case or lower case. In this book I'll write them in upper case to distinguish from table and column names and which are in lower case.

Now, you could run the above command in the SQLite shell, but another way to do this is by writing a Python script that does this for us. Indeed we should strive to have a script that can generate a new, empty database with our schema from scratch so that we can easily iterate as needed, including removing an old test database and creating a new one or trying out changes in the schema. A Python script that creates this table could look e.g. like the following:

```
import sqlite3

db = sqlite3.connect('mydb')
cursor = db.cursor()

cursor.execute('DROP TABLE if exists customers')
db.commit()

```

(continues on next page)

(continued from previous page)

```
9  cursor.execute('''
10         CREATE TABLE customers(id INTEGER PRIMARY KEY,
11                                name TEXT,
12                                address TEXT,
13                                zipcode TEXT,
14                                city TEXT)''')
15 db.commit()
16 db.close()
```

Let's go through this line by line:

- Line 1: We import the sqlite3 module which is included with Python.
- Line 3: We connect to a SQLite database called "mydb". This is the file name of the database. You can use whatever name you like. This function returns a database object. If the database doesn't yet exist then SQLite will automatically create it.
- Line 4: We obtain a *cursor* to the database which is an object allowing us to perform some database operations.
- Line 6: We *drop* the table "customers" if it already exists, i.e. delete it.
- Line 7: We *commit* our changes, i.e. write them in the file. Before this, the table removal was only stored in RAM but not written to the database file.
- Lines 9-14: We run our SQL statement to create a table. This uses Python multi-line strings using the ''' notation.
- Line 15: We commit our change to create the table.
- Line 16: We close the connection to the database.

Exercise: Run the above code. In addition, add code to create a table for the products. Call it "products". Each product should have an ID as the primary key, as well as name and size. The name and size can both be stored as text.

How about the relationships? There might not need to be a direct relationship e.g. between a customer and a product, but an order is always made by a specific customer. That means that the "orders" table will need to have another column, namely a value to *reference* the customer number of the customer who made the order. Furthermore we should tell SQLite that we intend to use this column to refer to an ID from another table as this way

SQLite is able to prevent invalid data which could occur if some rows were removed in one table but not in the other. Such a column is called a *foreign key*.

We can create the table "orders" with a foreign key using the following statement:

```
cursor.execute('''
        CREATE TABLE orders(id INTEGER PRIMARY KEY,
                            date DATE,
                            customer_id INTEGER,
                            FOREIGN KEY(customer_id)␣
↪REFERENCES customers(id))''')
```

Here, we define the column "customer_id" as a normal integer, but then include a line that tells this column is a foreign key which references the column "id" from the table "customers".

The field "date" holds a date of the order. When using SQLite with Python, we can create date fields by simply creating a string with format "YYYY-MM-DD" (ISO 8601 format).

Now that we have tables for customers, products and orders, we should come up with some way to describe which products were ordered with each order.

An order can include multiple products, and a product can be included in multiple orders (we don't take things like availability of a product in stock into account here; there can be multiple items of one product). This means that between an order and a product there is a *many-to-many* relationship. This is interesting because in SQL we need another table to model this kind of a relationship, namely a table that includes both products and orders as foreign keys (also called junction table). You can think of it as a mapping table describing which products belong to which orders, and vice versa. Such a table can be created like this:

```
cursor.execute('''
        CREATE TABLE products_ordered(id INTEGER PRIMARY KEY,
                                      order_id INTEGER,
                                      product_id INTEGER,
                                      FOREIGN KEY(order_id)␣
↪REFERENCES orders(id),
```

(continues on next page)

(continued from previous page)

```
                                    FOREIGN KEY(product_id)␣
↪REFERENCES products(id))''')
```

Here, we have a table with an ID like before, and two foreign keys, to orders and products. This table could look confusing at first glance, e.g.:

id	order_id	product_id
1	34	977
2	34	755
3	35	854

In this example we have three rows. The first two have the same order ID so they both describe the order number 34. For that order, products 977 and 755 were ordered. The last row describes order 35 for which product 854 was ordered.

Now, the only tables we're missing are those related to returning products. Remember, we want to note in the database when a customer wants to return products after ordering them for more automated return workflow at the warehouse. Here's one way we could define the table holding this information:

```
cursor.execute('''
        CREATE TABLE returns(id INTEGER PRIMARY KEY,
                             order_id INTEGER UNIQUE,
                             FOREIGN KEY(order_id) REFERENCES␣
↪orders(id))''')
```

Here, we define a table with two columns. The first one, "id" is our primary key like before. The second one, "order_id" is a foreign key almost like before, but we also include the keyword "UNIQUE". This causes SQLite to check that no two rows in this table have the same order_id. In practice this means our customers won't be able to send more than one return package from one order. We could enforce a policy like this to save shipping costs, but it also simplifies our code later.

The above table doesn't describe which products will be returned, or the reason for returning.

Exercise: Create a table for describing the return reasons. It needs to have an ID as a primary key as well as a text column that describes the reason.

Exercise: Create a table that describes which products were returned. It needs to describe the many-to-many relationship between ordered products and returns. Hence, apart from the ID as the primary key, it needs three more columns, all of which need to be foreign keys: the return ID, the reason ID and the ID to the table in "products_ordered", our mapping table describing the products in an order.

We now have our schema defined in code. It's often useful to also draw a diagram of the schema. In our case, it could look like this:

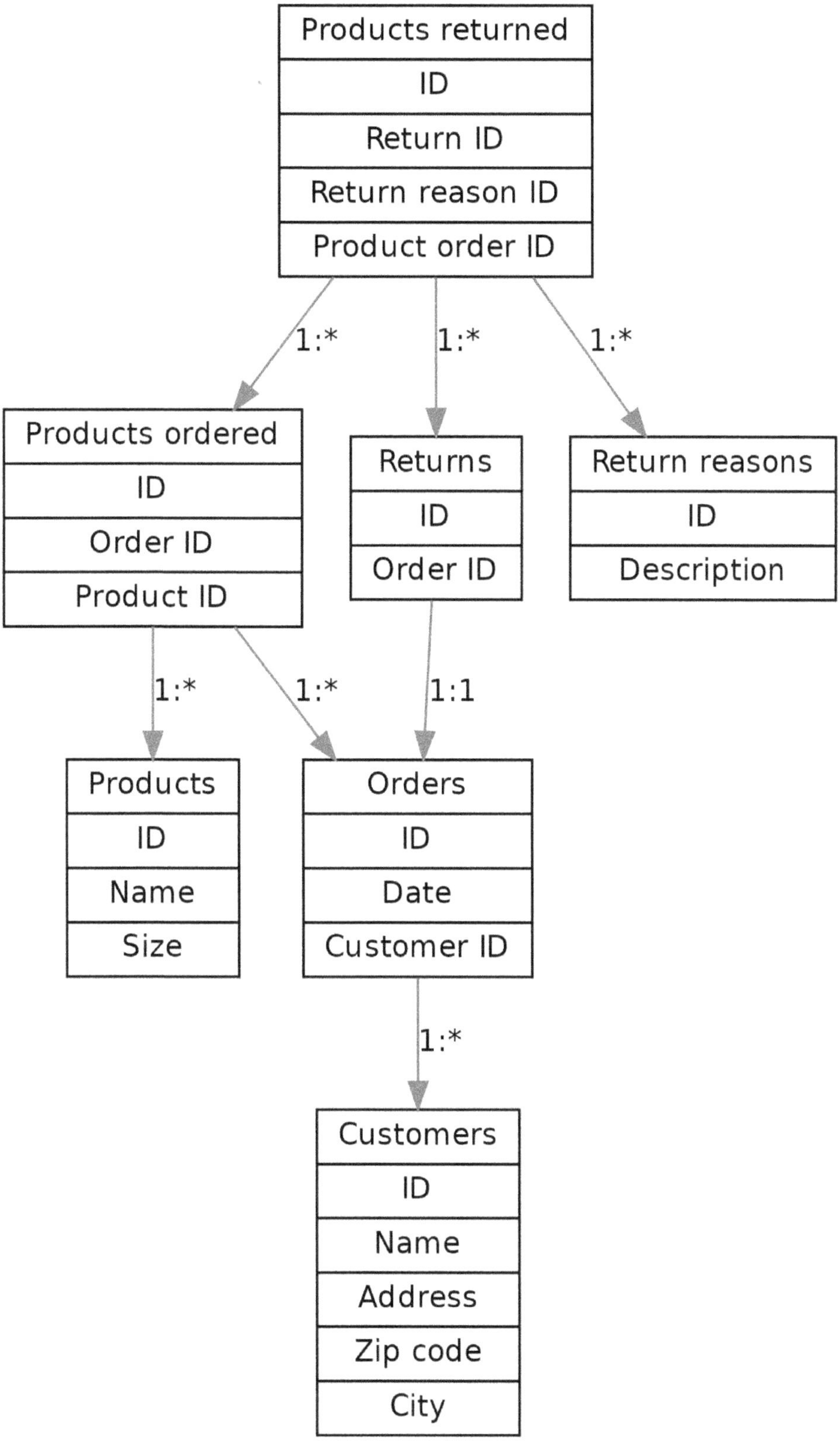
Products returned
ID
Return ID
Return reason ID
Product order ID
1:*
1:*
1:*
Products ordered
ID
Order ID
Product ID
Returns
ID
Order ID
Return reasons
ID
Description
1:*
1:*
1:1
Products
ID
Name
Size
Orders
ID
Date
Customer ID
1:*
Customers
ID
Name
Address
Zip code
City

Here, we have one box for each table, and one arrow for each foreign key reference. The labels describe the relationship between the tables, e.g. "1:*" between orders and customers reads as "one customer can have many orders, but one order is for exactly one customer". All relationships between the tables are one-to-many except the relationship between and order where each order can have (up to) one return. Several one-to-many relationships between tables lead to many-to-many relationships via junction tables, such that we have a many-to-many relationship e.g. between products and orders.

Now that we have our schema defined, the next step is using it by adding data to it.

4.3.2 Adding data to an SQL database

Now, we don't really have an online shop with products and customers so we have to generate some mock data. Python with its random number generator come into rescue here.

For example, for our products we have two columns we need to generate data for: the product name and size. Here's an example code snippet to generate 400 different products:

```
1  import random
2
3  # ... get hold of the database and the cursor here
4
5  for i in xrange(100):
6      color = random.choice(['Red', 'Green', 'Blue', 'Yellow',
   ↪'Black', 'White', 'Orange'])
7      gender = random.choice(["Men's", "Women's"])
8      clothing = random.choice(['Jeans', 'Shirt', 'T-Shirt',
   ↪'Cardigan', 'Skirt', 'Dress', 'Belt'])
9      name = '%s %s %s' % (color, gender, clothing)
10     sizes = random.choice([['S', 'M', 'L', 'XL'], ['36', '38',
   ↪'40', '42']])
11     for size in sizes:
12         cursor.execute('INSERT INTO products(name, size) VALUES(?
   ↪, ?)',
13                        (name, size))
```

Let's go through this line by line:

- Line 1: We import random, the Python random number generator library
- Line 5: We have a loop we loop through a 100 times
- Line 6: We select a random string, each describing a colour. The Python function random.choice() will select one item from a given list at random.
- Lines 7-8: We repeat the above for more descriptions of a clothing.
- Line 9: We combine our three words to one possibly nonsensical product name.

- Line 10: We select a list by random: either a list with elements 'S', 'M', 'L', 'XL' or with elements '36', '38', '40', '42'. Either way, a list of strings.
- Lines 11-13: We execute our SQL insert statement which inserts a new row into our "products" table, with our name and size as values.

Note that you'll need to run db.commit() before the changes are actually made persistent.

The insert statement deserves a bit more attention. There are the following things to take note of:

- One insert statement adds one row in the table. You need to supply the table you want the new data to be added for, and exactly what data you want to add.
- The columns for which data is added are provided in parentheses after the table name. In our case, these are "name" and "size". For the first column, "id", SQLite generates a number automatically (by picking a number not used before, typically one larger than the largest one currently in the database).
- We then provide the values for the columns in parentheses after the "VALUES" keyword. Because we want to read the values from our variables, we use the question marks as *placeholders* instead, and provide the variables as another parameter, in a tuple. SQLite will then replace the placeholders with the contents of the variables.

Hence, the insert statement will add random product data to our database.

The variable contents could also have been included in the insert statement using Python string syntax:

```
# Do NOT do this ever
cursor.execute('INSERT INTO products(name, size) VALUES(%s, %s)'
↪% (name, size))
```

However, the difference is that the Python string syntax (%s) inserts the variable contents in the string blindly while the SQLite built in syntax "(?)" *sanitises* the input first. This means that using the SQLite syntax is not a security hole unlike when the Python string syntax is used: if the variable name contents were dependent on user input, an attacker could craft an input string such as "foo'); DROP TABLE users; –" which, if inserted into the SQL statement blindly, would delete the table "users" in the database. Depending on the database the attacker could e.g. change or read passwords or other sensitive data. This kind of an attack is known as an *SQL injection*. To avoid this, use the SQLite built in syntax "(?)" when substituting variables in SQL statements.

Now that we have some mock products in our database, let's add some mock customers.

Exercise: Include the above snippet in a script that generates data in your database. Add another snippet that generates random customers: you'll need to generate and insert names, addresses, zip codes and cities for them. You can also use the function random.randint(a, b) which generates a random integer between a and b (both numbers inclusive), or random.shuffle() which randomly shuffles a list.

Note: You can set the *seed* of the Python random generator. E.g. running "random.seed(21)" before will set the seed to 21 for all future random numbers. This means that the random numbers will be *deterministic*, i.e. the output of the random functions will be the same every time you run your code. This can be useful for debugging and development purposes.

We now have some products and customers but there are no references between data. Generating some orders will help here. An order has a date column as well as a foreign key to the customer ID. Once we have generated a random year, month and day, we can turn them into a string using the following:

```
date = "%04d-%02d-%02d" % (year, month, day)
```

And once we have this and the customer ID, we can insert a new row in the "orders" table like this:

```
cursor.execute('INSERT INTO orders(date, customer_id) VALUES(?, ?)
↪',
        (date, customer_id))
```

Now, how do we get the customer ID? We could query for one, but there's another way. After an insert statement, SQLite provides the means to retrieve the primary key of the row that was just inserted like this:

```
cursor.execute('INSERT INTO customers(name, address, zipcode,␣
↪city) VALUES(?, ?, ?, ?)',
```

(continues on next page)

(continued from previous page)

```
        (name, address, zipcode, city))
customer_id = cursor.lastrowid
```

That is, the attribute "lastrowid" of the cursor object will provide the primary key.

Exercise: Generate some orders for your customers.

We now have some orders but the orders don't include any products so let's fix that. We can do this by generating some rows for the "products_ordered" table. What we'll need for this are the order ID as well as the product ID. How would we know what product IDs there are? One way is to store the returned primary key for each product table insert statement in a list. Alternatively, you can also *query* the product IDs after you've inserted them. The following code queries all product IDs in the database:

```
cursor.execute('SELECT id FROM products')
all_product_ids = cursor.fetchall()
all_product_ids = [x for (x,) in all_product_ids]
```

- The first line asks SQLite to execute a query to the "products" table such that the result of the query includes only the "id" column
- The second line fetches all the results of the query and stores them in a list
- When storing the results of a query, SQLite returns a list of tuples where each element in the tuple is one column of the row. When we query for only one column, the result is a list of tuples where each tuple has only one element (yes, such tuples exist, at least in Python). The third line converts this list of tuples to a list of integers using list comprehension.

Exercise: Generate a few rows for the "products_ordered" table. Use the order ID from the orders you've generated. You can either store the product ID in a list after inserting a product and reuse those, or query for the product IDs.

We now have customers, products, and customers ordering products. The final bit is returns.

Exercise: Generate some rows as return reasons for the "return_reasons" table. Note that SQLite requires the placeholder parameter for the insert statement to be a tuple so you may need a tuple with only one element.

Exercise: Generate some rows for the "returns" and the "products_returned" tables. You will need to keep hold of the order ID and the ID for the "products_ordered" table.

We now have some nice mock data. In the next section we'll learn how to query it in detail.

4.3.3 Querying SQL databases

In this section we'll learn how to query, or get data from our SQL database.

Querying an SQL database can be done using the select statement. We've already seen a couple of uses of this, e.g.:

```
cursor.execute('SELECT id FROM products')
all_rows = cursor.fetchall()
for row in all_rows:
    print row
```

This snippet will get all the product IDs from the database into a list of one-tuples and print the contents of those tuples.

Here's another query:

```
cursor.execute('SELECT count(id) FROM products')
row = cursor.fetchone()
print row # will print e.g. (400, )
```

- We tell SQLite we want to query for the *count* of IDs in the products table. The number of product IDs corresponds to the number of rows in the table so the result will indicate how many products we have stored in the database.
- Instead of using fetchall(), we can use fetchone() which will only give the first (and in this case, only) row of the query result.
- As before, the result will be a tuple, with one element in the tuple per column that was queried for. In this case, the result will be a one-tuple with an integer, namely the number of products.

Here's a bit more complicated query:

```
print 'distribution of return reasons:'
cursor.execute('''SELECT   return_reason_id, count(products_
↪returned.id)
                  FROM     products_returned
                  GROUP BY return_reason_id
                  LIMIT    5''')
for row in cursor.fetchall():
    print row
```

There are a few points to make here:

- We select the return_reason_id and the count of ids. The column names listed between SELECT and FROM define which columns are included in the table that will be returned.
- We specify we want to receive the count of the column "products_returned.id". In this case, simply typing "id" would've been enough, as we retrieve data from from the "products_returned" table. Generally, the table can be written before the column name to be clearer about which column you mean. In some cases, as we shall see, you must type the table name in order to clear ambiguity. (SQLite will return an error when the table name was required but not provided.)
- We want to *group* the result by the column "return_reason_id". This means that SQLite will, on the table that is the query result, group the column "return_reason_id" such that each ID will only appear once. In other words, the resulting table (the list that is returned by fetchall()) won't have any more elements than the number of return reasons we have in the database.
- We furthermore *limit* the number of rows in the resulting table to 5. This means, we only query for and receive the data for the first five reason codes.

Exercise: What would you expect the output of the above code snippet to be? Try it out.

You may ask yourself, for business analytics to be more useful, if you wanted to limit the output of the above query at all, you wouldn't limit it based on the reason code. Instead you'd want to know e.g. the most common return reasons. This can be done as well:

```
cursor.execute('''SELECT   return_reason_id, count(products_
↪returned.id)
                  FROM     products_returned
                  GROUP BY return_reason_id
                  ORDER BY count(products_returned.id) DESC
                  LIMIT    3''')
for row in cursor.fetchall():
    print row
```

Here, we include the keywords *order by*. This means we want to order by the count of the products returned ID, i.e. the number of products that were returned. If you wonder which column to order by, it may help to imagine the resulting table: we define the columns in the result after the SELECT keyword, so our table will have the columns "return_reason_id" and "count(products_returned.id)". As we furthermore group the return_reason_id i.e. have at most only one row per return reason, the column we'd want to order by would result to be the number of products returned.

The keyword "DESC" means we want to order in descending order, i.e. from the most to the least. (Alternatively the keyword "ASC" could be used for the opposite direction.)

Joins

Querying a single database table is fun enough, but things get more interesting when combining multiple tables.

Exercise: Let's say we want to find out our top five ordered products. How would we imagine the table to look like? What are the columns? How many rows would the table have? How would the table be ordered? Have a think.

We'd want to know the product ID, name, size and how often it was ordered, sort by the number of orders, and group by the product ID as we'd want no more than one row per product. The first three columns we can retrieve from the products table, while the fourth one (how often it was ordered) we can, as may be apparent from our database schema, retrieve by counting the products_ordered.id column.

The table could end up looking e.g. like this:

products.id	products.name	count(products_ordered.id)
158	Green Men's T-Shirt	349
30	Green Women's Jeans	341
86	Black Women's Belt	341
26	Yellow Men's Belt	338
71	Green Women's Cardigan	338

This query would look like this:

```
cursor.execute('''SELECT     products.id, products.name, products.
↪size, count(products_ordered.id)
                  FROM       products
                  INNER JOIN products_ordered ON products_
↪ordered.product_id = products.id
                  GROUP BY   products.id
                  ORDER BY   count(products_ordered.id) DESC
                  LIMIT      5''')
```

Now, this is similar to the previous example but we have two new interesting characteristics:

- On the first line we describe not only columns from the table we're querying data from, but also *another* table, namely "products_ordered".
- Because we need a column from another table in our result, we need to *join* the other table. Hence we include the keywords "INNER JOIN" to join the table "products_ordered".
- We need to tell SQLite *how* to join the other table, so we tell it to join "ON products_ordered.product_id = products.id" - meaning, if a row from the "products" table has the same ID as the "product_id" column in the "products_ordered" table then the two rows will be joined into one in the query result. It's worth noting here that products_ordered.product_id is a foreign key to products.id.

There are different kinds of joins like outer join, left join etc. but in practice inner join, where two tables are joined at the intersection (i.e. when a foreign key matches the primary key of a row in another table) is the most common.

Exercise: Try out the above statement.

But there's more! You can also join *multiple* tables using multiple joins in one statement. For example, if you wanted to find out which products were returned the most, you'd need to have the product ID in your query result and order by the number of products returned, i.e. products_returned.id. However, there's no direct link from the "products" table to the "products_returned" table because of the many-to-many relationship, so we'd need to also join the "products_ordered" table. In practice this query would look like this:

```
cursor.execute('''SELECT     products.id, products.name, products.
↪size, count(products_returned.id)
                  FROM       products_returned
                  INNER JOIN products_ordered ON products_
↪ordered.id = products_returned.product_order_id
                  INNER JOIN products         ON products.id     ␣
↪     = products_ordered.product_id
                  GROUP BY   products.id
                  ORDER BY   count(products_returned.id) DESC
                  LIMIT      5''')
```

This is very similar to the previous statement, but it has two joins: we query the table "products_returned", but join the table "products_ordered" to it such that the product order ID matches. We then join the "products" table such that the product ID between the "products" table and the "products_ordered" table matches.

Exercise: Try out the above statement.

Exercise: Find out which customers have put in the most orders. You'll need to select the customer ID as well as the customer name and the number of order IDs. Join the "orders" table with the "customers" table. Group by the customer ID. Order by the number of order IDs.

Exercise: Find out who has ordered most products. The query is similar to the previous exercise but you also need to join the "products_ordered" table.

Exercise: Find out the top five customers who have returned most products.

Another useful keyword is "WHERE" which allows you to filter which data you want in the result database. For example, we might want to see the details for the product with ID 123:

```
product_id = 123
cursor.execute('''SELECT *
                  FROM   products
                  WHERE  products.id = ?''', (product_id, ))
```

Here, we supply the wildcard "*" to SELECT which tells SQLite that we want all the columns from the queried tables. This way we don't need to specify all the columns manually.

Besides only looking for columns with a specific value, WHERE also allows for different operators such as boolean (AND, OR), arithmetic operators (>, <, etc.) or keywords like BETWEEN (values within a range) etc. You can look up the details at an SQL reference if you're interested.

Exercise: List the products ordered by customer 123.

We now have some knowledge around querying useful data from the database. In the next section we can put together some code to generate a return form.

4.3.4 Generating a return form

We now get to the meat of the chapter: generating the return form. We should have a program which has the following characteristics:

- As input, it should take the return ID
- As output, it should store a PDF in a file
- It should be possible to later easily refactor it to a function that could be called from a web app. This function should take the return ID as input and output a binary stream that represents the PDF that can be sent to the client over HTTP.

We'll do this in three steps:

- Fetch all the data we need for the form from our SQL database
- Generate the bar code
- Create an empty PDF, add all the data to it and save it

Fetching the data

We'll be needing the following columns:

- Customer name and full address
- The ID, name, size and return reason for all products that will be returned
- The order ID
- The return ID (provided as input parameter)

Exercise: Given the return ID, fetch the above data. You can either combine everything in one query, where e.g. the customer data is duplicated for each row, or use multiple queries where you first fetch e.g. the customer data and then the data for the products to be returned.

Furthermore we'll be needing the contents of the table holding the return reasons.

Exercise: Fetch the return reason codes and descriptions.

Generating the bar code

Let's generate the bar code next. Let's first recap the motivation for the bar code: the worst case would be the worker having to pick each returned item, walk to the correct place in our huge warehouse and put the item in the correct box. The ideal workflow would be that the worker who unpacks the return package can put each returned item into a box on a conveyor belt, such that a robot would then come and pick up each box and store it in the correct place in our warehouse. How would we achieve this? The worker should be able to easily let the robot system know that they will send a number of boxes to the robots, each box holding one specific item, and the robots then pick up the boxes and store the items correctly. In order to transfer the information, the act of scanning a bar code should inform the system of what products are incoming.

What should the bar code encode? It seems the easiest way to communicate the information about the products returned is the return ID. How can we do this? A quick search online for a Python barcode library reveals the existence of pyBarcode which can be installed using "pip install pybarcode". We'll furthermore need to decide what kind of bar code we use. The library seems to support a few, e.g. EAN-13, ISBN and Code 39. Now, from software development point of view it doesn't really matter which one we use but Code 39 seems to be general purpose enough that it's suitable for our purposes.

Looking at the pyBarcode documentation and adapting it a bit, we can then end up with this snippet:

```
import barcode
from barcode.writer import ImageWriter

bclass = barcode.get_barcode_class('code39')
code = bclass('123abc', writer=ImageWriter(), add_checksum=False)
fullname = code.save('barcode')
```

This will create a file "barcode.png" which will include a Code 39 barcode of the string "123abc".

Exercise: Create a barcode image with the return ID. You'll need to convert the ID from integer to string using str(number).

Creating the PDF

Now that we have our data and our barcode, the last bit is creating the PDF. Again searching online it seems there are several Python libraries for generating PDF files. For the purposes of this book I picked pyfpdf. It can be installed using "pip install fpdf".

Exercise: Install pyfpdf. Look up its reference online.

Now, the interface that pyfpdf provides for creating PDF files is quite a bit wider than the one from pyBarcode. We can create a very simple PDF file with the following code:

```
1 from fpdf import FPDF
2 
3 pdf = FPDF()
4 pdf.add_page()
5 pdf.set_font('Arial', 'B', 16)
6 pdf.cell(40, 10, 'Hello world', align='l')
7 pdf.output('output.pdf', 'F')
```

Going through this line by line:

- Line 1: import our library.
- Line 3: create a PDF object.
- Line 4: add a page.
- Line 5: Set font: Arial, bold, size 16.
- Line 6: Create a *cell* which will hold text. As per pyfpdf reference, its width is 40 units (in this case 40 mm - by default the unit is mm and the page format is A4) and its height is 10 mm. The text in the cell is "Hello world" and it's left aligned within the cell. (For reference, an A4 page is 210 mm wide and 297 mm long.)
- Line 7: We output our PDF to output.pdf.

Exercise: Create a test PDF. Look up the reference for the cell() member function.

You may ask yourself, where on the page does the cell with the text land up in. The answer is, the default location. Pyfpdf is a *state machine* in that it maintains the current location of new elements internally.

Here's a snippet that demonstrates the following concepts:

- Including images
- Designating the position of a text label
- Having multiple text labels, one after another (like customer name and address)

```
1  from fpdf import FPDF
2
3  pdf = FPDF()
4  pdf.add_page()
5  pdf.set_font('Arial', 'B', 16)
6  pdf.image('logo.png', 10, 10, 33)
7
8  pdf.set_xy(10, 45)
9  pdf.cell(40, 10, 'Hello world', align='l')
10
11 pdf.set_xy(10, 80)
12 pdf.cell(40, 10, "Text 1",  ln=1, align='l')
13 pdf.cell(40, 10, "Text 2",  ln=1, align='l')
14 pdf.output('output.pdf', 'F')
```

Let's look at this closer again:

- Line 6: We add the image "logo.png" in our PDF. The second and third parameters describe the position of the image. The fourth parameter designates the width of the image, here 33 millimetres. Pyfpdf calculates the height of the image automatically based on the width but if you wanted to stretch the image, as per pyfpdf reference, you could provide the height as the fifth parameter.
- Line 8: We set the X and Y coordinates of the next item to (10, 45).
- Line 12: We create our second text label. It will be created at position (10, 80) and have the width and height of 40 and 10 respectively. We pass the cell() member function the named parameter "ln" (line, or line break) with the value 1 which indicates that the next cell should appear below this cell (as opposed to to the right of it which is the default).
- Line 13: Because we passed ln=1 to the previous function call, the current X and Y positions are now shifted to right below the previous

cell. This means that the text "Text 2" should appear right below the text "Text 1".

We now have some tools available for starting to create our return form.

Exercise: Create the beginning of the return form: if you have a picture available that could be used as a logo, include it. Add a label that designates the name of your company. Add labels including the name and address of the customer. Include the barcode around top right, and a label for the order number below that.

You can also pick up an image file for the logo as well as the example PDF from the book web site.

Now, how about the table that describes the products that are being returned? Here are the clues that you need:

- By passing the named parameter "border=1" to pdf.cell(), the cell will have borders. You can construct a table by including borders for each cell in the table.
- If you don't include "ln=1", the next cell will be to the right of that cell. If you do include "ln=1", the next cell will be below the leftmost cell on the previous line.
- In order to have the table fit on the page, you may need to reduce the font size, e.g. to 12.

In other words, if you were to run e.g. this:

```
pdf.cell(40, 10, "Text 1", border=1, ln=0, align='l')
pdf.cell(80, 10, "Text 2", border=1, ln=0, align='l')
pdf.cell(30, 10, "Text 3", border=1, ln=1, align='l')
pdf.cell(40, 10, "Text 4", border=1, ln=0, align='l')
pdf.cell(80, 10, "Text 5", border=1, ln=0, align='l')
pdf.cell(30, 10, "Text 6", border=1, ln=1, align='l')
```

...then you'd end up with a 3x2 table, i.e. three columns and two rows. The widths of the columns would be 40, 80 and 30 mm. The heights of the rows would be 10 mm. The "ln" parameter controls the dimensions of the table.

Exercise: Put together the table showing all products that will be returned, including their product IDs, descriptions, sizes and reason code for return.

Now, the final bit missing in our PDF is the table describing the return reason codes.

Exercise: Add this table.

If you made it here, congratulations.

4.3.5 Web UI for our return form

Let's finish this chapter by putting together a simple (but ugly) web UI that allows a user to generate a return form.

We'll be using Flask for this exercise, and to keep things simple, we'll skip the JavaScript bit and *generate* all HTML on the server side. Flask makes this fairly easy as it integrates with the Jinja 2 templating language.

Products

To start things off, as an example, let's see how we could generate and display an HTML table consisting of Python data. Here's the relevant Python snippet:

```
from flask import Flask, render_template, request, make_response
app = Flask(__name__)

@app.route("/products/", methods=['GET'])
def products():
    my_list = [{'a': 1, 'b': 2}, {'a': 3, 'b': 4}]
    return render_template('products.html', my_list=my_list)
```

This returns an HTML file based on the template "products.html" which Flask will look for in the "templates" directory, but with a twist: it generates the HTML based on the contents of "my_list". The HTML template could look e.g. like the following:

```
<!DOCTYPE html>
<html lang="en">
    <head>
        <meta charset="UTF-8">
        <meta name="viewport" content="width=device-width">
        <title>Products</title>
    </head>
    <body>
        <p>
        List of all products
        </p>

```

(continues on next page)

(continued from previous page)

```
        <table border="1">
            <tr>
                <td>a</td>
                <td>b</td>
            </tr>
            {% for elem in my_list %}
            <tr>
                <td>{{ elem.a }}</td>
                <td>{{ elem.b }}</td>
            </tr>
            {% endfor %}
        </table>
    </body>
</html>
```

This makes use of the Jinja 2 *for* statement which will loop through a list provided to the template. In this case, it'll access the dictionary keys "a" and "b" of the input list and display the numbers 1, 2, 3 and 4 in the table.

You can include your SQLite database in your Flask application by calling the relevant functions at the top level, e.g.:

```
from flask import Flask, render_template, request, make_response
app = Flask(__name__)

import sqlite3

db = sqlite3.connect('mydb')
cursor = db.cursor()

# the rest of the code goes here
```

Exercise: Create the "products" page. Query your database for the products. Turn the result to a dictionary, write an HTML template and pass your data to your template. The page should display all the columns for all your products.

Orders

Now, it would be nice to be able to see all the orders by a customer. It would furthermore be nice to be able to write a URL like e.g. "http://127.0.0.1:5000/orders?customer_id=123" and get an overview of the orders made by customer 123. Let's do this next.

The part in the URL after the "?" is the query string and is accessible in Flask using the function "request.args.get()". In our case, the following line is what we need:

```
customer_id = request.args.get('customer_id', 1) # default to 1␣
↪if not given
```

Exercise: Create the Python handler for displaying the orders of a customer. Perform the relevant SQL query. Write an HTML template and provide the relevant data to the template. Also have the HTML display the customer ID for which the orders are shown. Do this by passing the customer_id variable to the template. You'll then be able to access the value in HTML using e.g. {{ customer_id }}.

Now that we're able to see what orders a customer has made, it would be nice to see the details of an order.

Exercise: In your table showing the orders, add another column which is a link to a more detailed page about the order. (We don't have the page yet so clicking on the link would make Flask return 404; this is fine for now.) You can create a suitable link using e.g. <a href="/order?order_id={{ order.id }}">Show details</a>.

Order details

We can now click on a link that would show order details but that page doesn't exist yet so let's create it. To make things more interesting, we can imagine we're writing this page for the customer with the goal that the customer should be able to start the return process from this page. We should have a flow that looks like this:

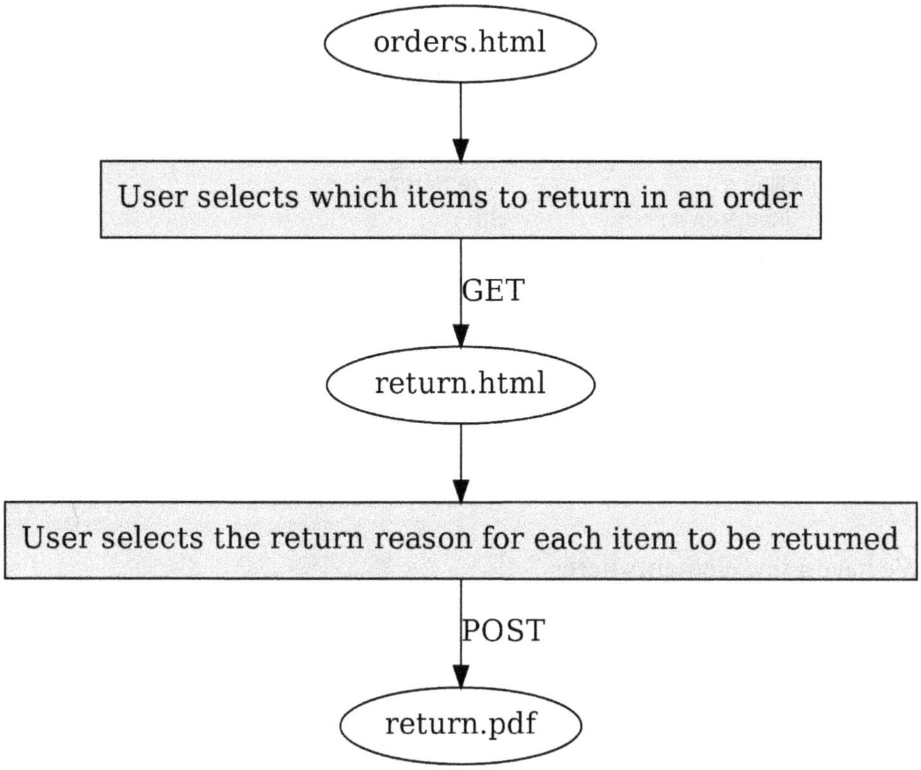

In other words, the customer would first select which items to return, then enter another page where they can provide a reason for the return, and submitting the form on that page will trigger a database update to enter the data about the return and send a PDF to the customer to print and include in the return package.

The order details page could look e.g. like this:

Product ID	Name	Size	Return
214	Red Men's Shirt	38	
200	Blue Women's Jeans	XL	
304	White Women's Cardigan	XL	
187	Black Women's Dress	40	
102	White Men's Dress	M	
280	Green Men's T-Shirt	XL	
333	Red Women's Skirt	S	

We have a few elements here:

- The order ID is shown
- A table listing all the products for the order is shown
- This page includes a *form*; the user can select a number of products using the check boxes and submit the selection to the server by pressing the button labelled "Return"

We should have a grip on displaying the order ID and the table without the check boxes by now. We can put together a form that sends the contents of the check boxes as well as the order ID using e.g. the following HTML:

```
<form action="/return.html" method="GET">
    <input type="hidden" name="order_id" value="{{ order_id }}">
    <table border="1">
        <tr>
            <td>Product ID</td>
            <td>Name</td>
            <td>Size</td>
            <td>Return</td>
        </tr>
        {% for product in product_list %}
        <tr>
            <td>{{ product.id }}</td>
            <td>{{ product.name }}</td>
            <td>{{ product.size }}</td>
```

(continues on next page)

(continued from previous page)

```
15                  <td><input type="checkbox" name="{{ product.id }}"/>
↪</td>
16              </tr>
17              {% endfor %}
18          </table>
19          <input type="submit" value="Return">
20      </form>
```

That is, we do the following:

- All the elements that are part of the form, including the submit button and the check boxes must be within the <form> tag
- The form tag should, with the "action" attribute, describe which URL will be loaded on the server side when the form is sent, i.e. to which URL the form contents are sent to
- The contents of the form can be defined using the <input> tag
- On line 15, we have an <input> tag describing the checkbox. We identify this checkbox by using the product ID which will be necessary later on.
- On line 19, we have another <input> tag which is the button to submit the form.
- On line 2, we have a *hidden* <input> tag which simply says the form will include the order ID.

Exercise: Put together the page to show the order details. Include the form. Submitting the form should result in requesting the page "return.html" with a query string including all the form information, but we don't have this page yet; this is fine for now.

Returning

The previous page should lead the user to a page where the user can describe the reason for returning each item and download the return form. It should look e.g. like this:

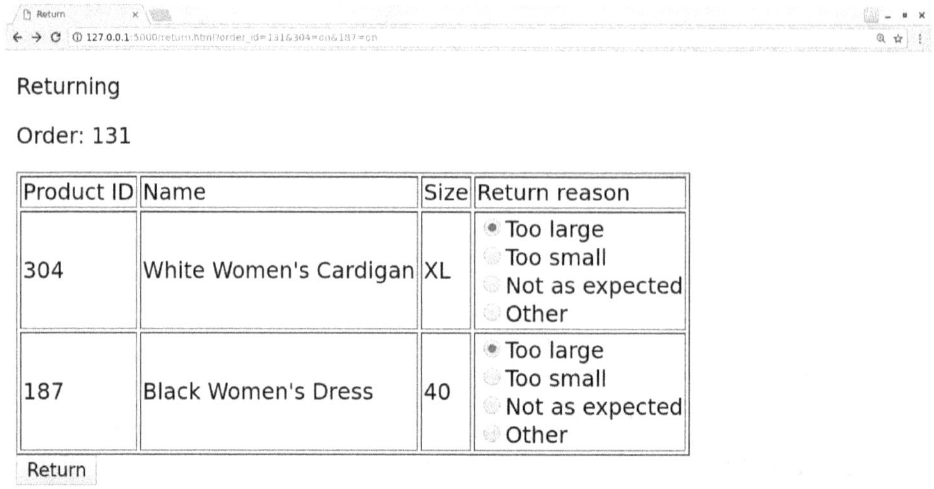

Now, this is similar to the previous one but with a few differences:

- Instead of including all products from the order in the table, we only display the products for which the user checked the checkbox
- We display the different return reasons as *radio buttons*. The first one is selected as the default. We'll need to send the information about which radio button was selected as the form is sent.

How would we know for which products the user checked the checkbox? The URL provides a hint: this information is included in the query string, which, again, is accessible in Flask using the request.args.get() function. We can get a list of all products the customer ordered from the database, and, for each product, check if the checkbox for that product was checked. As revealed by Flask documentation or general online search, the following statement will evaluate to True if the checkbox for ID 123 was checked and False otherwise:

```
request.args.get(str(123))
```

The parameter for get() must match the name given to the checkbox in the HTML. You'll need to use this to filter the list of products that are used for HTML generation.

As for the radio buttons, they can be displayed using e.g.:

```
<input type="radio" name="radio_button_1" value="Enable">Enable␣
↪widget<br/>
<input type="radio" name="radio_button_1" value="Disable">
↪Disable widget<br/>
```

The above will create one selection with two radio buttons such that the form query string will either include "radio_button_1=Enable" or "radio_button_2=Disable". In other words, the attribute "name", like with check boxes, defines the identifier for the radio box so your form handling code knows which variable is which. The attribute "value" describes the value that will be stored in the form if that button was selected.

In your code, you'll need to replace parts of the above using templates.

How would one define the default setting? This can be done using e.g. the following:

```
<input type="radio" name="radio_button_1" value="Enable" checked=
↪"checked">Enable widget<br/>
<input type="radio" name="radio_button_1" value="Disable">
↪Disable widget<br/>
```

In other words, setting the attribute "checked" to "checked" will make the radio button the default for that selection.

Exercise: Create the return page. Submitting the form can result in 404 for now. The page should display the products the user checked for returning, and include radio buttons to select the reason. Query the result reasons from the database. As submitting the form will eventually cause database changes, the form should perform a POST, not a GET. Again, include the order ID as part of your form as a hidden variable. To make a radio button the default, you can use the if-statement from Jinja 2. E.g.:

```
{% if default %}
<input type="radio" name="TODO" value="TODO" checked="checked">
↪TODO<br/>
{% else %}
<input type="radio" name="TODO" value="TODO">TODO<br/>
{% endif %}
```

You'll need to set the variable "default" in your Python code accordingly to determine which radio button is the default.

Return form

Now we have all the information from the user: which order ID they want to return products for, which products they want to return and why. Clicking the submit button on the previous page should result in the following:

- A new row is added in the database in the "returns" column, unless it already existed
- If any existing entries existed in the database already about returning products for this order, they should be removed, namely from the "products_returned" table
- We should add one row in the "products_returned" table for each product that will be returned, and commit this in the database
- We should then generate a PDF based on the order ID that we've been provided, reusing our existing PDF generation code
- We should finally send the generated PDF to the client

There are a few new concepts here so let's go through them one by one.

Add a new row except if it already existed

SQLite provides a practical way to do this:

```
cursor.execute('INSERT OR IGNORE INTO returns(order_id) VALUES (?)
↪', (order_id, ))
```

The above statement does what you'd expect: it inserts a new row in the table "returns" with the column "order_id" set to the value of the variable "order_id" - but, if this is not possible because it would violate our "UNIQUE" constraint - that is, that the "order_id" must be unique for all rows in the table as per our database schema definition from our "CREATE TABLE" statement at the beginning - then the insertion statement is simply ignored.

After the above statement, we can query for the "id" column in the "returns" table to retrieve the ID of the return for this order ID.

Deleting data in an SQL database

Now, if the user has already let us know that they'll be returning some products from an order but are now telling us they want to return some other products instead, then what we might want to do as a real online shop is to insist that the original return form, which might already have been received by our company, is the final one and no updates are allowed. However, as we're building our UI for testing and development purposes, it seems like the best way to handle this is to simply delete all references to old data and start afresh. This allows us to try out different things in our UI without polluting our database with conflicting data.

The following command would delete rows in the table "products_returned", namely those rows where the "return_id" field is set to the according variable:

```
cursor.execute('DELETE FROM products_returned WHERE return_id = ?
↪', (return_id, ))
```

After this we're ready to add the correct data in the database and commit our changes.

Reusing our existing PDF code to generate a PDF

Now, we already have a module in place for generating a PDF. If that file is in the same directory as our Flask code, then we can simply do:

```
import print_return # assumes the file is called print_return.py

@app.route(...)
def foo():
    pdf = print_return.generate_pdf(return_id)
    # do something with pdf
```

In other words, we can simply import the file and then call a function defined within that file. Note that you don't want to have any code defined at the top level of that file as that code would be run automatically at the import time. If you want code to be run when running the file directly, e.g. with "python print_return.py", then you can enclose that code in an if-statement, e.g.:

```
def generate_label(return_id):
    # code here

if __name__ == '__main__':
    pdf = generate_label(return_id)
    # do something with pdf
```

What this branch does is check whether the special variable __name__ is '__main__'. This is only the case if the script was invoked directly from the command line. In other words, if the above snippet was stored in foo.py, then the function generate_label() would only be called if the script was started as e.g. "python2 foo.py" but not if the file was imported from another Python file. Without this branch, the function generate_label() would be called when importing the file.

You may now be able to run your existing PDF code, or you may need to refactor the old code first, but the question remains: Once you have the PDF (either file or object), what do you do with it?

Sending the PDF to the client

As an online search will tell you, a good way to send a file to the client via HTTP using Flask is to have the file contents available as a binary stream, tell Flask to turn this binary stream into a response, set the response headers accordingly and then return this response in our Python code. Long story short, the code could look like this:

```
response = make_response(my_binary_stream)
response.headers['Content-Type'] = 'application/pdf'
response.headers['Content-Disposition'] = 'inline;␣
↪filename=return.pdf'
return response
```

That is, instead of using render_template() to send HTML to the client, we craft a response from binary data and send that instead.

If you're wondering how to get a binary stream from our PDF, then you're in luck because the pyfpdf library provides means to do exactly this:

```
# pdf is the pdf object, i.e. the return value from the function␣
↪FPDF()
my_binary_stream = pdf.output('', 'S')
```

Now we should have everything we need to finish this task:

Exercise: Put everything together and see if you can download the PDF. You'll need to do the following:

- Call your existing code to generate a PDF. You should be able to call a function which takes a return ID as the input parameter and returns a PDF object (not a file object or a file name). Refactor your existing code if necessary. Make sure you set the SQL database contents correctly beforehand.
- Convert the PDF object to a binary stream.
- Send the binary stream to the client using Flask.

If you succeeded in the above exercise, you've finished our chapter around SQL and return forms. Congratulations! As you may have seen, our simple UI is nice for demonstration purposes but it lacks some features, like authentication, and as such should not be used for real online shops without significant additions. However the code does serve to demonstrate the key concepts around displaying, using and updating database contents.

4.4 Final bits

4.4.1 Software licenses

As a software engineer it's often useful to have some understanding of the different software licenses. This may be useful not only to understand whether you can use certain software, or what the limitations are, but also something to consider when writing your own software and making it available to others. This section provides an overview. Note that none if this is legal advice. If necessary please consult a lawyer.

Proprietary software

Proprietary software, or non-free software, refers to software where another entity than the user, such as the software publisher, owns the software and retains major rights. This typically means that the user may not be allowed to e.g. copy, modify, distribute or sell the software, or receive the source code of the software.

Open source licenses

We've used lots of different open source software in this book, from the compilers and interpreters (e.g. Python, gcc, clang and all main JavaScript engines) to various libraries (SQLite, SDL2, Flask) and other tools (most shells, Make, git, vim). In addition, several components of modern operating systems may be open source, from the kernel to the file system utilities (commands such as "ls", "grep" etc.) and commonly used desktop software such as the browser. There are several different open source licenses and here only some of the most popular ones are covered.

A note on terminology: open source and free software are used interchangeably in this section. They're often treated as synonyms of each other although "free software" emphasises freedom (as in speech, not as in beer) while "open source" emphasises the practicality of being able to access and modify the source.

Permissive licenses

Permissive free software licenses are licenses that have very little requirements on the usage of the software. Most common permissive free software licenses include the *MIT license* and the *BSD licenses*. Typically, permissive licenses allow the use, copying, modification, distribution and selling of the software as long as the relevant copyright notice is stated, i.e. the original author is credited.

E.g. clang, the main Python interpreter, SDL2 and Flask are licensed under a permissive free software license.

GNU General Public License

GNU General Public License (GPL) is a *copyleft* license. This means that, similarly to the permissive license, the license allows the use, copying, modification, distribution and selling of the software, but under the condition that any software distribution of the original or modified software must retain the same license terms. This means that were one to e.g. obtain the source code of a program licensed under GNU GPL, and modify it, any recipient of the modified software has the right to access the modified source code. Similarly, were one to obtain a program licensed under GNU GPL in binary form (i.e. only the machine code but not the source code), the recipient has the right to receive the source code for the received machine code.

E.g. gcc, the Linux kernel and git are licensed under GNU GPL.

Public domain

Software under public domain or licensed under a public domain equivalent license allows the use, copying etc. of the software without any limitations.

E.g. SQLite is placed under public domain.

Open source license compatibility

One may ask the question: "what happens when one incorporates multiple pieces of software licensed under different terms?" Generally speaking, it may make things tricky from legal perspective, but often it is possible to check the different licenses for *compatibility*.

License compatibility refers to whether different software components licensed under different license terms can be combined. It's typically allowed to incorporate software licensed under more permissive license terms under less permissive license. For example, one could take various pieces of software that are all placed under public domain and license them under the MIT license which is a permissive license. Another example is combining various pieces of software licensed under permissive licenses with software licensed under GNU GPL, and license the final product under GNU GPL. This is because a permissive license may be *compatible* with GNU GPL but not the other way around. In other words, one may not e.g. license software originally licensed under GNU GPL using the MIT license as this would conflict with the GNU GPL license terms.

4.4.2 NP-hard problems

In the chapter "First touch of algorithms" we discussed the run times of various algorithms (O(log n) etc.). There's more to this, namely problems which, to the best of current knowledge of mankind, are *hard*. Hard here means that the run time of an algorithm to solve the problem is expected to be high, and it's not known how to construct an algorithm that has a run time polynomial to n, i.e. the complexity class isn't $O(n^x)$ for any x but rather e.g. exponential ($O(2^n)$, i.e. incrementing n by one doubles the run time).

There are several classifications from classical Computer Science for problems, such as *P* (solvable in polynomial time), *NP* ("NP" standing for non-deterministic polynomial time) etc. which are not in the scope for this book, but the summary is that for certain problems, fast solutions are not known. This section discusses one of such problems in detail, namely the *Travelling salesman problem.*

Travelling salesman problem (TSP)

TSP is one of the classical Computer Science problems. Imagine set of cities with distances defined between all cities, and a salesman who intends to visit all of the cities. The goal is to find the shortest path to visit all the cities and return to the starting point.

Let's see if we can solve this. Let's start with generating the input data. The following should get you started:

```
import random

random.seed(21)
N = 5

input_data = list()
for i in xrange(N):
    x = random.randint(0, 100)
    y = random.randint(0, 100)
    input_data.append((x, y))
```

Here, we set the *random seed* to a predefined number, causing the random number generator to always generate the same numbers each time our code is run. This is useful for us as we'll be running our code multiple times and want to keep the problem the same each time. We furthermore set N, the number of cities, to 5, and generate N coordinates where the X and Y values are integers between 0 and 100.

The following diagram displays an example of TSP, for N=7:

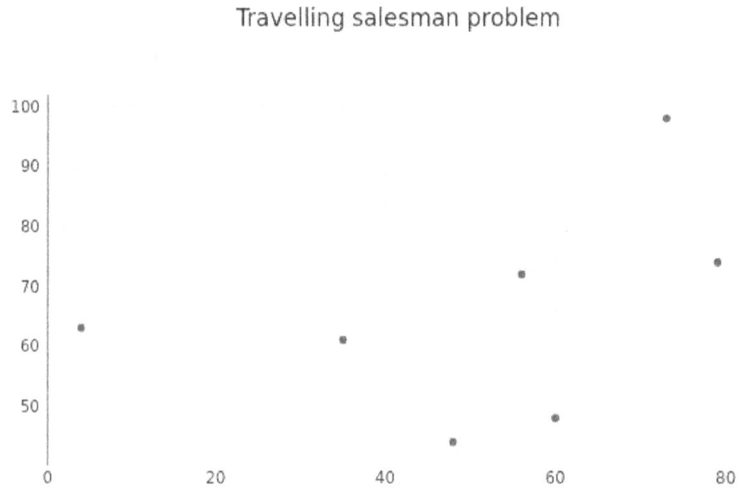

The most naive way to solve TSP is *brute force search*: trying out all combinations and picking the best one. Before we can implement this, let's write a few helper functions.

Exercise: Write a function that returns the distance between two cities using the Pythagorean theorem.

Exercise: Write a function that returns the total length of the path. It should, as input, take a list of tuples, whereby each element in the list is a city. The total length of the path is the sum of the distances between each city in the list. Test your function with some simple dummy data.

Now we can get to the meat of the problem and implement the brute force search.

Exercise: Implement the brute force search function which shall find the shortest path between the different cities. Note that the path must begin and end at the same location. You can find all the *permutations*, i.e. all the possible path combinations by running the following Python code:

"all_permutations = list(itertools.permutations(input_data))" (you'll need to "import itertools" first). Print out the shortest path and the length of the path.

The following diagram displays an example of a brute force search solution to TSP, for N=7:

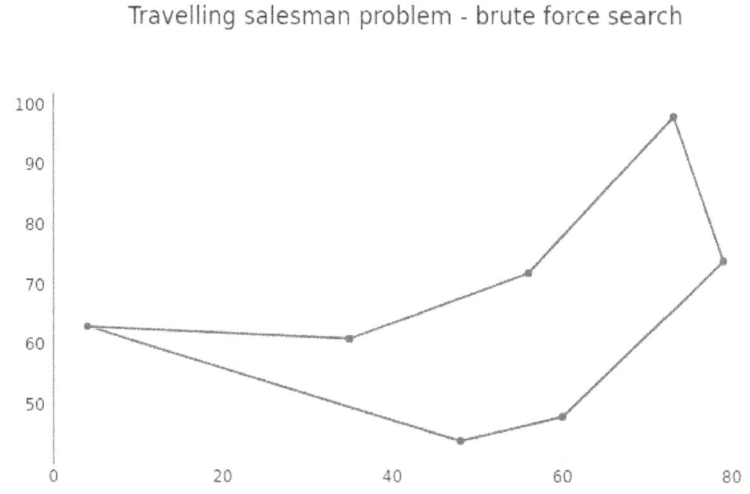

Now, things get interesting if we increase N. The brute force search to TSP has the runtime complexity of O(n!), that is, each time N is incremented, the runtime is *multiplied* by N. The number of permutations for N=5 is 5 * 4 * 3 * 2 * 1 = 120. For N=6 it is 120 * 6 = 720.

If we assume we require four bytes to store each permutation in RAM (in practice it'll be more with our data structure), how much memory would we require to store all the permutations for different values of N?

Exercise: With the above assumption, calculate the possible memory requirements. You can use "math.factorial(n)" to calculate the factorial in Python, and convert bytes to kilobytes by dividing by 1024.0, or to megabytes by dividing by 1024.0 * 1024.0, or to gigabytes by dividing by 1024.0 * 1024.0 * 1024.0. Find out the memory requirements for N from 1 to 20.

Now, let's examine the run time of our brute force search.

Exercise: Try to increment N from 5, one at a time. Measure the impact on the run time of your script. You can use the command "time" to measure time to execute a command in Unix shell (e.g. "time python2 tsp.py"). Don't increase N to a higher number than you have RAM available on your machine (or if you do, save any of your work before).

Now, the brute force search may be slow for increasing N, but it does find the optimal solution. Can you come up with a faster algorithm? Have a think.

One possible approach is called the *next neighbour algorithm*. This algorithm works as the following:

1. Pick any city as the starting city (current city).
2. Find the city that is nearest to the current city that hasn't yet been visited.
3. Set the nearest city as the current city and mark it as visited.
4. Repeat until all cities have been visited.

Now, this may seem like it could result in the optimal solution. In some cases it does, but in most cases it produces a longer path than the optimal. Indeed, in some cases it may produce the worst possible path. An algorithm that produces an approximate solution but is faster than finding the optimal solution is called a *heuristic*.

The following image displays an example path found by the next neighbour algorithm.

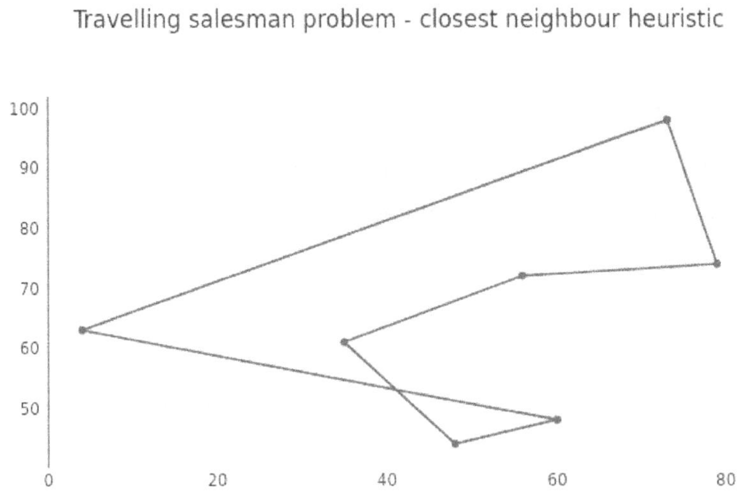

Here, it's possible that the algorithm started at (60, 48). It found the nearest neighbour at (48, 44), then at (35, 61) and so on, until the final city at (4, 63) and the return to the starting point.

Exercise: Implement the next neighbour algorithm. Compare the resulting path length between this and the brute force search for various N, e.g. N=8.

The next neighbour algorithm is a *greedy algorithm*. A greedy algorithm is an algorithm which attempts to find the locally optimal solution repeatedly with the hope of arriving as close to the globally optimal solution as possible. It only looks at the local state such that the decision e.g. to set a city as the current city does not consider all solutions or future decisions. Algorithms that combine the solutions of subproblems and do consider all solutions and future decisions are called *dynamic programming* algorithms. The fastest algorithms to find the optimal solution to TSP utilise dynamic programming; they have a run time complexity of $O(n^2 2^n)$ which is still exponential but much better than factorial.

Apart from greedy algorithms, there are other heuristics that can help provide reasonable solutions to difficult problems. Another heuristic is *stochastic optimisation*, where, e.g. for TSP, multiple paths are generated at random and compared against each other, selecting the best one in the end. These can furthermore be improved e.g. by attempting to combine features of various paths.

Were it actually necessary for you to find good and fast solutions to TSP, the best way to do this would probably be to use one of multiple libraries designed to solve TSP, which may incorporate years of optimisation and research to provide the best algorithms. Never the less, basic understanding of the problem space can be helpful in daily programming life. Furthermore, typical Computer Science topics are often a popular subject in technical interviews for software development positions.

4.4.3 Concurrency

Concurrency refers to multiple tasks being executed, at least seemingly, the same time.

In the section "Unix shell scripting" we already touched upon the concept of a *process* - a program running on a computer. Modern OSes support having lots of processes at the same time; you may have e.g. the web browser and a terminal open at the same time, and the terminal may have several windows e.g. the shell, the editor and the compiler. Furthermore, modern OSes support running several processes at once; you may e.g. start the compiler which could run for a while, and at the same time use the editor without the computer locking up.

Typically, each process, when running, runs on a *CPU core*; modern CPUs may have multiple cores, more or less independent from each other, each one being able to process instructions individually. Hence, if your CPU e.g. has four cores, it is able to run four processes at the same time (*in parallel*).

Digression: What if I want to run even more processes at the same time? What if I only have one CPU core?

More processes can be run concurrently than a computer has CPU cores available. However, they won't run in parallel - they won't *really* run at the same time. Instead, modern OSes will change the process running on a CPU core every few milliseconds, creating *the appearance* that more processes than CPU cores are being executed at once, even though in reality the execution is interleaved. This changing of the process that is being executed on a CPU core is called a *context switch*.

Conversely, if you have certain computations you want the CPU to process, and your CPU has several cores which you would like to use, you need to somehow be able to split your work across the different CPU cores.

Processes are one way to do this; you may be able to run multiple processes, each doing part of the work. You may need your processes to communicate with each other ("*Interprocess communication*, or IPC); we've seen a few different ways processes can communicate with each other, such as files, sockets (even on a single computer) or the Unix pipe.

Apart from processes, you can use *threads* to split the work. Threads work such that you may start a new thread in your code, such that, as a result, you now have two threads running your code at the same time. They share the same memory space, e.g. variables, so communication between threads can be relatively simple.

Digression: What is memory space?

When you check the pointer value of a variable, e.g. 0x7fffe7d8, this address, on a modern OS, does not really refer to the *physical address* in your memory. Instead, modern OSes typically employ *virtual addresses* - they let each program have their own *virtual address space*, and whenever the program tries to access memory, the CPU performs a *translation* from virtual address to the physical address on the physical memory. This way it's usually not possible for processes to read each others' memory. Indeed one of the main distinctions between a thread and a process is that when a thread is created, it shares the virtual address space with the thread that created it, while a process receives its own virtual address space from the OS on creation.

Simple example

Let's put together a simple threading example by writing a program that has two threads, both of them writing some characters to stdout. A common C API to manage threads is the *pthreads* API. It provides e.g. the following function:

```
int pthread_create(pthread_t *thread,
                   const pthread_attr_t *attr,
                   void *(*start_routine) (void *),
                   void *arg);
```

This function takes four parameters:

- thread: a *handle* to a thread. We simply need to create a local variable of type pthread_t and pass its address to the function. The function will fill its contents such that if we need to refer to the thread later, we can use this variable.
- attr: attributes of the thread. We can simply pass NULL which causes pthreads to use the default attributes.

- start_routine: this is a function pointer to the function that the thread should start executing. The function must take one parameter of type void pointer (pointer to anything) and return a void pointer.
- arg: the parameter to pass to start_routine when the thread runs.

pthreads also allows us to wait until a thread has finished:

```
int pthread_join(pthread_t thread, void **retval);
```

- thread is the thread handle.
- retval is a pointer to a void pointer. With this pointer we can retrieve the return value of the function that the thread executed.

Now, let's create two threads, one of which printing 100,000 lines filled with the character 'x', the other printing 100,000 lines filled with the character 'y':

```
#include <stdio.h>
#include <stdlib.h>
#include <pthread.h>

void *print_text(void *d)
{
    char char_to_print = *(char *)d;
    for(int j = 0; j < 100000; j++) {
        for(int i = 0; i < 50; i++) {
            printf("%c", char_to_print);
        }
        printf("\n");
    }
    return NULL;
}

int main(void)
{
    pthread_t x_thread;
    pthread_t y_thread;
    int ret;
    void *res;

```

(continues on next page)

(continued from previous page)

```
24     char x_param = 'x';
25     char y_param = 'y';
26 
27     ret = pthread_create(&x_thread, NULL, print_text, (void *)&x_param);
28     if(ret) {
29         fprintf(stderr, "Could not create thread x\n");
30         exit(1);
31     }
32     ret = pthread_create(&y_thread, NULL, print_text, (void *)&y_param);
33     if(ret) {
34         fprintf(stderr, "Could not create thread y\n");
35         exit(1);
36     }
37 
38     ret = pthread_join(x_thread, &res);
39     if(ret) {
40         fprintf(stderr, "Could not join thread x\n");
41         exit(1);
42     }
43     ret = pthread_join(y_thread, &res);
44     if(ret) {
45         fprintf(stderr, "Could not join thread y\n");
46         exit(1);
47     }
48 
49     return 0;
50 }
```

Let's go through this line by line:

- Line 3: We #include <pthread.h>, declaring the functions from the pthreads API.
- Lines 5-15: We define our function that the threads will execute. It will use printf() to write characters to screen. It takes a void pointer, which is in this case a pointer to char, which is the character we want to print. On line 7 we cast the void pointer to a char pointer, and dereference it to obtain our char.

- Lines 19-20: We define our variables of type pthread_t which are our handles to our two threads.
- Lines 24-25: We define our characters, the addresses of which we pass as parameters to the thread function.
- Lines 27-36: We start our two threads using pthread_create. We want both of them to run the same function, and we pass them the addresses to characters 'x' and 'y' respectively. The threads will start running directly after pthread_create is called.
- Lines 38-47: We wait until both threads are finished by calling pthread_join which will block until the function call finishes.

Note that although the two threads can share variables, they both have their own stacks. This means that the local variable e.g. in the function print_text() is *not* shared between the two threads. However, if you have variables with are pointers, they might point to the same memory.

When compiling this program the compiler flag "-pthread" needs to be passed to the compiler (at least in case of gcc and clang; e.g. "gcc -pthread -O2 -Wall -o th1 th1.c"). This enables pthread support during compilation.

Exercise: Compile and run the above program. Bonus points if you type it instead of copy-pasting. Run it multiple times. What output would you expect? Is the output always the same?

When running the program you may see characters "x" fill the screen. When this happens, the first thread is running and writes its output to the screen. Other times you may see characters "y" on the screen. Although both threads may be running at the same time, only one of them is allowed to write to the screen at once (this is typically enforced by the OS).

Incrementing

Now, let's assume we have a task: we need to increment an integer very many times. To make things interesting, we use two threads to increment the integer.

While this example is hardly very realistic, it does demonstrate some key concepts around threads. Generally, if we had multiple integers to increment, i.e. if our problem was *parallelisable*, using threads might make sense.

In this case, because we only have one integer, using multiple threads won't help performance, but we can anyway see what happens.

Take a look at the following program:

```
#include <stdio.h>
#include <stdlib.h>
#include <pthread.h>

struct thread_param {
    int num_increments;
    int *variable_to_increment;
};

void *increment(void *d)
{
    struct thread_param *param = (struct thread_param *)d;
    for(int j = 0; j < param->num_increments; j++) {
        (*param->variable_to_increment)++;
    }
    return NULL;
}

int main(int argc, char **argv)
{
    if(argc != 3) {
        fprintf(stderr, "Usage: %s <num increments 1> <num increments 2>\n",
                argv[0]);
        exit(1);
    }
    pthread_t thread1;
    pthread_t thread2;

    int our_value = 0;
    int ret;
    void *res;

    struct thread_param param1;
    struct thread_param param2;

    param1.num_increments = atoi(argv[1]);
```

(continues on next page)

(continued from previous page)

```
37      param2.num_increments = atoi(argv[2]);
38
39      param1.variable_to_increment = &our_value;
40      param2.variable_to_increment = &our_value;
41
42      ret = pthread_create(&thread1, NULL, increment, (void *)&
   ↪param1);
43      if(ret) {
44          fprintf(stderr, "Could not create thread 1\n");
45          exit(1);
46      }
47      ret = pthread_create(&thread2, NULL, increment, (void *)&
   ↪param2);
48      if(ret) {
49          fprintf(stderr, "Could not create thread 2\n");
50          exit(1);
51      }
52
53      ret = pthread_join(thread1, &res);
54      if(ret) {
55          fprintf(stderr, "Could not join thread 1\n");
56          exit(1);
57      }
58      ret = pthread_join(thread2, &res);
59      if(ret) {
60          fprintf(stderr, "Could not join thread 2\n");
61          exit(1);
62      }
63
64      printf("Final value: %d\n", our_value);
65      return 0;
66  }
```

- Lines 5-8: We define a struct which holds the data we want to pass to our two threads. It holds the number of increments we want each thread to perform, and the pointer to the one integer that should be incremented.
- Lines 10-17: We define the function the threads will run. We cast the void pointer to a pointer to thread_param, and then have our loop where we perform a number of increments to the integer in question.

- Line 29: We define our integer that needs to be incremented.
- Lines 33-40: We define the contents of the parameters we pass to our threads. The number of increments are read from command line parameters for each thread. We use the C standard library function atoi() to convert a char pointer to an int, and ensure the threads receive the address of our one integer.
- Line 64: After running our threads and waiting until they've finished, we print out the final number.

This program could be used e.g. like the following:

```
$ ./th2 1000 1000
Final value: 2000
```

Here, we ask both threads to increment the integer by 1,000. As expected, the final value is 2,000.

Exercise: Compile and run the above program. Bonus points if you type it instead of copy-pasting. Run it multiple times. Try with large values, e.g. 100,000 for both threads. What output would you expect? Is the output always the same?

What happens here is that because both threads access the same memory, i.e. the same variable "our_value" from main, the result of one thread may interfere with the other. The x86-64 assembly for the incrementing could look e.g. like the following, with compiler optimisations disabled for clarity (output in the output file by the compiler after passing the "-S" flag):

```
movl    (%rax), %edx
addl    $1, %edx
movl    %edx, (%rax)
```

Here, the first instruction loads the value from the address stored in the register rax (param->variable_to_increment) to the register edx. The second instruction increments edx by one. The third instruction moves the value from register edx to the address stored in rax (param->variable_to_increment). In other words, because the addition instruction works with data stored in registers, the data is fetched from memory for the addition, incremented, and then written out again, in a loop.

(The assembly code using compiler optimisation flags looks different but has the same effect in principle.)

Now, because we have two threads accessing the same memory concurrently, the end result may be incorrect. It could be that the first thread performs all of its calculation, then the second thread kicks in and clears the result of the first thread, such that the final result is only affected by the calculations of the second thread. This could happen, for example, if one of the threads performs the addition but is then *preempted*, i.e. temporarily moved out from a CPU core to let another thread run, and then later moved back to the CPU core. In this case the thread would then perform the move of the (now obsolete) data to memory. This is called a *race condition*. However, we can solve this.

Incrementing with mutual exclusion

pthreads offers *mutexes*, a portmanteau from "mutual exclusion", as a synchronisation mechanism. Mutex, also called a *lock*, can be used to limit the access to a *critical section*, i.e. code where shared data is being accessed and modified. A thread can lock a mutex, perform the increment, and then unlock the mutex. If another thread at the same time attempts to lock the mutex, it will block until the mutex has been unlocked. Hence, only one thread will be performing the increments at once.

To do this, we should define a mutex. It needs to be defined in main because the mutex must be shared between threads. A mutex can be defined like this:

```
pthread_mutex_t our_mutex = PTHREAD_MUTEX_INITIALIZER;
```

Now that we have a mutex, we should ensure our threads have access to it. We can do this by adding a field in the struct definition:

```
struct thread_param {
    int num_increments;
    int *variable_to_increment;
    pthread_mutex_t *mutex;
};
```

Here, the last field in the struct is a pointer to a mutex handle. We can then, in main, before starting our threads, set this field to the address of our mutex:

```
param1.mutex = &our_mutex;
param2.mutex = &our_mutex;
```

Finally we can use the mutex in our function that the threads will run:

```
int ret = pthread_mutex_lock(param->mutex);
if(ret) {
    fprintf(stderr, "Could not lock\n");
    return NULL;
}
(*param->variable_to_increment)++;
ret = pthread_mutex_unlock(param->mutex);
if(ret) {
    fprintf(stderr, "Could not unlock\n");
    return NULL;
}
```

Here, we lock the mutex before the increment and unlock it directly after, within our loop. Locking and unlocking a mutex in an inner loop like this may ruin our performance because mutex locking and unlocking could be a heavy operation, requiring relevant kernel code to be executed - a better way would be to perform the lock and unlock before and after the loop - but for demonstration purposes that'll do.

Exercise: Make the required changes to the previous program such that the critical code is protected by a mutex. Does the output of the program change?

Exercise: What would happen if a thread forgot to unlock a mutex? This might not happen in this case but could be more plausible in code with several branches, or multiple return points from a function, or C++ exceptions.

While our use case for using threads was somewhat non-realistic, better uses of threads do exist. For example, an HTTP server may have several threads serving the various clients that connect to the server, such that a client doesn't need to wait until another client has been served. Another example is splitting the work: for example, our Sudoku solver solved a series or Sudoku puzzles in series. To improve performance, it could be rewritten to use threads, such that each thread picks one of the unsolved puzzles and solves it. This way, the run time of solving a set of puzzles could be dramatically decreased. While pthreads could be used with C++, C++ (like most modern programming languages) also provides its own API for managing threads.

4.4.4 Tech behind this book

This chapter describes the technology used for creating this book.

The text is written using vim, in a format called *reStructuredText* (rst). Rst is fairly simple to write and looks like this:

```
Title
-----

This is some text.

.. code-block:: python

  print 'foo'

Here's an image.

.. image:: ../material/foo/bar.png
```

After I've written a section in rst, I feed it to *Sphinx*. Sphinx is a Python tool that can generate documentation for a piece of software, but it can apparently also be used for books. It takes rst as input and can generate output in various formats such as HTML and LaTeX (which can be converted to PDF - which can be printed to a physical book). Sphinx also extends rst by defining some additional directives, for example for generating a table of contents.

I had Sphinx generate a Makefile for myself so after I've written a new section, I can run e.g.:

```
$ make latexpdf html
```

This command will generate both HTML and PDF from the input rst files which are defined in the main table of contents.

It's worth going a bit more into detail on LaTeX. LaTeX (often pronounced "lah-tech" - as in "technical") is a typesetting system which takes LaTeX files as input and outputs files such as PDF. LaTeX input files, again, look e.g. like this:

```
\section{Javascript}
\label{\detokenize{js_index:javascript}}\label{\detokenize{js_
↪index::doc}}

\subsection{Guessing game in JS}
\label{\detokenize{js:guessing-game-in-js}}\label{\detokenize
↪{js::doc}}
Let's write a guessing game. This game is fairly simple: the␣
↪computer thinks of a number between 1 and 25, and you need to␣
↪guess what it is. The computer will give hints such as "my␣
↪number is smaller" or "my number is bigger" on wrong guesses.
```

In other words, it supports several different commands that describe what the output should be like. Sphinx generates LaTeX files from the rst input, and also generates and runs a Makefile which runs the Perl script latexmk which runs pdflatex which actually generates the PDF. In order to make the page layout as I wanted - with page breaks only where I wanted them and nowhere else - I needed to write some *LaTeX code*. You see, LaTeX (and TeX, the language it builds upon) is *Turing complete* - it, like all common programming languages, can be used to describe any computation, and hence supports e.g. branches, variables, and loops. This comes in handy when the document writer wants e.g. a page break before every section except the first section in the chapter, like in my case.

The following diagram displays the overall flow. The grey boxes represent applications while the white spots are data.

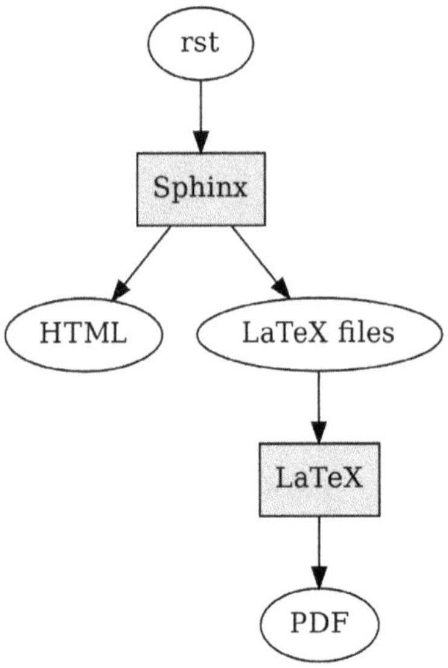

Apart from using Sphinx, another alternative I read about afterwards was Asciidoctor, which is software that takes files written in AsciiDoc syntax as input (which has some similarities to rst, e.g. is also plain text) and can generate various outputs such as HTML and PDF.

Diagrams

The dot format was discussed in section "Graphs", and this book uses that format, with some additions for subgraphs, and the Graphviz tool for most of the diagrams.

There are a few diagrams not generated with Graphviz, though. When I needed to create some diagrams manually or needed specific symbols, like with the diagrams on electric circuits, I used draw.io which is an online diagram maker. The diagrams created using draw.io can be exported and imported as XML. Furthermore, draw.io can turn the diagrams to images such as .png files.

Apart from Graphviz and dot, in the chapter "Quadratic formula" as well as the section "NP-hard problems" I needed to generate images of a quadratic function and points on a plane respectively. For this I used a *Jupyter notebook*. Jupyter notebook is a web application that allows the user to write Python code and display the results. Because Jupyter notebooks make it easy to load, analyse and visualise data and share the results, they're popular among people who need to work with data.

Within the Jupyter notebook, I used the Python libraries *plotly* and *numpy*. Plotly makes it easy to create plots within Python code, and numpy makes it easy to work with numbers in larger scale in Python, such as multi-dimensional arrays and matrices.

The following screenshot illustrates the Jupyter notebook used for generating the quadratic function diagram:

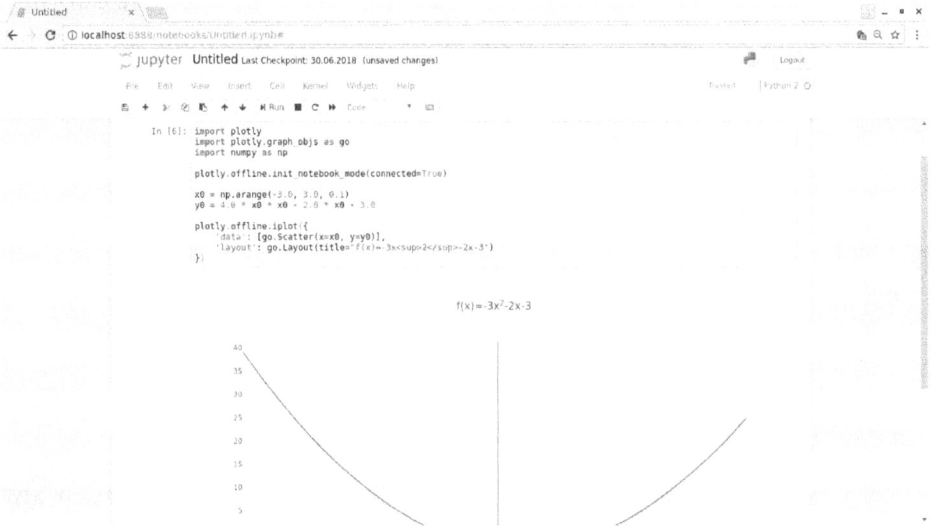

Here, the Jupyter server is started on localhost and connected to using the browser. The code at the top is the code needed for generating the plot. The variables x0 and y0 use numpy constructs to generate arrays of the data to display: x0 is an array with values from -3 to 3 with steps of 0.1, and y0 is an array where each value depends on the corresponding element in x0 as described in the formula. Finally, the two arrays are provided to plotly for generating the diagram. Plotly supports exporting the diagram to a PNG file.

Miscellaneous

The screenshots, where necessary, were created using scrot. Scrot is a Unix command line tool that can create screenshots. I typically instruct it to wait for two seconds (so I can bring the relevant window to focus), then take a screenshot of the currently active window and store it as a pre-defined file name. This workflow works fairly well as it saves me from having to cut, crop or save images.

Another command line suite which came very handy is ImageMagick which allows easy modification of images (cropping, resizing, converting between formats etc.) from the command line.

While generating the PDF for the print version, I noticed many of the diagrams generated using dot had too low DPI (dots per inch). I found out I can increase the DPI by passing the command line flag "-Gdpi=300" to dot, but this meant I needed to regenerate all the PNG files from the dot files. The following command took care of this for me (split to multiple lines for readability):

```
1 for file in $(find . -name '*.dot')
2 do
3     pushd $(dirname $file)
4     dot -Tpng -Gdpi=300 $(basename $file) > $(basename $file .
↪dot).png
5     popd
6 done
```

Let's see what this does:

- Line 1: We find all the dot files within the current directory or any subdirectories, and loop over them
- Line 3: We first capture the *directory* where the file resides using shell expansion ("$(...)"), and then *push* this directory to a stack. Bash supports a stack for directories such that one can push a directory in the stack, which changes the current working directory and also allows the directory to be *popped* later which changes the current working directory back to what it was before the push.
- Line 4: We capture the *base name* of the dot file - this is the file name without the directory part. We also run "$(basename $file .dot).png" which first removes the ".dot" suffix from the file name and then adds the ".png" suffix to it. Running this dot command for e.g. a file "foo.dot" effectively runs dot on "foo.dot" to generate a "foo.png".
- Line 5: We pop the directory from the stack, arriving at the previous directory. Doing this allows our script (or one-liner) to end up in the directory we started in.

(I later discovered that Sphinx can run dot as part of the HTML and LaTeX generation as well.)

GitHub provides a hosting service for hosting web pages which I also experimented with for the purposes of this book. There's a command to publish the generated HTML on GitHub pages ("git subtree push –prefix _build/html/ origin gh-pages") but as this command was difficult to remember I created a simple shell script "publish.sh" with only this command as the contents. This way, once I've committed a new section, I could run "git push origin master && ./publish.sh" which would upload all the changes online.

The dependency diagrams were generated using dot. I have the master dot file which describes the actual dependencies, but this dot file doesn't include the actual section titles, only the file names. I then wrote a simple shell script to read the section titles from the rst files and generate dot statements which cause the titles to be used as labels in the diagram. These generated dot statements, together with a dot header and the master dot file are then concatenated to the final dot file which describes the dependencies between the sections.

After the dependencies between sections are described in a dot file, another dot file is generated from this input which describes the dependencies between chapters (one chapter can include multiple sections). This is done in a simple Python script which parses a) the section dependencies from the dot file, and b) which sections belong to which chapters from the rst files. Finally, a shell script is run which passes the two dot files to "tred" to remove unnecessary edges and creates the final PNG images from the dot files. This flow is run as part of the Makefile invocation.

The source code for the book is versioned using git and is publicly available in GitHub at https://github.com/anttisalonen/progbook.

4.4.5 Further reading

As mentioned in the introduction, this book aims to contain an overview of almost everything that I think is important for software developers. However, depending on your future projects, you may find the need to go more in depth in some topics. This final section lists some books and other resources that I can recommend when going more in depth.

C programming language: The C Programming Language by Brian Kernighan and Dennis Ritchie

C++ programming language: The C++ Programming Language by Bjarne Stroustrup

JavaScript: Eloquent JavaScript: A Modern Introduction to Programming 2nd Edition by Marijn Haverbeke

Algorithms: The Algorithm Design Manual by Steven S Skiena

Programming in general:

- The Pragmatic Programmer by Andrew Hunt
- Programming Pearls by Jon Bentley
- Coders at Work by Peter Seibel

Compilers and interpreters:

- Structure and Interpretation of Computer Programs by Harold Abelson, Gerald Jay Sussman, Julie Sussman
- Types and Programming Languages by Benjamin C. Pierce

Other:

- The Art of UNIX Programming by Eric S. Raymond
- Unix Network Programming, Volume 1: The Sockets Networking API by W. Richard Stevens
- The Mythical Man-Month: Essays on Software Engineering by Frederick P. Brooks Jr.

4.4.6 Chapter dependencies

The following diagram describes the dependencies between chapters.

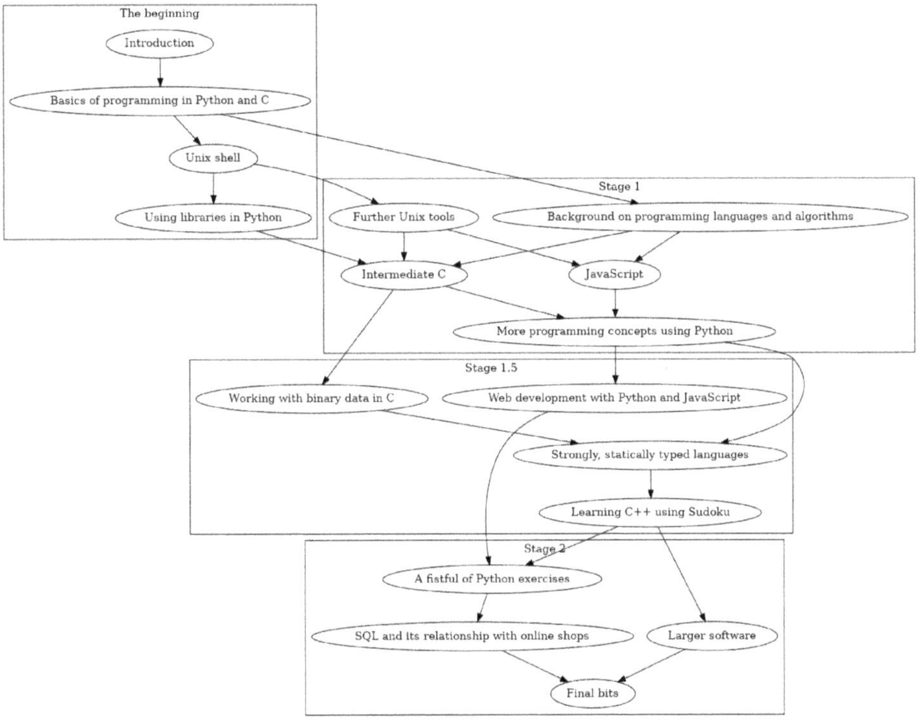

www.ingramcontent.com/pod-product-compliance
Lightning Source LLC
Chambersburg PA
CBHW060643060326
40690CB00020B/4494
9781722834920